OXFORD Children's Pocket Book of Knowledge

OXFORD UNIVERSITY PRESS

Oxford University Press, Walton Street, Oxford OX2 6DP

Oxford New York Athens
Auckland Bangkok Bombay Calcutta
Cape Town Dar es Salaam Delhi
Florence Hong Kong Istanbul Karachi
Kuala Lumpur Madras Madrid Melbourne
Mexico City Nairobi Paris Singapore
Taipei Tokyo Toronto

Oxford is a trade mark of Oxford University Press

First published 1995

This book was originally prepared for Weetabix Ltd. and issued as the *Weetabix Oxford Illustrated Book of Facts* and was subsequently published as the *Oxford Children's Pocket Book of Facts.*

1 3 5 7 9 10 8 6 4 2

British Library Cataloguing in Publication Data
Data available

ISBN 0 19 910015 2

Printed in Italy

Aborigines

▲ **Aborigine playing a didgeridoo (a wind instrument).**

Aborigines were the first people to live in Australia. They lived there for thousands of years before Europeans arrived, moving from place to place, hunting animals and gathering plants for food.

Aborigines worshipped the land, which they believe their ancestors made for them in a time they call Dreamtime. They wrote many songs and dances about Dreamtime.

After the Europeans arrived, over 200 years ago, the Aborigines lost their lands, and many of them were killed. They only had spears and boomerangs to defend themselves against the guns of the settlers.

There are now far fewer Aborigines. Most have lost their traditional way of life, and take a full part in Australian politics, religion, law, sport and the arts. Some places which are holy to the Aborigines are now being given back their original Aborigine names. Today Aborigines prefer to be called Kooris.

Did you know?

■ Aborigines spoke more than 300 different languages before the Europeans arrived in Australia.

■ There are now about 150,000 Aborigines in a total population of over 17 million Australians.

Acid rain

Did you know?

■ Vast areas of forest in northern and central Europe are dying because of acid rain. It has also killed fish in the lakes of Scandinavia, North America, Scotland and Wales.

Acid rain is caused by gases from power stations and factories, and by the exhaust fumes from motor vehicles. Up in the atmosphere these gases form weak acids, which fall to the ground in rain or snow. Acid rain harms plants and animals, and attacks stone, metal and concrete.

Aerosols

Paints, polishes, deodorants, fly-killers and oven cleaners can all be sprayed by aerosol cans. The can contains the substance to be sprayed, together with a liquid known as a propellant. The propellant turns into a gas when released and forces the substance to spray out through the nozzle.

Propellants called chlorofluorocarbons (CFCs for short) may be damaging the protective ozone layer around the Earth. Aerosols that contain safe propellants have 'Ozone Friendly' written on the side.

▼ **Many hair sprays come from an aerosol can like this.**

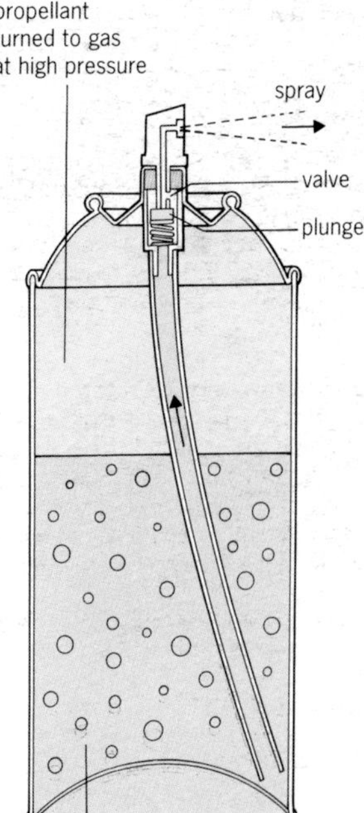

Africa

Africa is the world's second largest continent. Its many countries have very different features. There are three large deserts, Sahara, Kalahari, and Namib.

In Central Africa there is tropical rainforest. Away from the forest, grasslands are home to many of Africa's larger animals, such as lions, giraffes and elephants. Many animals live in national parks, such as the Serengeti in Tanzania. Four of the world's largest rivers, the Nile, the Zaïre, the Niger and the Zambezi, flow through Africa.

People speak more than 14,300 languages in Africa. Some speak European languages in those places which used to be ruled by Britain, France, Belgium and Portugal.

Islam is now the fastest growing religion in Africa, and there are also many Christians.

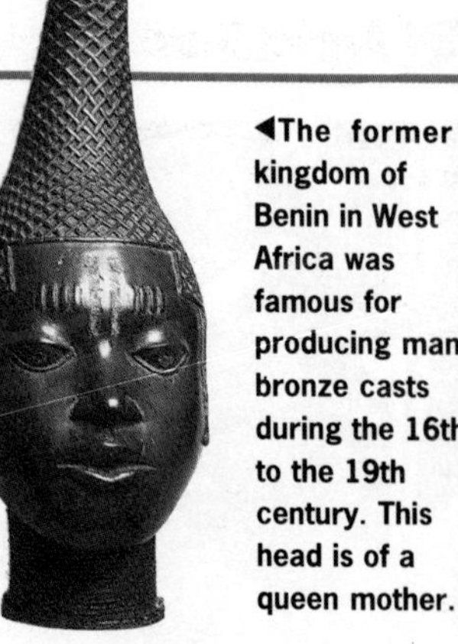

◀The former kingdom of Benin in West Africa was famous for producing many bronze casts during the 16th to the 19th century. This head is of a queen mother.

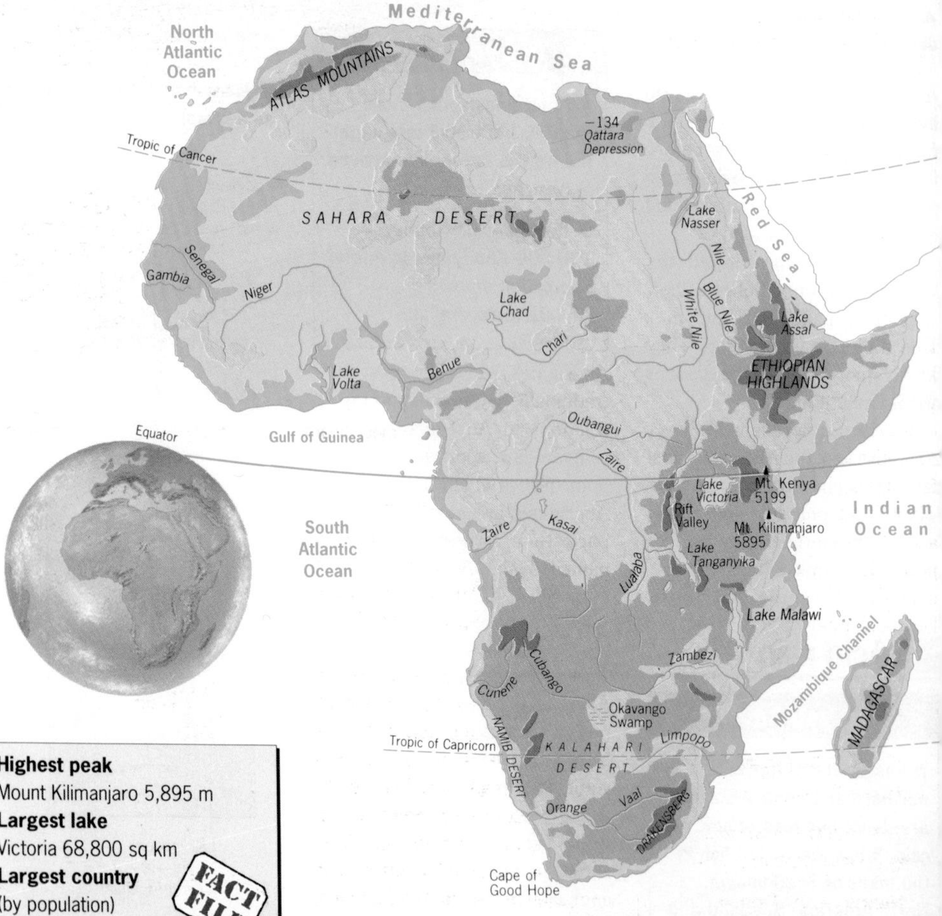

Highest peak
Mount Kilimanjaro 5,895 m
Largest lake
Victoria 68,800 sq km
Largest country
(by population)
Nigeria 105,000,000

FACT FILE

Agriculture

Most types of agriculture produce food for people to eat. Cereals, such as wheat, corn (maize) and rice, are the main food sources for most people, and for many farm animals.

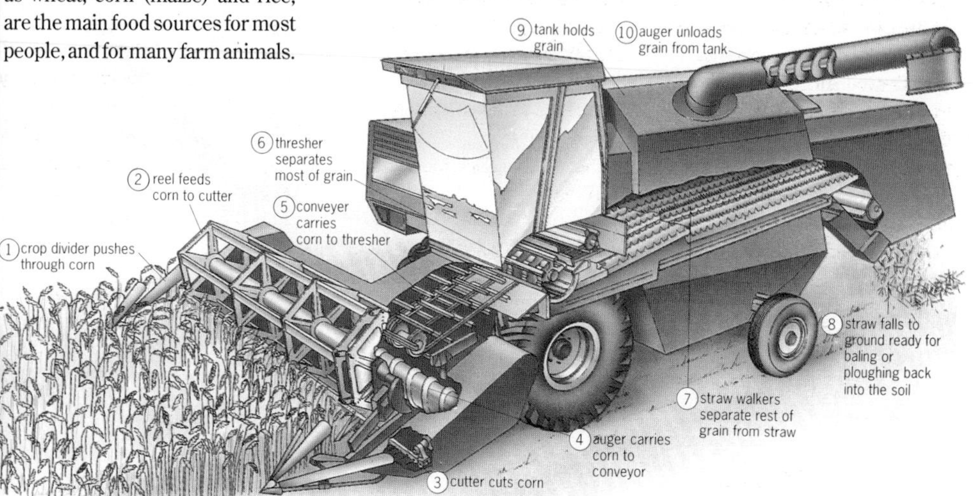

▼ **Combine harvesters cut the corn and separate the grain from the straw.**

Dairy farming produces milk, butter and other dairy products, while mixed farming involves both crops and livestock.

Many farmers practise intensive farming to improve their yields. They use lots of machinery as well as chemical fertilizers and pesticides. Organic farmers do not use artificial chemicals on the land, and their animals roam in the open air.

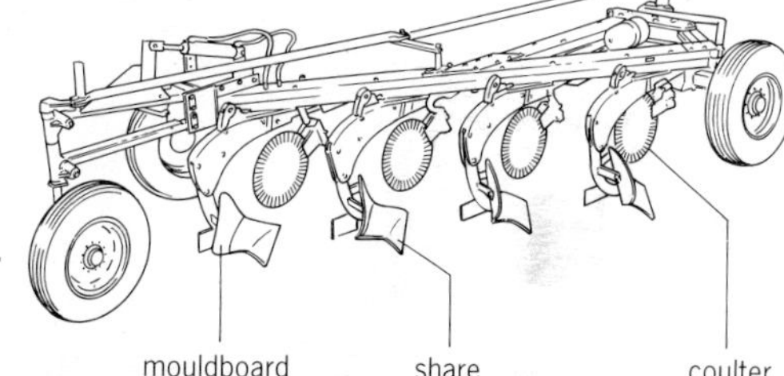

▶ **Ploughs prepare the soil ready for planting the seeds.**

Did you know?

- **Farmers first grew crops before 9,000 BC.**
- **The USA is the world's biggest exporter of grain.**
- **Nearly every African country imports grain.**

Air

Air is the mixture of gases we breathe. You cannot see, smell or taste air, but without it the Earth would be an empty desert with no living creatures.

Air consists mainly of oxygen and nitrogen, together with small amounts of argon, carbon dioxide and other gases. It also contains dust, water vapour, pollen, seeds, tiny animals, bacteria and pollution from factories. Mountain air is much cleaner, but it contains less oxygen. On very high mountains, climbers have to carry their own oxygen supply in cylinders.

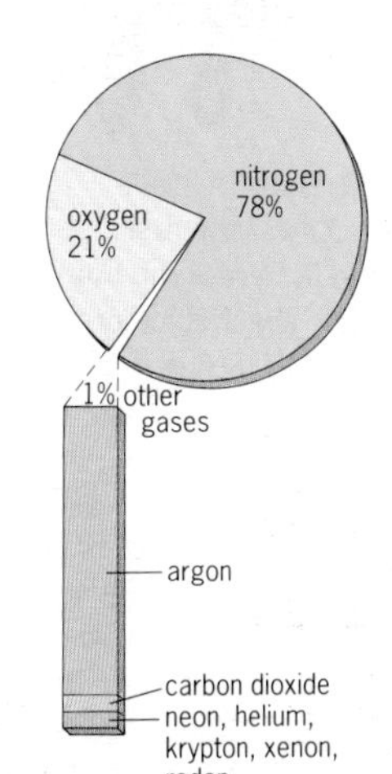

▲ **Gases in the air.**

Aircraft

The Wright brothers' *Flyer* made the first-ever powered flight in 1903, in the USA. The flight lasted just 12 seconds.

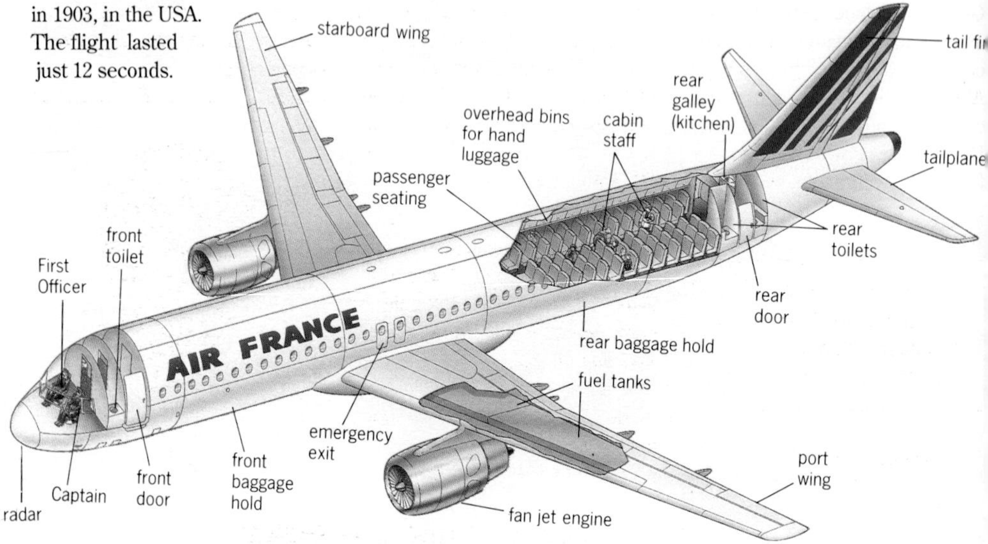

▼ This Airbus can seat up to 179 passengers. It needs a flight crew of only two people. The plane's computers help to manage its engines and controls.

▼ Harrier jets.

▼ Aerial photograph of Heathrow Airport, Terminal 4.

In 1909, Louis Blériot's *Blériot XI* was the first plane to fly across the English Channel. The first jet aircraft, the Heinkel HE178, flew in 1939. Most jets were developed after World War II.

The 747 (jumbo jet) was the first wide-bodied jet. The latest 747 can carry over 600 passengers and fly non-stop a third of the way round the world. Concorde, the first supersonic airliner, crosses the Atlantic in 3 hours at twice the speed of sound.

Alexander the Great

Alexander was born in 356 BC. He became King of Macedonia in Greece at the age of 20. He led his armies to many victories and conquered the Persian empire. Alexandria in Egypt is one of the cities built and named after him. He was only 32 when he died of a fever in Babylon.

Did you know?

■ When his horse Bucephalus died in the east, Alexander built a city and named it after him.

Algeria

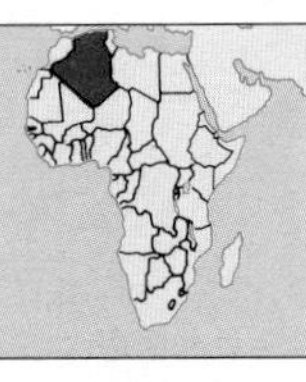

Algeria stretches from the Mediterranean Sea to the middle of the Sahara Desert. It is ten times the size of Britain. Most Algerians live close to the coast because the soil there is good for growing food. There is oil and natural gas in the desert for Algeria to export.

Algeria was ruled by France before it became independent in 1962. Many Algerians still speak French as well as Arabic.

FACT FILE

Capital
Algiers
Population
26,401,000
Currency
1 dinar = 100 centimes

Alfred the Great

Alfred was born in 849. He became king of Wessex at 22. He was a brave fighter who led his people against the invading Danes.

In 878 his army won the battle of Edington, and the Vikings left Wessex. Alfred set laws and built towns for his people. He died in 899 at the age of 50.

▶ This ornament was found near the Isle of Athelney in Somerset in 1693. It was made in the 9th century and has an inscription: *Aelfred mec heht gewyrcan.* It means 'Alfred ordered me to be made'. The portrait shows a man holding two sceptres. This is probably Alfred himself.

Did you know?

■ Once Alfred hid from the Vikings in a cottage. He fell asleep and the cakes baking on the fire burnt. Alfred is known as 'the king who burnt the cakes'.

Alligators and crocodiles

Alligators and crocodiles are large, carnivorous reptiles found in rivers and lakes in the warmer parts of the world. They have few natural enemies: adults can reach lengths of around 6 m, and all have thick leathery skins armoured by tiny bone plates. For most of their lives they feed mainly on fish, small mammals, birds and frogs. As they get older, crocodiles especially, begin to hunt larger prey, sometimes even trapping humans or their livestock.

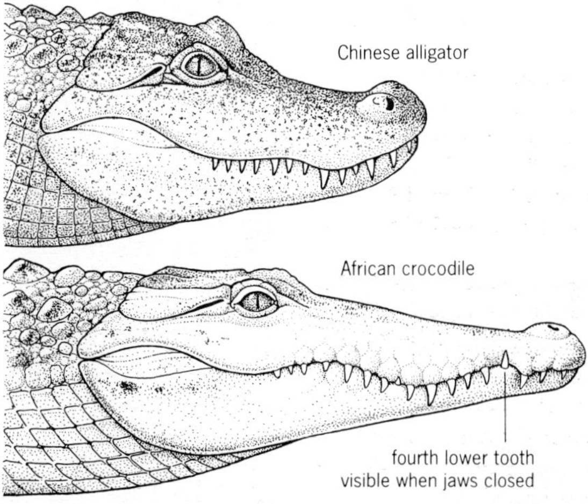

Alloys

Most pure metals are weak and soft, but if other substances are added to them, the mixture, which is known as an alloy, may be very different.

In Mesopotamia, before 4,000 BC, people added tin to molten copper to make bronze. Bronze is harder than pure copper, and it does not rust or corrode.

Did you know?

■ **An alloy of aluminium and copper, called duralumin, is used to make aircraft bodies.**

Alphabets

Alphabets are the letters we use to make words. Most alphabets have between 20 and 30 letters. English has 26. Most of the letters in our alphabet came from the Romans. The letters J, U and W were added in the Middle Ages.

There are about 50 different alphabets used in the world today.

Ancient Greek	Α Β Γ Δ Ε Ζ Η Θ Ι Κ Λ Μ Ν Ξ Ο Π Ρ Σ Τ α β γ δ ε ζ η θ ι κ λ μ ν ξ ο π ρ σ τ
Cyrillic	А Б В Г Д Е Ё Ж З И Й К Л М Н О П Р С Т У Ф а б в г д е ё ж з и й к л м н о п р с т у ф
Devanagari	अ आ इ ई उ ऊ ऋ ए ऐ ओ औ अं अः क ट ठ ड ढ ण त थ द ध न प फ ब भ
Hebrew	א ב ג ד ה ו ז ח ט י כ ל מ נ ס ע פ צ ק ר ש ת
Arabic	ج ح خ د ذ ر ز س ش ص غ ف ق ك ل م ن و هـ ي

▲ **Samples from various alphabets.**

Did you know?

■ **The Chinese do not use an alphabet. They draw out in shapes whole words. These 'idea' shapes are called ideograms.**

American history

The first humans reached America from Siberia about 12,000 years ago. In the 16th century people began to arrive from Europe, many of them in search of religious freedom.

In 1776 they declared their independence. The United States of America was originally made up of thirteen states. The new nation grew as more people arrived and

▲ **Slaves on a South Carolina estate in 1862. They would have been freed in 1865.**

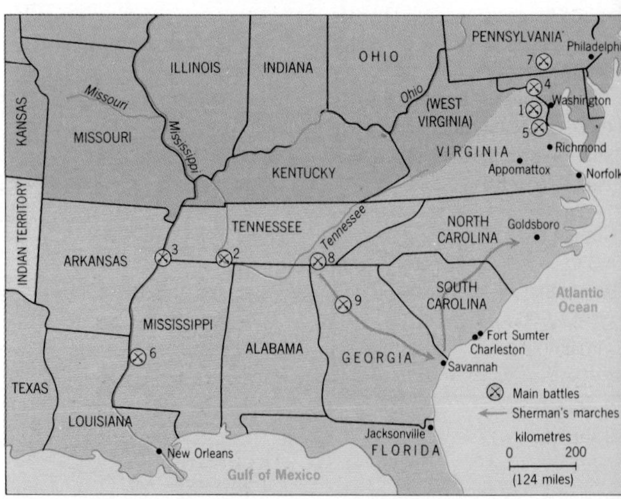

moved west, driving out the native 'Indians'.

In the south, many people owned black slaves as workers on farms and cotton plantations. In 1861 some southern states left the Union and fought the Civil War against the anti-slavery north. Over half a million people died before the north won in 1865.

The USA became one of the richest nations of the 20th century. It helped to win two World Wars, and Americans were very proud to be the first nation to land men on the moon in 1969.

Did you know?

- **In 1803 the USA doubled in size by buying land from France (the Louisiana Purchase).**
- **It was against the law to sell alcohol in America from 1919 to 1933. This was called 'Prohibition'.**

◄ This map shows which states were on the Union and Confederate sides in the American Civil War. The 11 Confederate states are coloured pink. These are the names of the main battles.
1 Bull Run
2 Shiloh
3 Memphis
4 Antietam
5 Fredericksburg
6 Vicksburg
7 Gettysburg
8 Chattanooga
9 Atlanta

American Indians

▲ A Yanomami woman and child in their home in the Amazon rainforest of Brazil.

European explorers thought they had arrived in the East Indies when they reached America, so they called the people they saw there 'Indians'.

Some of the better-known Indian nations are the Aztec of Mexico, the Inca of South America, and the Cherokee, Apache, Sioux and Navajo of North America.

In the 16th and 17th centuries, Indians were killed in the Caribbean islands by Europeans who wanted their land. The same thing happened in North America in the 19th century when Indians were driven west by whites. Even today Indians in South America are losing their tropical forests, as settlers from the coast of Brazil burn down large areas of rainforest to make huge cattle farms. Now, throughout America, Indians are beginning to fight for their rights, and prefer to be known as Native Americans.

Did you know?

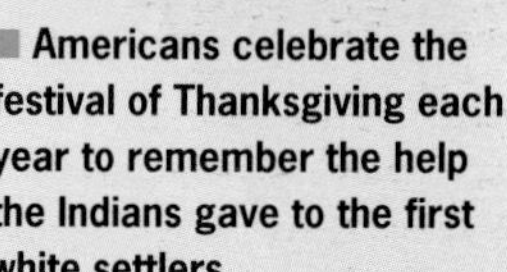

- **Americans celebrate the festival of Thanksgiving each year to remember the help the Indians gave to the first white settlers.**
- **When the Cherokee were driven from their lands they called the route they followed 'The Trail of Tears'.**

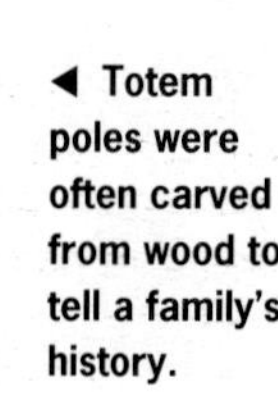

◄ Totem poles were often carved from wood to tell a family's history.

Amoebas

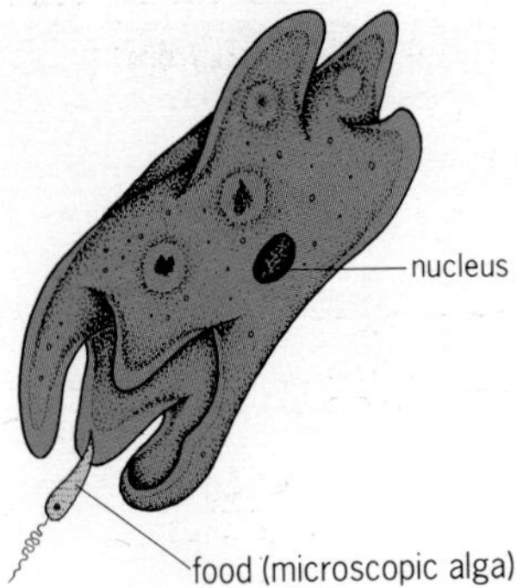

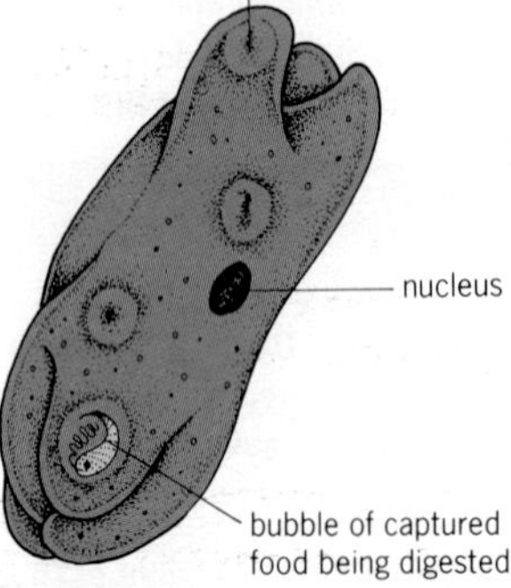

▲ An amoeba surrounds and traps its food in a bubble called a food vacuole. Digestive juices dissolve the food so it can be absorbed into the cell. Amoebas feed on bacteria, algae and other microscopic organisms.

Amoebas are microscopic single-celled animals which live in watery places, such as streams and wet soil. Amoebas move and feed by changing shape, and they reproduce simply by splitting in half.

Did you know?

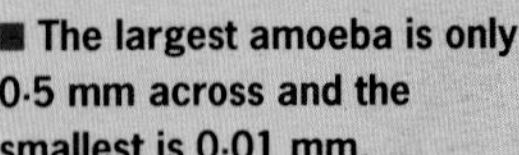

■ **The largest amoeba is only 0·5 mm across and the smallest is 0·01 mm.**

Amphibians

There are three main kinds of amphibians. **Caecilians** have no legs and are usually blind. They are found only in the Tropics and are unusual amphibians as only one species lives in water. **Newts and salamanders** mostly look a little like lizards. **Frogs and toads** are tailless, with very long hind legs for jumping.

▼ Caecilians burrow underground and are rarely seen.

Ancient world

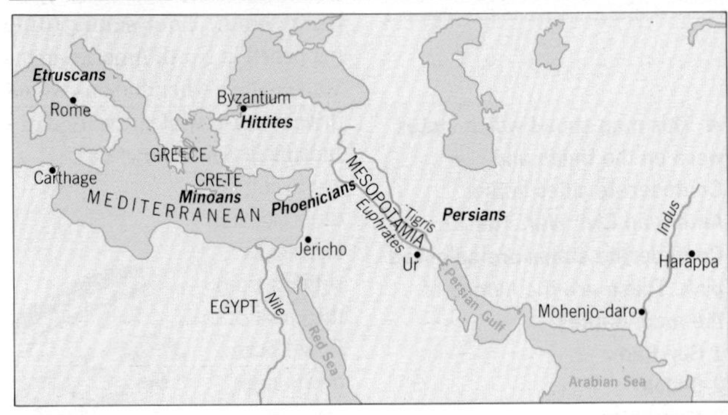

▲ Some of the most important cities and peoples of the ancient world

The 'seven wonders of the ancient world' were all built in the ancient countries which grew up around the Mediterranean Sea. They are:

- the Pyramids of Egypt
- the Hanging Gardens of Babylon
- the Temple of Artemis at Ephesus
- the Statue of Zeus at Olympia
- the Mausoleum of Halicarnassus
- the Colossus of Rhodes
- the Pharos of Alexandria

Anglo-Saxons

The first Anglo-Saxons came to Britain from north Europe when the Romans were the rulers. In the 4th and 5th centuries more Anglo-Saxons arrived. They set up small kingdoms such as East Anglia, Mercia and Wessex.

■ **English comes from the Anglo-Saxons' language.**

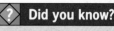

Animals

Animals are living things that feed by eating other living things. This is the main thing that distinguishes them from plants. Those that eat meat are called carnivores; those that eat plants are herbivores, and those that eat both are omnivores. There are at least 1 million species of animal and 99% of these are smaller than humans. Most of these do not have a backbone. These are the invertebrates which include insects, worms and jellyfish. Animals with backbones are called vertebrates.

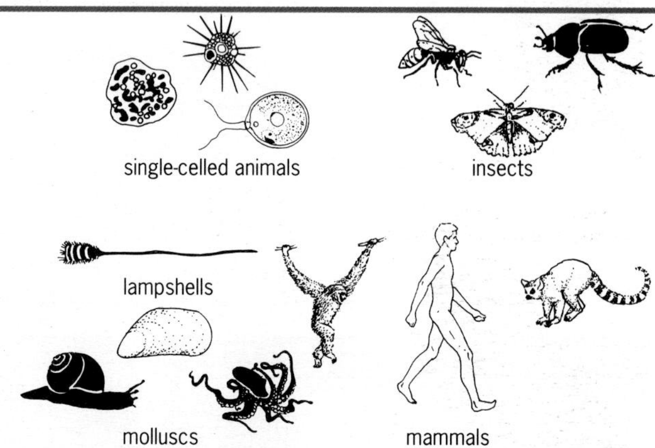

▲ **Some of the groups that makes up the animal kingdom.**

Antarctica

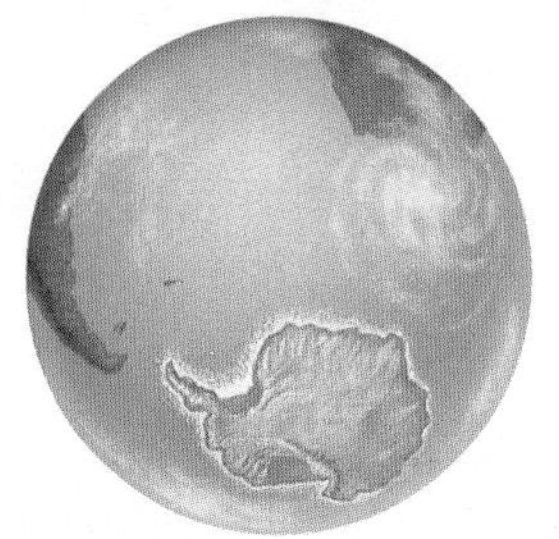

Antarctica, the fifth largest continent in the world, is at the South Pole. It is covered with ice over 3 km thick. Pieces of this ice break off to form icebergs. The lowest temperature ever recorded in Antarctica was -89·2° C. No land animals can live there, but seals and penguins live in the sea and at its edge.

Thirty-nine countries, including Britain, have signed the Antarctic Treaty, promising to use the area for peaceful scientific research only.

FACT FILE

Highest point
Vinson Massif 5,140 m
World's longest glacier
Lambert Glacier 400 km

Ants

Ants are social insects. This means they live together in large colonies. There maybe 100,000 ants in a colony but they all have the same mother, the queen ant, the only female in the colony who can lay eggs. The ants you see most are the workers. These are all females.

Apes

Chimpanzees, gorillas, gibbons and orang-utans make up the apes, our closest relatives. There are many similarities: apes usually live in family groups; give birth to only one baby at a time and care for it for a number of years; and have long lifespans of about 50 years.

▶ **Apes have long fingers and toes so they can grasp things.**

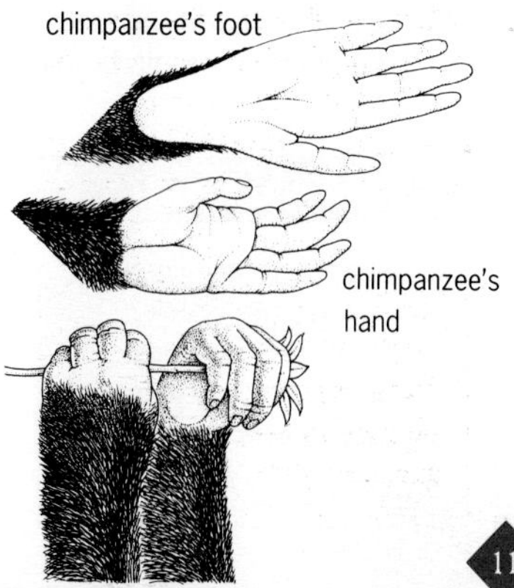

Arabs

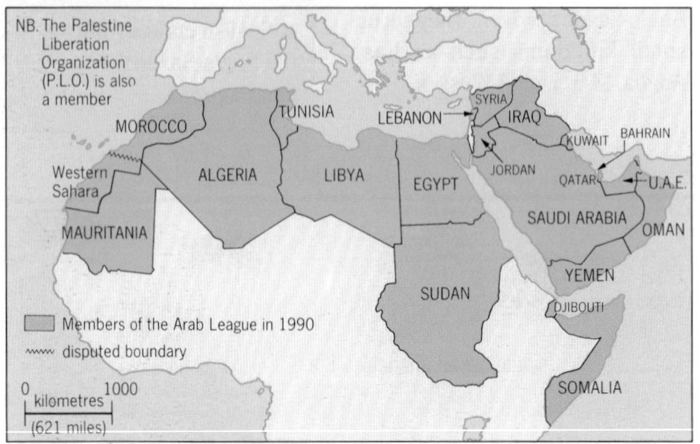

Over 200 million Arabs live in the 20 countries which stretch from Morocco to Saudi Arabia. All Arabs speak Arabic and most are Muslims. Some Arab countries are rich because much of the world's oil is found there.

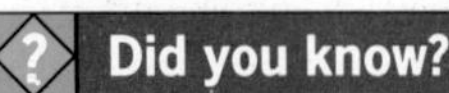

Did you know?

■ The numbers we use for counting (1,2,3,4,5,6,7,8,9) are Arabic numerals.

Archaeology

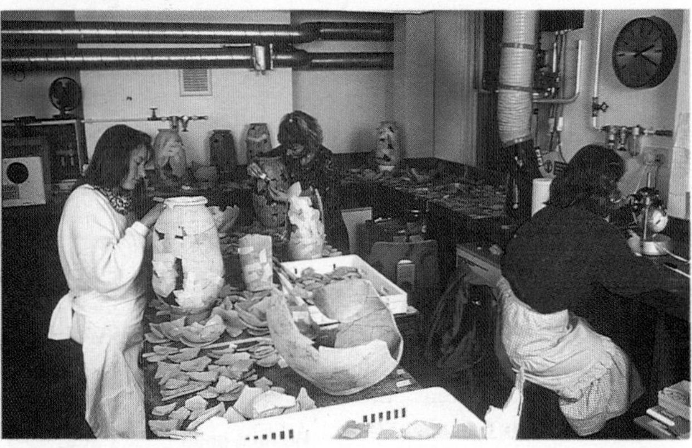

▲ **Piecing together jars broken before 1150 BC.**

Archaeologists try to find out what happened long ago by studying remains. These can be small objects, such as bones from a meal or bits of pottery. They may be the ruins of a large house or even a whole town, such as Pompeii, which was destroyed by the volcano Vesuvius in 79 AD and discovered in 1748.

These days archaeologists use modern techniques such as aerial photography and radioactive carbon dating, to say exactly how old remains are.

Very often archaeological finds are put on display in museums. The Jorvik Viking Centre in York shows us what life was like in Viking times.

Did you know?

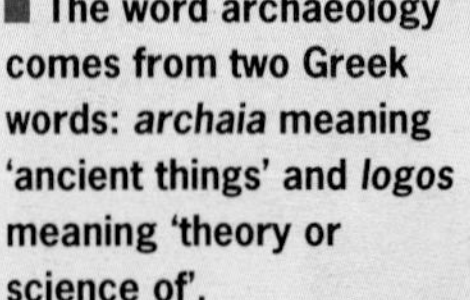

■ The word archaeology comes from two Greek words: *archaia* meaning 'ancient things' and *logos* meaning 'theory or science of'.

Archaeopteryx

▼ ***Archaeopteryx*, 'ancient wing', resembled a small dinosaur with feathers.**

Archaeopteryx found in Germany in 1861, is one of the earliest known fossils of a bird. It was found in rock from the Upper Jurassic period, 145 million years old. Scientists see it as the 'missing link' between dinosaurs and birds. The fossil shows an almost complete skeleton of an animal about the size of a pigeon, with teeth, slender bones and a long bony tail. But the imprint of feathers can be seen surrounding the skeleton, which also has a bird-like wishbone. Only four specimens have been discovered since 1861.

Argentina

Argentina means 'Land of Silver'. This is what it was called by Spanish explorers who hoped to find silver there but were disappointed. Now most of Argentina's wealth comes from oil in Patagonia and from ranches on the pampas, the grassy plains where farmers grow wheat and maize. They also rear cattle, sheep and pigs to sell abroad.

In 1982 Argentina invaded the British Falkland Islands and claimed them as her territory. After a ten-week war Argentina was defeated at a cost of about 1,000 lives.

FACT FILE

Capital
Buenos Aires
Population
33,070,000
Currency
1 Argentine austral = 100 centavos

Armour

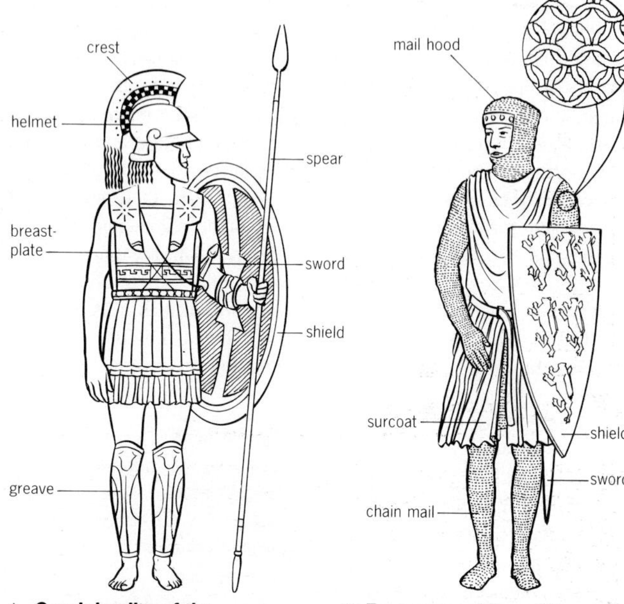

▲ **Greek hoplite of the 5th century BC.**

▲ **European soldier of the early 13th century.**

Soldiers have worn armour to protect themselves, for thousands of years. Ancient Greeks wore bronze helmets, breastplates and leg guards. From Roman times onwards, soldiers wore armour made of metal links, called chain mail.

When guns replaced swords and lances, metal armour virtually disappeared, except for the metal helmet.

Arthur and his knights

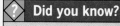

Arthur is a mythical king. He was taught as a boy by the wizard Merlin. He pulled the sword, Excalibur, from a stone to become king. The Knights of the Round Table met at his castle in Camelot. They fought the wicked and helped the weak.

Did you know?

■ **A Celtic chief of 1,400 years ago may have been the real Arthur.**

Asia

Asia is the world's largest continent. It has one third of the planet's land area and half the world's people. Because it is so huge, there are many different landscapes and peoples.

In northern Siberia, the land is frozen. Further south there are forests and grasslands with rich, fertile soil. But much of Asia from the Red Sea to Mongolia is desert. The biggest desert is the Gobi. Asia also has the world's highest mountain range, the Himalayas. In south Asia, near the Equator, there are damp jungles and swampy sea shores. Countries on the Pacific coast, such as Japan, experience earthquakes. Sometimes there are tidal waves too.

Most Asians live in the area that used to be the USSR, China and India. The wealthiest countries are Japan, Singapore, and South Korea. Their industries make many goods for export to other countries. But most Asians make their living from farming. Rice and wheat are the main crops. On the plains of central Asia, there are herds of cattle, goats and yaks.

Many Asians are moving to live in cities. There are now over a dozen cities in Asia with more than 5 million people living there.

FACT FILE

Highest peak
Mount Everest 8,863 m
Largest lake
Caspian Sea 370,000 sq km
Largest country
(by population)
China 1,165,888,000

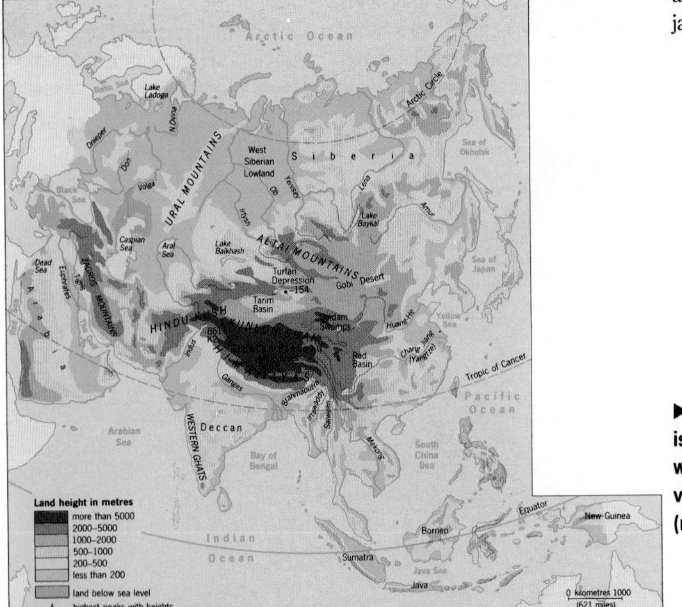

Athletics

There are two types of athletics. Track events are races on a 400 m track. The shortest is a 100 m sprint. The longest is 10,000 m. In some races runners leap over hurdles.

◀ The hammer is a heavy metal ball joined by a wire to a handle (men only).

Field events involve jumping and throwing. There are four jumps: long jump, high jump, triple jump, and pole vault. The throwing events are hammer, discus, shot and javelin.

▶ The pole vault is a high jump with the aid of a vaulting pole (men only).

▶ **The javelin is a spear thrown from a run-up (men and women).**

▶ **The shot is a heavy metal ball (men and women).**

Some athletes do five events in one competition called the pentathlon. The decathlon, with ten events, is probably the hardest athletics contest of all.

▼ **Hurdling race lengths are 100m and 400m for women and 110m and 400m for men.**

Atmosphere

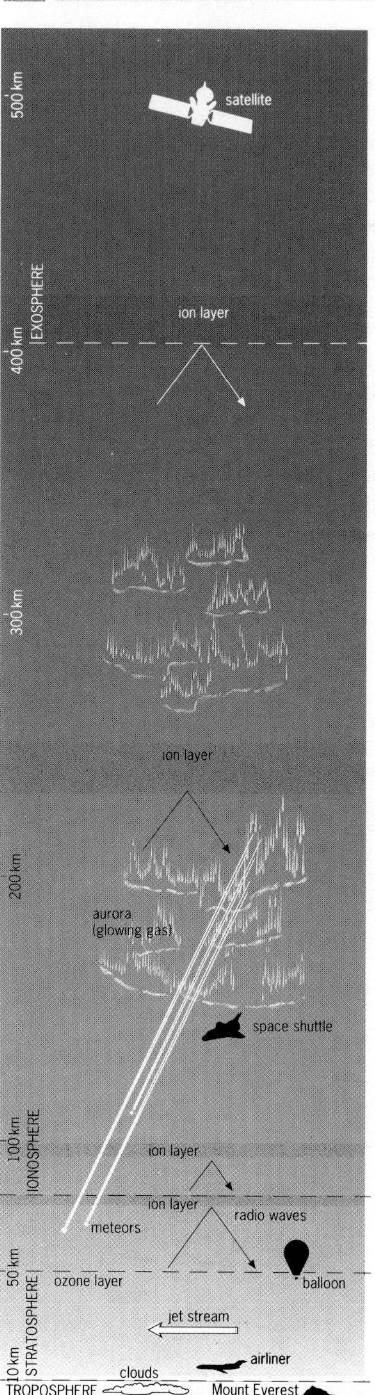

The Earth is surrounded by a layer of air called the atmosphere. This diagram shows the different layers of the atmosphere.

The **exosphere** contains tiny amounts of hydrogen and helium. Here, the Earth's atmosphere really becomes part of space.

In the **ionosphere**, electrical particles called ions help to bounce radio signals around the Earth.

The air in the **stratosphere** is much thinner than in the troposphere. Long-distance aircraft fly in this layer. It contains ozone, a gas which absorbs harmful ultraviolet rays from the Sun.

The **troposphere** is the layer we live in. It contains 90 per cent of the air in the atmosphere. Clouds form in the troposphere, and weather balloons are sent up through it.

Atoms

An atom is the smallest amount of an element (see pages 56 and 185) you can get. Over 4,000,000,000 atoms would fit on the dot of this i.

Atoms are made up of smaller particles called protons, neutrons and electrons. Electrons move at high speed like smeared clouds, around a nucleus of protons and neutrons.

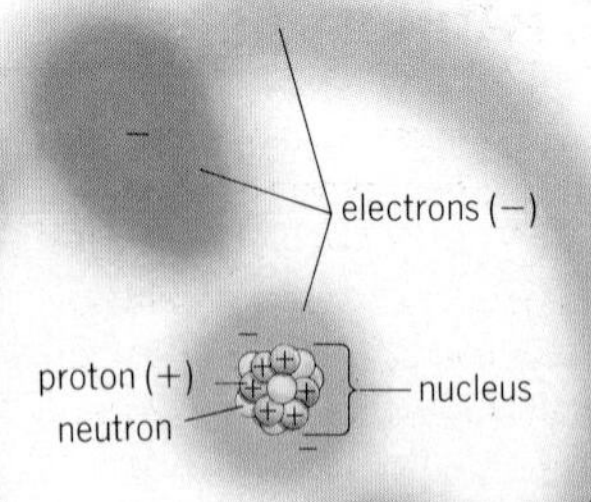

◀ **Model of a carbon atom.**

> **? Did you know? ?**
>
> **■ Protons and neutrons weigh 2,000 times more than electrons.**

Australia

Australia is the sixth largest country in the world. Inland Australia is called 'the outback'. Much of this is desert. Animals found there include koalas, kangaroos, wombats, emus and budgerigars.

Eighty per cent of Australians live on the coast : over 3 million in Sydney alone. Large inland farms grow wheat, and rear cattle and sheep. Australia also produces oil, gas and minerals, such as iron ore.

> **FACT FILE**
>
> **Capital**
> Canberra
> **Population**
> 17,562,000
> **Currency**
> 1 Australian dollar = 100 cents

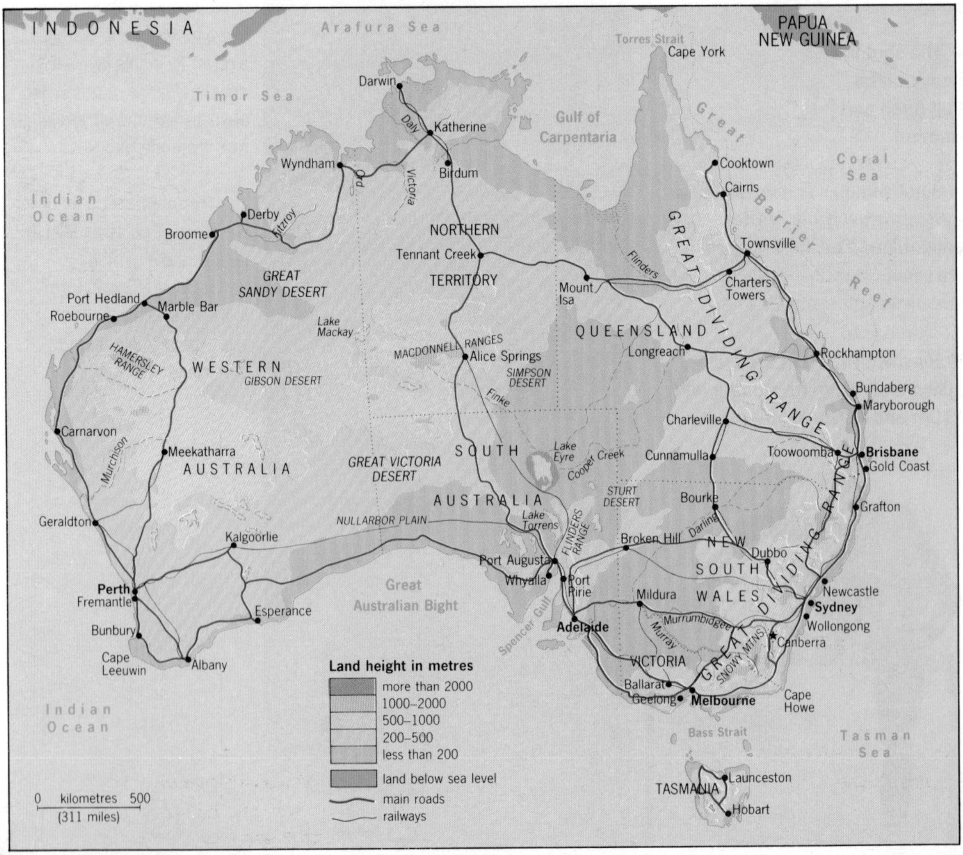

INDONESIA
Arafura Sea
Torres Strait
Cape York
PAPUA NEW GUINEA
Timor Sea
Darwin
Daly
Katherine
Gulf of Carpentaria
Great Barrier Reef
Wyndham
Ord
Victoria
Birdum
Cooktown
Cairns
Coral Sea
Indian Ocean
Derby
Fitzroy
Broome
NORTHERN TERRITORY
Tennant Creek
GREAT DIVIDING RANGE
Townsville
Flinders
Charters Towers
Mount Isa
GREAT SANDY DESERT
Port Hedland
Marble Bar
Roebourne
Lake Mackay
QUEENSLAND
MACDONNELL RANGES
Alice Springs
Longreach
Rockhampton
HAMERSLEY RANGE
WESTERN AUSTRALIA
GIBSON DESERT
SIMPSON DESERT
Finke
Bundaberg
Maryborough
Carnarvon
Charleville
Meekatharra
Murchison
SOUTH AUSTRALIA
Lake Eyre
Cooper Creek
Cunnamulla
Toowoomba
Brisbane
Gold Coast
GREAT VICTORIA DESERT
STURT DESERT
Bourke
Grafton
Geraldton
NULLARBOR PLAIN
Lake Torrens
FLINDERS RANGE
Darling
Kalgoorlie
Broken Hill
NEW SOUTH WALES
Dubbo
Port Augusta
Whyalla
Port Pirie
Perth
Fremantle
Great Australian Bight
Spencer Gulf
Mildura
Newcastle
Sydney
Esperance
Murrumbidgee
Murray
Adelaide
Wollongong
Bunbury
SNOWY MTNS
Canberra
Cape Leeuwin
Albany
VICTORIA
Ballarat
Geelong
Melbourne
Cape Howe
Indian Ocean
Bass Strait
Tasman Sea
TASMANIA
Launceston
Hobart

Land height in metres
- more than 2000
- 1000–2000
- 500–1000
- 200–500
- less than 200
- land below sea level
- main roads
- railways

0 kilometres 500
(311 miles)

Austria

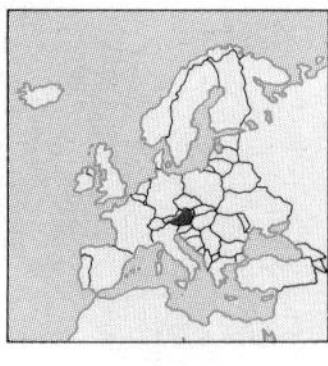

Austria is in central Europe. The Alps, Europe's largest mountain range, stretches from east to west across the country. In winter, many Austrians and tourists enjoy skiing in the Alps.

Some Austrians produce dairy products on family farms. Others work in the paper industry in the forests.

Capital
Vienna
Population
7,857,000
Currency
1 schilling = 100 groschen

Badminton

Badminton is a game for two (singles) or four (doubles) played on a court. Players use rackets to hit a shuttlecock over a high net. The aim is to score points by hitting it over the net so that your opponent cannot hit it back.

Aztecs

The Aztecs lived in what is now Mexico. They moved south into the Valley of Mexico over 1,000 years ago. They built the city of Tenochtitlán in about 1345 and it became the capital of the Aztec empire.

Although hunted and attacked by enemies, the Aztecs began to conquer neighbouring nations. In time they became rulers of Mexico.

Tenochtitlan was a huge city of about 350,000 inhabitants. It was crossed by canals which took the place of streets. The markets of the city were filled with produce from all over the empire.

Most Aztecs were farmers, but they also made superb sculptures and buildings, particularly their pyramid-shaped temples. The Aztecs worshipped many gods, including Quetzalcóatl, the Plumed Serpent.

In 1519, the Spaniard Hernan Cortés arrived at Tenochtitlán. He captured the Aztec emperor, and tried to rule the country himself. The Aztecs rebelled but they were no match for the heavily armoured Spaniards. After fierce fighting the Aztecs were defeated. Within two years the Spaniards were ruling Mexico. They destroyed the temples and the city of Tenochtitlán and built a new city on the ruins.

Ballet

Ballet is a kind of dancing. Men and women can be ballet dancers. Some children start training at a very young age. They have to learn a lot of positions and practise certain movements. Many of these have French names. A turn is a *pirouette*. The *jeté* is a type of jump. Ballet dancers use special shoes with strengthened toes, so that they can dance on tip-toe. This is called 'on *pointe*'.

▶ Scene from the ballet *Sleeping Beauty*.

A dancer ▶ practising *pointe* work. She is in fifth position.

Balloons

In 1783, the Montgolfier brothers in France built the first hot-air balloon to carry a person. The air inside it was heated by a fire on the ground. Modern hot air balloons carry burners to do this. The heated air makes the balloon rise.

In 1988, a hot-air balloon reached an altitude of 19·8 km (12·3 miles).

In 1992, Richard Abruzzo and Troy Bradley flew for over 144 hours non-stop in a balloon when crossing the Atlantic Ocean. Richard Branson and Per Lindstrand made the first transatlantic flight in a hot air-balloon in 1987.

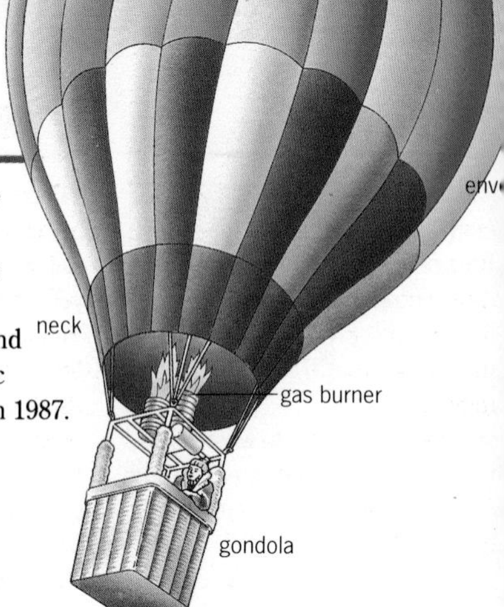

▶ This hot-air balloon is 16 m across and can carry 3 people.

Bangladesh

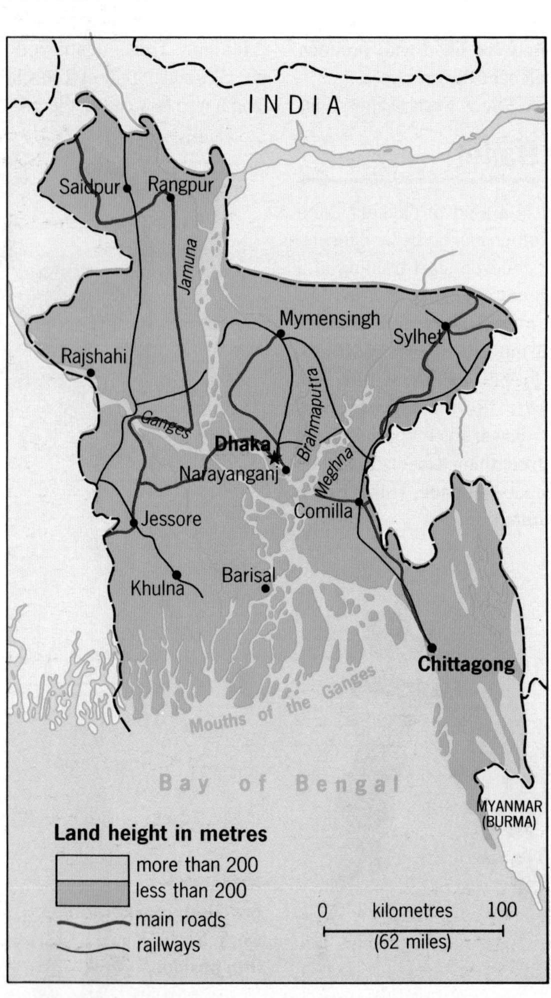

Bangladesh is one of the most crowded countries in Asia. It has only existed as a separate country since 1971. Before that it was East Pakistan. The land is flat and criss-crossed by rivers. More than 2,000 mm of rain falls on most of the country each year. Floods and storms cause a lot of damage and sometimes kill many thousands of people.

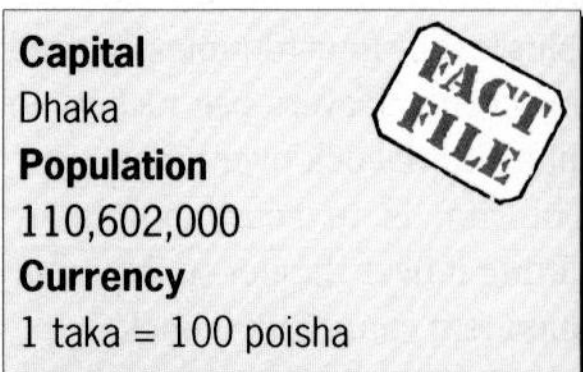

Capital
Dhaka
Population
110,602,000
Currency
1 taka = 100 poisha

Barnacles

▶ Goose barnacles attach themselves by fleshy stalks to the bottom of ships. They feed by combing tiny particles of food from the water with their hairy feet.

Baseball

Baseball is a nine-a-side bat-and-ball game. Batters try to score runs by hitting the ball thrown by the pitcher, and running round the bases. Batters can be struck out, caught out, and run out. When three batters are out, the inning is over. Each side has nine innings.

ball
bat
catching mitt

Baseball is the most popular summer game in the USA. Each year the winners of the two main baseball leagues play each other in a seven game series called the World Series.

Basketball

Basketball is a five-a-side game played on a court. The aim is to score points by shooting the large ball through the other team's 'basket'. This is a metal hoop 3·05 m above the floor. The ball can be passed or dribbled (bounced) by hand around the court. Players must not touch each other. Two points are usually scored for a basket, and the team with the most points wins the game.

- **Basketball began in its present form in 1891 when some young Americans wanted an indoor game.**

Bats

There are 951 species of bat and they make up almost a quarter of all living mammal species. Nearly all are nocturnal. They avoid obstacles and locate their prey by echolocation: they produce high-pitched sounds which bounce off nearby obstacles causing an echo which is picked up by the bat's large ears.

Did you know?

- **Largest bat**
  Flying fox:
  head and body length over 40 cm;
  wingspan 2 m.
- **Smallest bat**
  Kitti's hog-nosed bat:
  head and body length 3 cm;
  wingspan 15 cm.

Echolocation is so accurate that even very tiny insects can be detected.

▲ Mouse-eared bat. Bats are the only mammals capable of true flight. Their wings are made of a double membrane only 0·3 mm thick.

Batteries

Small electric batteries are used to run torches, radios and watches. The electricity comes from chemicals sealed inside the battery. When they are used up, the battery is 'flat'. Some can be recharged, but others must be thrown away.

▶ A 'dry' zinc-carbon battery.

brass cap
carbon rod
ammonium chloride jelly
manganese dioxide and carbon
zinc case (negative terminal)

Bears

Bears usually live alone in large territories coming together for only a short time to breed. Females can give birth to as many as four cubs, but more often they will have two. The cubs weigh less than 0·5 kg (1 lb) at birth.

Bears are primarily meat-eaters, but they also eat a variety of other foods including ants, birds' eggs, berries and honey.

Did you know?

- **The biggest bear, the polar bear, is the largest meat-eating animal on land, three times the size of a lion.**
- **Polar bears can run at up to 56 km (35 miles) an hour.**

Bees

Bees are social insects like ants and termites, and so live mostly in large family groups. Each hive has a queen, the mother of all the bees. She lays eggs that are tended by her infertile daughters, the worker bees. Only a small number of the bees in a hive are males; these are the drones. The drones have only one function: to mate with the queen. After this they die. The queen may live for about five years so the hive is quite long-lived.

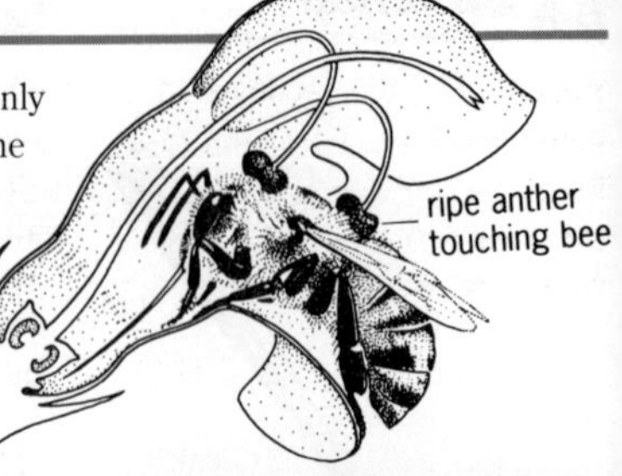

workers looking after the queen while she lays eggs

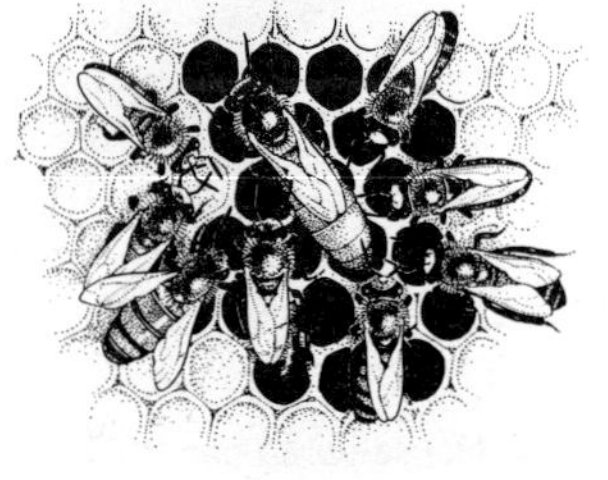

workers constructing a honeycomb

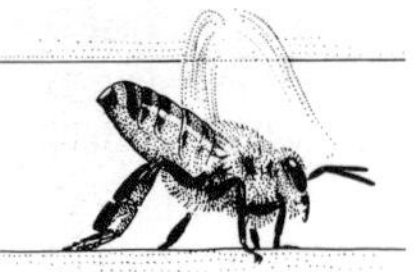

worker at hive entrance beating its wings to drive in cool air

Did you know?

■ Worker bees change their jobs as they get older: they first clean empty cells in the honeycomb ready for eggs or honey and pollen. Then they feed the developing larvae, before producing wax to make new honeycomb. They then become guards, or beat their wings at the nest entrance to drive fresh air through the hive. Finally they visit flowers to collect nectar and pollen.

Beethoven, Ludwig van

Beethoven was born in Bonn, Germany in 1770. His father and grandfather were both musicians, and he followed in their footsteps.

As a young man he moved to Vienna, Austria, and was soon much in demand as pianist and music teacher. But by 1796 he began to go deaf, and by 1802 his deafness was serious. He fought off his growing despair and spent more and more of his time writing music. He wrote nine great symphonies before his death in 1827. Many of his pieces were considered unplayable at the time but are now accepted masterpieces played all over the world.

Portrait of Beethoven, by an unknown artist.

Belgium

Belgium is in western Europe. The people in the north speak Flemish and those in the south speak French.

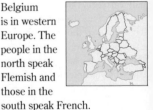

Most Belgians live in towns and cities. Antwerp is a major port and centre for the diamond industry. Brussels is the heaquarters of the European Community.

Capital
Brussels
Population
10,021,000
Currency
1 Belgian franc = 100 centimes

Bicycles

Modern bicycles range from ultra-light racers to sturdy mountain bikes for cross-country riding. Most bicycle frames are hollow, with a light, strong structure and a triangular-shaped design. Early cycles had iron wheels and later, solid rubber ones which made them bumpy to ride. Air-filled tyres were introduced in 1888.

Pedalling is made easier by changing gear. For hills, a low gear gives plenty of force but not much speed. On the flat, a high gear gives less force but more speed.

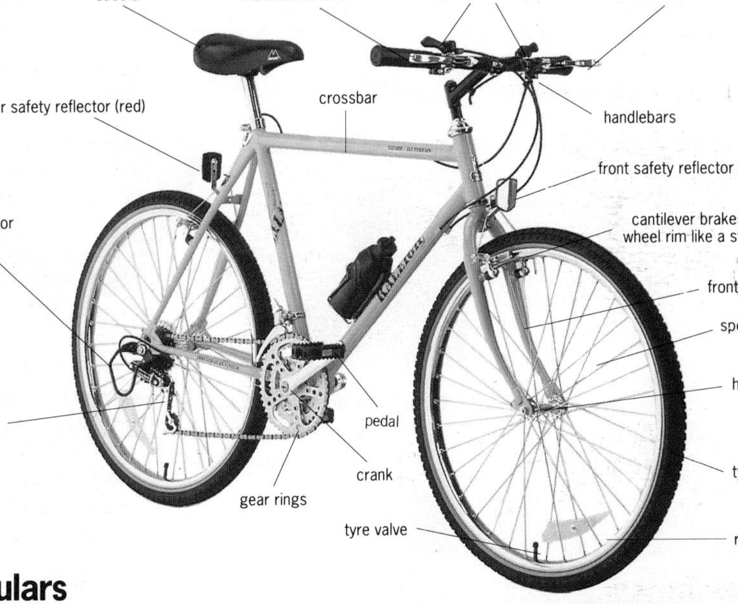

saddle
front brake lever
gear selectors
rear brake lever
rear safety reflector (red)
crossbar
handlebars
front safety reflector (white)
gear protector
cantilever brakes grip the wheel rim like a strong hand
front forks
spokes
derailleur gears have a range of gear wheels which help you to pedal easily up hills or on the flat
hub
pedal
crank
tyre
gear rings
tyre valve
rim

Binoculars

adjustable eyepiece to get the clearest picture for each eye
ocusing wheel
o get a clear
icture
eyepiece lenses
prisms to reflect light
objective lens
light

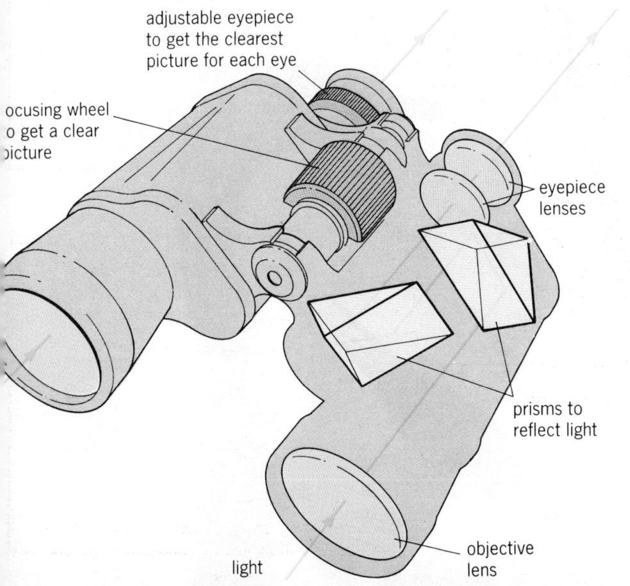

Did you know?

■ If binoculars are marked 8 x 30 it means they have a 30 mm lens and make things look eight times larger.

◄ Binoculars are really a pair of telescopes, side by side. Most have glass prisms inside them. These are needed to turn the picture the right way up.

Birds

There are about 8,700 living species of birds and their variety is amazing. One of the most noticeable differences between species is the shape of their bills. Many wading birds have long, strong bills for probing mud in search of worms and shellfish. Birds of prey have hooked bills for tearing meat. Finches have short strong bills for cracking seeds. Flamingos' bills act like filters: there are hair-like combs along their edges to filter food from mud and sand. Pelicans have large, fleshy pouches beneath their bills which they use for catching fish.

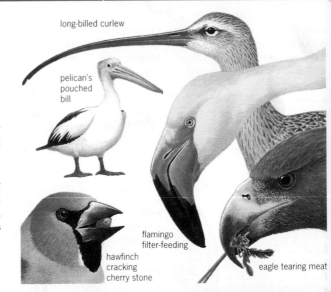

long-billed curlew
pelican's pouched bill
flamingo filter-feeding
hawfinch cracking cherry stone
eagle tearing meat

▲ **Birds' bills are useful tools for feeding, and some are highly specialized.**

Bird record-breakers

Largest wing-span:
Wandering albatross, up to 4 m
Smallest bird:
Bee hummingbird, 6 cm long
Largest bird:
Ostrich, 2·5 m high
Longest non-stop flight by small bird:
4,100 km (2,500 miles) by Greenland wheatear
Fastest bird:
Peregrine falcon, 180 km/h (112 mph)

Did you know?

- **Out of every 100 robins hatched in one year, only 28 are likely to survive until the following spring.**
- **The arctic tern migrates further than any other bird, covering up to 40,000 km (25,000 miles) a year.**

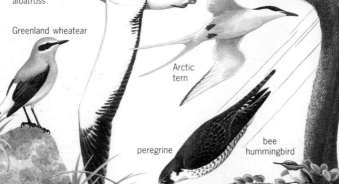

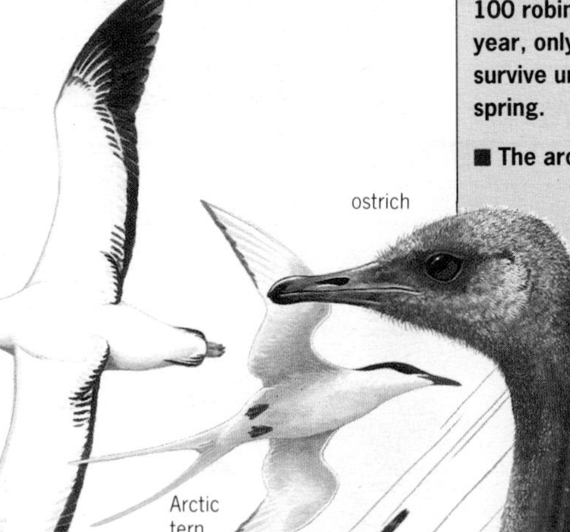

wandering albatross
Greenland wheatear
peregrine
bee hummingbird

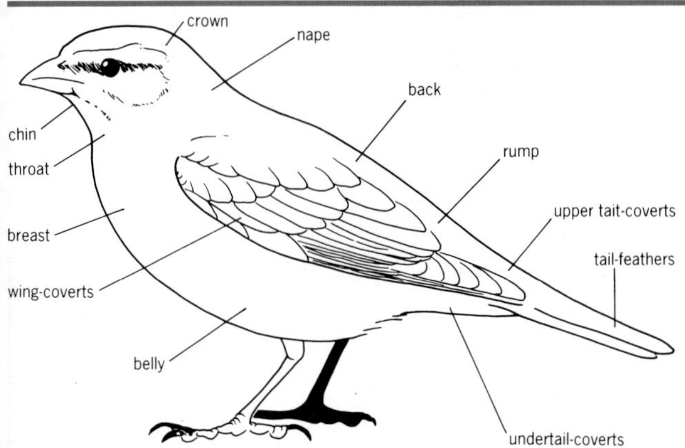

Garden birds

The most common garden birds in Britain are sparrows, starlings, blackbirds, chaffinches, blue tits, great tits, song thrushes, greenfinches, robins and dunnocks. Magpies and collared doves are becoming increasingly common.

You can feed the birds! During the winter put out unsalted peanuts, cheese rinds, cooked potato, seeds, berries, and bread and cake crumbs. Don't forget to put out some water too, and remember to keep it free from ice.

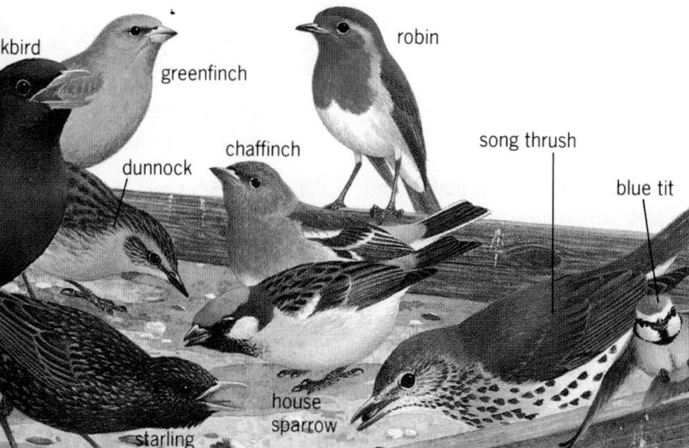

▶ Swallows, like some other northern hemisphere birds, migrate each year to spend the winter in warmer, food-rich places. They face many dangers on their journey.

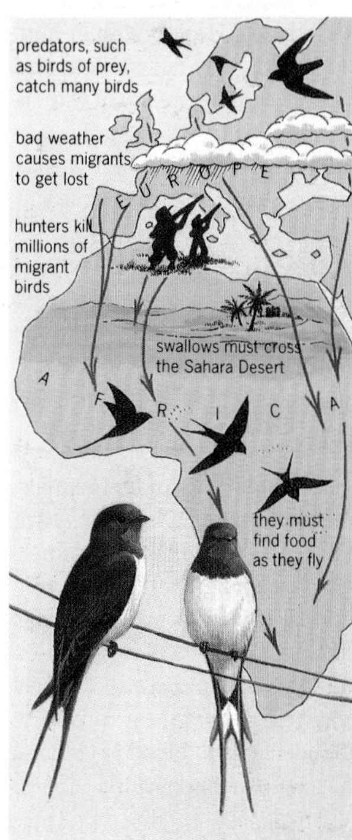

Did you know?

■ **Birdsong is generally the male declaring that he has found a nesting site. It is to attract females and deter other males.**

Feathers

The vane of the feather is made up of barbs and barbules. The barbules are like hooks, holding the barbs together so the feather is wind-resistant for flying. Feathers also keep the bird dry and warm.

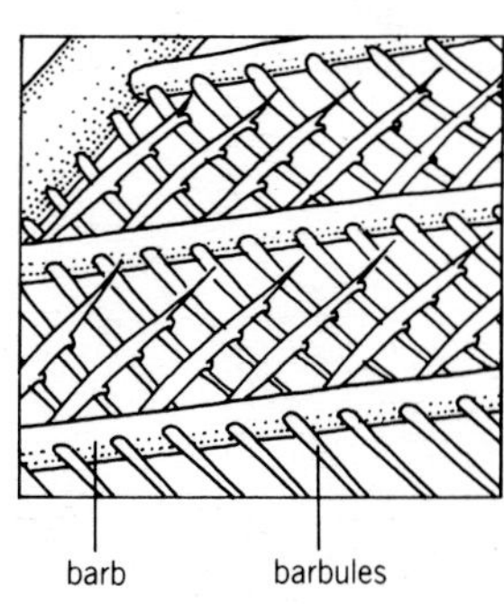

Black holes

A 'black hole' is a very strange kind of star. It sends out no light and pulls in anything near to it with its strong gravity. Black holes are probably formed when a star explodes and the inside of the star falls in on itself.

A black hole with the Sun's mass would be about 6 km (4 miles) wide. Some black holes may be millions of times more massive.

Blood

Only some of the simplest animals, such as corals and flatworms have no blood. The blood of animals with backbones is made up of a fluid called plasma, with blood cells floating in it. Blood cells have a number of different functions: they may carry oxygen, produce antibodies, help blood to clot and destroy invading bacteria.

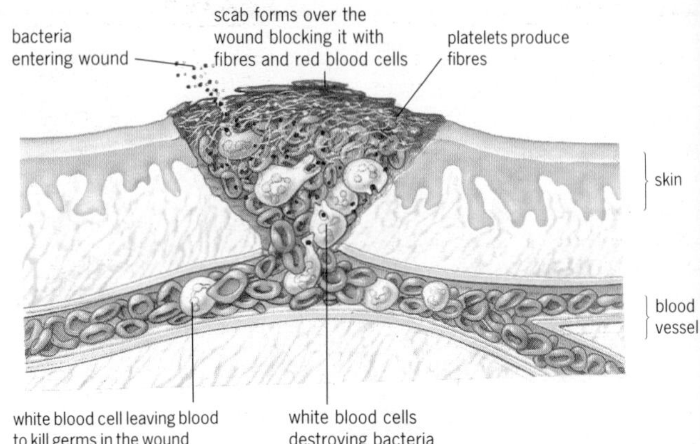

▲ **When you bleed, platelets in the blood send out fibres which form a mesh and trap red blood cells. This forms a blood clot, which blocks the wound.**

Did you know?

- **A drop of blood contains about 100 million red blood cells.**
- **Lobsters' blood is pale blue.**

Bones

Bones are alive. This is why they can mend and regrow after they break. They are as strong as some kinds of steel but only a fifth as heavy. Bones are made out of a mixture of a tough protein, called collagen, and tiny hard mineral crystals which contain calcium and phosphorus. This mixture gives the bones their strength.

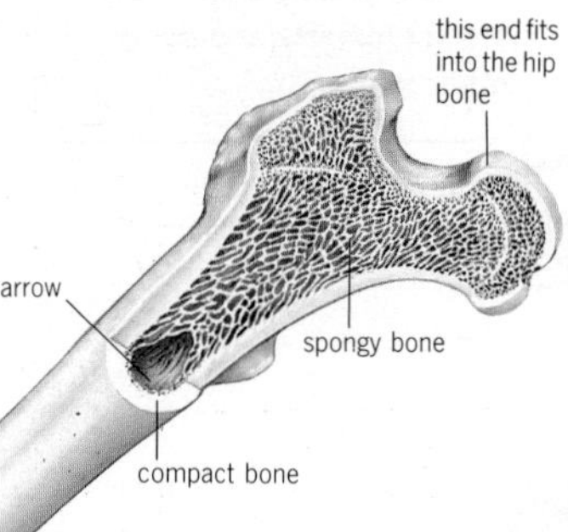

At the centre of many bones is a soft tissue called bone marrow. This contains blood vessels which supply the bone with food and oxygen. New red and white blood cells are made in the bone marrow.

A baby's bones develop slowly in the womb. To begin with they are made of the softer substance, cartilage. The tip of your nose and your ears are made of cartilage. During growth, most of the cartilage is turned into bone. Cartilage is still found in adults' bones: it forms the smooth surfaces where bones slide against each other in joints.

Did you know?

- **A deer's antlers are bones that grow from the skull.**
- **The thigh bone is the longest bone in the human body. Its head fits into the socket in the hip bone, and the other end forms part of the knee joint.**

Books

Some books contain stories. These are called fiction. Others are about real life. They are called non-fiction.

William Caxton printed the first books in England in 1476. Now over 6,000 new children's books are printed in Britain each year.

- **The first printed book was made in China in 868 AD.**
- **The first European printed book was the Bible, printed in Germany between 1452 and 1456.**

Brakes

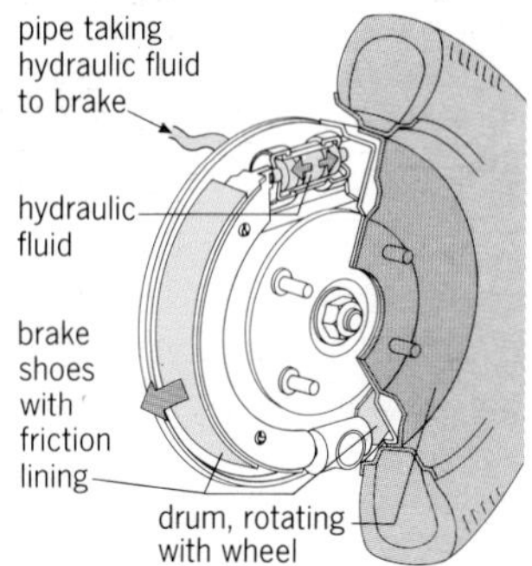

▲ **Drum brake.**

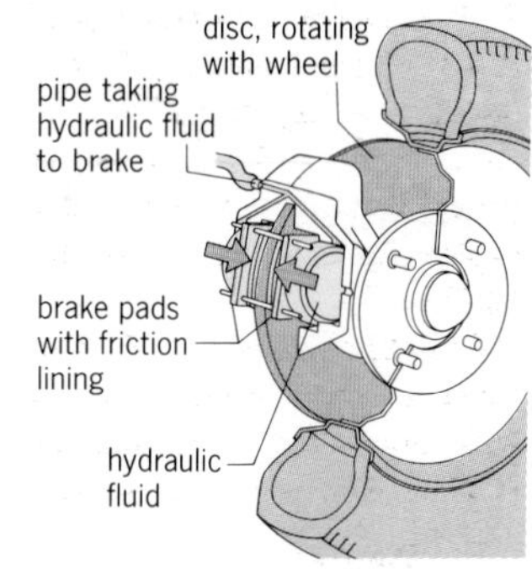

▲ **Disc brake.**

Most cars have disc brakes on the front wheels and drum brakes on the back wheels. When the driver brakes, hydraulic fluid in the disc brake pushes two brake pads against a metal disc which rotates with the front wheel. On the back wheel, the hydraulic fluid pushes two curved brake shoes against a metal drum which rotates with the wheel.

Brazil

Brazil covers nearly half of South America. It borders with every other country there except Ecuador and Chile.

In the north, the river Amazon is surrounded by the world's largest rainforest. Jaguars, monkeys, and many other animals are found there. But more and more of the forest is being cleared to make way for cattle ranches.

Brazil's crops include, coffee, sugar cane and tobacco. There are deposits of iron ore used to make steel for the manufacture of cars, trains, railway lines and ships.

Brazil is one of the ten biggest industrial nations in the world, but most Brazilians are poor.

Capital
Brasília
Population
151,381,000
Currency
1 cruzeiro real = 100 centavos

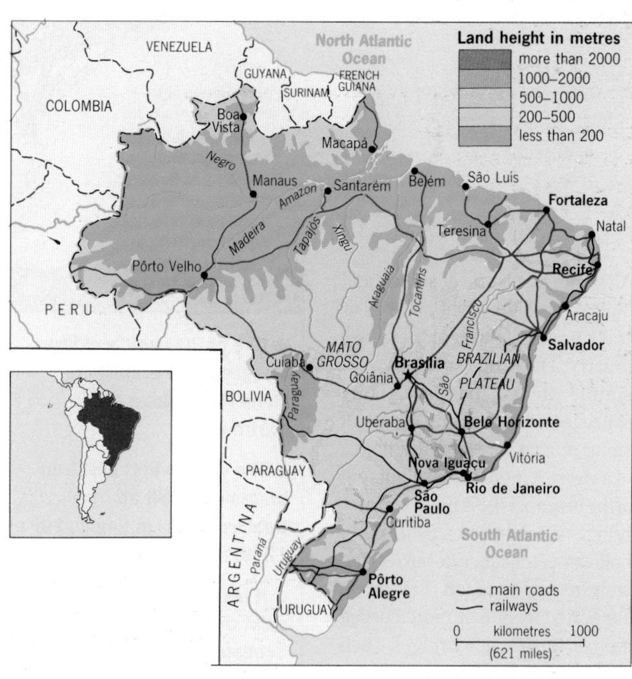

Bridges

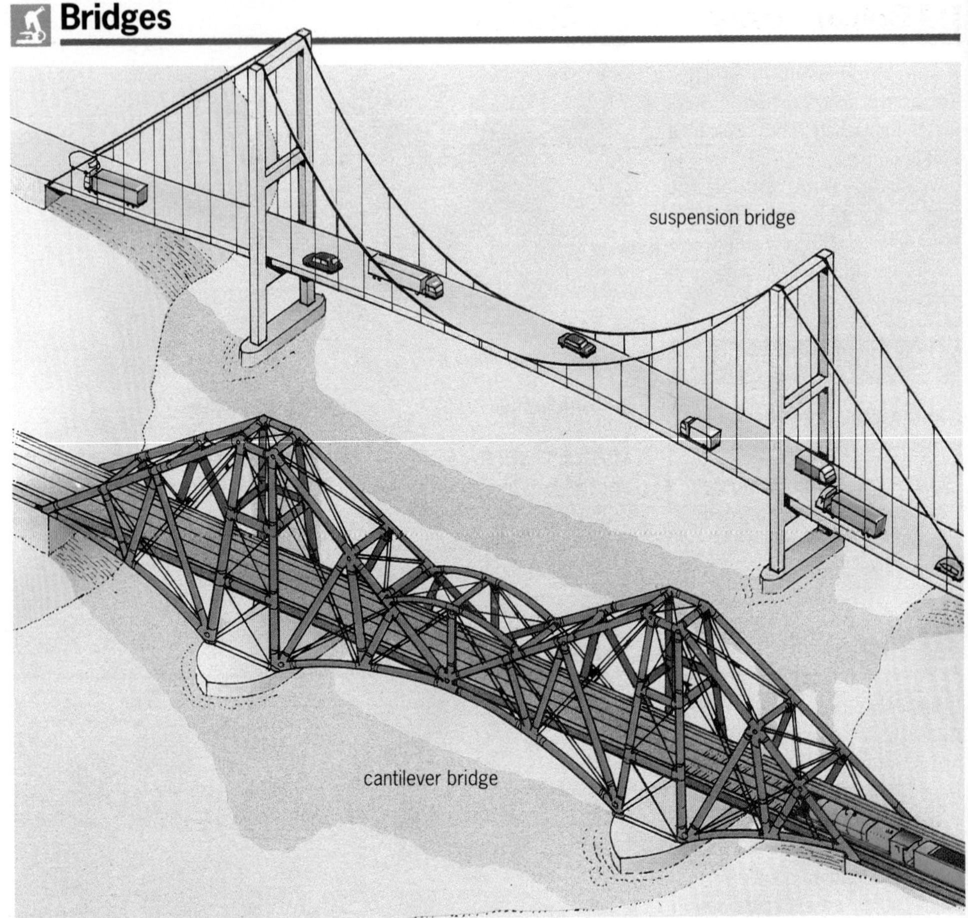

All bridges must be designed and built so that they will not sag or crack under the weight they have to carry. The earliest bridges were simple beam bridges. They consisted of a tree trunk or slab of stone resting between the banks of a river. A modern development of the beam bridge is the box girder bridge which has beams made of hollow steel or concrete boxes. The weight on an arch bridge is supported by one or more curved arches. Suspension bridges, such as the Golden Gate bridge across San Francisco Bay, USA, are best for very large spans.

Did you know?

■ One of the world's oldest bridges is the prehistoric stone Post Bridge on Dartmoor.

■ The world's first cast iron bridge was built at Coalbrookdale in England in 1779.

■ It takes three years to paint the Forth Bridge in Scotland. As soon as the painting is finished, it is time to start again.

▲ The roadway on a suspension bridge is suspended from steel cables which hang between towers. The ends of the cables are anchored in the banks. The world's longest suspension bridge is the Akashi-Kaikyo bridge, Japan.

▲ A cantilever bridge has long, rigid sections. Each section is supported in the middle. The world's longest cantilever bridge is the Québec railway bridge across the St Lawrence River, Canada.

British history

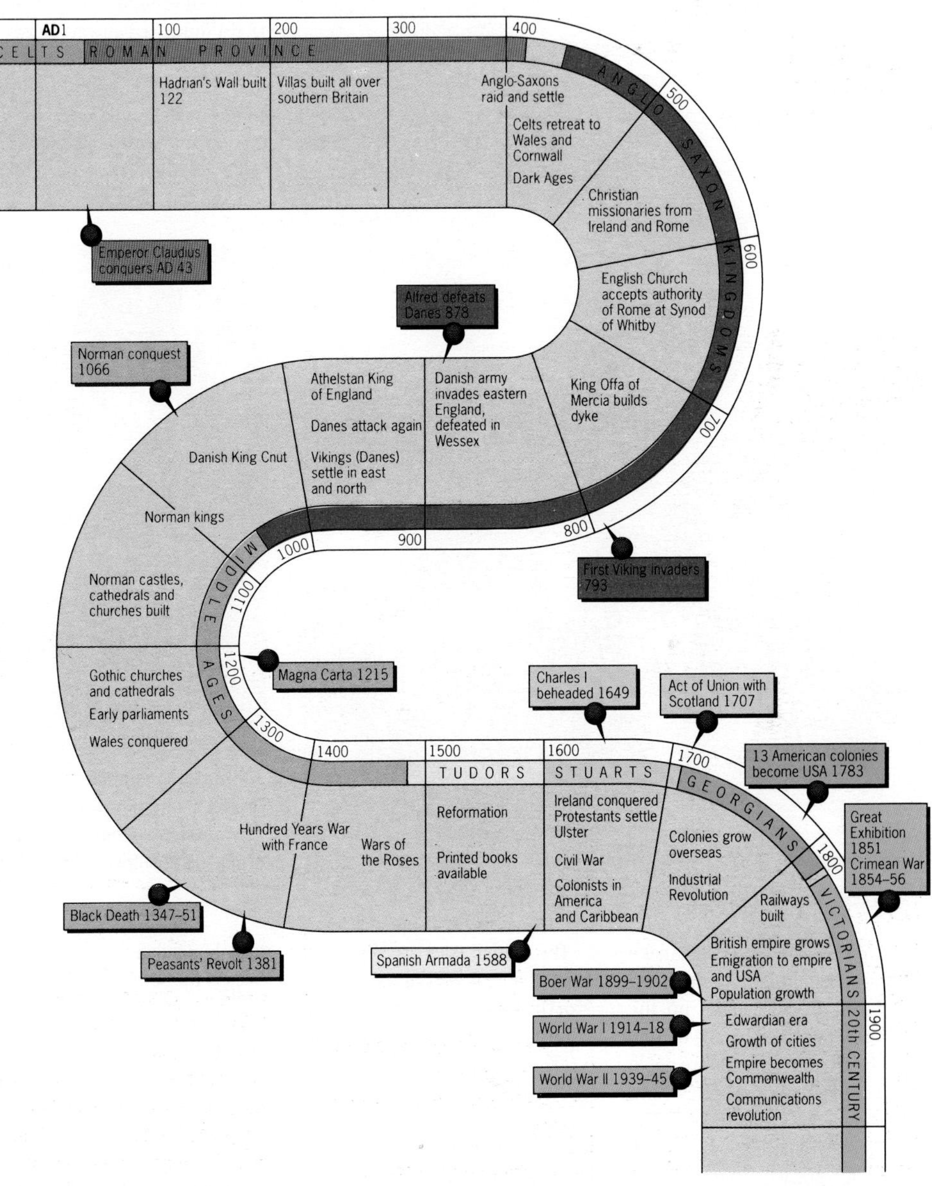
AD1
100
200
300
400
500
600
700
800
900
1000
1100
1200
1300
1400
1500
1600
1700
1800
1900
CELTS
ROMAN PROVINCE
ANGLO SAXON KINGDOMS
MIDDLE AGES
TUDORS
STUARTS
GEORGIANS
VICTORIANS
20th CENTURY
Hadrian's Wall built 122
Villas built all over southern Britain
Anglo-Saxons raid and settle
Celts retreat to Wales and Cornwall
Dark Ages
Christian missionaries from Ireland and Rome
English Church accepts authority of Rome at Synod of Whitby
King Offa of Mercia builds dyke
Danish army invades eastern England, defeated in Wessex
Athelstan King of England
Danes attack again
Vikings (Danes) settle in east and north
Danish King Cnut
Norman kings
Norman castles, cathedrals and churches built
Gothic churches and cathedrals
Early parliaments
Wales conquered
Hundred Years War with France
Wars of the Roses
Reformation
Printed books available
Ireland conquered
Protestants settle Ulster
Civil War
Colonists in America and Caribbean
Colonies grow overseas
Industrial Revolution
Railways built
British empire grows
Emigration to empire and USA
Population growth
Edwardian era
Growth of cities
Empire becomes Commonwealth
Communications revolution
Emperor Claudius conquers AD 43
Alfred defeats Danes 878
Norman conquest 1066
First Viking invaders 793
Magna Carta 1215
Charles I beheaded 1649
Act of Union with Scotland 1707
13 American colonies become USA 1783
Great Exhibition 1851
Crimean War 1854–56
Black Death 1347–51
Peasants' Revolt 1381
Spanish Armada 1588
Boer War 1899–1902
World War I 1914–18
World War II 1939–45

▲ **Time-line showing the different rulers of Britain, and some of the major historical events since the Roman invasion.**

British Isles

England, Scotland and Wales make up Great Britain. Great Britain and Northern Ireland make up the United Kingdom. The Isle of Man and the Channel Islands are not in the United Kingdom. They have their own laws and taxes. The southern part of Ireland is the Irish Republic. But when you add the Isle of Man, the Channel Islands and the Irish Republic to the United Kingdom, you have the British Isles.

The British Isles are separated from the rest of Europe by the North Sea and the English Channel. They extend about 1,000 km from the top of the Shetland Isles to Lizard Point in Cornwall. The most mountainous areas are the highlands of Scotland, the English Lake District and Snowdonia in Wales. About three quarters of the land is used for farming, but most people live and work in towns and cities. The most heavily populated part of the British Isles is the south east of England, around London.

FACT FILE

Population
61,297,000
Highest peak
Ben Nevis (Scotland)
1,344 m
Longest river
Shannon (Irish Republic)
386 km

Brunel
Isambard Kingdom

Isambard Kingdom Brunel (1806-1859) built a railway between London and Bristol, which was one of the finest engineering achievements of its day. His ship the *Great Britain*, launched in 1843, was the first modern metal, transatlantic steamship.

▲ This famous photograph of Brunel shows him standing by the massive anchor chain of one of his great ships.

Bulgaria

Bulgaria is a country in south eastern Europe. The river Danube separates it from Romania to the north. Bulgarians grow cereals, fruit, cotton, tobacco and grapes for wine making. They also export coal, steel and chemical products.

Capital
Sofia
Population
8,985,000
Currency
1 lev = 100 stotinki

FACT FILE

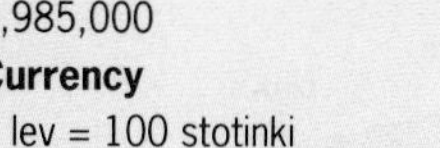

Cacti

Cacti are plants adapted to life in the desert. They have a spreading network of roots so they can absorb as much water as possible after rain. The water is stored in the fleshy stem, which is surrounded by a thick skin to reduce water loss by evaporation. After rain the cactus swells, then gets slowly thinner as it uses the water, which may last for up to two years of drought.

▶ During a drought the stem of a giant saguaro cactus shrinks and develops deep pleats. But after heavy rain it swells, the stem expands, and the pleats almost disappear.

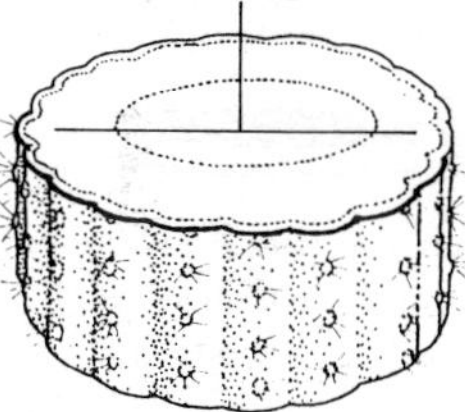

stem swollen after rain

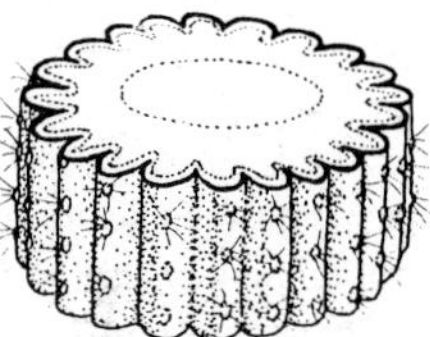

stem shrivelled after drought

Butterflies

▲ Cairn's birdwing butterfly, one of the largest butterflies.

Did you know?

- **There are 20,000 species of butterfly.**
- **Birdwing butterflies have a wingspan of up to 28 cm.**
- **The females die after they have laid their eggs.**

Caesar, Julius

Julius Caesar was a general in ancient Rome. In 55 and 54 BC he led his army on two invasions of Britain. He marched them back into Italy in 49 BC to fight a civil war against his rival Pompey. He won in 45 BC and made himself 'dictator for life'. Before this time two 'consuls' had shared the rule; Caesar had been a consul since 60 BC. But many did not wish to be ruled by one person and his opponents plotted against him and stabbed him to death in Rome in 44 BC, aged about 57.

Camels

Did you know?

■ Camels can go for weeks without drinking anything, and lose up to 40% of their body weight. When a camel does reach water it can drink up to 57 litres (12.5 gallons) without a pause.

▲ Camels are mammals used as a means of transport in the desert.

Cameras

When you take a picture with a camera, the lens takes in light from the person or scene and makes a small upside-down picture on the film inside. The light-sensitive film must be kept in the darkness until it is processed and the finished photographs are produced. The shutter and the aperture (hole size) are set so that the camera lets in the same amount of light whether it is dull or sunny.

The first real camera, made by Frenchman Joseph Niepce in 1826, made a picture on a metal plate. In 1947 an American, Edwin Land, invented a camera that produced instant photos.

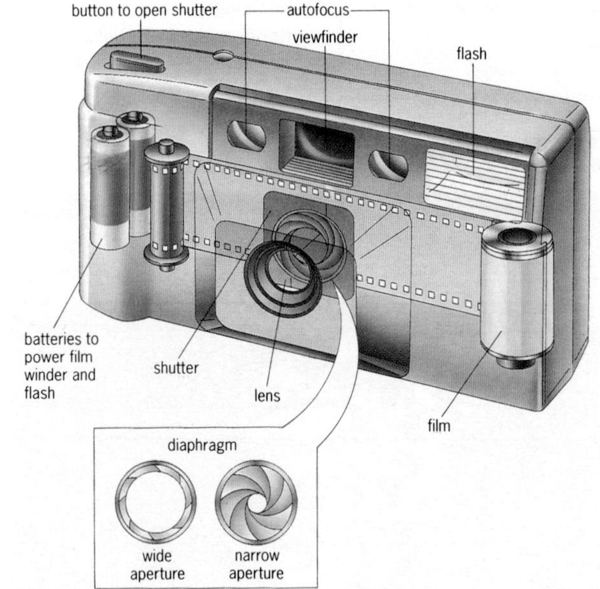

▶ **In a camera, a lens is used to make a tiny picture on a film.**

Making a pin-hole viewer

Cover one end of a cardboard tube with foil, and the other with tracing paper, shading it with extra card. Make a large pin-hole in the middle of the foil and point this at a bright window (but never at the Sun). The pin-hole acts like a lens and makes an upside down picture.

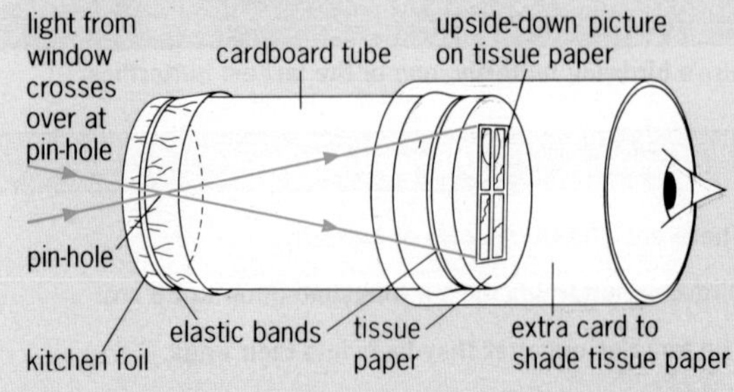

Canada

Canada is the world's second largest country, after Russia. It stretches over 5,000 km from the Pacific to the Atlantic Ocean. A trip across Canada by aeroplane takes about eight hours. A car journey can take up to eight days.

The northernmost parts of Canada are inside the Arctic Circle. In the winter months much of Canada is covered in snow. Most of Canada's cities are found round the Great Lakes — St Lawrence Seaway. Around 5 million people live in the two largest cities, Toronto and Montréal.

Canada contains many valuable resources, which are exported to other countries. Its wheat feeds many millions, and its forests provide timber and paper. Gold, nickel, asbestos and platinum are mined for export.

Canada has two official languages. Most people speak English as their first language, but one in five Canadians speaks French as a first language and learns English in school. Canada's 500,000 native people, the Inuit (Eskimo) and 'Indians', also have their own languages.

FACT FILE

Capital
Ottawa
Population
27,737,000
Area
9,970,610 sq km
(3,849,674 sq miles)
Currency
1 Canadian dollar = 100 cents

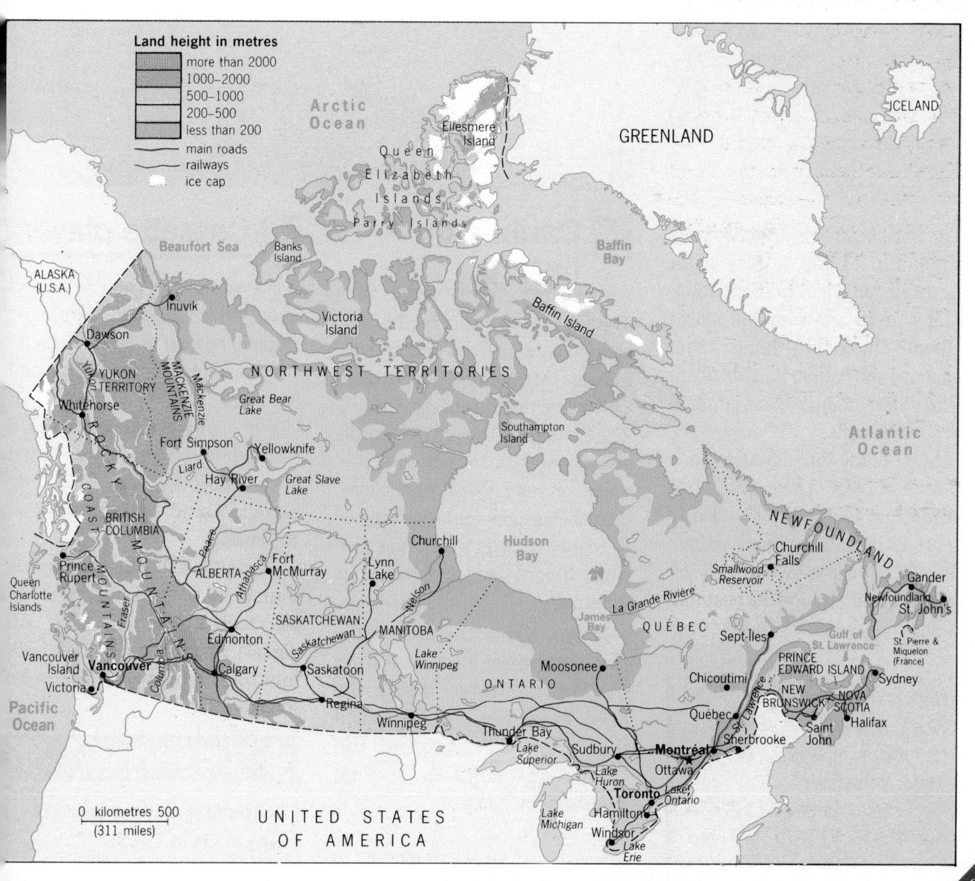

Caribbean

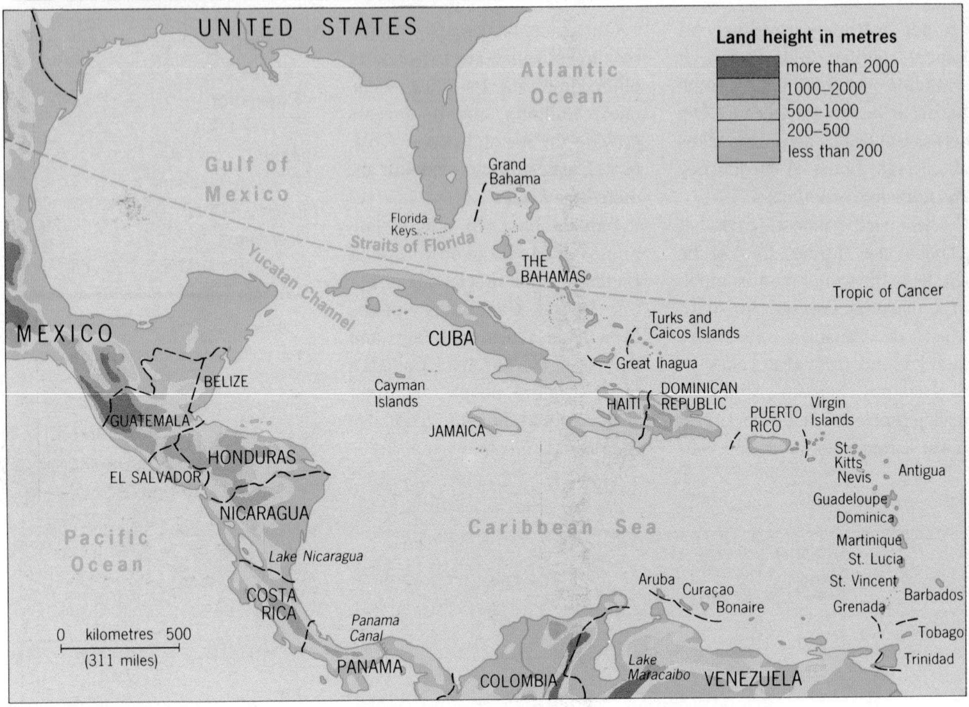

The Caribbean Sea stretches over 3,000 km (1,900 miles) from Central America to Barbados. Many crops grow in the warm climate, including sugar cane, bananas and coffee. Bauxite, from which aluminium is made, is mined in some islands.

Most of the time, gentle winds blow across the sea, but sometimes, during the rainy seasons, hurricanes cause serious damage. Tourists love to visit the Caribbean because of the beautiful weather and scenery.

FACT FILE

Highest peak
Pico Duarte
(Dominican Republic) 3,175 m
Major volcanoes
Mont Pelée (Martinique) 1,397m
Soufrière (St Vincent) 1,234m

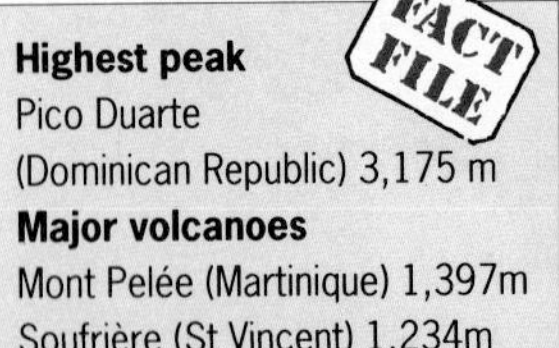

Caribbean history

The first people who lived in the Caribbean were Carib and Arawak Indians. Many were killed after 1492 when the Europeans arrived. The Europeans brought in African slaves to work in the fields to grow crops to send to Europe. Many Caribbean people today speak Creole languages with French or English words, and mainly African grammar.

In 1804 slaves rose up to make Haiti the first free black state in the Caribbean. Others fought for freedom too, but it was not until the 1960s that most of the Caribbean countries became independent states.

Cassette player

A cassette player can record and play back speech, music or computer data. The plastic cassette case contains magnetic tape and two reels.

When you record your voice, a microphone changes the sound into electric signals. A record/playback head records these on the tape.

During playback, the tape is pulled back past the record/playback head. This gives off signals which are changed back into sound by an amplifier and a loudspeaker.

Did you know?

- **The first modern cassette was made in 1963.**

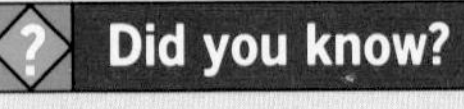

Castles

Castles were built as fortified homes for kings and nobles. The best known castles in Europe were built in the Middle Ages. Most were built of stone on high ground. Larger ones had room for local people to shelter behind the walls if an enemy army was attacking.

Enemy armies sometimes surrounded a castle. These sieges could last a long time as attackers tried to break in and defenders tried to keep them out. In the 15th and 16th centuries, the invention of gunpowder made it harder to defend castles.

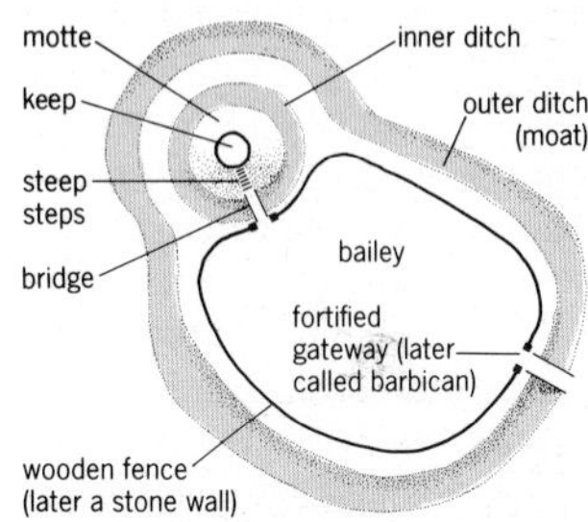

▲ Plan of a Norman motte-and-bailey ('mound and yard') castle.

▼ Harlech Castle, North Wales.

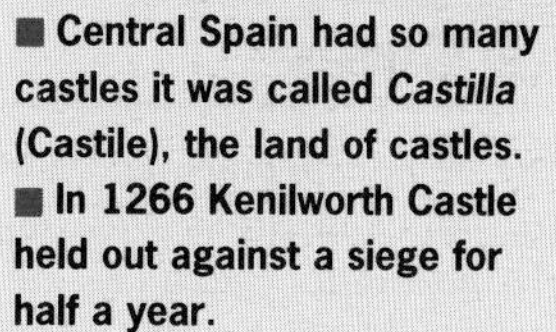

Did you know?

- **Central Spain had so many castles it was called *Castilla* (Castile), the land of castles.**
- **In 1266 Kenilworth Castle held out against a siege for half a year.**

Cats

Your pet cat is a member of the cat family. There are many different breeds of domestic cat but they can all breed together. This shows that they all belong to the same species. There are 37 species of cat including the big cats, such as the lion. Cats were first tamed by the ancient Egyptians 3,500 years ago. The Egyptians worshipped cats and the punishment for harming one was sometimes death.

All wild cats are hunters depending almost entirely on their kills for food. Cats hunt by ambushing their prey and then making a short dash for the kill. Most cats are very fast over a short distance but give up if their quarry escapes to run further. Many cats hunt at night and have large whiskers to improve their sense of touch in the dark.

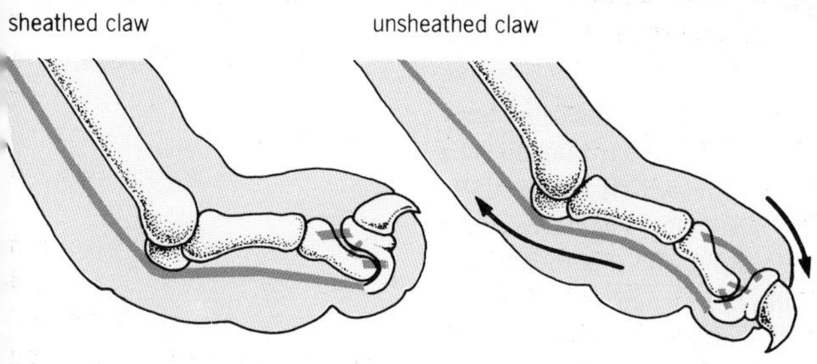

▲ A cat can retract its claws into sheaths in the pads of its paws, so they are not worn down and blunted when it walks. When making a kill, strong muscles pull against the toe bones on which the claws grow, so they extend, to hold and tear the prey.

Did you know?

- **The largest cat is the Siberian tiger which is 2·8 m long, excluding tail, and weighs as much as 360 kg.**

Cattle

Cattle were first domesticated 8,000 years ago. Today there are about 200 breeds. They are cud-chewing animals which means they have complex four-part stomachs. Food, usually grass, passes without much chewing, into the rumen and reticulum where it is partly broken down by bacteria. The cow then 'chews the cud' by regurgitating food and chewing it thoroughly. Food then returns to the reticulum and is passed into the omasum and abomasum where digestion is completed.

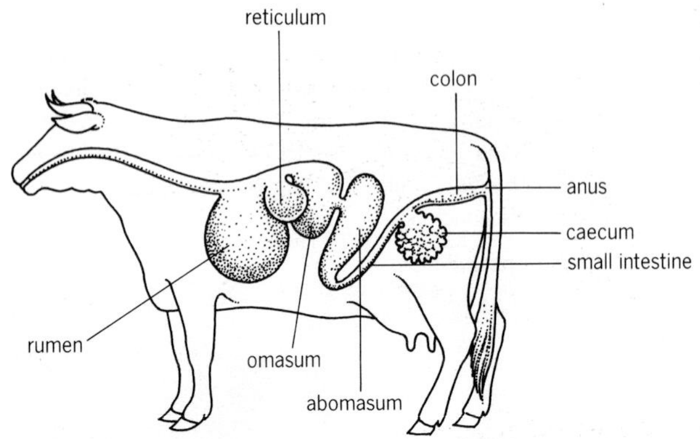

Caves

The most spectacular caves are found in areas with lots of limestone, such as the Mendip Hills in England. Water gradually widens cracks and joints in the porous limestone, and underground rivers wear it away.

The Mammoth Cave system in Kentucky, USA has 560 km (348 miles) of caves and passages. The world's deepest cave (1,602 m deep) is in France.

▼ **Caves are made by water gradually eroding rock.**

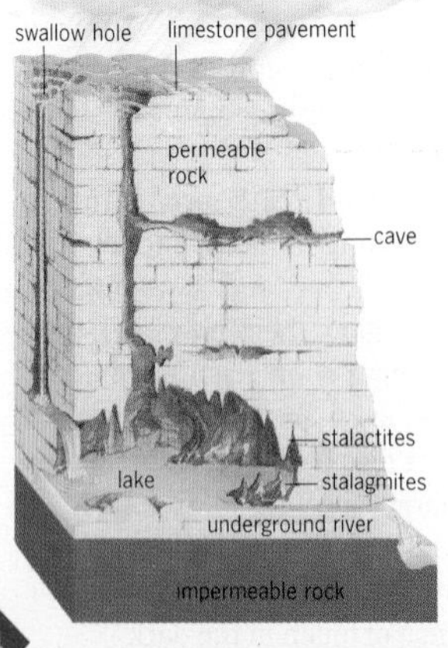

Cells

Cells are the living building blocks from which microbes, plants and animals are made. Microbes and very simple plants and animals, such as amoebas, have only one cell. Most living things are made up of large numbers of cells grouped together. Your body is made up of billions of cells. Groups of cells of the same type are called tissues.

Most cells have the same basic parts. Each are surrounded by a membrane which holds them together. Plant cells have a thick cell wall outside this membrane. Inside the membrane, the cell is divided into two parts: the nucleus and the cytoplasm. The nucleus contains the body's genes, which are made of DNA. These control the manufacture of protein and, together with other chemicals, make all the substances in the body. The cytoplasm surrounds the nucleus and contains a number of different cell 'organs', called organelles, with a range of functions. Cells reproduce by dividing in two.

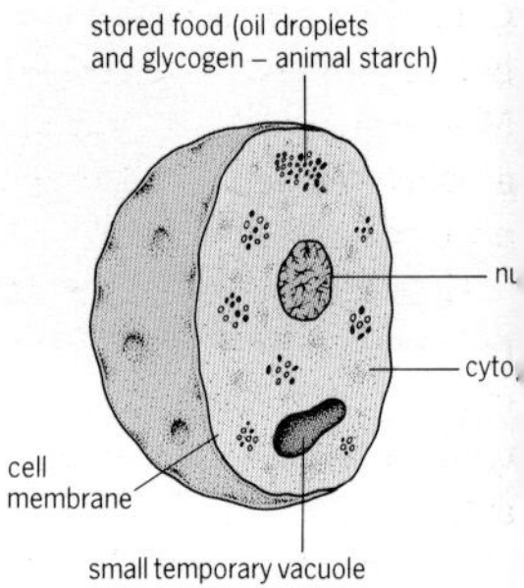

▲ **A typical animal cell.**

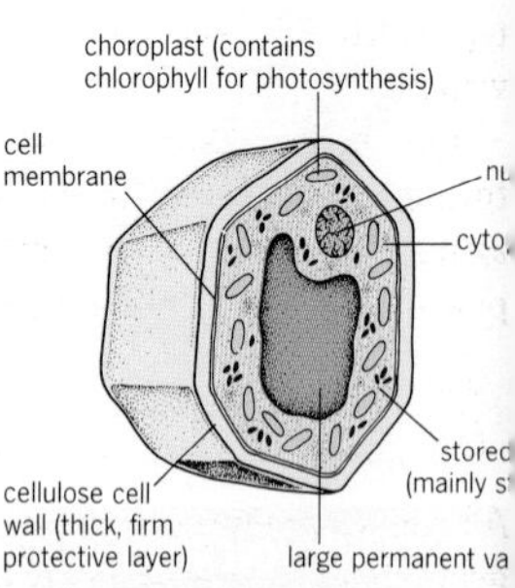

▲ **A typical plant cell.**

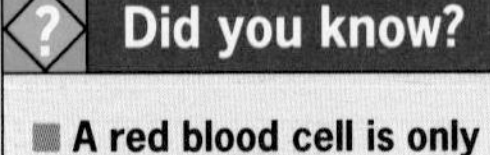

■ **A red blood cell is only 0·007 mm across.**

Centipedes

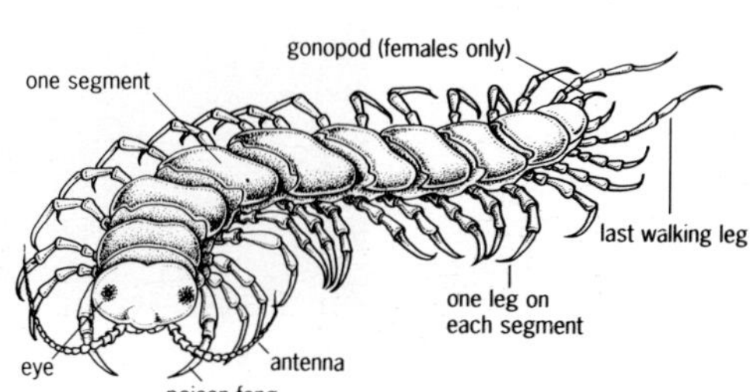

The name centipede means 'hundred feet'. Though most centipedes have fewer than this some have been known to have over 350 legs. Centipedes are hunters and have poison fangs with which to overcome the insects and worms which are their main food.

The largest centipede is over 30 cm in length, and is found in South America. It hunts mice and lizards, as well as insects, for its food.

Central heating

Central heating can heat a whole building using a single heat source. Most systems use water, heated in a boiler, which is fuelled by gas, oil, electricity or solid fuel.

Hot water is pumped round the radiators to heat the rooms. An electric timer controls this and turns the heating on and off automatically.

Hot water from the boiler also heats water for the hot taps. It flows through a coiled tube in the storage tank connected to the hot taps and the shower, and heats the water.

The same water circulates through the boiler over and over again. This stops the boiler and its pipes from scaling up like a kettle.

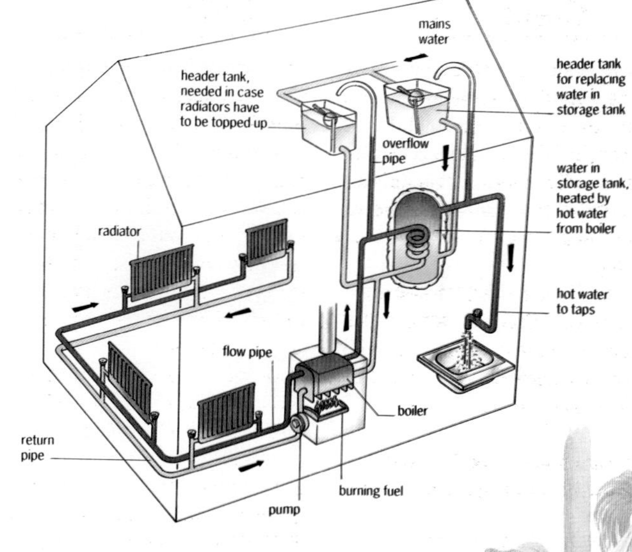

Cereals

All cereals are types of grass. We grow them for the seeds, which are called grains. These grains have carbohydrate, protein, vitamins, minerals and fibre. All these can be good for us.

The main cereals are rice, wheat, maize, rye, barley and millet. Some are used to make breakfast cereals, others are ground into flour for baking.

Did you know?

■ The first breakfast cereal was Shredded Wheat. It was first produced in 1893.

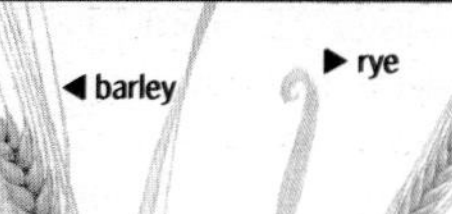

Chameleons

Chameleons are small lizards that can blend into their backgrounds by changing colour. In brilliant sunshine they are a rich green, whilst at night they become paler. A frightened chameleon may turn pale, while an angry one goes a blackish green.

A chameleon's eyes are like little swivelling turrets, and each eye can look in a different direction.

Channel Tunnel

The 50 km long Channel Tunnel is one of the world's longest underwater tunnels. It links France and Great Britain. Huge machines were built to cut through the clay 50 m (150 ft) beneath the sea-bed. On 1 December 1990, English and French tunnel workers reached the same spot beneath the English Channel. The tunnel opened in 1994.

▶ **Channel Tunnel under construction.**

Chaucer, Geoffrey

Geoffrey Chaucer was born in London in about 1340. He did a number of jobs for the king before he became a writer. His most famous stories are *Troilus and Criseyde* and *The Canterbury Tales*. In 1386 Chaucer was made Member of Parliament (MP) for Kent. He died in 1400 and is buried in Westminster Abbey.

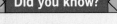

Did you know?

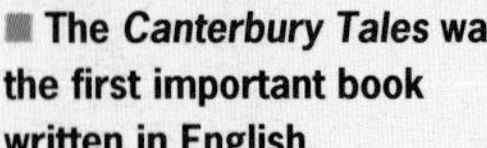

■ **The *Canterbury Tales* was the first important book written in English.**

Charles I

Charles I was born in Scotland in 1600. After he became king in 1625, he quarrelled with Parliament. By 1642 the rows had turned into a civil war.

Parliament won the war, and when Charles tried to start another war, he was arrested. In 1649 he was publicly beheaded.

Chimpanzees

Chimpanzees are apes and our closest living relatives. They live in small groups in African rainforests, feeding mostly on leaves and fruit. But they will also sometimes hunt small monkeys, in highly organized groups, much as our early ancestors must have done. Chimpanzees also use tools. They use crushed leaves as sponges to soak up water to drink, and long twigs for 'fishing' termites from their nests.

Chimpanzee language includes at least 24 sounds, each with a special meaning. They also use a wide range of gestures and facial expressions to communicate.

China

▲ **Bicycle park in Si-an.**

▲ **The Li River, Guilin.**

More people live in China than in any other country. As much of the land is desert or mountain, China has difficulty in feeding all its people. Most Chinese families live in the country and work on the land. Their main crop is rice, which they eat with vegetables.

Those who live in cities usually have small houses or flats with only one or two rooms. Very few own cars. Most Chinese use bicycles, buses and trains.

Capital
Beijing
Population
1,165,888,000
Currency
1 yuan = 100 fen

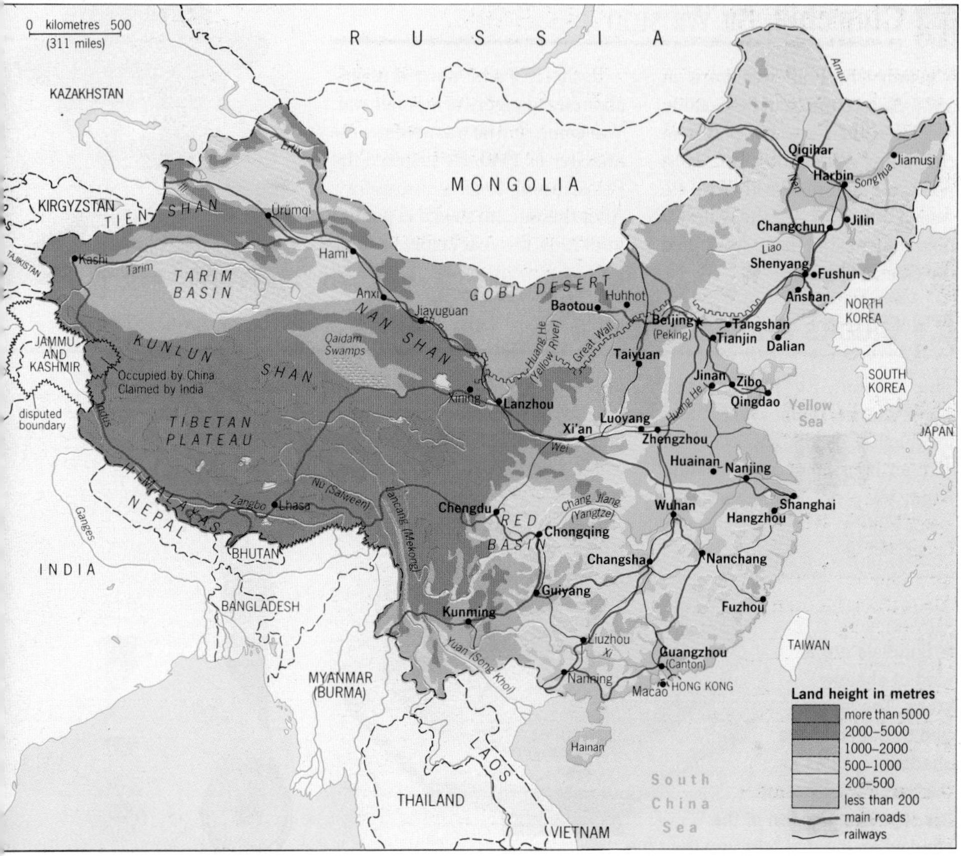

0 kilometres 500 (311 miles)

Land height in metres
- more than 5000
- 2000–5000
- 1000–2000
- 500–1000
- 200–500
- less than 200
- main roads
- railways

China's history

China was ruled by emperors for about 3,000 years. The first emperor was Yu of the Xia dynasty, in about 2100 BC. The Great Wall of China was built in the Qin dynasty in 221 BC to keep out foreigners.

The last emperor, Pu Yi, was overthrown in 1912. In 1949 Mao Zedong set up the People's Republic and China became a communist country.

◀ **14th-century Chinese plate.**

Paper, printing, compasses, canal locks and gunpowder were all used in China long before they reached Europe.

▼ **When Zheng ('The First Emperor') died in 210 BC, 6,000 models of soldiers were buried with him to serve him in the after-life. His tomb was uncovered in 1974.**

Churchill, Sir Winston

Winston Churchill was born in 1874. As a young man he became a soldier, then a war reporter in the Boer War, and finally a politician. Before World War I he was a minister in the Liberal government, but later he joined the Conservatives.

In the 1930s he warned people about the dangers of another war. War came, and he was made prime minister in 1940. He inspired the British people to carry on to victory. After the war, he stayed in politics until 1964, the year before he died.

Clocks and watches

The ancient Egyptians used water clocks to measure time. Mechanical clocks and watches, with an hour hand and a minute hand, were not made until the 17th century. Atomic clocks are the world's most accurate timekeepers. They are accurate to within one second in 1·6 million years.

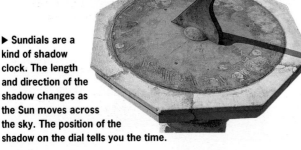

▶ **Sundials are a kind of shadow clock. The length and direction of the shadow changes as the Sun moves across the sky. The position of the shadow on the dial tells you the time.**

▼ **An analogue watch uses hands and a dial to show the time. When you look at the hands, it is easy to see that there are 15 minutes to go before four o'clock.**

▼ **A digital watch uses numbers to show the time. It keeps time very accurately, but you cannot see at a glance how long it is until four o'clock. You have to work it out for yourself.**

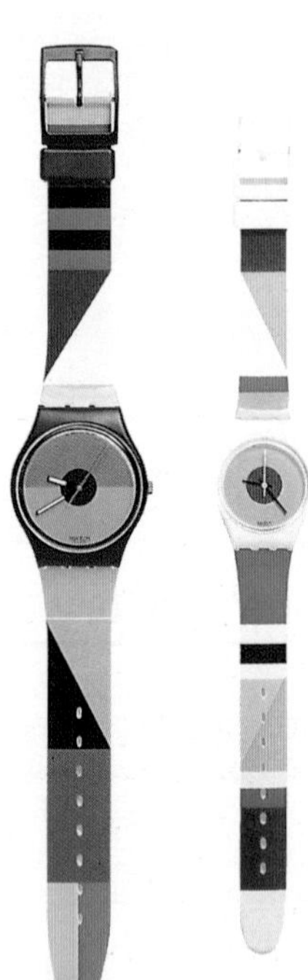

▲ **Lots of modern watches are brightly coloured and inexpensive. They use the natural vibrations (100,000 times per second) in a quartz crystal to keep time, and their power comes from tiny batteries.**

Clouds

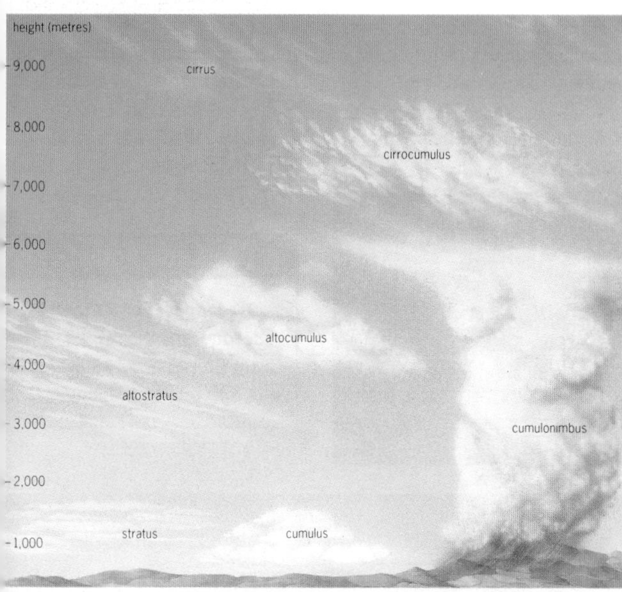

When water vapour condenses into billions of tiny droplets we see these as clouds in the air. Different types of clouds form at different heights above the ground. These are the names of some of the cloud formations.

Cirrus clouds may form up to 13 km (8 miles) up.

One form of **cirrocumulus** is the 'mackerel sky' which means that rain is on the way.

Stratus is the low type of cloud which often turns to fog, drizzle or rain.

Cumulonimbus is a thunder cloud.

Altocumulus are blob-shaped clouds seen in summer, late evening or early morning.

Coal

Coal is the fossilized remains of plants which grew millions of years ago. As the dead plants decayed, they formed peat. Layers of sand, clay and gravel above the peat eventually turned to rock. They squashed the peat until it became hard and turned into coal.

- **In the early 19th century young children dragged heavy tubs of coal underground in the mines.**
- **Chemicals from coal are used to make nylon, explosives, medicines and fertilizers.**

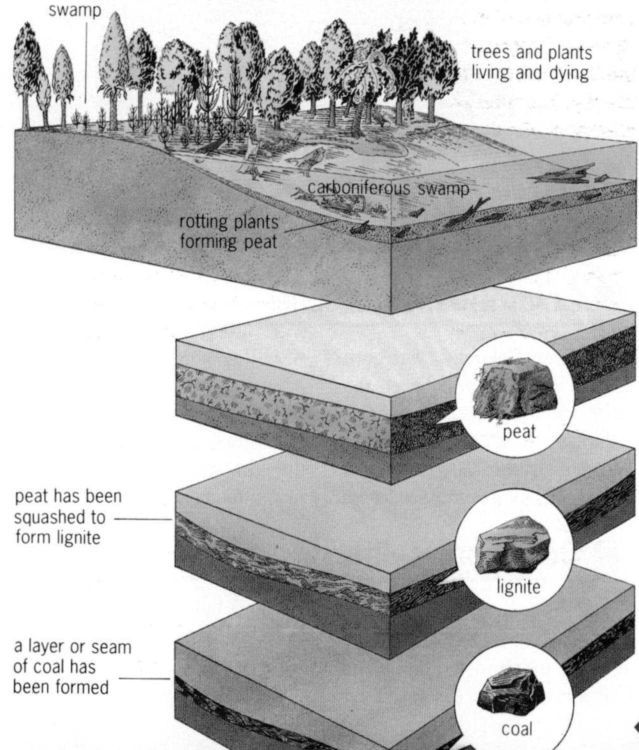

▶ **How coal is formed.**

Colour

When light beams of different colours are mixed together, only red, green and blue (the primary colours) are needed to make all the other colours. White light is made up of coloured light.

▼ **A glass prism splits white light.**

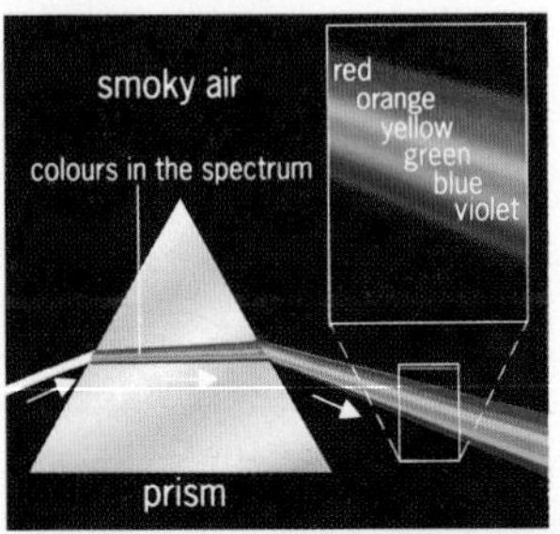

▼ **Mixing coloured beams of light.**

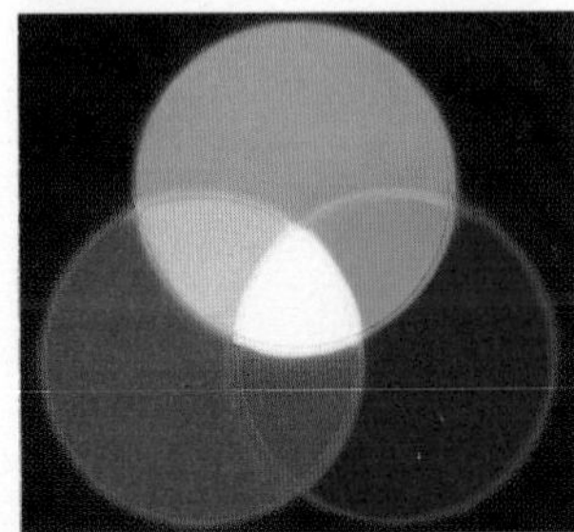

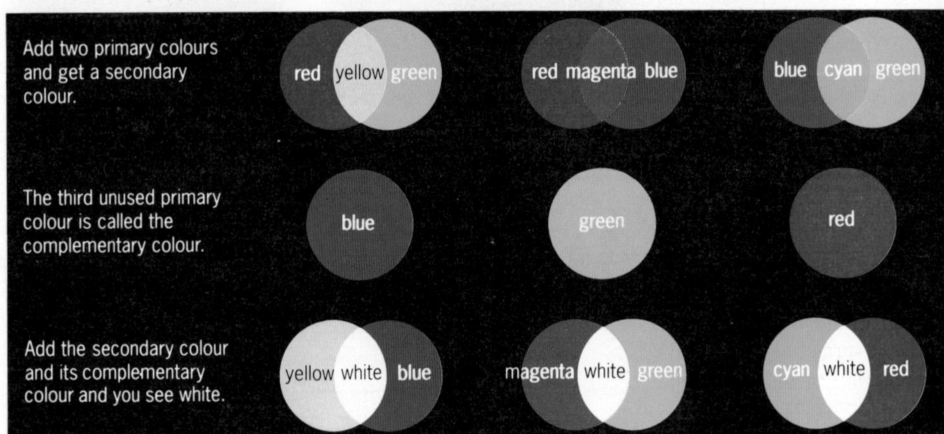

Comets

Comets are made of ice, gas and dust. They orbit the sun and shine because they reflect sunlight. Halley's Comet, first spotted in China in 240 BC, was last seen in 1986. It can be seen from the Earth every 76 years.

Did you know?

■ **The longest comet tail recorded was that of the Great Comet of 1843, which was 330 million km long.**

Columbus, Christopher

Christopher Columbus was born in Italy in 1451. He believed the Earth was round so he wanted to sail west to reach the countries of the east. Queen Isabella of Spain paid for his expedition. He sailed with three ships, *Santa Maria*, *Ninã* and *Pinta*, and about 90 men.

In 1492 they reached the Bahamas, which Columbus thought was the East Indies. He made four voyages across the Atlantic reaching the Caribbean and the mainland of Southern Central America, before his death in 1506.

Commonwealth

The Commonwealth is a group of about 50 countries which used to be in the British Empire. As well as Australia, Canada, New Zealand, India and Pakistan, there are Commonwealth countries in the Caribbean, Africa and Asia. The Secretary-General, Chief Emeka Anyaoku, sets up regular meetings for the leaders of Commonwealth countries.

Computers

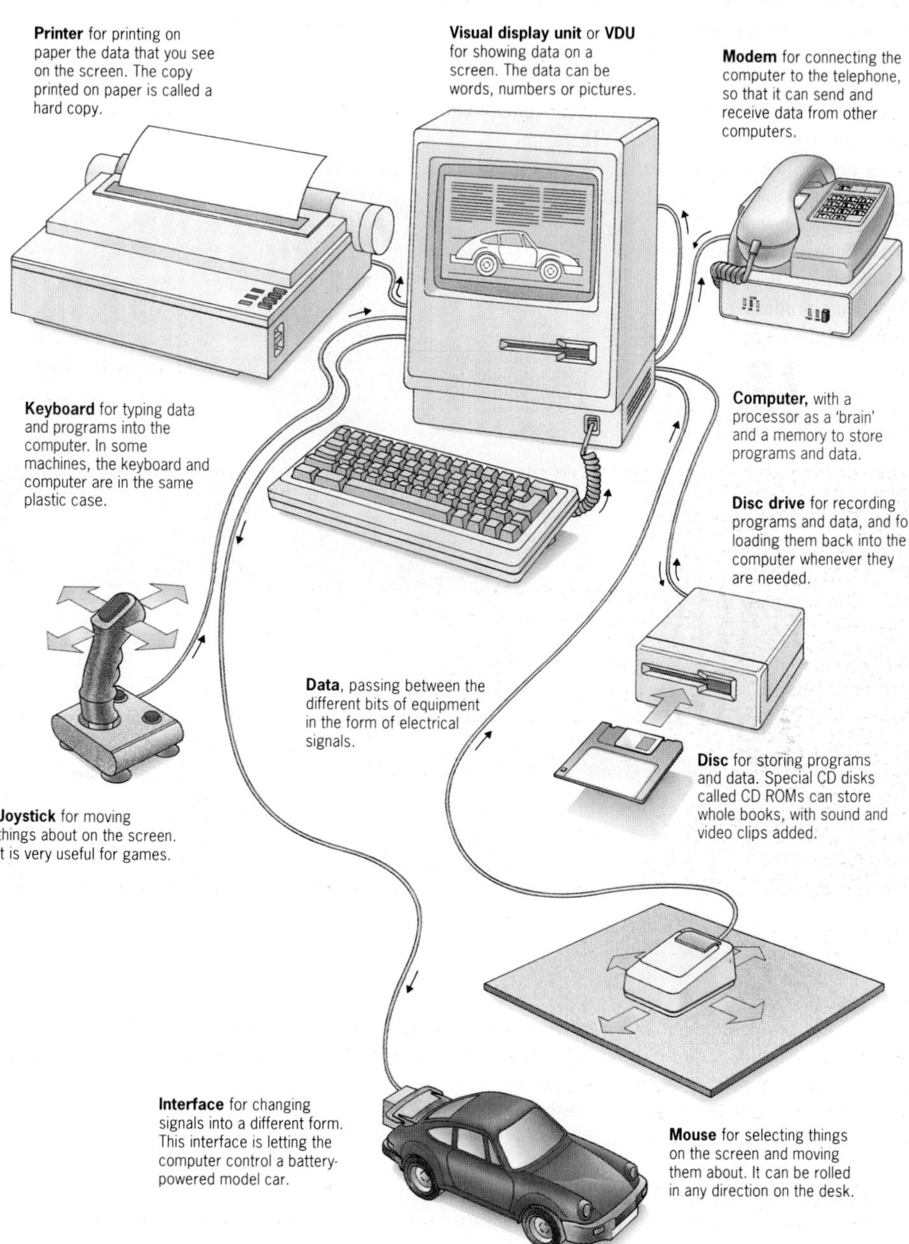
Printer for printing on paper the data that you see on the screen. The copy printed on paper is called a hard copy.
Visual display unit or **VDU** for showing data on a screen. The data can be words, numbers or pictures.
Modem for connecting the computer to the telephone, so that it can send and receive data from other computers.
Keyboard for typing data and programs into the computer. In some machines, the keyboard and computer are in the same plastic case.
Computer, with a processor as a 'brain' and a memory to store programs and data.
Disc drive for recording programs and data, and for loading them back into the computer whenever they are needed.
Data, passing between the different bits of equipment in the form of electrical signals.
Disc for storing programs and data. Special CD disks called CD ROMs can store whole books, with sound and video clips added.
Joystick for moving things about on the screen. It is very useful for games.
Interface for changing signals into a different form. This interface is letting the computer control a battery-powered model car.
Mouse for selecting things on the screen and moving them about. It can be rolled in any direction on the desk.

Conifers

Conifers are woody plants which bear cones containing seeds. Most are evergreens and found mainly in cold northern areas, such as Canada and Scandinavia. They grow faster than deciduous trees, so they are frequently grown for timber.

▼ Male cones grow in clusters and are smaller than female cones. They produce huge numbers of pollen grains which are carried by the wind to fertilize the seeds attached to the scales of the female cones.

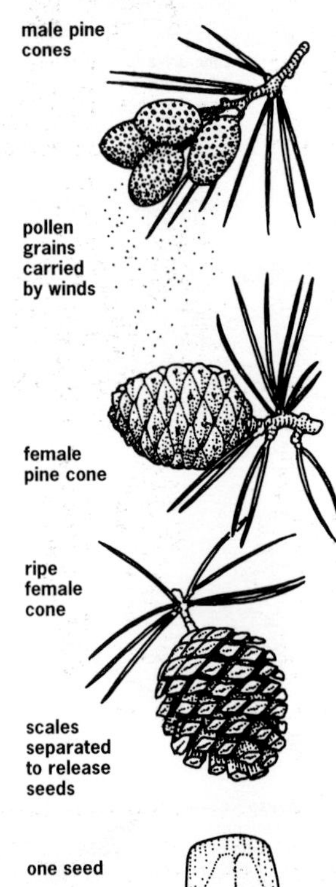

Constellations

A constellation is a named group of stars that seem to make a pattern when seen from Earth. Some of the 88 constellations in the sky were named by the Greeks 2,000 years ago.

If you live in the northern hemisphere, some easy constellations to find in winter are Orion (the Hunter), Leo (the Lion) and Gemini (the Twins).

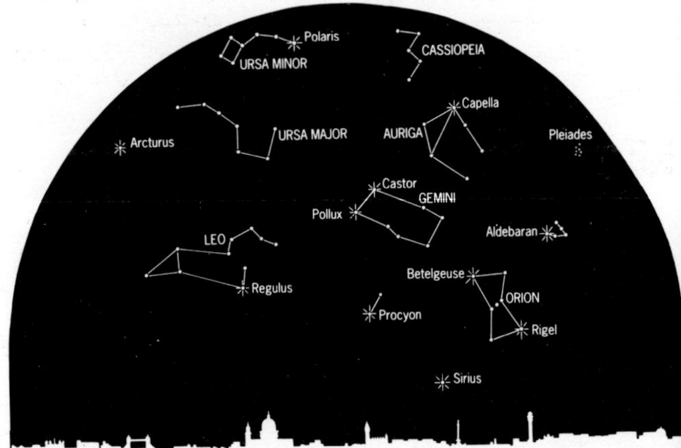

Continents

The large masses of land on the Earth's surface are called continents. They cover 29 percent of the Earth's surface. Most geographers agree that there are seven continents.

The continents were once joined together in a supercontinent called Pangaea. About 200 million years ago Pangaea began to break up into separate pieces which moved slowly apart.

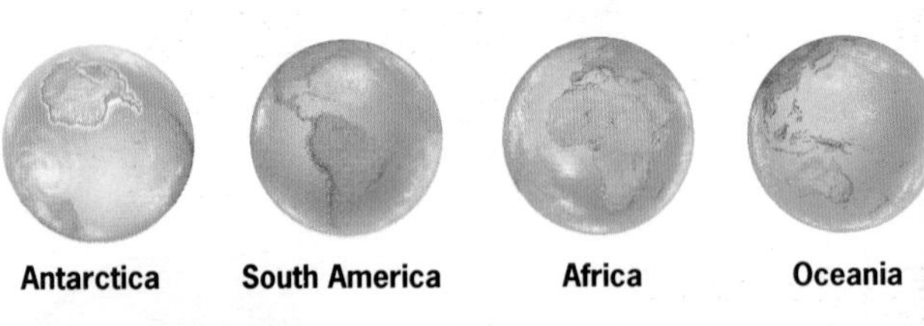

North America

Europe

Asia

Coral

Coral polyps are small animals related to sea anemones. The polyp produces a hard, cup-shaped limestone skeleton around itself, which remains after it has died. Coral reefs are made up of the skeletons of millions of polyps. Living corals often appear dead as most coral polyps stretch out their tentacles to feed only at night.

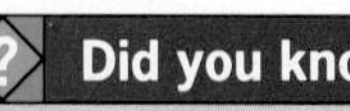

Did you know?

■ **The Australian Great Barrier Reef, is so large that it can be seen from the moon. It is over 2,000 km (1,250 miles) long.**

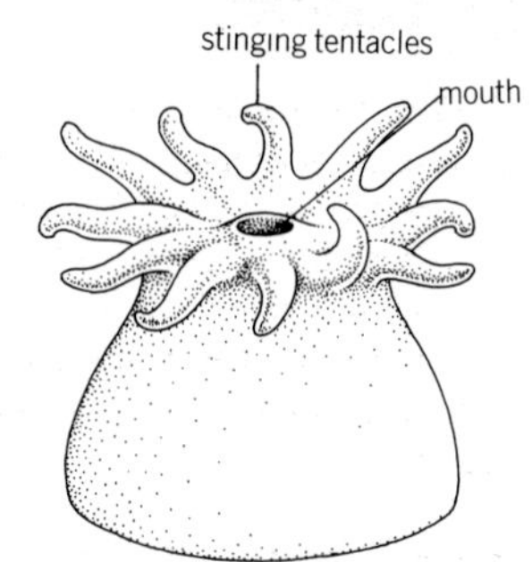

▶ **The bodies of coral polyps are filled with fluid. Their mouths are ringed with stinging tentacles, used to catch food.**

Costume

Celtic

Roman

Norman 1060s–1100s

Medieval 1390s–1430s

Late Medieval 1460s–1480s

Tudor 1530s

Elizabethan 1580s–1600s

Stuart 1630s

Georgian 1750s

Regency 1815–1820

Victorian 1870s

Edwardian 1900s

1920s

1960s

Cowboys

Cowboys, or cowhands, are workers who look after cattle in North America. In South America they are called *gauchos*. During the 20 years after 1870 there were about 40,000 cowboys. They rode the range in all weathers, and faced danger from rustlers (cattle thieves).

Today there are about 20,000 cowboys. They still ride horses, but also use trucks and aircraft, and communicate by two-way radio.

Did you know?

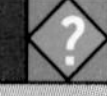

■ **The cowboy's chief tool is still the lasso.**

Cranes

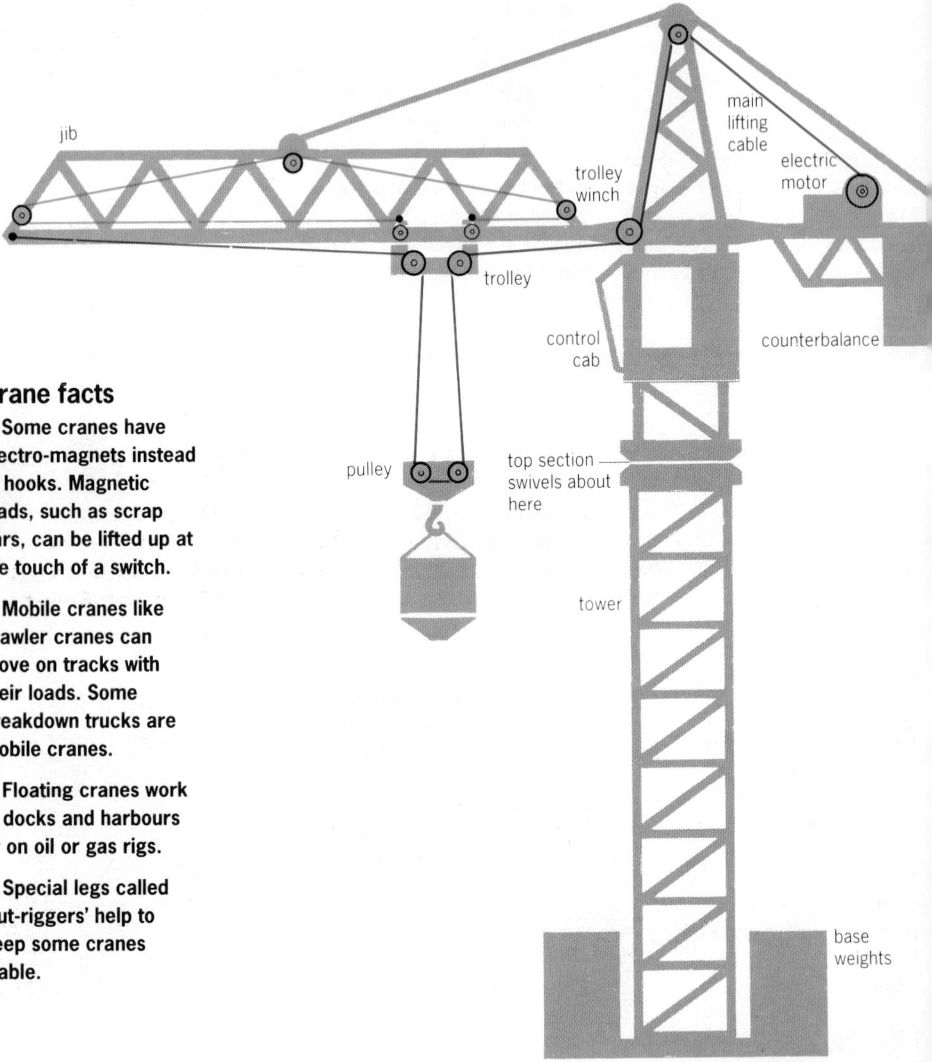

jib
main lifting cable
electric motor
trolley winch
trolley
control cab
counterbalance
pulley
top section swivels about here
tower
base weights

Crane facts

- **Some cranes have electro-magnets instead of hooks. Magnetic loads, such as scrap cars, can be lifted up at the touch of a switch.**
- **Mobile cranes like crawler cranes can move on tracks with their loads. Some breakdown trucks are mobile cranes.**
- **Floating cranes work in docks and harbours or on oil or gas rigs.**
- **Special legs called 'out-riggers' help to keep some cranes stable.**

Cranes help us lift and move heavy loads. The arm of the crane (the jib) is a long lever. The hook is attached to it by wires, ropes or cables which run round a drum.

The jib and tower usually consist of a metal framework made of triangles which are strong and resist bending. To balance the weight of the load, a heavy block called a counterbalance is attached to the other end of the jib.

Did you know?

- **A crane over 28 metres wide was tested to lift a 2,232-tonne load in the USA.**

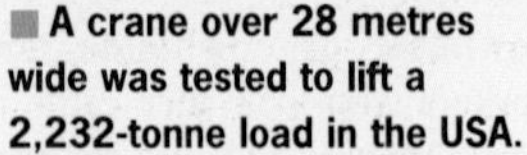

- **The Romans lifted heavy loads using slaves to turn the crane's cable drum.**

Cricket

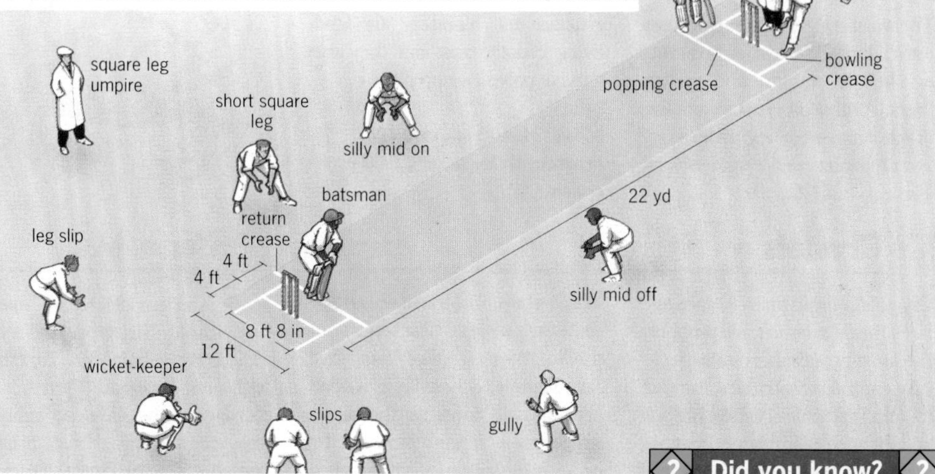

Cricket is a bat-and-ball game played by two teams of eleven. The batting side try to score runs by hitting the ball and running between the wickets. The fielding side try to get the batting side out.

The main cricket playing countries are England, West Indies, Australia, New Zealand, Pakistan, India, Sri Lanka, South Africa and Zimbabwe.

Did you know?

■ There are ten ways of being out, but bowled, caught and leg before wicket (LBW) are the main ones.

Cromwell, Oliver

Oliver Cromwell was one of Parliament's leaders in the Civil War. He led his own cavalry, the 'Ironsides', and later commanded the New Model Army. After Parliament defeated the king, Cromwell became the most powerful man in England. In 1653 he was given the title of 'Lord Protector'.

Did you know?

■ Parliament offered Cromwell the crown, but he refused to become 'King Oliver'.

▶ Oliver Cromwell.

Crusades

Crusades were medieval wars fought by European Christians against the Muslims of the Middle East. Amongst other things the crusaders wanted to seize the holy city of Jerusalem and protect pilgrims travelling there. There were four main crusades between the 11th and 13th centuries.

Crusaders took Jerusalem in 1099, but it was taken back by Saladin in 1187. The Muslims then took other Christian cities. The last to fall was Acre in 1291.

The word 'crusade' comes from the Latin word *crux*, which means 'cross'. The first crusaders had sewn Christian crosses to their clothes.

Did you know?

■ Thousands of children set off on a children's crusade in 1212. Those who did not die on the way were sold into slavery.

Crustaceans

The word crustacea means 'crusty ones': they all have a jointed crust or shell to support and protect them. Almost all crustaceans live in water and most begin life as tiny swimming larvae. Crabs, lobsters, shrimps and barnacles are all crustaceans. Woodlice are land-living crustaceans, but they can survive only in damp places .

▶ The 31,400 species of crustacean includes 4,500 crab species.

Crystals

Crystals come in many shapes and sizes, but diamonds are probably the most beautiful crystals of all. Like emeralds and rubies, they are rare and valuable crystals. But salt and sugar are also made of crystals, and so are materials such as metal and plastics.

Try growing your own crystals by adding two teaspoonfuls of salt to half a cupful of warm water. Stir until the salt has dissolved. Pour the liquid into a saucer and leave on a windowsill for a day or so. Salt crystals will form as the water evaporates. If you look at the crystals under a magnifying glass you will see that they all have the same basic shape : a cube.

Curie, Marie

Marie Curie (1867-1934) spent her whole life working with radioactive substances. Together with her husband Pierre, she discovered the element radium. She received two Nobel prizes, one shared with Pierre. Years of working with radioactive materials eventually killed her.

Czech Republic

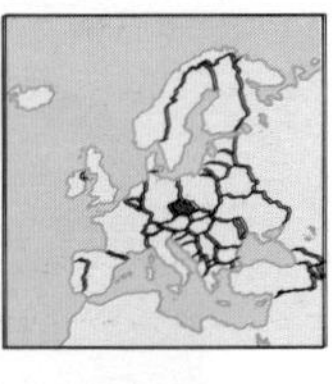

The Czech Republic became independent in 1992, when the central European country of Czechoslovakia was divided in two. It is made up of Bohemia and Moravia, the most industrialized regions of the former Czechoslovakia, where Skoda cars and Pilsner beer are produced.

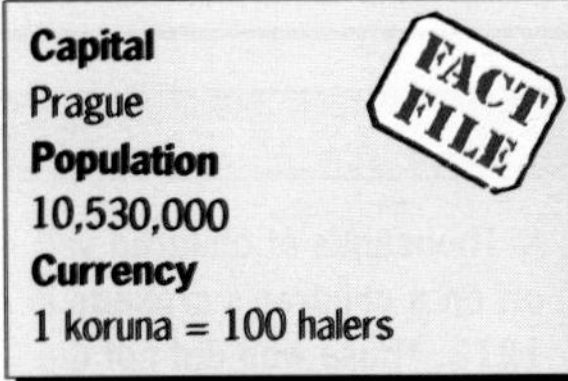

Capital
Prague
Population
10,530,000
Currency
1 koruna = 100 halers

Dams

Most modern dams are either embankment dams (piled earth) or masonry dams (built of concrete). Most have a wide base with a narrow top. The Aswan Dam in Egypt is one of the world's largest embankment dams.

The world's highest dam is being built at Rogunskaya in Russia. It will be 335 m high. The Hoover Dam, USA, helps to generate electricity for Arizona, Nevada and southern California.

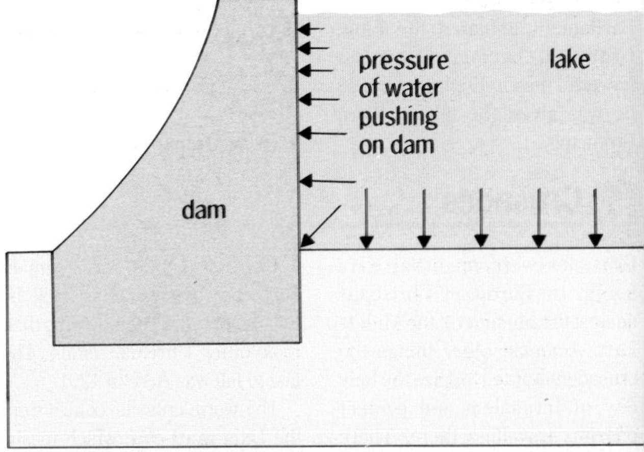

▲ The base of this masonry dam is made of concrete. The pressure of water pushing on the dam is greatest at the bottom of the dam.

 Darwin, Charles

Charles Darwin, born in 1809, was a great biologist who is best known for his theory about the evolution of plants and animals. During a five-year journey on a naval survey ship, HMS *Beagle*, Darwin visited the Galapagos Islands off the coast of South America. There he saw plants and animals that were found nowhere else in the world. Darwin knew that even animals of the same type had slightly different features. He suggested that the animals whose features made them best suited to their surroundings were most likely to survive. Therefore, these features would be passed on to their young. In this way a population of animals would evolve (slowly change). He called this natural selection.

Darwin published his ideas in 1859 in *The Origin of the Species*. The book caused an uproar and many people thought, wrongly, that he was claiming that humans had descended directly from apes. Darwin died in 1882 aged 73.

Day and night

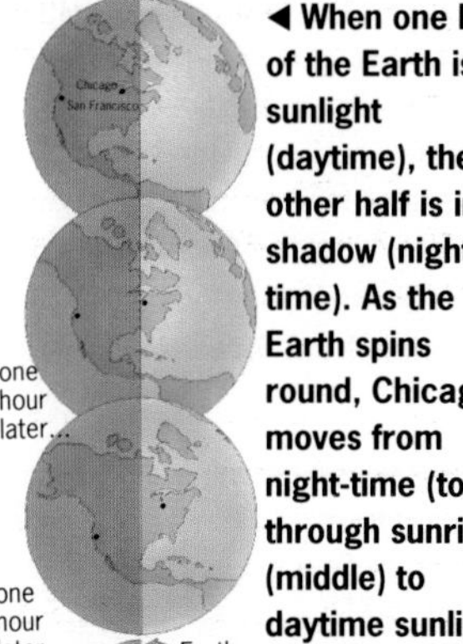

◀ **When one half of the Earth is in sunlight (daytime), the other half is in shadow (night-time). As the Earth spins round, Chicago moves from night-time (top), through sunrise (middle) to daytime sunlight (bottom).**

 **Did you know?** 

- **When you see the Sun rise, it is already up at places further east. So when it is 7 o'clock in the morning in New York, it's already midday in London.**
- **At places near the Arctic and Antarctic, the Sun never sets in the middle of summer and never rises in the middle of winter.**

 Denmark

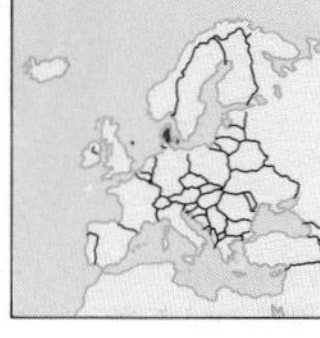

Denmark is in Scandinavia. Greenland and the Faroe Islands also belong to Denmark. Its mild climate and flat countryside is perfect for farming, and its main exports are butter, condensed milk, ham, bacon and beer. The Danish fishing fleet lands millions of tonnes of fish each year.

Capital
Copenhagen
Population
5,167,000
Currency
1 Danish krone = 100 øre

Deserts

About an eighth of the world's land area is true desert, mostly near the tropics of Cancer and Capricorn. Geographers say that deserts are areas which have less than 250 mm of rain in an average year. But true deserts have almost no rain, while semi-deserts have a short rainy season. The world's longest drought (400 years) ended in 1971 when rain fell in the Atacama Desert, Chile.

▼ **Deserts of the world.**

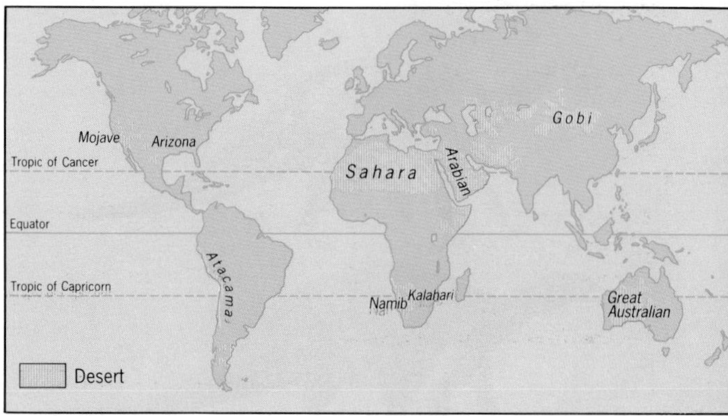

Dickens, Charles

Charles Dickens was born in 1812. As a boy he was forced to earn a living in a shoe polish factory when his father was imprisoned for debt. He became famous in both Britain and America at the age of 24 when his story *The Pickwick Papers* was published in 1836. He wrote many more books, including *Oliver Twist*, *A Christmas Carol* and *David Copperfield*. Many of Dickens's stories appeared as serials in magazines before they were published as books. He died of a stroke in 1870.

◀ **A scene from *Bleak House*.**

Diets

The type of food you eat most of the time is your diet. This should give you all the things you need for growth and health. If you eat too many fats, oils and sweet foods, they can make you fat and can cause heart disease. But fruit, cereals and vegetables can give you the energy, vitamins and minerals you need.

Some people need special diets. Diabetics follow low sugar diets, and vegetarians do not eat meat.

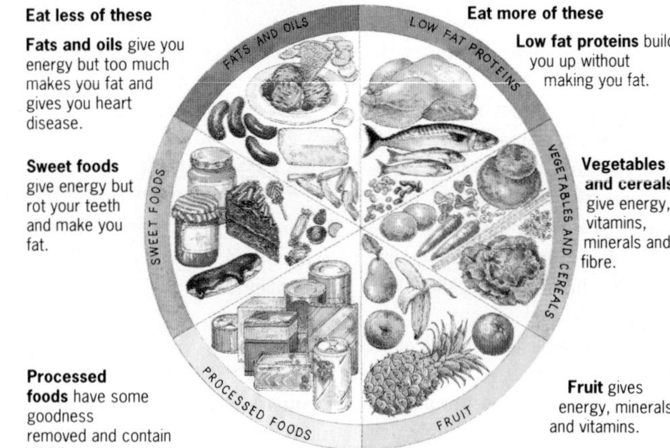
Eat less of these
Fats and oils give you energy but too much makes you fat and gives you heart disease.
Sweet foods give energy but rot your teeth and make you fat.
Processed foods have some goodness removed and contain additives.
Eat more of these
Low fat proteins build you up without making you fat.
Vegetables and cereals give energy, vitamins, minerals and fibre.
Fruit gives energy, minerals and vitamins.
FATS AND OILS
LOW FAT PROTEINS
VEGETABLES AND CEREALS
FRUIT
PROCESSED FOODS
SWEET FOODS

Dinosaurs

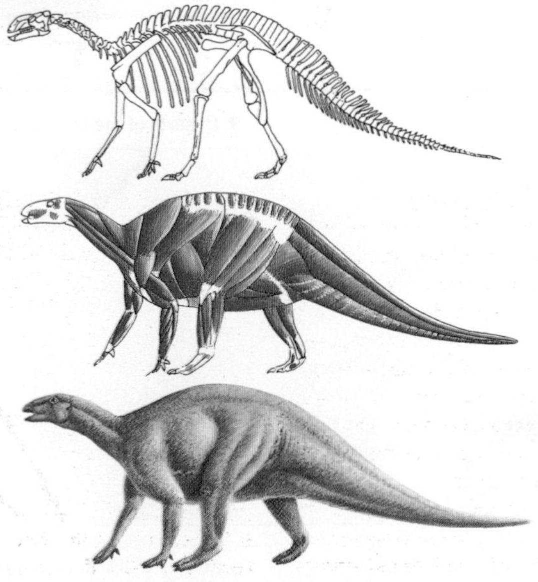

When a dinosaur skeleton is discovered scientists can build up a picture of what that dinosaur may have looked like by reconstruction. First the skeleton is made up from the bones found. Usually some of the bones are missing, so these are replaced with plaster or fibreglass replicas. The skeleton tells them the general size and shape of the dinosaur, and how it stood.

Next, the size and position of the main muscles of the body are guessed at, and the likely outline of the belly. In this way overall body shape can be worked out.

Finally the scientist must guess at what the scales and skin were like and what colour the animal was when it was living.

Dogs

Dogs were the first animals to be domesticated, and all tame dogs are descended from the same wild ancestor, the wolf. Their domestication began at least 12,000 years ago when wolves probably scavenged from prehistoric hunters. As wolves can run faster than people a hand-reared pup was a useful hunting aid, but it took several thousand years to transform wild wolves into tame dogs. By 10,000 years ago dogs were playing an important part in people's lives.

The dog family also includes foxes, coyotes and jackals. African hunting dogs, and the dingo, which has lived unchanged in the wild for at least 8,000 years, are known as wild dogs.

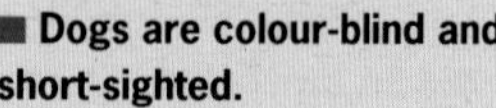

■ Dogs are colour-blind and short-sighted.

■ In 18th-century China Pekinese dogs were so pampered that human wet-nurses were employed to feed them as puppies.

■ There are more than 100 breeds of dog but they all belong to the same species and can interbreed.

Dracula

Bram Stoker wrote a book called *Dracula* in 1897. Count Dracula was a vampire, one of the 'undead'. He lay in a coffin during daylight, and drank human blood.

Vlad the Impaler was a prince in Romania who killed people by driving wooden stakes through their hearts. Some people think Dracula was based on Vlad. Many films have been made about the legend of Dracula.

Dragons

People have made up stories about dragons for centuries. They are mythical creatures, a mixture of bird and snake. The ancient Egyptians and Christians thought dragons were evil. St George supposedly killed one in the Middle East, and in time became patron saint of England.

In the Far East, dragons are good. The Chinese dragon, *Long*, lives in water and roams the skies.

▲ Chinese celebrating New Year's Day with a dragon dance.

Drake, Sir Francis

Francis Drake, born in 1543, worked for Elizabeth I as a pirate looting Spanish ships. In 1577 he set out with five ships, to raid Spanish colonies in South America. Three of his ships were lost at sea, and one turned back. In the last ship, the *Golden Hind*, Drake sailed right round the world. Elizabeth knighted him when he returned.

In 1588 Drake helped defeat the Spanish Armada. He died at sea in 1596.

Ducks

There are over 110 species of duck worldwide. Different species of duck have different methods of finding food: the shoveller filters the surface water; the tufted duck dives to the water bottom and the mallard up-ends to feed in shallower water.

Ducks are flightless for several weeks of the year as they moult all their flight feathers at the same time.

▼ Mallards are dabbling ducks, feeding in shallow water.

Drums

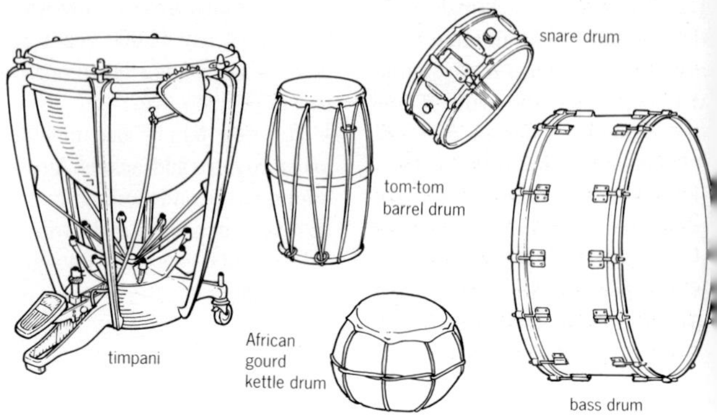

Dynamos

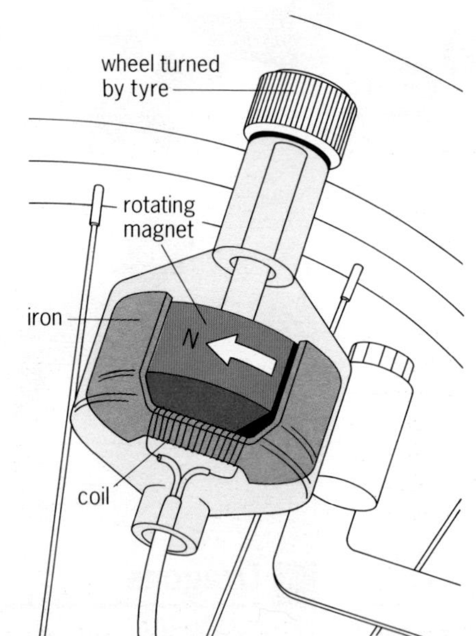

◀ This dynamo is producing enough electricity to run the lights on a bicycle. The dynamo is turned by the bicycle tyre. Inside the dynamo, a magnet rotates and generates electricity in a coil of wire.

Did you know?

- **Dynamos are machines that produce electricity. They are sometimes called generators. Large dynamos generate the electricity in power-stations. Bicycle dynamos, or generators which produce alternating current (a.c.), are called alternators.**
- **The principle of the dynamo was discovered by an Englishman, Michael Faraday, in 1831.**

Ears

Sound waves are chanelled into the ear by the funnel-shaped outer ear. The sound waves make the eardrum vibrate. When the eardrum vibrates, tiny bones called ossicles also vibrate. The vibrating ossicles cause sensory hairs in the cochlea to vibrate. As these are attached to nerves, every time they vibrate a message is sent to the brain where we hear the sound.

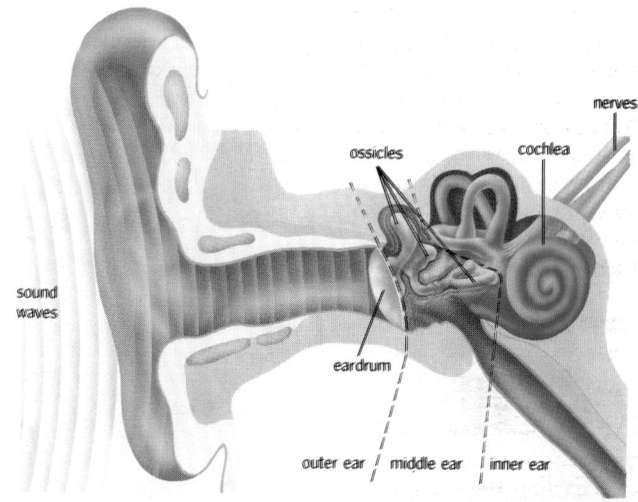

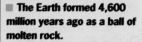

▶ **Inside the human ear.**

Earth

The Earth is not like all the other planets in the Solar System. It has an atmosphere containing oxygen and this has allowed complex life forms to evolve.

The Earth is tiny when compared with many other planets, or the Sun. The Sun is over a million times bigger than the Earth. We live on the outer part, called the crust. The inside of the Earth is very hot (5,000 C° at the core).

◀ **Satellite photographs show the Earth as a blue ball covered with swirling clouds.**

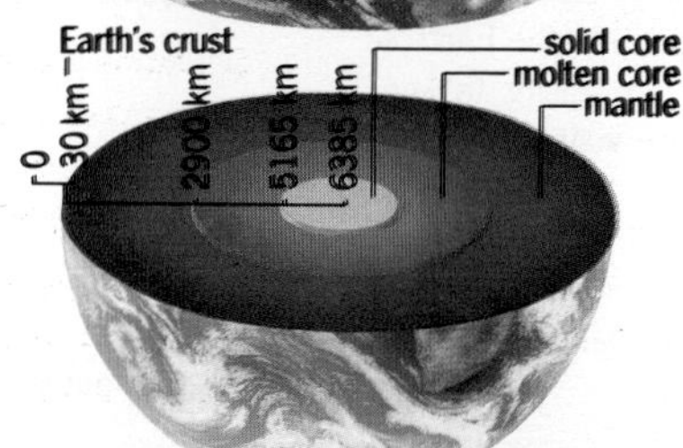

This cross-section of the Earth shows the main layers under the Earth's crust, which is so thin that it only ◀ shows as a line.

Did you know?

- **The Earth formed 4,600 million years ago as a ball of molten rock.**
- **The first forms of life lived without oxygen, and date from 3,500 million years ago.**
- **The Earth has a mass of 5,976 million million million tonnes.**

Earthquakes

When an earthquake happens, the Earth's surface jumps and cracks. This can make houses fall into huge holes, roads split and the water in lakes disappear. Earthquakes happen when two of the great plates in the Earth's crust jerk against each other. The San Andreas Fault in California, where major earthquakes occurred in 1906, 1989 and 1994, marks the boundary of two plates.

The size and effect of every earthquake is measured on a scale from 1 to 10, called the Richter scale. Some instruments can detect earthquakes thousands of miles away. Each year scientists record 800,000 earthquakes which are too small to be felt by people. At least 100 earthquakes a year cause considerable damage to buildings.

Effects of shallow shocks in populated areas	Richter scale	Number of earthquakes per year
Damage nearly total	more than 8·0	0·1-0·2
Great damage	more than7·4	4
Serious damage, rails bend	7·0–7·3	15
Considerable damage to buildings	6·2–6·9	100
Slight damage to buildings	5·5–6·1	500
Felt by all	4·9–5·4	1,400
Felt by many	4·3–4·8	4,800
Felt by some	3·5–4·2	30,000
Not felt but recorded	2·0–3·4	800,000

Eclipses

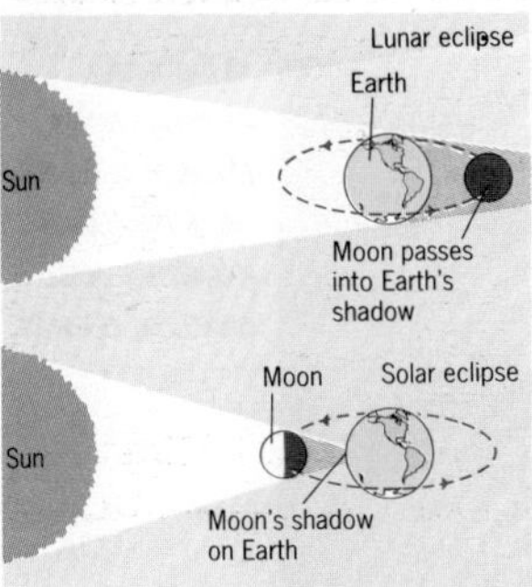

If the Moon gets between the Earth and the Sun, there is an eclipse of the Sun. A total eclipse only lasts a few minutes: the Sun's disc appears to be blotted out by the Moon, the sky goes dark and the Sun's corona, a faint halo of glowing gas, can be seen around the Moon.

Eclipses of the Moon occur when the Moon moves into the Earth's shadow. They are easier to see because they are visible from all the places where the Moon has risen, and they last for several hours. During an eclipse, the Moon looks darker and reddish.

Ecosystems

Plants, animals and their environment together form an ecosystem. An ecosystem may be as small as a pond or as large as an ocean. Each one has food chains. The Sun is the main source of energy in any ecosystem as green plants use sunlight to make their food. The plants are food for plant-eating animals (herbivores), such as rabbits. Herbivores are food for meat-eating animals (carnivores), such as foxes. The carnivores may be food for larger carnivores.

The dead remains of plants and animals break down into simple substances in the soil. Plants use these substances to help make food. In this way all living things in the ecosystem depend on each other, and the ecosystem is in balance.

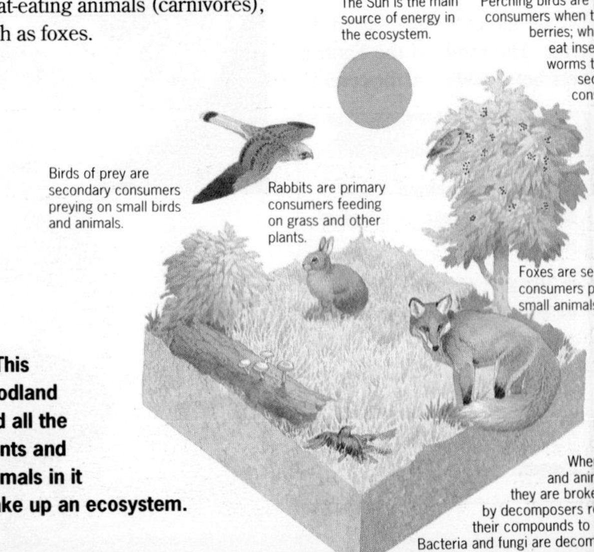

The Sun is the main source of energy in the ecosystem.
Birds of prey are secondary consumers preying on small birds and animals.
Rabbits are primary consumers feeding on grass and other plants.

▶ This woodland and all the plants and animals in it make up an ecosystem.

Egypt

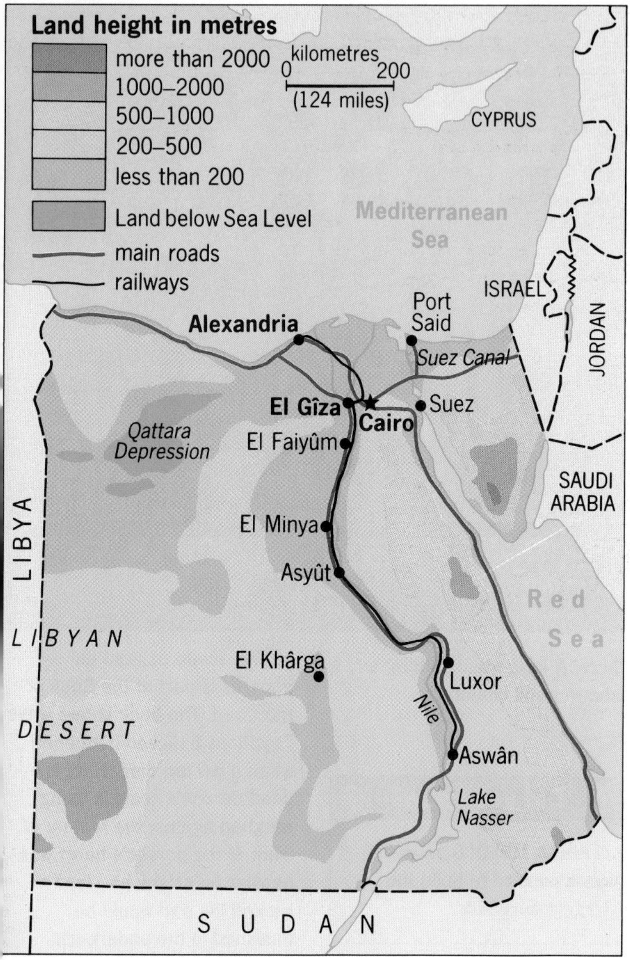

Land height in metres
more than 2000
1000–2000
500–1000
200–500
less than 200
Land below Sea Level
main roads
railways

kilometres 0 200 (124 miles)

CYPRUS
Mediterranean Sea
ISRAEL
JORDAN
Port Said
Suez Canal
Alexandria
El Gîza
Cairo
Suez
Qattara Depression
El Faiyûm
SAUDI ARABIA
LIBYA
El Minya
Asyût
Red Sea
LIBYAN DESERT
El Khârga
Luxor
Nile
Aswân
Lake Nasser
SUDAN

More people live in Egypt than in any other Arab country, and 15 million live in the capital, Cairo. Ninety-five per cent of the people live by the River Nile, where they grow sugar cane, cereals, vegetables and fruit. Away from the Nile, the land is desert. After centuries of ancient civilization, Egypt has had many different rulers. It was conquered by Persians and by Greeks, and then became a part of the Roman empire. By AD 200 many Egyptians had become Christians, and the church, called the Coptic Church was strong. But when the Arabs invaded in the 7th century, Egypt became mainly Muslim, though a Coptic Christian community survives.

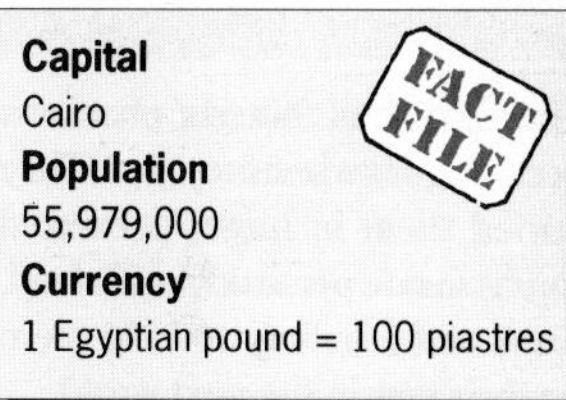

Capital
Cairo
Population
55,979,000
Currency
1 Egyptian pound = 100 piastres

Egyptian ancient history

Egypt is one of the oldest countries in the world. Its people used the water of the River Nile to grow crops. They were so grateful for the Nile that they saw it as a god, called Hapi.

Rulers of Egypt were called 'pharaohs'. A pharaoh was High Priest, chief judge and leader of the army. The pharaoh usually married his own sister and their son would become the next pharaoh.

The Egyptians were very religious and believed the gods played a great part in their lives. They also believed there was life after death.

◄ Sculpture of the pharaoh Rameses II, dated about 1250 BC.

The Egyptians thought pharaohs became gods when they died. They buried them in huge, decorated tombs inside pyramids, with food, drink and jewellery to help them on their way in the next world.

They thought the dead person made a journey to the next world and continued to live the same life there. A king was still king and a labourer still laboured.

Did you know?

■ **About 100,000 people were needed to build the largest pyramids.**

▲ This scene painted on papyrus is part of the *Book of the Dead*. The book shows what Egyptians believed happened when a person died. Here the dead person's heart is being weighed against the feather of truth. If the person's heart was heavier he or she had lead a wicked life and would be punished in the underworld.

Einstein, Albert

Albert Einstein (1879-1955) was one of the world's greatest physicists. His theories about time and space, and about how atoms and their particles behave are important parts of modern physics. Although his ideas were used to develop nuclear weapons, Einstein campaigned strongly for world peace. He tried to persuade world leaders to abandon nuclear weapons.

Did you know?

■ **When Einstein was awarded the Nobel prize for science in 1921, he travelled third class with his violin under his arm to receive it. Without Einstein's theories, lasers, computers and space travel may never have been developed.**

Electricity

Electricity makes clingfilm stick to your hands and it crackles when you comb your hair. It can power televisions and trains, and can cause lightning. Electricity is lots of tiny particles called electrons. Electrons are parts of atoms, and since everything in the world is made of atoms, there is electricity in everything.

Electricity can come from tiny batteries or huge generators. The mains electricity that we use in our homes comes from power stations, where huge magnets turn round in a generator, making electricity. The generator is powered by water or high-pressure steam. Electricity can be very dangerous and must always be treated with care.

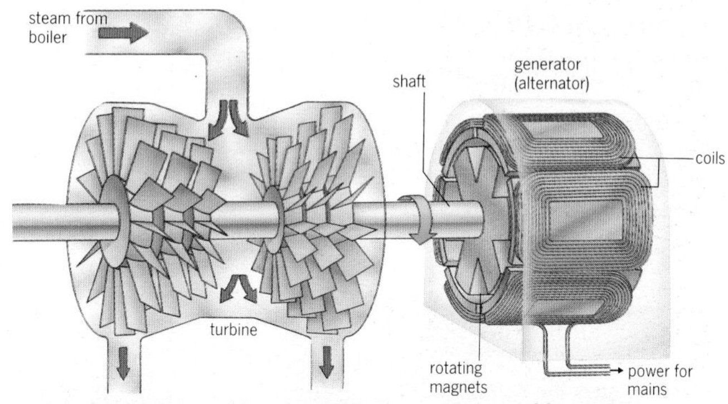

▲ **In many power stations the generators are turned by steam turbines.**

 **Did you know?** 

A flash of lightning has a voltage of 100 million volts. A torch battery has a voltage of 1½ volts.

The wire in a light bulb gets so hot that it glows white and gives off light.

Large power stations can generate 1,000 million watts of electrical power. Each light bulb in your home uses between 40 and 150 watts.

When popular TV programmes end, the demand for electricity can increase by 10 per cent as people start to make hot drinks.

▼ **Power is carried across country by overhead transmission lines. The voltage is stepped down in stages as the power is distributed to towns and factories.**

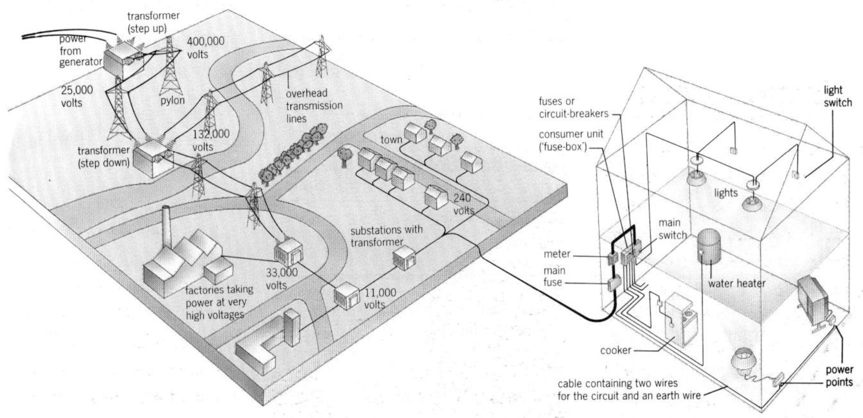

Elements

Everything on Earth and in the whole Universe is made of elements. Over 90 different elements are found in nature. Scientists have made 16 new ones. You will find a table of elements on page 185.

Did you know?

- **Oxygen is the commonest element on Earth, and hydrogen is the commonest element in the Universe.**
- **Most elements are solids at normal temperatures. Only 2 are liquids and 11 are gases.**
- **Sugar is made from the elements hydrogen, oxygen and carbon.**

Elephants

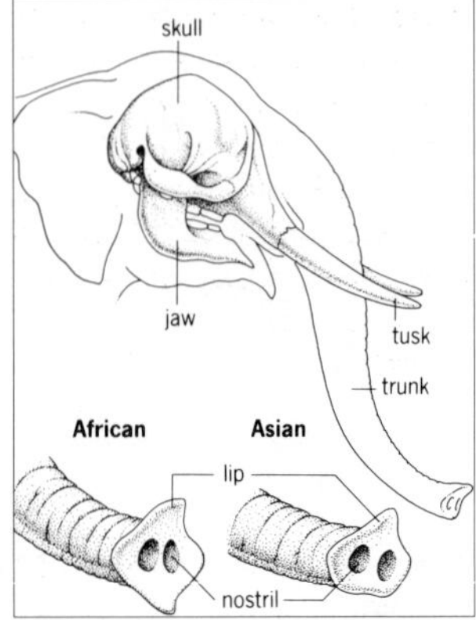

The elephant's skull accounts for a quarter of the elephant's body weight. Its tusks are actually its front teeth.

The trunk is a sense organ of touch and smell. It can also squirt water and dust, and is strong enough to lift trees. It has one or two finger like lips sensitive enough to pick up small pebbles.

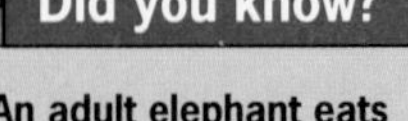

- **An adult elephant eats about 150 kg (300 lb) of grass, leaves, twigs and fruit each day.**
- **Elephant pregnancies last for 22 months.**
- **Elephants have a lifespan of up to 70 years.**
- **African elephants are the largest elephants, weighing up to 7,500 kg (16,538 lb) with a shoulder height of up to 4 m (12 ft) and a head-and-body length of up to 7·5 m (22·5 ft).**
- **The heaviest single tusk weighed 107 kg.**

Elizabeth I

Elizabeth was born in 1533, the daughter of Henry VIII and Anne Boleyn. When she was 2, her mother was executed.

Elizabeth became queen in 1558. Everyone expected her to marry, but she did not. She could be very stubborn and hated to spend money. Instead of fighting an expensive war against Philip II of Spain, she secretly encouraged sailors like Drake to attack his ships and colonies. She was an inspiring war leader when the Spanish Armada was sent to invade England. Elizabeth died in 1603.

Did you know?

- **As a child Elizabeth had four different stepmothers after Anne Boleyn's death.**

Elizabeth II

Elizabeth II, born in 1926, is the 42nd ruler of England since 1066. She became Queen in 1952 when her father, George VI, died. Her husband is Prince Philip. They have four children, Charles, Anne, Andrew and Edward.

As Queen she has more than 400 public engagements a year, and often makes visits to other countries.

Endangered species

Some of the most endangered species in 1995:

Species	Threat to survival
Black rhino (Sub-Saharan Africa)	Poaching for horn
River terrapin (S.E. Asia)	Hunting, pollution
Greater bamboo lemur (Madagascar)	Forest clearance
Salmon-crested cockatoo (Indonesia)	Collection for pets
Green pitcher plant (USA)	Collecting

Energy

Almost all of the energy that we use originally came from the Sun. Energy is stored in the food we eat, and in the coal, oil and gas that we burn.

An average 11-year-old needs about 10,000 kilojoules of energy every day. One gram of nuclear fuel contains about 600,000 kilojoules of energy.

At the centre of the Sun, nuclear reactions produce huge amounts of energy which radiate from the surface as heat and light. There is enough nuclear energy left in the Sun to keep it shining for another 5,000 million years.

Millions of years ago, plants and tiny animals took in energy from the Sun as they grew. When they died, they gradually turned into the fossil fuels: coal, oil and natural gas.

We take the fossil fuels from the ground and release their energy by burning them. Coal is mined, and oil and natural gas are pumped from underground. The coal is burned in power-stations, the oil is refined to make petrol, jet fuel and diesel, and the natural gas is used for cooking and heating.

Energy from the Sun
At the Sun's centre, nuclear reactions give enormous amounts of energy which radiate from the surface as heat and light.

Energy in plants and animals
Green plants use the Sun's energy to make their food from simple materials like water, and carbon dioxide gas in the air. Like other living things, plants need food to live and grow. We get our energy by eating plants, or eating meat from animals which have fed on plants. So our energy really comes from the Sun.

Energy from the Sun
On average, each square metre of the Earth's surface receives the same energy from the Sun as it would do from a one-bar electric fire.

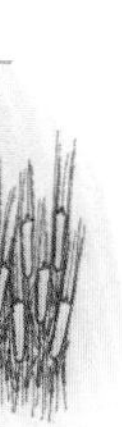

Energy in fossil fuels
Fossil fuels, such as coal, store energy which once came from the Sun.

Energy from fossil fuels
To get the energy in fossil fuels, we mine coal, and pump oil and natural gas from underground. The oil is refined to make other fuels, including petrol, kerosene (jet fuel) and diesel fuel. We release the energy from fossil fuels by burning them. This happens in heating systems, in power-stations, and in the engines of cars, trucks, trains, ships and aircraft.

Energy for living
The food we eat gives us energy. We need it, even when we are asleep, to stay warm and keep the organs of our body working. When we are active, we need more energy to move our muscles.

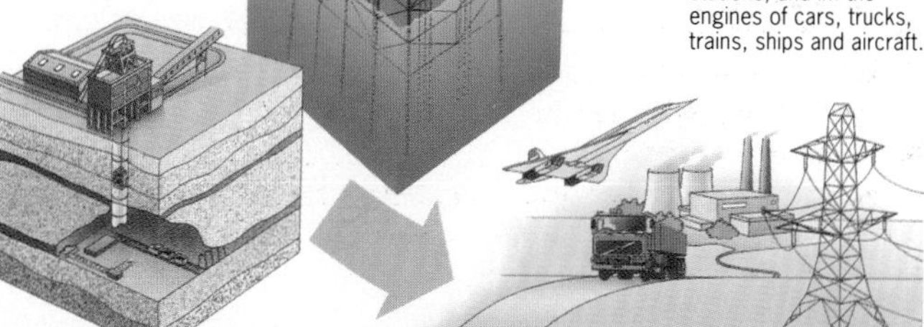

England

England is the largest part of the United Kingdom, with a population of over 47 million people. Many live in the south near London, England's capital city. Much of the land is used to grow food, but most people work in factories and offices. There are differences between life in the north of England and life in the south, for example there are more of the older industries, such as coal mining in the north; housing is more expensive in the south.

FACT FILE

Highest peak
Scafell Pike 978.4 m
Largest lake
Windermere 26 sq km
Longest river
Thames 336 km

English Civil War

Between 1642 and 1649 King Charles I and Parliament fought a war to decide who should have the most power. In January 1642 Charles tried to arrest five leading Members of Parliament. War followed.

Supporters of the king were called Royalists or Cavaliers. The supporters of Parliament were nicknamed Roundheads.

The king's army was led by Prince Rupert. At first, Parliament's army was badly organized. Then Oliver Cromwell and other leaders set up the New Model Army, which won the war for Parliament.

Charles I was arrested, but fighting started again in 1648. Parliament's leaders decided to behead the king in 1649.

Did you know?

■ **Some of the main battles were:**

Edgehill	**1642**
Marston Moor	**1644**
Naseby	**1645**

◀ **Soldiers in the Civil War were armed with muskets. This man is a Royalist.**

English language

English is spoken all over the world. Around 450 million people use it as their main language. It is the main language in Britain, North America, the Caribbean, Australia, New Zealand, and parts of India and Africa.

The first sort of English was Old English. It was spoken by the Anglo-Saxons about 1,500 years ago. When the Normans came in 1066 they introduced Latin and French words. English became Middle English. Words from other languages are being added to the English language all the time.

British and American English

Familiar things with different names

British	American	British	American
autumn	fall	pavement	sidewalk
biscuit	cookie	petrol	gasoline
bonnet (of car)	hood	post	mail
dustbin	garbage can	pushchair	stroller
holiday	vacation	queue	line
lift	elevator	railway	railroad
lorry	truck	rubber	eraser
motor car	automobile	sweets	candy
nappy	diaper	tap	faucet

The same word with different meanings

	British	American
homely	warm and friendly	plain and dull, or even ugly
mean	stingy	nasty
nervy	nervous	cheeky
pants	underpants	trousers
public school	private fee-paying	ordinary

Different spellings

British	American	British	American
analyse	analyze	mould	mold
catalogue	catalog	pyjamas	pajamas
colour	color	sulphur	sulfur
defence	defense	theatre	theater

Did you know?

■ **'Yacht' is a Dutch word, 'kiosk' is Turkish and 'bungalow' is Hindi.**

Equator

The Equator is an imaginary line which runs round the Earth, halfway between the North and South Poles.

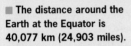

? Did you know? ?

- The distance around the Earth at the Equator is 40,077 km (24,903 miles).
- At any place on the Equator the Sun is directly overhead at midday on 21 March and 23 September.
- At the Equator, day and night are roughly the same length all year round.

Ethiopia

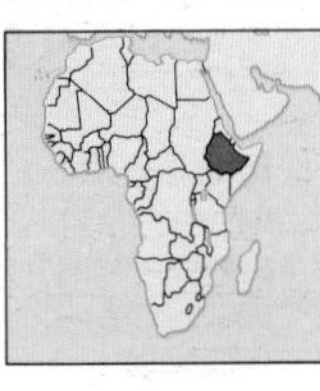

Ethiopia is in north east Africa. The high land is cool, but the lowlands are hot and dry.

Most Ethiopians live in small villages and grow food. Some coffee is grown for export. In the 1970s and 1980s drought ruined crops and killed farm animals. Many people starved until food aid came from other countries. Famine remains a great problem. There was also civil war in Ethiopia between 1975 and 1991, which caused many deaths.

Capital
Addis Ababa
Population
50,345,000
Currency
1 birr = 100 cents

Europe

Europe is the smallest continent, but about one eighth of the world's people live there. More than 20 per cent of everything made in the world is made in Europe.

FACT FILE

Highest peak
Mount Elbrus (USSR) 5,642 m
Largest lake
Caspian Sea 370,000 sq km

European Community

After World War II some countries in western Europe wanted to work closer together. In 1957 six signed the Treaty of Rome to form the European Community (EC). By 1995 fifteen countries were involved.

Since 1993 the EC has been known as the European Union, and anyone from a member country can work or start a business just as easily in another member country as in their own.

Members of the European Parliament are elected by voters in each member state. The Parliament meets partly in Luxembourg and partly in Strasbourg.

? Did you know? 

- The first six members were Belgium, France, (West) Germany, Italy, Luxembourg and the Netherlands. Denmark, Irish Republic and the UK joined in 1973; Greece in 1981; Portugal and Spain in 1986; Austria, Norway and Sweden in 1995.

European history

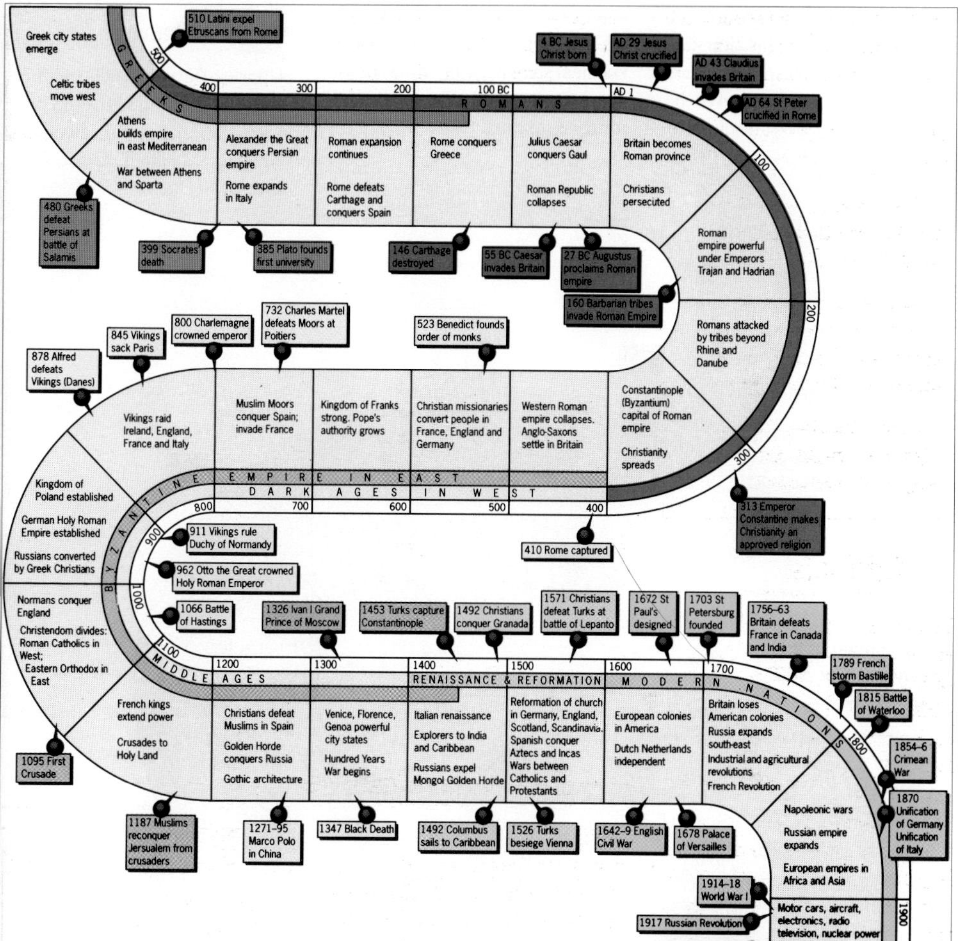

Greek city states emerge

Celtic tribes move west

GREEKS

500 | 400 | 300 | 200 | 100 BC | AD 1 | 100 | 200 | 300 | 400 | 500 | 600 | 700 | 800 | 900 | 1000 | 1100 | 1200 | 1300 | 1400 | 1500 | 1600 | 1700 | 1800 | 1900

510 Latini expel Etruscans from Rome

480 Greeks defeat Persians at battle of Salamis

Athens builds empire in east Mediterranean

War between Athens and Sparta

399 Socrates' death

385 Plato founds first university

Alexander the Great conquers Persian empire

Rome expands in Italy

Roman expansion continues

Rome defeats Carthage and conquers Spain

146 Carthage destroyed

Rome conquers Greece

ROMANS

Julius Caesar conquers Gaul

Roman Republic collapses

55 BC Caesar invades Britain

27 BC Augustus proclaims Roman empire

4 BC Jesus Christ born

AD 29 Jesus Christ crucified

AD 43 Claudius invades Britain

AD 64 St Peter crucified in Rome

Britain becomes Roman province

Christians persecuted

Roman empire powerful under Emperors Trajan and Hadrian

160 Barbarian tribes invade Roman Empire

Romans attacked by tribes beyond Rhine and Danube

Constantinople (Byzantium) capital of Roman empire

Christianity spreads

313 Emperor Constantine makes Christianity an approved religion

410 Rome captured

Western Roman empire collapses. Anglo-Saxons settle in Britain

EMPIRE IN EAST

DARK AGES IN WEST

523 Benedict founds order of monks

Christian missionaries convert people in France, England and Germany

Kingdom of Franks strong. Pope's authority grows

732 Charles Martel defeats Moors at Poitiers

Muslim Moors conquer Spain; invade France

800 Charlemagne crowned emperor

845 Vikings sack Paris

878 Alfred defeats Vikings (Danes)

Vikings raid Ireland, England, France and Italy

BYZANTINE

Kingdom of Poland established

German Holy Roman Empire established

Russians converted by Greek Christians

911 Vikings rule Duchy of Normandy

962 Otto the Great crowned Holy Roman Emperor

Normans conquer England

Christendom divides: Roman Catholics in West; Eastern Orthodox in East

1066 Battle of Hastings

1095 First Crusade

French kings extend power

Crusades to Holy Land

MIDDLE AGES

1187 Muslims reconquer Jersualem from crusaders

Christians defeat Muslims in Spain

Golden Horde conquers Russia

Gothic architecture

1271–95 Marco Polo in China

1326 Ivan I Grand Prince of Moscow

Venice, Florence, Genoa powerful city states

Hundred Years War begins

1347 Black Death

RENAISSANCE & REFORMATION

1453 Turks capture Constantinople

Italian renaissance

Explorers to India and Caribbean

Russians expel Mongol Golden Horde

1492 Christians conquer Granada

1492 Columbus sails to Caribbean

Reformation of church in Germany, England, Scotland, Scandinavia.

Spanish conquer Aztecs and Incas

Wars between Catholics and Protestants

1526 Turks besiege Vienna

1571 Christians defeat Turks at battle of Lepanto

MODERN NATIONS

European colonies in America

Dutch Netherlands independent

1642–9 English Civil War

1672 St Paul's designed

1678 Palace of Versailles

1703 St Petersburg founded

Britain loses American colonies

Russia expands south-east

Industrial and agricultural revolutions

French Revolution

1756–63 Britain defeats France in Canada and India

1789 French storm Bastille

1815 Battle of Waterloo

Napoleonic wars

Russian empire expands

European empires in Africa and Asia

1854–6 Crimean War

1870 Unification of Germany Unification of Italy

1914–18 World War I

1917 Russian Revolution

Motor cars, aircraft, electronics, radio television, nuclear power

1939–45 World War II

European empires end

1957 Treaty of Rome

New nation states in Europe, Africa and Asia

▲ **Time-line of European history from 500 BC to the 20th century.**

To begin with there were no separate countries in Europe. Romans, Germans and Arabs conquered different parts of Europe. Gradually people who spoke different languages split into nations. England, France, Spain, Portugal and Sweden all became countries.

In the 17th century there were wars between Catholics and Protestants. France became strong. Napoleon set out to conquer all Europe before he was beaten at the battle of Waterloo in 1815.

There were two world wars in the 20th century. After World War II eastern Europe was ruled by communist governments. Most of these lost power in the 1980s and 1990s.

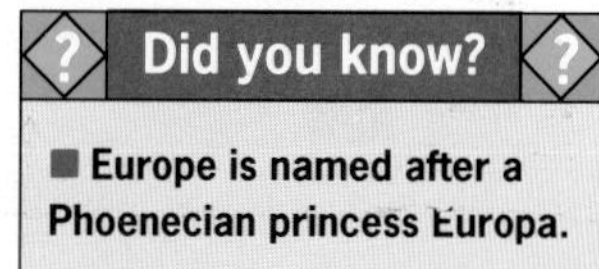

Did you know?
■ Europe is named after a Phoenecian princess Europa.

Evolution

Evolution of life began about 3,500 million years ago. This time-line shows the last 500 million years only. As scientists can never be sure of the exact time an animal or plant evolved it shows only when something was living rather than when it first appeared. Some of the species shown living millions of years ago are still alive today, but most are extinct.

Darwin

Charles Darwin (1809-1882) is famous for his theory of evolution by natural selection. This is explained in the biography of Darwin.

SEA
LAND
trilobite
Vauxia (sponge)
no life on land
500
Pikaia
Hallucigenia
land plants
Cooksonia
400
starfish
bryozoans (moss animals)
sea scorpion
jawed fish
wingless insects
Rhyniella

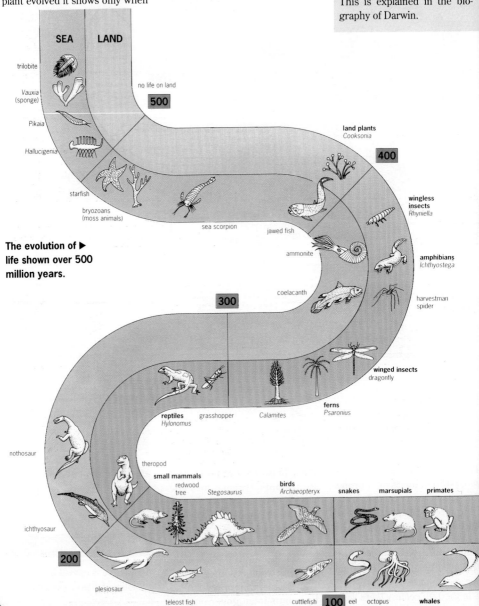

The evolution of ▶ life shown over 500 million years.

ammonite
amphibians
Ichthyostega
coelacanth
harvestman spider
300
winged insects
dragonfly
ferns
Psaronius
reptiles
Hylonomus
grasshopper
Calamites
nothosaur
theropod
small mammals
redwood tree
Stegosaurus
birds
Archaeopteryx
snakes
marsupials
primates
ichthyosaur
200
plesiosaur
teleost fish
cuttlefish
100
eel
octopus
whales

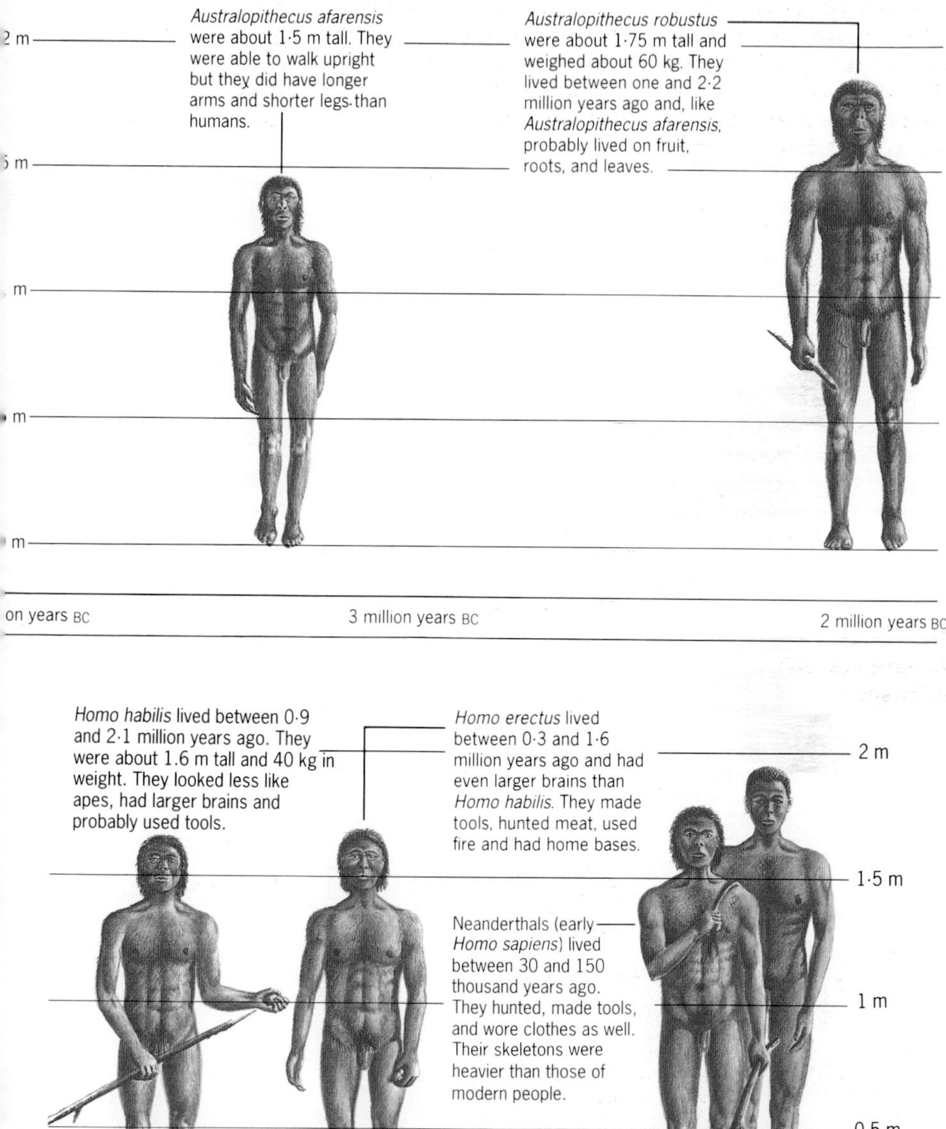

Australopithecus afarensis were about 1·5 m tall. They were able to walk upright but they did have longer arms and shorter legs than humans.

Australopithecus robustus were about 1·75 m tall and weighed about 60 kg. They lived between one and 2·2 million years ago and, like *Australopithecus afarensis*, probably lived on fruit, roots, and leaves.

Homo habilis lived between 0·9 and 2·1 million years ago. They were about 1.6 m tall and 40 kg in weight. They looked less like apes, had larger brains and probably used tools.

Homo erectus lived between 0·3 and 1·6 million years ago and had even larger brains than *Homo habilis*. They made tools, hunted meat, used fire and had home bases.

Neanderthals (early *Homo sapiens*) lived between 30 and 150 thousand years ago. They hunted, made tools, and wore clothes as well. Their skeletons were heavier than those of modern people.

A more modern kind of *Homo sapiens* lived at the same time as the Neanderthals and eventually replaced them.

Explorers

There have always been people who want to discover new lands. Many of the early explorers travelled by sea. We still hear stories of famous Greek explorers such as Jason and Ulysses. But there were also explorers from China and Polynesia. The Polynesians covered vast distances sailing through the south Pacific between 2000 BC and AD 950 when they reached New Zealand.

One of the most famous explorers of the Middle Ages was Marco Polo from Venice. He travelled to China and was away for more than twenty years. At that time there were also many Muslim explorers. The story of Sinbad the Sailor is based on the adventures of one. After Columbus discovered America many European explorers followed. Some of them simply wanted to become rich on American Indian gold and silver.

In later centuries, explorers wanted to find out about the geography and biology of the lands they visited. Gradually the gaps on the maps of the world were filled in. In the 18th century new sea routes were discovered such as the Bering Strait off Siberia, named after the Danish explorer Vitus Bering. Captain James Cook sailed round New Zealand and Australia. In 1804 Lewis and Clark explored the American West and found a route from the Missouri River over the Rocky Mountains to the Pacific.

Explorers have taken on new challenges in the 20th century. The North and South Poles were reached; high mountains were climbed; and spacecraft went to the Moon.

Did you know?

- **The oldest maps found are Babylonian. They were drawn on clay tablets more than 2,000 years BC.**
- **The world's highest peak, Everest in the Himalayas, was first climbed in 1953.**
- **The first astronaut in space was Yuri Gagarin of the USSR in 1961.**

Extinct animals

Did you know?

- **99 % of all the animal species that have ever lived are now extinct.**

There have been living things on Earth for about 3,500 million years and millions of animals have come and gone in that time. Some, like the dinosaurs, are well known but most have been forgotten.

Eyes

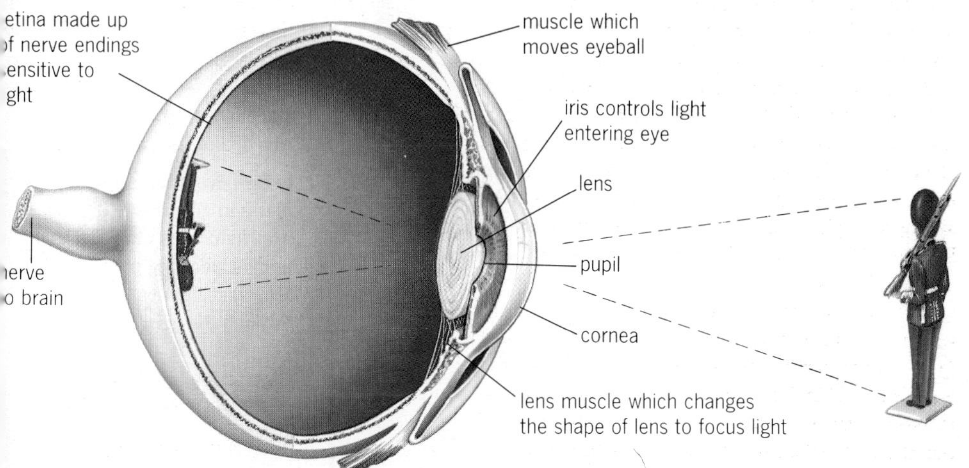

▲ **The internal structure of the eye. Nerve cells pass messages to the brain. The image at the back of the eye is upside down because this is how we really see it, but the brain interprets the image the right way up.**

An eye is a living camera. It focuses light from surrounding objects to form a picture which can be understood by the brain. Humans, and other animals with backbones, have eyes all built in the same way. Each of your eyes contains about 142 million light-sensitive nerve endings, 10 million of which are sensitive to colour. You can see objects as small as 0·1 mm across and tell the difference between 10 million different shades of colour.

Insects and crustaceans have eyes very different to ours. They are made up of hundreds or even thousands of narrow light-sensitive tubes. Each one cannot make a proper picture but together they can. Eyes like this are called compound eyes.

▲ **Insect compound eyes vary in size from huge ones like these of a horsefly, with thousands of facets, to the tiny eyes of some ants which have about a dozen facets.**

Did you know?

Through blinking you spend half an hour of your waking day with your eyes closed.

Faraday, Michael

Michael Faraday (1791-1867) was a great 19th-century scientist who discovered the principle of electricity generation. He found that if he moved a magnet in and out of a hollow coil, an electric current flowed in the coil. He had invented the dynamo, now used in modern power-stations. Faraday also invented the transformer, used in most modern electrical equipment, and discovered the chemical benzene, and the process of electrolysis.

Faraday is also known for his skill in explaining science to ordinary people. In 1826 he started the famous Royal Institution lectures which have been held every year since then, except for three years during World War I.

Feet and hands

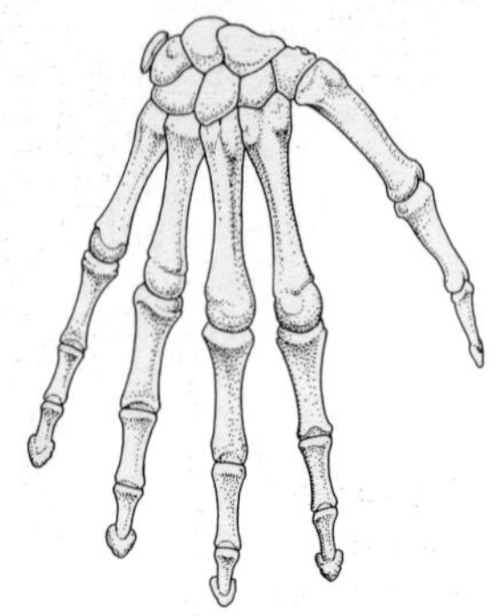

Human hand

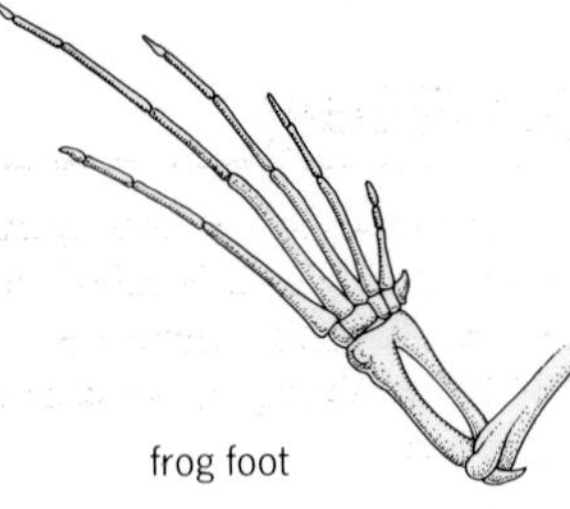

frog foot

The human hand has the same basic structure as the frog foot, because we have descended from the same fish-like ancestors.

Fingerprints

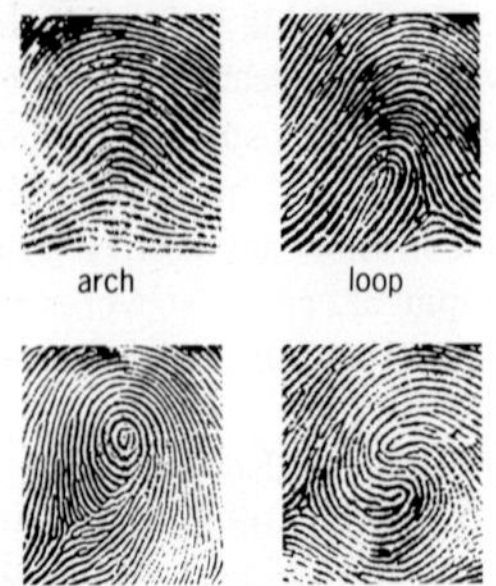

There are only four basic kinds of fingerprint, but each of your fingerprints is different and no one else has the same fingerprints as you.

Finland

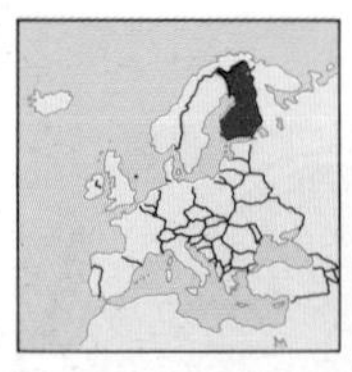

One third of Finland is inside the Arctic Circle. Two-thirds are covered by forests of fir, pine and spruce trees. Timber from the forests is used for paper and furniture making. Finland has long cold winters and warm summers.

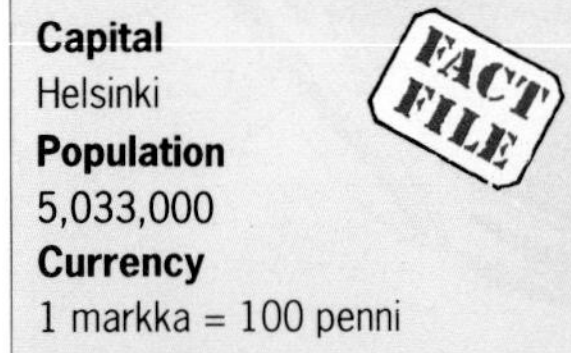

Capital
Helsinki
Population
5,033,000
Currency
1 markka = 100 penni

FACT FILE

Fire

Prehistoric people used fire to keep wild animals away, and to cook food. Later they learned how to 'fire' clay pots to make them hard and leakproof. They also discovered that fire could be used to work metals.

Today we use fire to provide most of our power. We burn coal, oil or gas in power-station boilers to help make the steam which turns the generators.

Did you know?

- **The temperature of the flames from a gas cooker is about 2,000 °C.**
- **All fires need three things: fuel, heat to start them off and oxygen.**
- **Fuels such as paraffin or coal must turn into a gas before they can burn.**

Fish

There are two types of fish: **cartilaginous fish** and **bony fish.** Sharks and lampreys are cartilaginous fish as they have gristly skeletons. Most fish have skeletons of true bone and so are called bony fish.

▶ Gill covers cut away to show gills and gill rakers. Gill rakers are like combs attached to the bone supporting each gill. They let water, but not food, pass out through the gills.

▲ The porcupine fish inflates itself with water when it is alarmed. When undisturbed it has a similar shape to most other fish and its spines lay flat.

Did you know?

- **The largest fish is the whale shark, which grows up to 18 m (54ft) in length and weighs over 40 tonnes. There are more species of fish than there are of mammals, birds, reptiles and amphibians put together.**
- **Most kinds of fish lay huge numbers of eggs: a large codfish lays about 9 million eggs, an ocean sunfish can lay as many as 300 million eggs.**

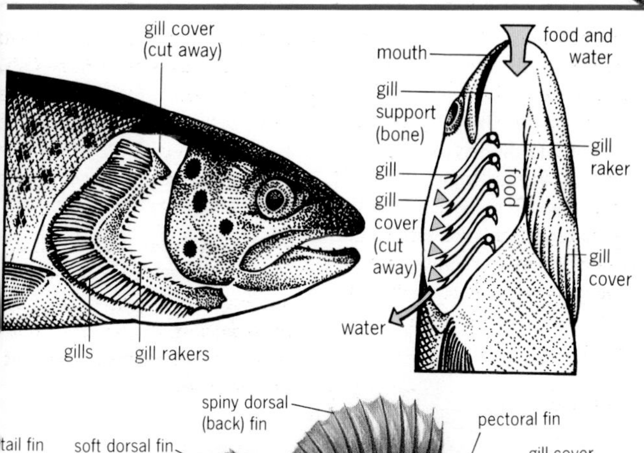

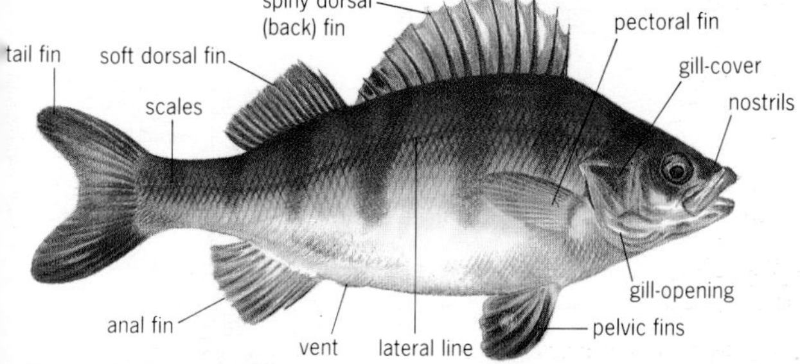

▲ Fish are covered with protective scales and are streamlined so they move easily through water. Their tail fin pushes them forwards, and the other fins are for steering and keeping the fish upright in the water.

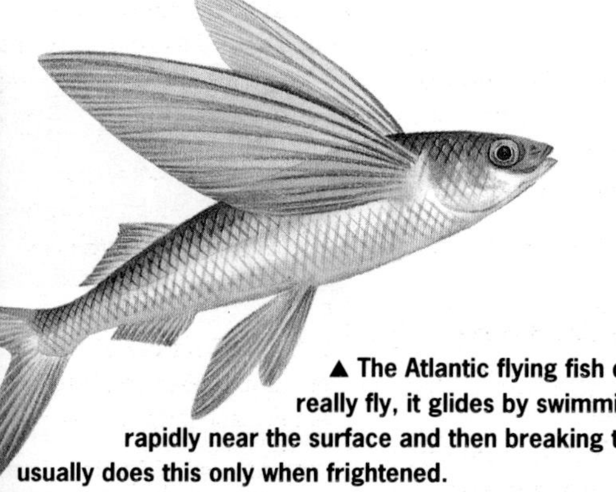

▲ The Atlantic flying fish does not really fly, it glides by swimming very rapidly near the surface and then breaking through. It usually does this only when frightened.

Fishing industry

The average world fish catch is 92 million tonnes a year. Most of the catch comes from the deep oceans. The Japanese catch 12 million tonnes of fish a year.

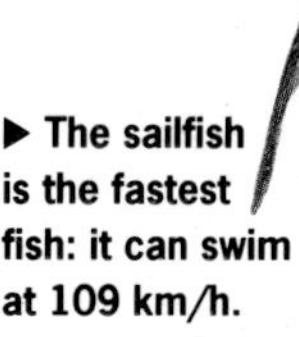

▶ The sailfish is the fastest fish: it can swim at 109 km/h.

Fishing

Fishing is the most popular 'sport' in many countries. In Britain there are about 4 million active anglers and in Japan the figures are nearer 20 million.

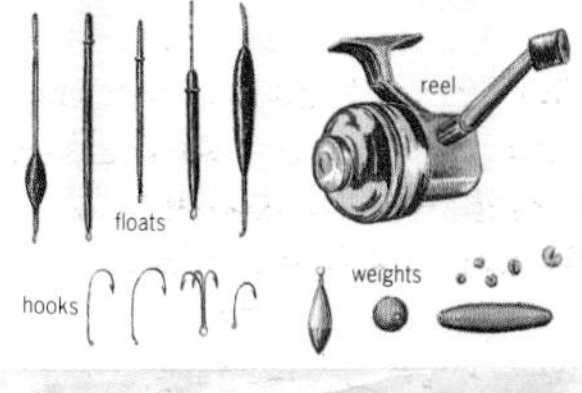

▲ Coarse fishing is the most popular form of fishing. The word 'coarse' refers to the type of fish. Many of those caught are not edible.

Flight

Watching birds and experimenting with gliders helped early inventors understand that air moving over a wing can create lift. Most aircraft have wings with a cross-section like those of birds, but as they cannot be flapped air must be kept flowing over them.

The aircraft in the picture is moved forward using a propeller which is turned quickly by the engine. As the aircraft builds up speed, the air rushing over the wings creates the lift needed to raise it into the sky. The aircraft will stay in the sky as long as it keeps moving fast enough for the lift created to be the same as or greater than, its weight.

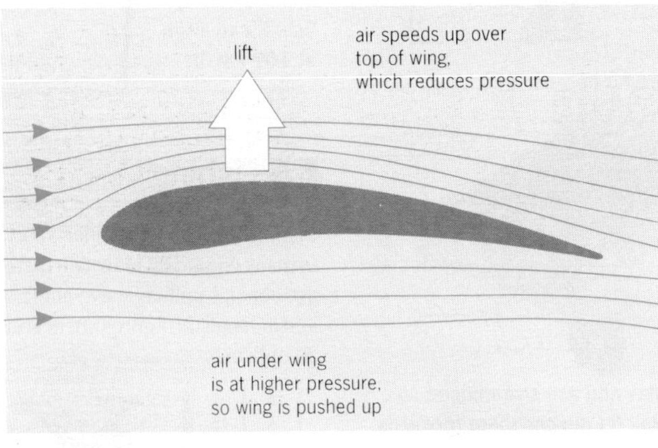

▲ **Air flow across a wing.**

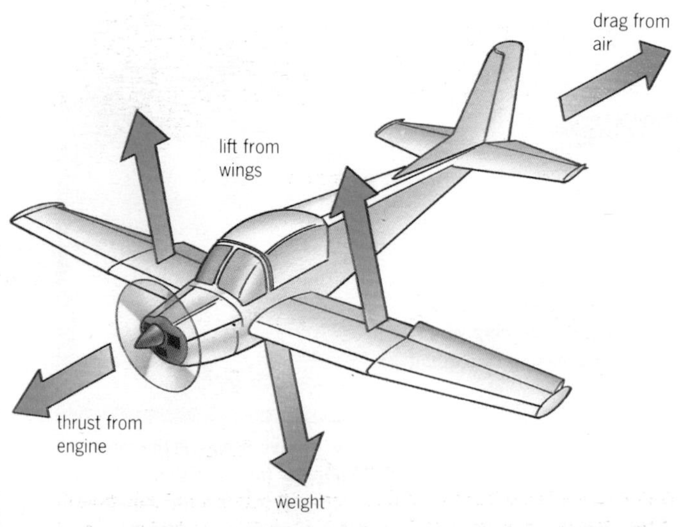

▲ **The forces on an aircraft in flight.**

Flowering plants

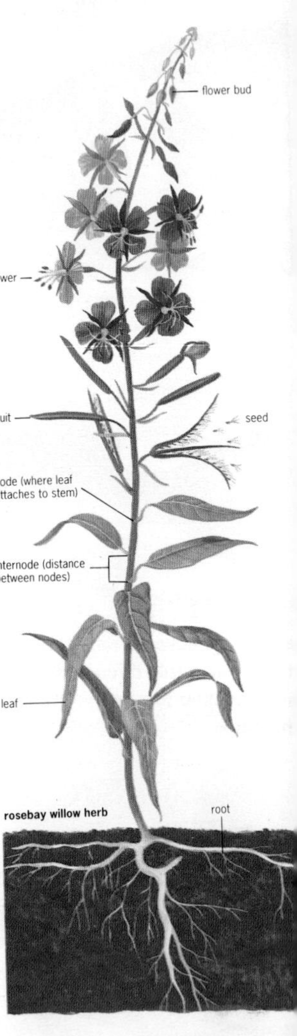

There are about 235,000 species o
flowering plants. The smallest is
duckweed called *Wolffia*, 1 mm
across. The tallest is a eucalyptus
tree, over 100 m in height
Flowering plants have roots, and
shoot which produces leaves and
flowers. The flowers contain se
organs that produce seeds and frui

Flowers

◀ A flower contains a plant's reproductive organs. The male parts are called stamens and they produce pollen. The female parts are called carpels, and after fertilization they produce fruits and seeds.

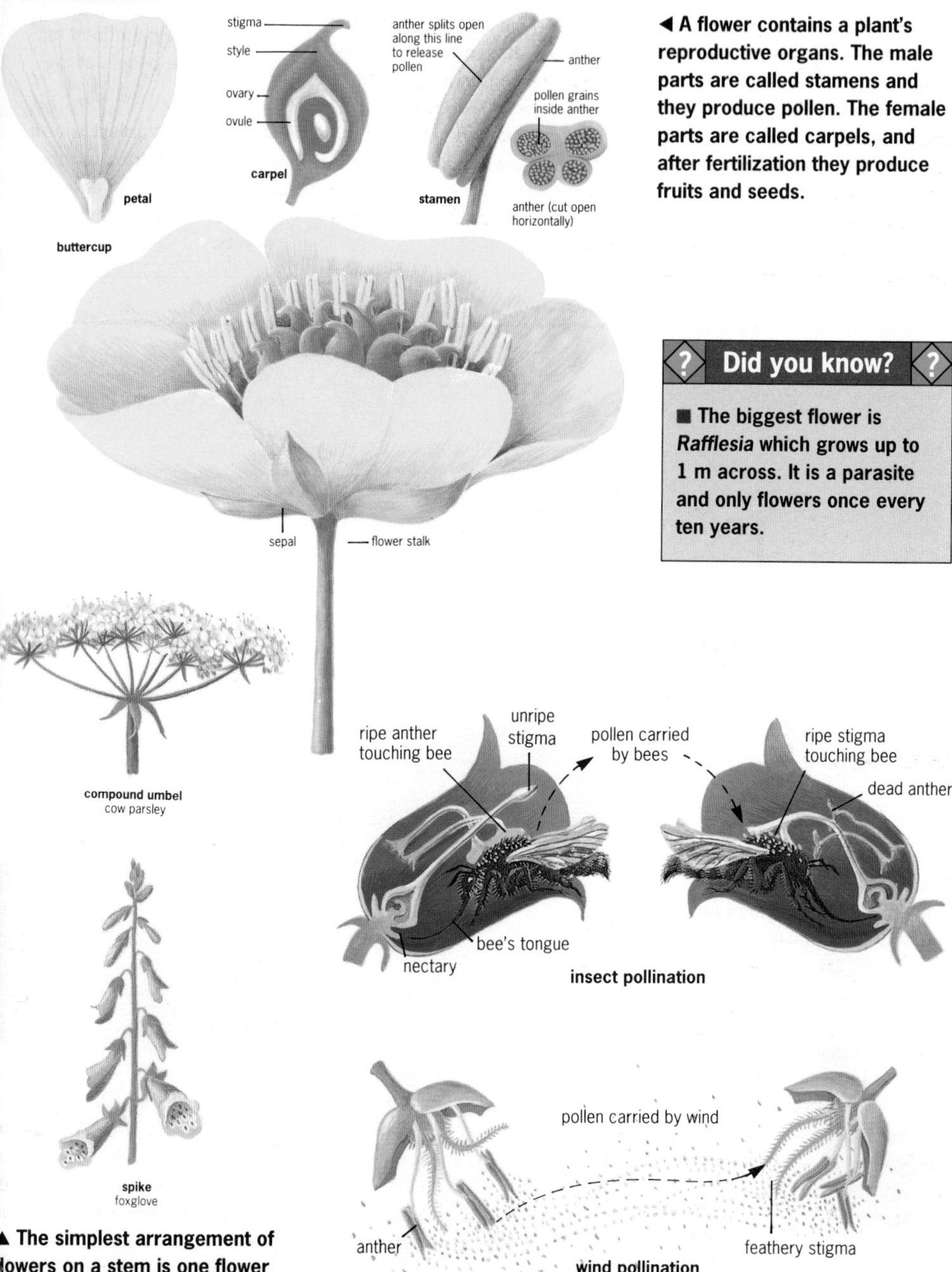

Did you know?

■ The biggest flower is *Rafflesia* which grows up to 1 m across. It is a parasite and only flowers once every ten years.

▲ The simplest arrangement of flowers on a stem is one flower on the end of a stalk, but flowers are also arranged in other ways.

▲ Pollination is the transfer of pollen from the anthers of one flower to the stigmas of another of the same kind. Pollen can be transferred by wind or insects.

Food

You eat food for energy and to stay well. Your muscles use energy when you move and your brain uses it when you think. Carbohydrates and fats supply energy. Protein, vitamins and minerals repair damaged parts and give you healthy blood and bones.

Different countries grow and eat different foods. Too many people do not get enough to eat. This is especially bad for children.

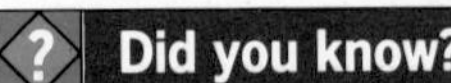

■ Rice is the main food for over half the people of the world.

■ One of the earliest known recipes was written on stone by the Egyptians in about 1600 BC. It was for making sweets.

Food chains and webs

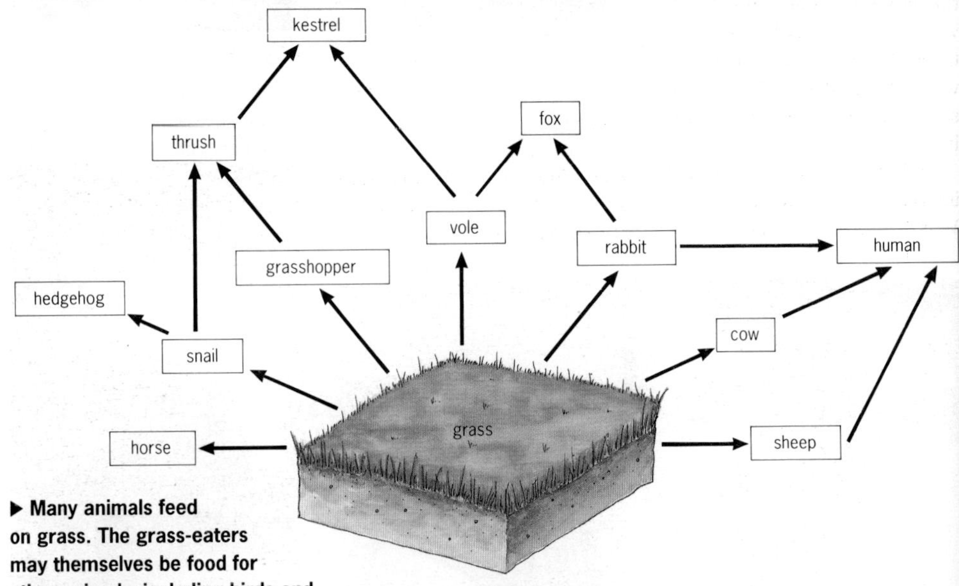

▶ Many animals feed on grass. The grass-eaters may themselves be food for other animals, including birds and mammals. The top carnivores are not killed for food by any other animals. This is just one of many food webs.

All living things need food to stay alive. Animals need to spend a lot of time either feeding or searching for food, but green plants make their own food. Using sunlight energy they combine water and carbon dioxide gas to make sugar. This is called photosynthesis. All animals depend on plants for their energy and so are part of a food chain that begins with plants.

Plant-eating animals (herbivores) get their energy from the plants they eat. Herbivores then may be eaten by flesh-eating animals (carnivores), which, in their turn, may be eaten by other carnivores. Each animal is a link in the chain which begins with plants. But food chains are rarely simple as they often criss-cross with other food chains to form complicated food webs.

As living things are so closely linked together in food webs it is easy to see why a change in the numbers of animals or plants in one part of the web can affect all other parts of the web.

▼ A simple food chain.

grass → vole → kestrel

Football

Football is a game played by two teams of eleven. They try to score by kicking or heading the ball into the other team's goal. Ten of the players cannot use their hands. The goalkeeper can handle the ball to stop it going into the goal.

Games similar to football have been played for many centuries. The rules of the modern game were written down in 1863. In England, the FA (Football Association) Cup was first played for in 1872. In the same year England played Scotland in the first game.

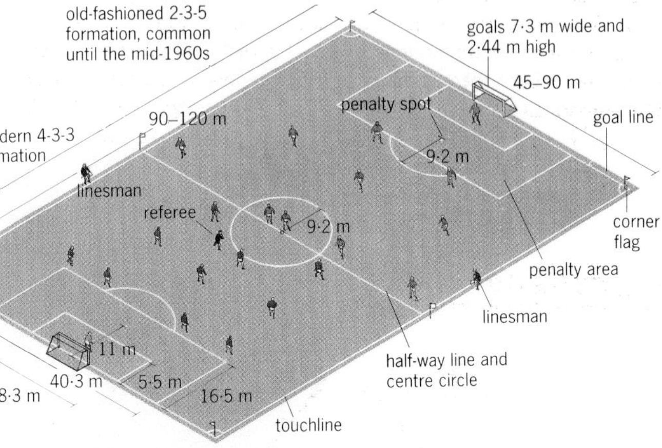

Today the most important international competition is the World Cup, which takes place every four years. In the 1994 finals in the USA Brazil won a record fourth title.

▲ England versus Cameroon in the 1990 World Cup.

Did you know?

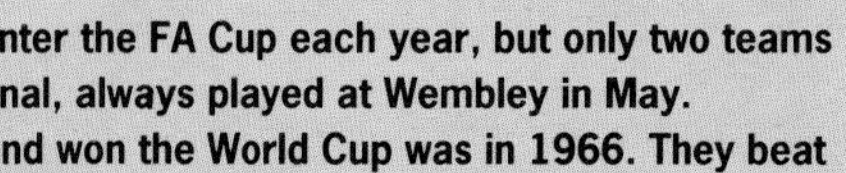

■ Over 500 clubs enter the FA Cup each year, but only two teams will make it to the final, always played at Wembley in May. The only time England won the World Cup was in 1966. They beat West Germany 4-2 at Wembley.

■ Other types of football include Australian Rules and Gaelic football.

American football

American football is more like rugby than soccer. It is played with an oval ball. Teams have 40 players, but only eleven are on the field at one time. A touchdown (6 points) is scored when the ball is caught or carried into the end zone. Players can handle the ball, run with it, and throw it forward. Defenders can block and even tackle opponents who do not have the ball.

Each year the top two teams in the USA play in the Superbowl.

Forests

▶ **Emergent trees rise through the canopy where there is wind to distribute seeds.**

▶ **The canopy of spreading treetops is so dense it may be 8 m thick in places.**

▶ **The understorey provides shelter for many forest animals.**

▶ **The shrub layer contains few shrubs if the canopy is dense.**

▶ **The forest floor is so dark that few plants grow there. Forest decay takes place here.**

▲ **Tropical rainforests may have as many as 750 species in an area of 1 sq km.**

▲ **Deciduous forests are found in temperate climates and follow a seasonal pattern, shedding their leaves in winter.**

▲ **Coniferous forests are the largest in the world; one in Siberia covers an area of 11 million sq km.**

Fossils

Fossils are the remains of plants and animals that once lived on the Earth. The word 'fossil' means 'dug up'. The commonest fossils are ancient sea shells, because most of the rocks that contain fossils were laid down in the sea. In coal-mining areas you can see the outlines of twigs, stems and fern-like leaves in big lumps of non-shiny coal.

Dinosaurs are only preserved as fossils if their remains ended up on river- or sea-beds. The earliest fossil mammals were found in Lesotho and are thought to be over 200 million years old.

▶ **Fossils of the shells of the extinct mollusc, ammonite.**

Foxes

The red fox is found over more of the world than any other carnivore: from the Arctic tundra through grassland to temperate forest. It can survive on a wide variety of foods, such as rabbits, earthworms, carrion and fruit. In season wild berries, apples and rosehips can make up 90 % of its diet.

 Did you know? 

■ **Foxes can run at speeds of 48 km/h (30 mph) over long distances, jumping obstacles and swimming through water.**

France

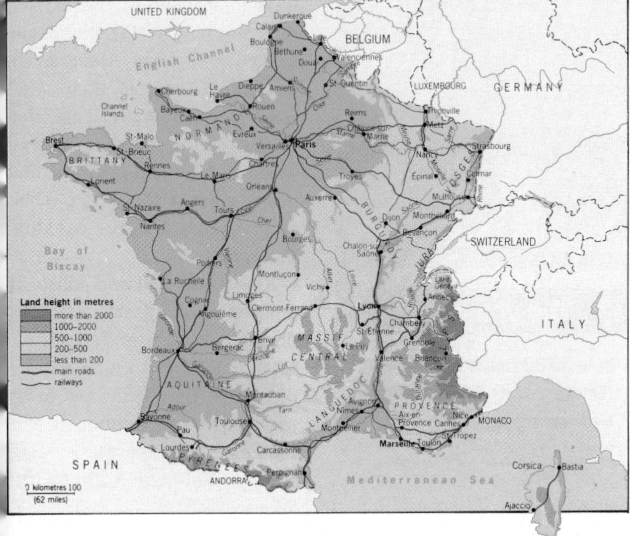

France is the largest country in western Europe, and is bordered by the English Channel ('la Manche' in France), the Atlantic and the Mediterranean. The Alps separate France from Italy. The highest mountain in the French Alps is Mont Blanc.

French farms grow wheat, maize and sunflowers. Dairy cows are kept for milk used in famous cheeses such as Camembert. Vineyards produce wine for sale all over the world. Industries such as car-making are based around Paris. But new science industries are growing in the south of France.

Capital
Paris
Population
57,289,000
Currency
1 franc = 100 centimes

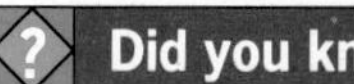 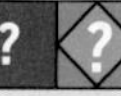

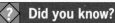

■ **The Tour de France is one of the world's most famous cycle races. The route includes sections in all the mountainous areas of France, where the competitors face long, steep hill climbs.**

▼ **The tricolore (three-colour), one of the symbols of the Revolution, has been the French flag ever since.**

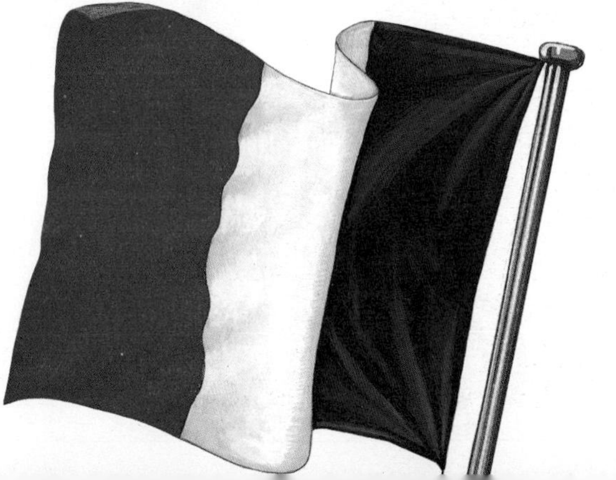

France's history

In the 1st century BC France was conquered by Julius Caesar and became part of the Roman Empire, for 500 years. When the Romans left, France was invaded by the Franks. Their king, Clovis, became a Christian and settled in Paris. His reign gave France her name, her religion and her capital city.

In the late Middle Ages plague, famine and war brought misery to the French. English kings, descendants of William of Normandy, claimed part of France and from 1337 to 1453 the two countries were at war. Joan of Arc is remembered by the French partly because she helped drive the English out of France.

▲ **A painting depicting the storming of the Bastille, the huge prison in Paris. There weren't many prisoners inside, but the act of capturing it symbolized the destruction of the monarchy.**

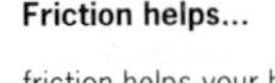

? Did you know? ?

■ **In 1789 Louis XVI wrote in his diary 'July 14: nothing.' How wrong he was!**

French Revolution

In 18th-century France many people were unhappy. On 14 July 1789 the poor of Paris stormed a prison called the Bastille. This was the start of the French Revolution. After storming the Bastille, people formed a National Assembly (a parliament) so that they could lower the price of bread and stop shopkeepers, peasants, and workers being kept down and overworked by the nobles. Their slogan was 'liberty, equality, fraternity'.

King Louis XVI was killed by guillotine and 17,000 more died during the Reign of Terror from 1793 to 1794. But the Revolution did make life better for many people. The Revolution is still remembered in the words of the French National Anthem, the 'Marseillaise'.

Friction

Sometimes friction is useful, sometimes it is a nuisance. When you ride a bike, friction helps you to grip the handlebars, stops you when you brake, and helps your feet to grip the pedals and your tyres to grip the road. But it also slows you down, and slows the pedals and wheels of your bike.

Meteorites entering the Earth's atmosphere from outer space are burned up by the heat caused by friction with the air. This same friction causes spacecraft to overheat.

Friction helps...

friction helps your hands grip the handlebars

friction stops you when you put the brakes on

friction helps your feet grip the pedals

friction helps the tyres grip the road

Friction is a nuisance...

air friction slows you down

friction slows the pedals

friction slows the wheels

Frogs

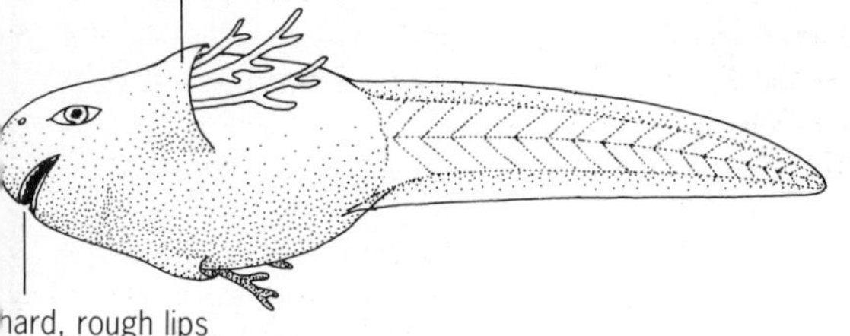

◀ **Frogs are amphibians. A frog hatches out of its egg as a tadpole, with gills for breathing and a tail for swimming. At first it uses yolk inside its body for food. Later it eats water plants and finally it eats small water animals. At around three months the froglet is able to leave the water.**

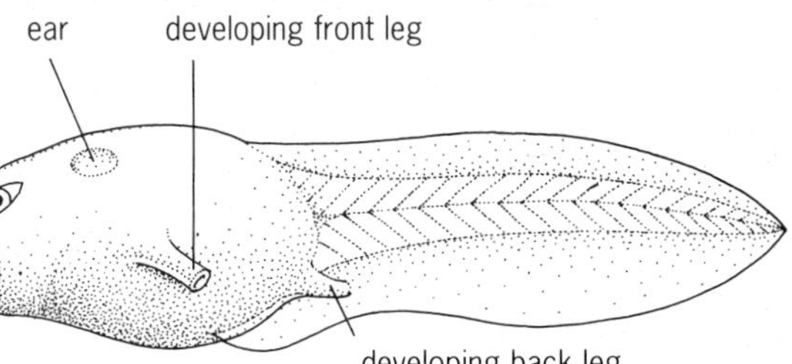

Did you know?

■ **The golden dart-poison frog from South America is so poisonous that one adult contains enough poison to kill 2,200 people.**

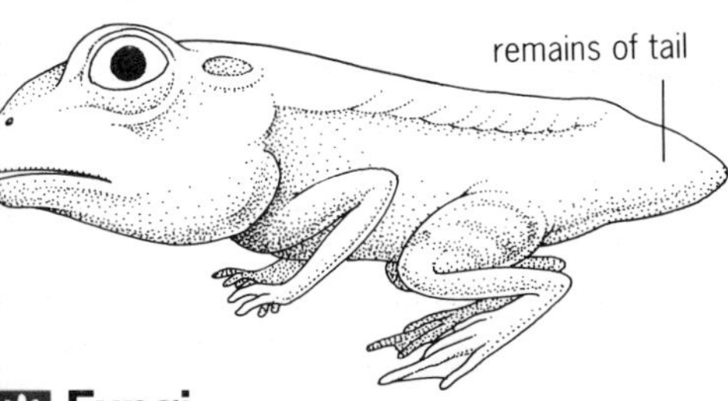

Fungi

Fungi live either on the dead remains of animals or plants, or as parasites on living things. All fungi, except yeasts, are made of fine threads of cells called hyphae. These form a tangled mass called mycelium.

▶ **Bracket fungus growing on a dead tree. You can only see part of the fungus; the rest, the mycelium, is growing inside the tree.**

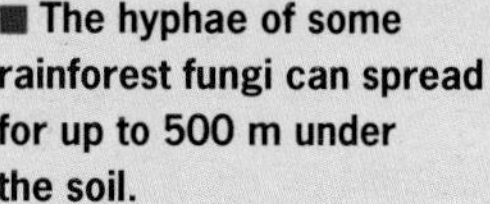

Did you know?

■ **The hyphae of some rainforest fungi can spread for up to 500 m under the soil.**

■ **Fungi grow so fast that a single spore can produce more than 1 km of hyphae in 24 hours.**

Galaxies

The Sun and many of the stars you can see in the night sky belong to a giant family of stars called a galaxy. The name of our galaxy is the Milky Way. Andromeda, the nearest big galaxy to ours, is just over 2 million light years away: its light has taken over 2 million years to reach us.

▶ **The spiral galaxy Andromeda, with two small elliptical galaxies close to it.**

Galilei, Galileo

Galileo (1564-1642) dramatically changed the science of astronomy. As the first person to use a telescope for looking at the Sun, Moon and planets, Galileo realized the Earth and other planets orbit the Sun.

Gandhi, Mohandas

Mohandas Ghandi was born in India in 1869. He became a lawyer and worked in South Africa for 21 years.

Back in India he led the National Congress party in a non-violent campaign against British rule. He was sent to prison three times for his beliefs and actions.

When India and Pakistan became independent in 1947, Gandhi worked for peace between Hindus and Muslims. He was assassinated by a gunman in 1948.

Georgian Britain

Four Georges ruled Britain from 1714 to 1830. Robert Walpole became Britain's first prime minister while George I was on the throne.

Many wealthy people had big houses and lots of land. But poor people suffered because they were badly fed and housed. Some things did get better. Britain began to sell more goods abroad, and travel improved as roads and canals were built.

▲ **A coach in a London street at the beginning of the century.**

The Public Conveyances from the York House, Bath, Royal Mail Office, Are constructed upon the most approved principles of safety

Should any irregularities occur it is requested that immediate application be made to William Lane.

ROYAL MAIL AND GENERAL COACH OFFICE,

YORK HOUSE, BATH.

Royal Mails.

LONDON—through Devizes, Marlborough, and Reading, every Evening at a quarter past Seven.

LONDON—through Chippenham and Calne, every Evening at Eight.

EXETER—through Wells, Bridgewater, Taunton, every Morning at Seven.

PLYMOUTH direct—

PORTSMOUTH

▶ **Timetable for the Royal Mail at the General Coach Office, Bath.**

Germany

Germany has more people than any country in Europe apart from Russia. After 1948 there were two countries, East Germany and West Germany. They reunited in 1990. This has caused some problems because East Germany had a communist government and many businesses were in a poor condition. Although Berlin is the official capital now, the government is likely to remain in Bonn for some time.

There are now sixteen Federal States (Lander). Each has a government to look after such things as education. There is also a Federal Government to take charge of the whole country.

Germany has a reputation for making high-quality products, including motor vehicles, machine tools, electrical goods and chemicals. Farms grow wheat, maize and potatoes.

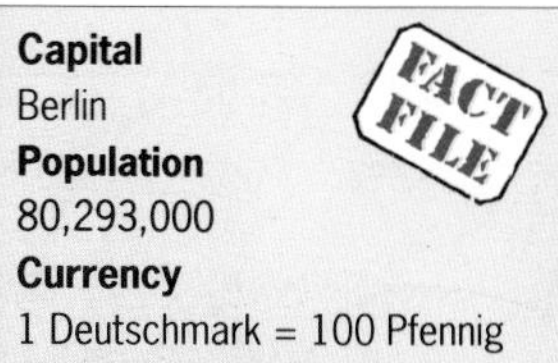

Capital
Berlin
Population
80,293,000
Currency
1 Deutschmark = 100 Pfennig

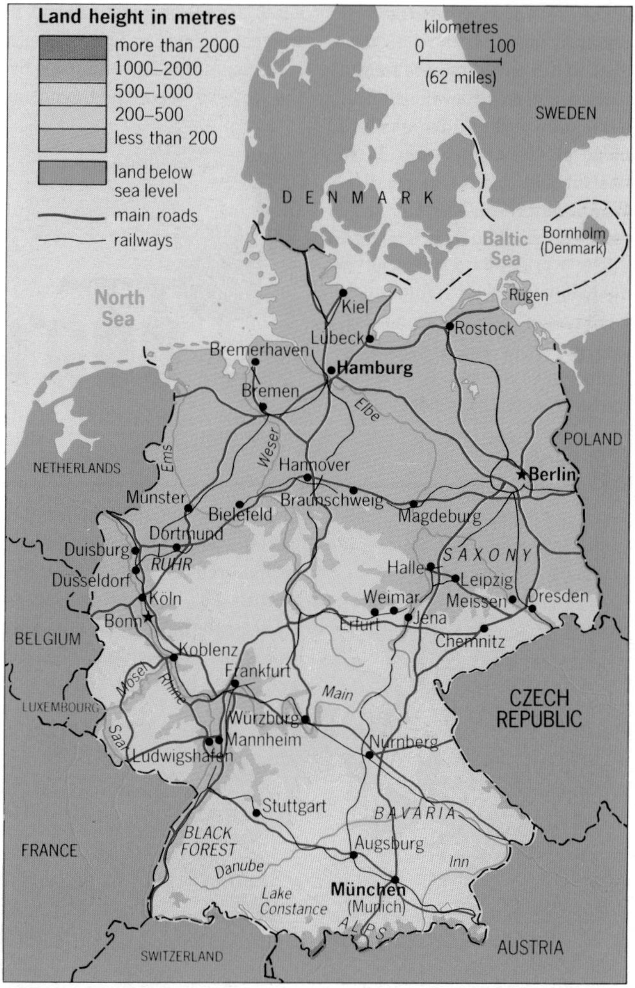

Land height in metres
more than 2000
1000–2000
500–1000
200–500
less than 200
land below sea level
main roads
railways

kilometres
0 100
(62 miles)

SWEDEN
DENMARK
Baltic Sea
Bornholm (Denmark)
Rügen
North Sea
Kiel
Lübeck
Rostock
Bremerhaven
Hamburg
Bremen
Elbe
POLAND
NETHERLANDS
Ems
Weser
Hannover
Berlin
Münster
Bielefeld
Braunschweig
Magdeburg
Dortmund
Duisburg
RUHR
SAXONY
Halle
Leipzig
Düsseldorf
Köln
Weimar
Meissen
Dresden
Bonn
Erfurt
Jena
BELGIUM
Chemnitz
Koblenz
Mosel
Rhine
Frankfurt
Main
LUXEMBOURG
CZECH REPUBLIC
Saar
Würzburg
Mannheim
Nürnberg
Ludwigshafen
Stuttgart
BAVARIA
BLACK FOREST
FRANCE
Augsburg
Inn
Danube
Lake Constance
München (Munich)
ALPS
SWITZERLAND
AUSTRIA

Ghosts

People have imagined ghosts for centuries. Ghosts are believed to be the spirits of dead people. Most make no trouble, but others are said to terrify human beings.

The night before All Saints' Day (1 November) is Hallowe'en when ghosts and witches were supposed to roam the world.

Giraffes

Giraffes are the tallest mammals, they reach up to 5·3 m in height. They live in the African savannahs where their long necks enable them to reach food too high for other ground-living animals. Giraffes can run at speeds of up to 56 km to escape dangers.

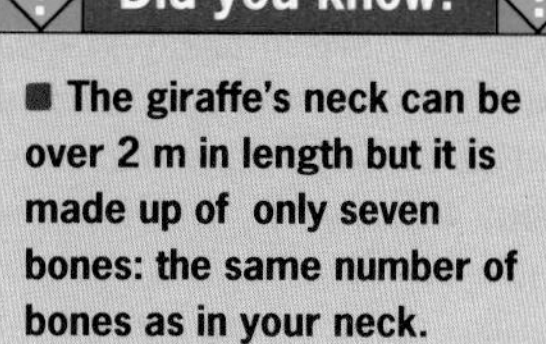

Did you know?

- **The giraffe's neck can be over 2 m in length but it is made up of only seven bones: the same number of bones as in your neck.**

Glaciers

A glacier is a moving sheet of ice. It can be as much as 100 m (330 ft) thick. If it is on a slope, the weight of the ice makes the whole sheet move downhill. Most glaciers move at speeds between 1 cm (0·4 in) and 1 m (3 ft) per day. When they reach the sea, large pieces break off to form icebergs.

The world's largest glacier is the Lambert Glacier in Antarctica. It is 514 km (320 miles) long. The fastest glacier is the Quarayac Glacier in Greenland, flowing at a rate of 20 m (65 ft) per day.

Glass

Glass is made mainly from sand. It was being made in Syria at least 5,000 years ago, and in Europe by the 7th century BC. The Egyptians were the first people to blow molten glass. Today, only quality glass products are still blown by hand.

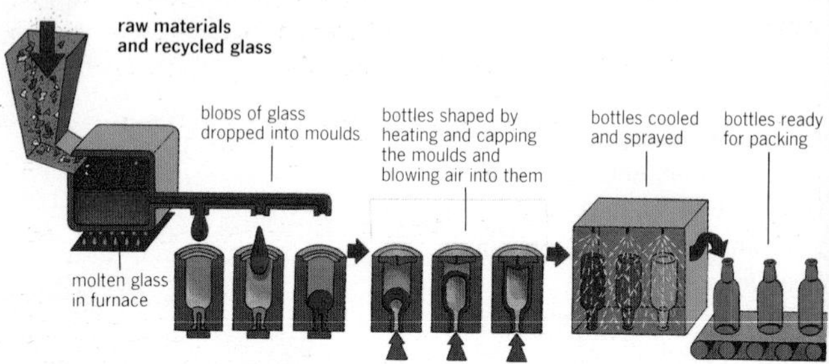

Golf

In golf players use clubs to hit a ball into a hole in the ground. It can be hundreds of metres from the tee to the hole on the green. Golfers try to get the ball into the hole with as few hits as possible. A full sized golf course has eighteen holes.

Did you know?

- **Golf has been played in Scotland since the 15th century.**

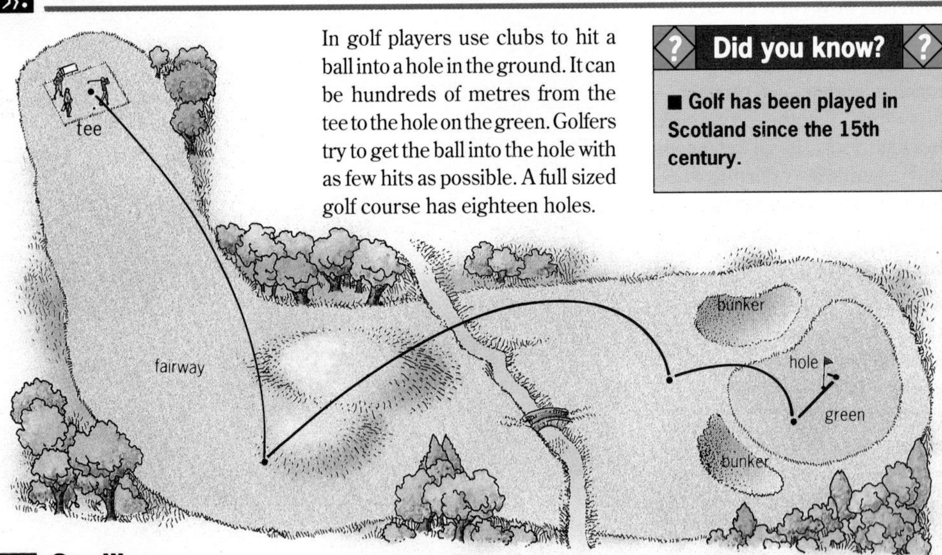

Gorillas

Gorillas are the largest of the great apes. They live in family groups led by a big male, called a silverback. Babies are weaned at about 4 years old, and females begin breeding at about age 9. Gorillas are now rare because of hunting and rainforest destruction. There are fewer than 400 mountain gorillas in the wild.

Did you know?

- **Gorillas grow up to 1·75 m tall and have an armspan of up to 2·75 m.**
- **Gorillas live up to 50 years of age in the wild.**

Grammar

Grammar is the way we put words together to say something. If you want people to understand what you mean you have to use the right kinds of words and put them in the right order.

'May I have a cake?' is good grammar. It makes sense. 'May a cake I have?' does not make sense because it is bad grammar.

Words can be grouped into different parts of speech. The parts of speech include nouns (which name things), verbs (which tell you what is happening) and adjectives (which describe things).

These parts of speech are put together into sentences. Nearly all sentences have a verb and most have nouns.

Interjections are words that you call out (oh, gosh, hey)

definite article (the)

nouns tell you what is being talked about (cake, brother, love)

pronouns stand for people and things already known or mentioned (she, me, it, you)

indefinite article (a)

'Ouch!' cried the hairy gorilla as he fell clumsily in a heap.

verbs tell you what is happening or what someone is doing (sit, push, be, love)

adjectives describe things (red, big, fat, fast)

conjunctions join phrases and sentences (and, because, if)

adverbs tell you the way in which things happen or are done (suddenly, easily, fast)

prepositions tell you about position (in, on, to, off)

Grasses

Grasses are the biggest and most successful family of plants. Wheat, maize, sugar cane and bamboo are all grasses. Grasses survive because they grow quickly and soon produce seed. They grow from the base so even if their tops are eaten they can carry on growing.

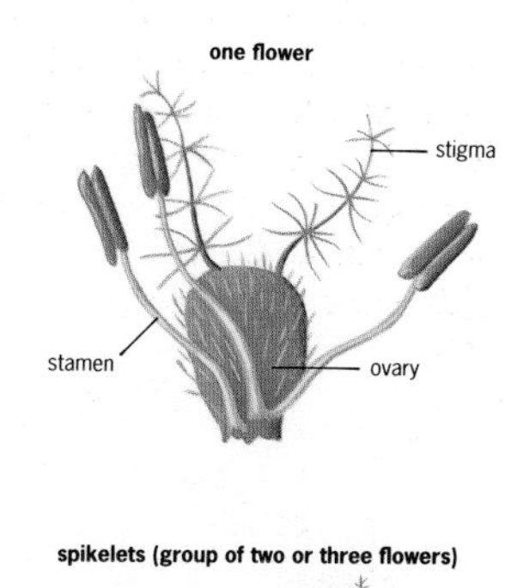

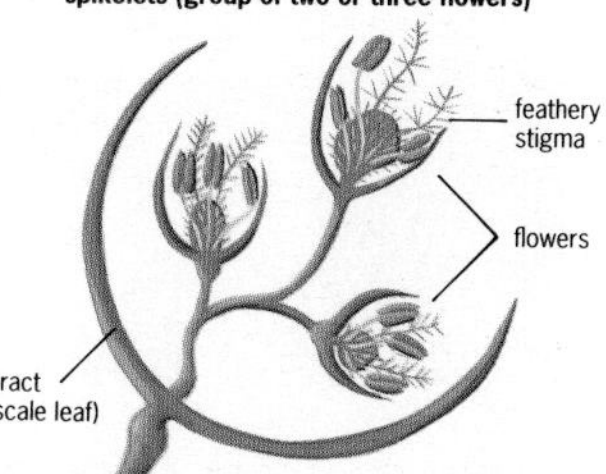

▶ The parts of the oat plant. Grass flowers grow in clusters of two or three flowers, called spikelets. They have no petals, because they are pollinated by the wind and so do not need to attract insects. The male anthers hang outside the flower so the wind can carry the pollen to other plants. The female stigmas are feathery to catch the wind-blown pollen.

Gravity

Gravity is the pulling force which every object has, including you and me, towards everything else. The Earth's gravity is a very strong pull that holds us all down on its surface.

Gravity holds the Moon in its orbit around the Earth, and the Sun and 100,000 million stars in a group called our Galaxy.

Gravity gives us our weight. You weigh about six times as much on Earth as you would on the Moon. On the planet Jupiter you would weigh three times more than on Earth.

Greece

Greece is in south eastern Europe. It is about the same size as England, but one fifth of the country is made up of islands. Greece has over 15,000 km (9,330 miles) of coastline. Nowhere is more than 130 km (80 miles) from the sea.

Many Greeks make their living from fishing and shipping. Farmers grow olives, oranges, lemons, grapes, cotton and tobacco. Greek houses have flat roofs. They can be used for drying fruit in summer and collecting rainwater in winter.

▲ The Acropolis in Athens.

▲ The island of Santorini.

Capital
Athens
Population
10,288,000
Currency
1 drachma = 100 leptae

FACT FILE

Greek ancient history

We remember the ancient Greeks for their splendid buildings and works of art. They also gave us our political system, 'democracy', meaning people's rule. In the cities of Greece all male citizens made laws by voting at big public meetings. Women, children and slaves had no vote.

The Greeks fought several wars against Persia. When the Persians were finally defeated in 479 BC, the Greek city state of Athens ruled an empire. A magnificent temple, the Parthenon, was built on the Acropolis in the centre of the city. Athens also had schools and the world's first university.

The main rival city state was Sparta, where all men had to be in the army. Sparta controlled most of the southern parts of Greece, called the Peloponnese. Athens and Sparta began the Peloponnesian War in 431 BC. Athens had more people, but the Spartan army was too strong. In the end Sparta won and took over the Athenian empire. Greek democracy came gradually to an end.

Later the Macedonians, under kings such as Philip and Alexander, took over most Greek cities. By the 2nd century BC, Roman armies had conquered most of Greece.

▲ **A cutaway view of a house in classical Greece. This house was built around an inner courtyard. This allowed light into the rooms (notice there are only little windows on the outside) and made the house cool in summer. Some houses were two storeyed.**

 **Did you know?** 

■ **The first 'Olympic' games with events such as discus and javelin throwing, were held by the Greeks in 776 BC to honour their chief god Zeus.**

◀ **Athens had its own 'high city', the Acropolis. This is what it looked like in 5th century BC.**

1 Sanctuary of Zeus

2 Parthenon (Temple of Virgin Athene)

3 Theatre of Dionysus

4 Erechtheum (temple of Athene and Poseidon)

5 Statue of Athene

6 Sanctuary of Artemis

7 Propylaea gateway

Greek gods

Each god has two names, one Greek and one Roman. The Romans worshipped many of the same gods as the ancient Greeks.

Greek	Roman	
Aphrodite	**Venus**	Goddess of beauty and of love.
Apollo	**Phoebus**	God of prophecy, music and medicine. The Romans also thought that he ruled the Sun.
Ares	**Mars**	God of war. Protector of Rome.
Artemis	**Diana**	Goddess of the Moon; a great huntress.
Athene	**Minerva**	Goddess of wisdom and of war. Protector of Athens.
Demeter	**Ceres**	Goddess of crops and harvest.
Dionysus	**Bacchus**	God of wine, dancing and theatre.
Hades	**Dis or Pluto**	Ruler of the underworld.
Hephaestus	**Volcanus**	God of fire.
Hera	**Juno**	Goddess of marriage.
Hermes	**Mercury**	Messenger-god, with a winged helmet and sandals. He shepherded dead souls to the underworld.
Poseidon	**Neptune**	God of the sea and of earthquakes.
Zeus	**Jupiter**	Sky-god, ruler of gods and mortals.

Green issues

Did you know?

■ The Irish Sea is one of the world's most radioactive seas because of the radioactive water released into it.

■ By recycling 75 per cent of the world's paper, over 35 million trees could be saved each year.

■ A typical Western family produces over 12 tonnes of carbon dioxide each year which contributes to the greenhouse effect.

■ More than 105,000 sq km (40,000 sq miles) of forest are destroyed every year (an area larger than Ireland and Wales).

Greenhouse effect

Some of the gases such as CO_2 in the Earth's atmosphere act like greenhouse glass and trap the Sun's heat. We produce too much of these gases for the Earth's plants to absorb, and so the Earth is slowly warming up. Melting ice-caps means that sea-levels could rise by over 1 m by the year 2030, making 15 million people homeless in Bangladesh.

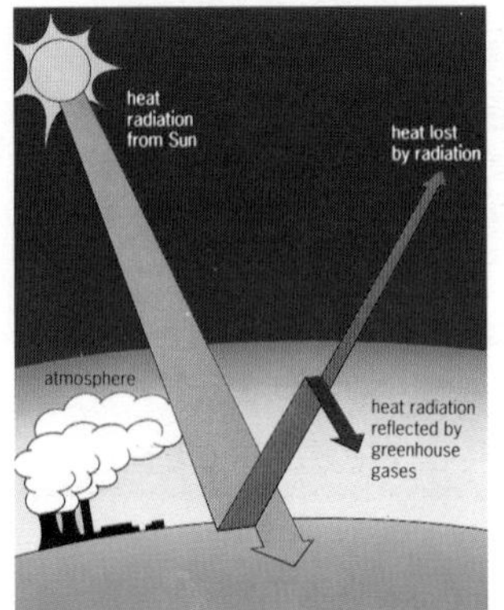

▶ **The Earth loses heat by radiation, but some of this heat is reflected back.**

Gymnastics

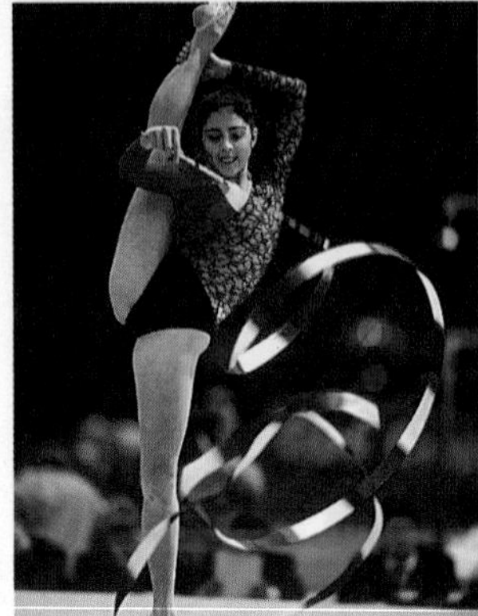

Gymnastics is a sport where people perform exercises. Some of these need special equipment such as the vault, the beam, and the parallel bars. The best gymnasts go in for competitions. They are given marks by judges. The best possible mark they can get is 10.0

Did you know?

■ The Greeks and Romans used gymnastic exercises to train their soldiers.

Growth

The time it takes for an animal to grow to breeding age varies enormously. Usually the larger the animal the longer it takes to grow, although a notable exception is the 17-year cicada.

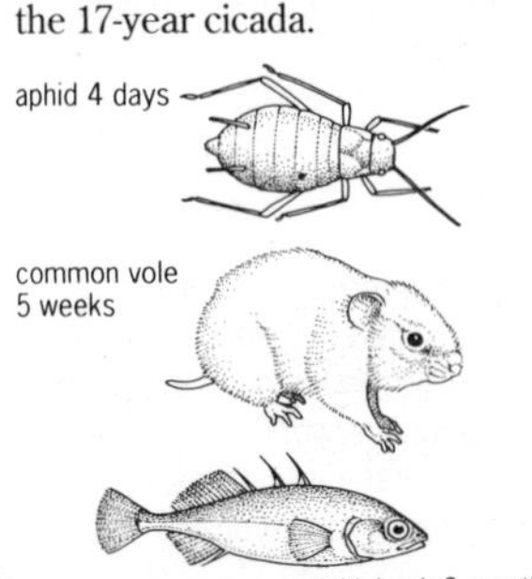

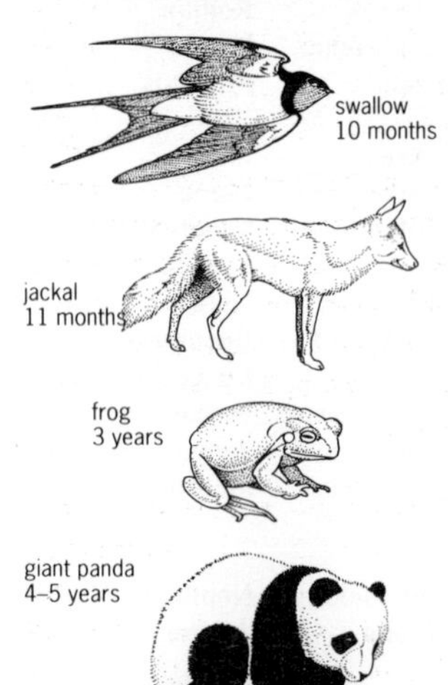

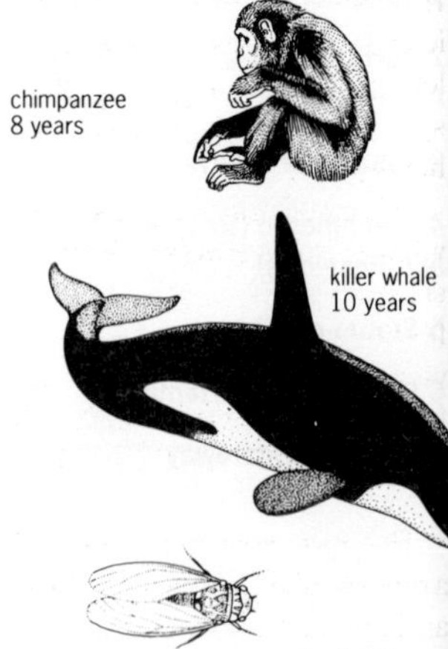

Heart

▼ This is what the heart looks like sliced open. It has four hollow chambers with muscular walls. The valves in the heart ensure that the blood flow is only one way.

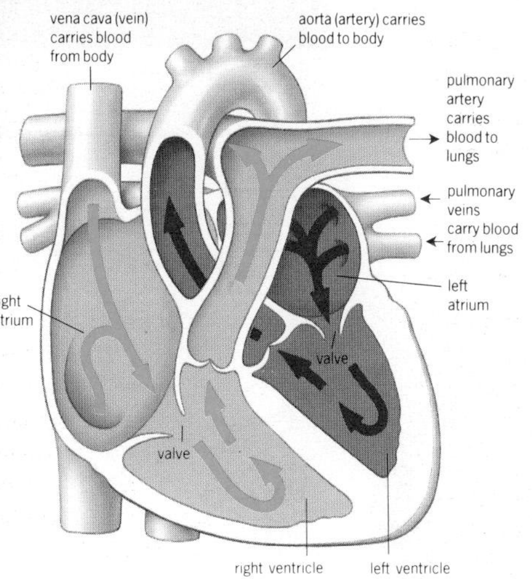

▼ Blood movement around the body. The blood travels from the heart to the lungs and back to the heart. It then travels to the rest of the body, before returning to the heart.

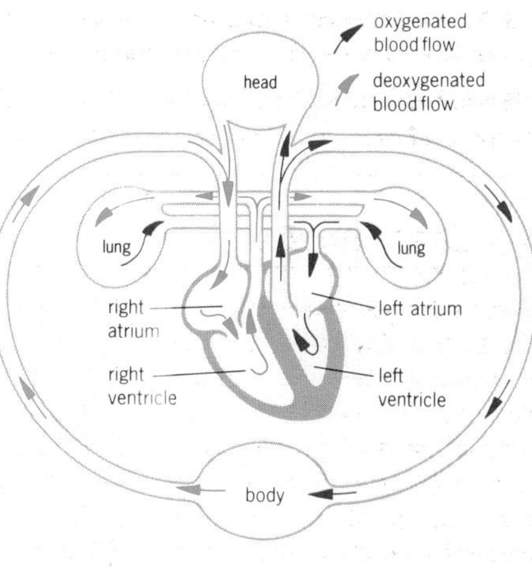

Heat

Heat is a type of energy. Radiant heat can travel through empty space. Heat from a fire travels to your skin in the same way as heat and light reach you from the Sun. Heat also makes objects increase in size. In bridges, small gaps are left between the girders to allow space for the metal to expand on hot days.

When a solid is heated, its atoms vibrate more quickly. A spoon sticking out of a cup of hot tea soon feels hot because the faster vibrations at the hot end are transmitted to the cooler end. This movement of heat is called conduction.

The movement of hot air round a room is called convection. This is an important method of heating houses.

Hedgehogs

▲ The hedgehog's skin is larger than is necessary to cover its body. When it curls up it pulls its skin down over its head and rump, so it is completely protected by its 3,000 or more spines.

Hedgehogs are active at night and may travel up to 2 km (over 1 mile) looking for food. They eat insects, snails, slugs and the occasional frog or lizard.

Helicopters

The long thin blades on top of a helicopter are turned by its engine. They push air downwards and this lifts the helicopter up. The pilot tilts the blades to make the helicopter move forwards, backwards or sideways. The first practical helicopter was the Focke Fa-61, made in Germany in 1937. A helicopter's maximum speed is about 400 km/h (250 mph).

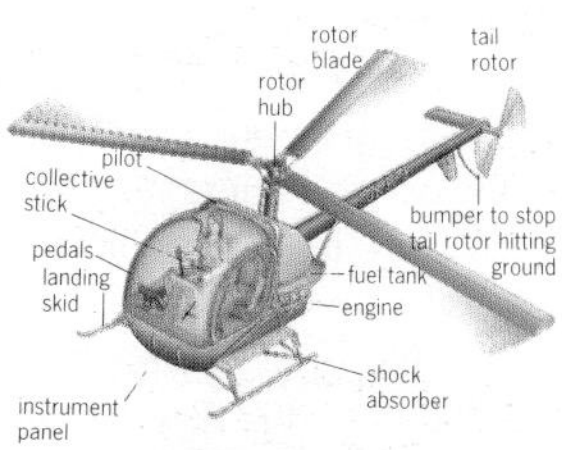

Henry VIII

Henry, born in 1491, became king in 1509. He wanted a son to follow him, but his wife, Catherine of Aragon, had only one child, a daughter. The Pope refused to give Henry a divorce, so he broke away from the Church of Rome.

He married Anne Boleyn (divorcing Catherine later) and made himself Head of the English Church. Henry had four more wives before he died in 1547. They were Jane Seymour, Anne of Cleves, Catherine Howard and Katherine Parr.

Hieroglyphics

This is a type of writing which uses pictures instead of words. The Egyptians used hieroglyphics from about 3100 BC to the end of the 4th century AD. They had over 700 signs. The Maya and Aztec Indians also used hieroglyphics.

People learned again how to read Egyptian hieroglyphics after the Rosetta Stone was found in 1799. It had an inscription on it written in Greek and Egyptian. As the Greek could be read the Egyptian hieroglyphics could also be deciphered.

Crocodile *Cipactli*

Wind *Ehecatl*

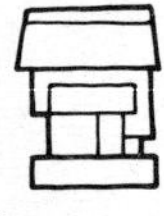

House *Calli*

Lizard *Cuetzpellin*

Serpent *Coatl*

Deer *Mazatl*

Rabbit *Tochtli*

Water *Atl*

Dog *Itzcuintli*

Monkey *Ozomatli*

Grass *Malinalli*

Reed *Acatl*

Eagle *Cuauhtli*

Flint knife *Tecpatl*

Rain *Quiahuitl*

Flower *Xochitl*

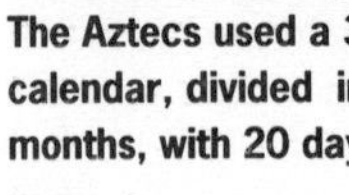

▶ The Aztecs used a form of writing in which ideas and objects were shown as pictures (pictograms) or symbols. These are some of the signs for days. The Aztecs used a 365 day calendar, divided into 18 months, with 20 days in each.

Highwaymen

Highwaymen were robbers who held people up on the road. They usually carried guns to stop stagecoaches, in the days before motor vehicles and trains. One day in 1698 three highwaymen robbed over 30 people on Hounslow Heath outside London.

Dick Turpin, a very famous highwayman, was said to have ridden from London to York on his horse Black Bess, to escape arrest. In fact, this ride was done by another highwayman, William Nevinson or 'Swift Nicks'.

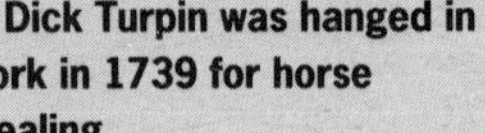

Did you know?

■ Dick Turpin was hanged in York in 1739 for horse stealing.

Hillforts

▲ **This is Maiden Castle in Dorset, one of the largest hillforts. Its earth banks and ditches enclose an area of 18 hectares. Archaeologists found stores of sling stones near one entrance. One store had over 20,000 pieces of stone ammunition.**

▶ **This is the entrance to the hillfort in Crickley Hill in Gloucestershire. If enemies broke through the outer gate they would then be trapped in the slingers' crossfire in front of the inner gate.**

Hillforts were built more than 2,000 years ago. They had huge walls of earth, and sometimes stone, to protect people from enemy tribes and wild animals. Inside there were workshops and food stores.

Entrances to the forts had to be easy to defend. Some were like mazes, where attackers could be trapped and killed.

Did you know?

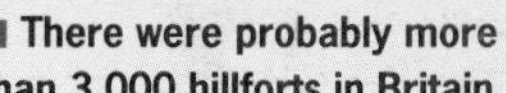

■ **There were probably more than 3,000 hillforts in Britain.**

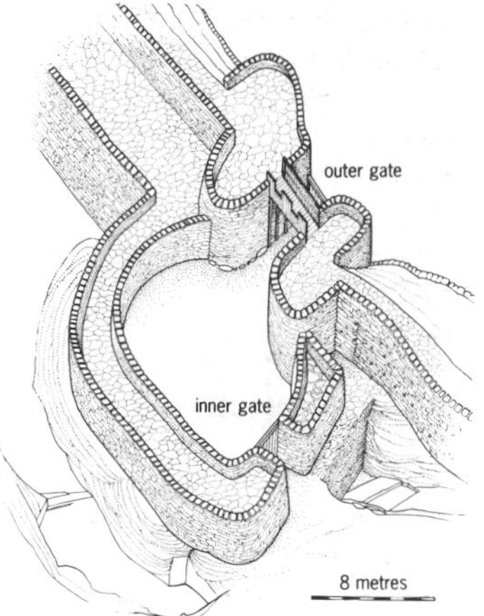

Hippopotamuses

▲ **Male hippos use their huge lower canine teeth as weapons, when fighting for females and territory. Hippos are mammals.**

Hitler, Adolf

Adolf Hitler was born in 1889. After World War I he became leader of the National Socialist (Nazi) Party. He thought that all Germany's problems were the fault of Jews and communists, and that Germany needed a strong *Führer* (leader) to be great again.

Hitler became Führer in 1934. All who opposed him were crushed, and Jews gradually lost all their rights. In 1938 and 1939 his armies invaded Austria and Czechoslovakia and then attacked Poland.

This started World War II. Hitler took command of the German forces, and ordered the deaths of 6 million Jews. When he was defeated in 1945 he shot himself in his underground shelter.

Hockey

Hockey is a game played by two teams of eleven. Players use a stick with a curved end to hit the ball into the other team's goal. Only goalkeepers can handle the ball, and wear gloves, face-mask, and padding for protection.

Holocaust

The word Holocaust means 'a burnt sacrifice', but now it has come to mean one particular event in history. During World War II, the Nazis took over many European countries. In all those countries, and in Germany itself, the Nazis began to arrest all the Jews they could find.

From 1941 to 1945 they built huge death camps and transported Jews to them in their thousands. Altogether about 6 million Jews were killed. This wiping out of 85 per cent of Europe's Jews is now called the Holocaust.

Holograms

A hologram is a 3D picture which is made using a beam of laser light. You also need laser light to see some holograms, although others, like the ones on credit cards, can be seen with ordinary light. In factory testing, holograms show up small differences in objects which should be identical. They were used on the Space Shuttle to show which of its protective tiles had become loose.

Hong Kong

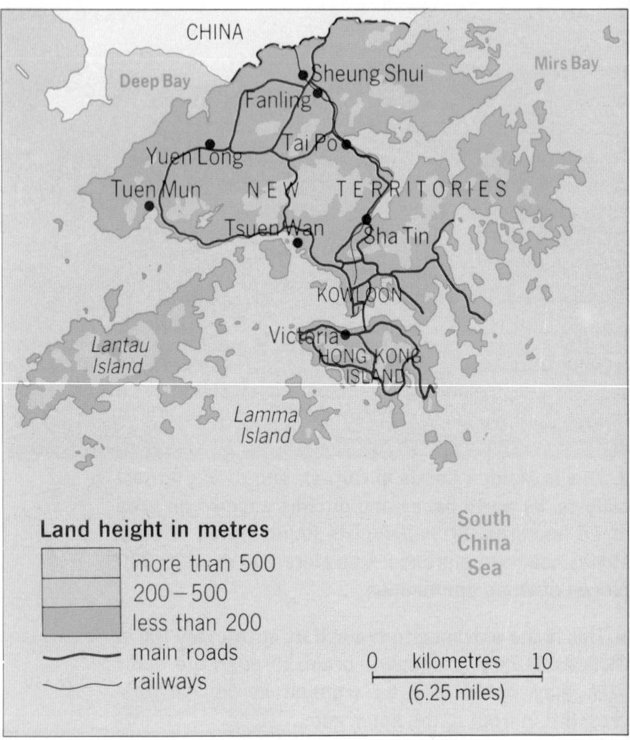

FACT FILE

Capital
Victoria
Population
5,800,000
Currency
1 HK dollar = 100 cents

Hong Kong is made up of a peninsula and over 200 islands on the south coast of China. It belongs to Britain, but is to be given back to China in 1997.

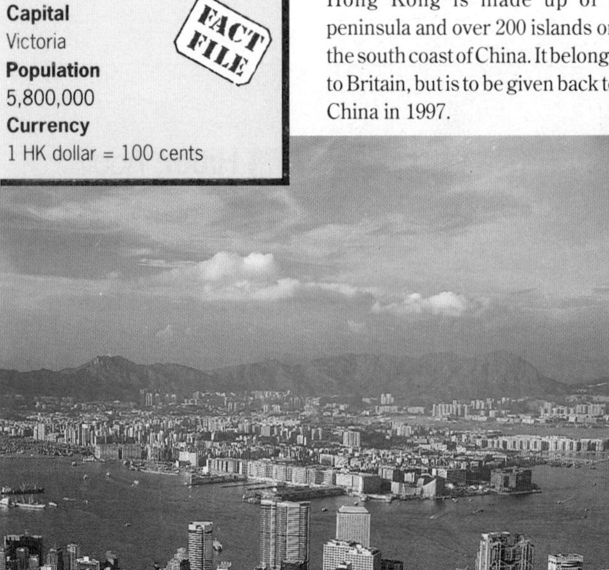

▶ **More than 100,000 people per sq km live in parts of Kowloon, which lies across the harbour from Hong Kong Island.**

Horses

A horse is measured at the shoulder in hands, using a measurement of 4 inches (10·16 cm), the width of a man's knuckles.

Horses were first domesticated by prehistoric people in Central Asia over 6,000 years ago. They are now virtually extinct in the wild.

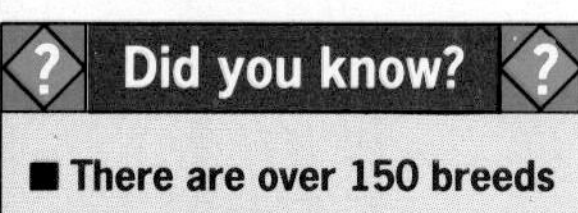

■ **There are over 150 breeds of domestic horse.**

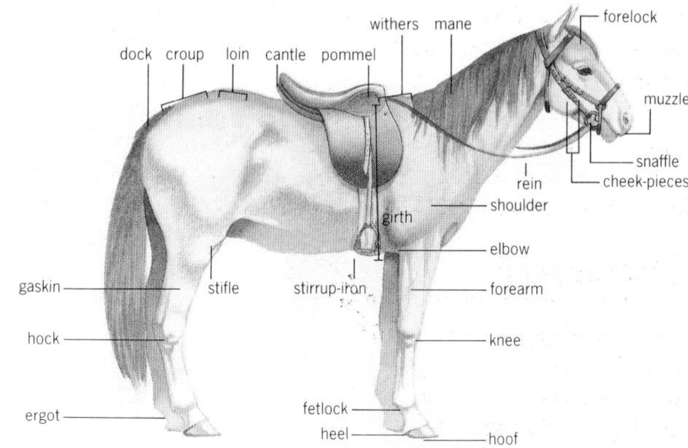

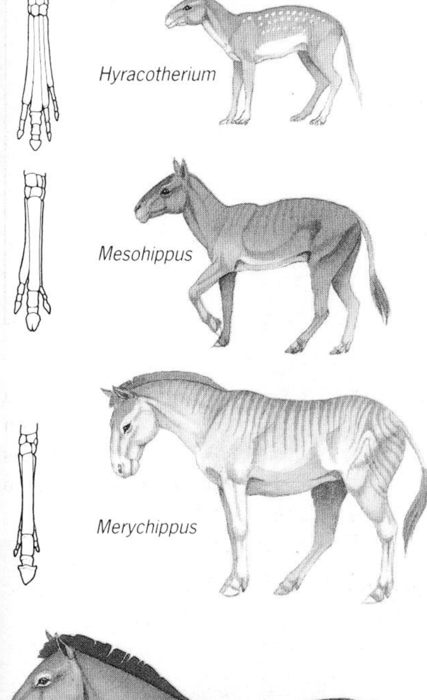

◀ ***Hyracotherium* lived about 58 million years ago, and was the size of a miniature poodle. It lived in forest and had four toes on its front feet and three on its hind.**

◀ ***Mesohippus* lived 36 million years ago. It had three toes on each foot, which were protected by large toenails.**

◀ ***Merychippus* was the first plains horse and lived 25 million years ago. It had three toes but only the middle one touched the ground.**

◀ ***Equus* is the modern horse, and has only one toe on each foot. It took nearly 60 million years to evolve from *Hyracotherium*.**

Hovercraft

A hovercraft floats on a cushion of air, which is kept in by large rubber skirts. The vehicle is pushed forwards by aircraft-like propellers.

Hovercraft have been used as ferries for cars and passengers. They are much faster than normal ferries, cruising at 80 km/h (50 mph). The first hovercraft, the SRN1, flew from the Isle of Wight to England in 1959. It was designed by the British engineer Sir Christopher Cockerell.

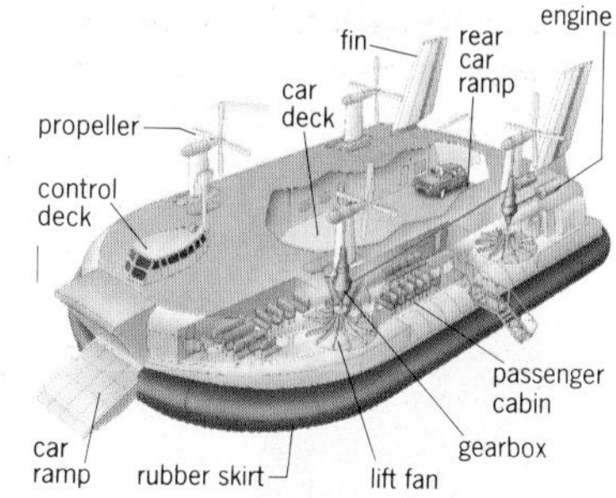

▲ **A hovercraft does not touch the surface over which it travels, but floats above it on a cushion of air kept in by its rubber skirt.**

Human body

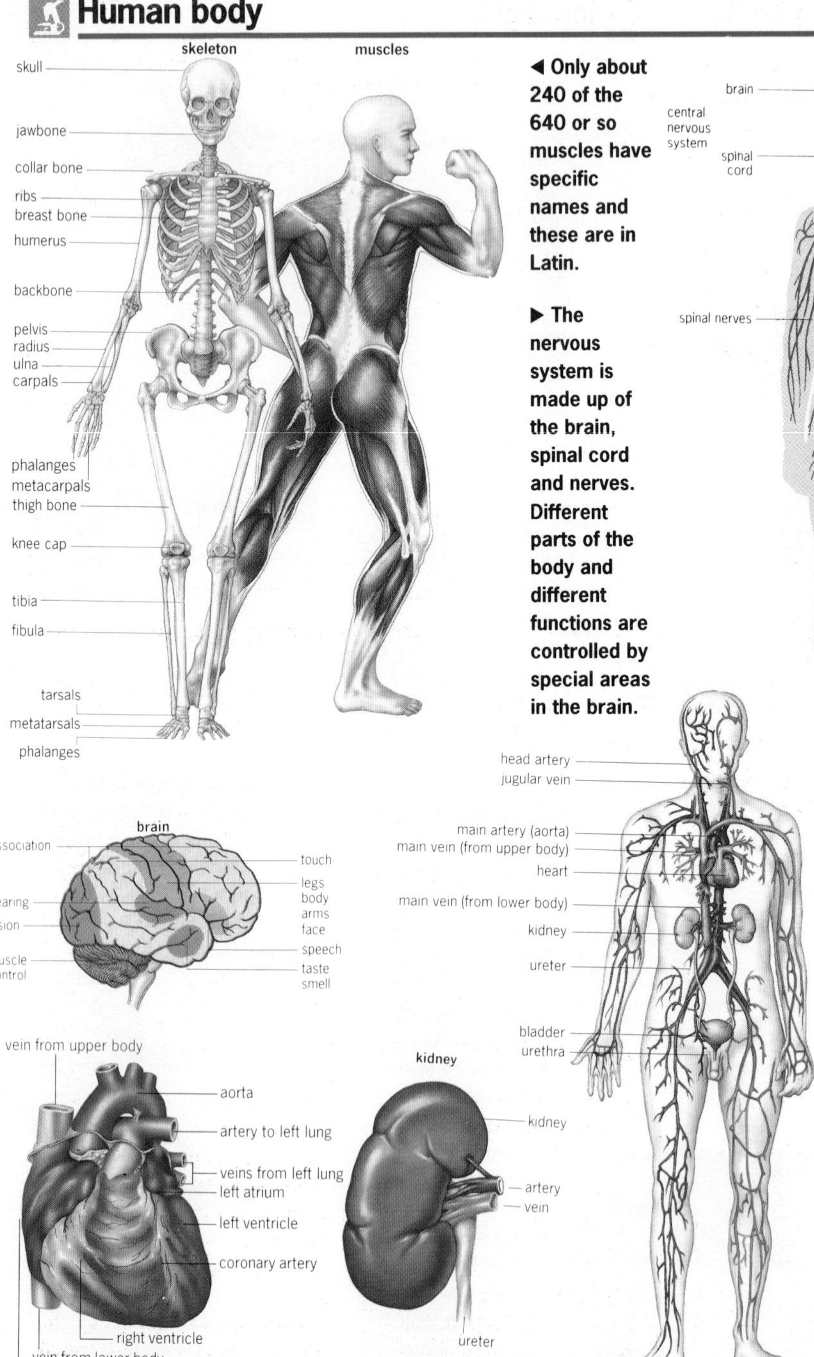

◀ **Only about 240 of the 640 or so muscles have specific names and these are in Latin.**

▶ **The nervous system is made up of the brain, spinal cord and nerves. Different parts of the body and different functions are controlled by special areas in the brain.**

◀ **The heart pumps blood around the body through the blood vessels. Arteries carry blood away from the heart. Veins carry blood back to the heart. The kidneys filter the blood and remove waste.**

Hummingbirds

Hummingbirds hover while feeding, beating their wings at more than 70 times a second. The Cuban bee hummingbird is the smallest bird in the world, it is under 6 cm long from bill-tip to tail-tip.

▲ A humming-bird's wings can move in all directions from the shoulder.

Hungary

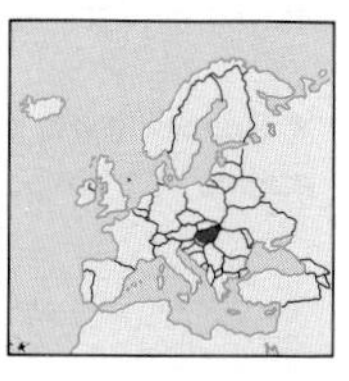

Hungary is in central Europe. The land is very good for farming. Hungary also sells machinery, trucks and buses to other countries.

Capital
Budapest
Population
10,303,000
Currency
1 forint = 100 fillérs

FACT FILE

Ice ages

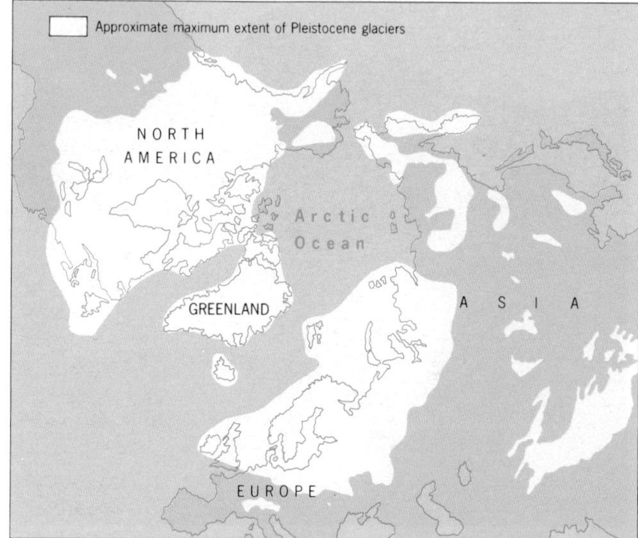

▲ Ice covered parts of the northern hemisphere during the last ice age.

▲ A reconstruction of an ice age showing mammoths and a glacier.

Did you know?

■ The most recent ice age started about 1,800,000 years ago and ended about 10,000 years ago.

Ice ages were times long ago when ice-sheets covered many parts of the world. The land was frozen and there was a lot of ice in the sea. Even in places as hot as the Sahara Desert rocks have scratch marks made by moving ice-sheets in the ice ages.

Many animals had to move to warmer places or change their living habits. Some died out altogether.

Incas

▲ **The ruins of the Inca city Machu Picchu.**

Incas were South American Indians who ruled an empire in the 15th and 16th centuries. Their capital city was Cuzco in Peru. From Cuzco they built roads over the mountains to all parts of their empire which extended 4,500 km from north to south.

▼ **A sacred puma fashioned from gold.**

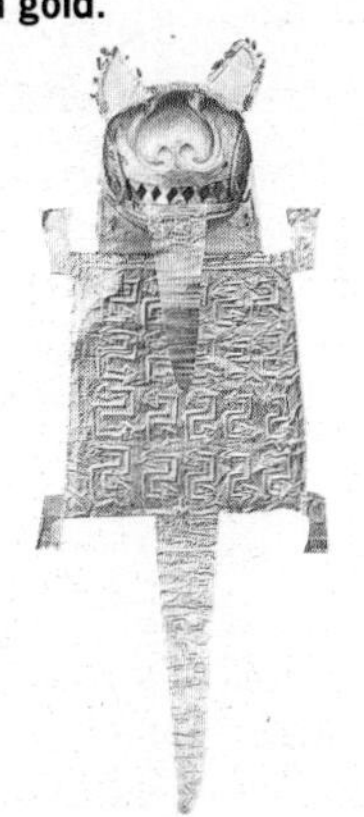

The Incas were farmers, and kept llamas and alpacas for food and wool. Everyone had to give food and goods to the government, run by the emperor. In return the government made sure that no one starved.

The last Inca emperor was Atahualpa. In 1532 Spanish invaders, led by Francisco Pizarro, arrived in Peru. Pizarro captured Atahualpa and asked for a roomful of gold and silver as a ransom. Pizarro took the gold and silver, but still had Atahualpa killed. By the 1570s the Incas had been utterly crushed by the Spanish conquerors.

Did you know?

■ **The Incas had no system of writing. Messages were learned by heart and taken all through the empire by relays of runners.**

India

▲ **The Taj Mahal at Agra, northern India was built in the 17th century.**

India is the sixth largest country i the world in terms of area, and onl China has more people. There ar sixteen main languages and man others besides.

Four out of five people work o the land. In the north wheat is th main crop. People use wheat flou to make chapatis (flat bread). I the south and east, where it i warmer and wetter, they grow ric There are other important crop such as bananas, sugar cane, te and cotton. India now produce enough food for its own people an has some left over for export.

▼ **Bullock carts are a common means of transport.**

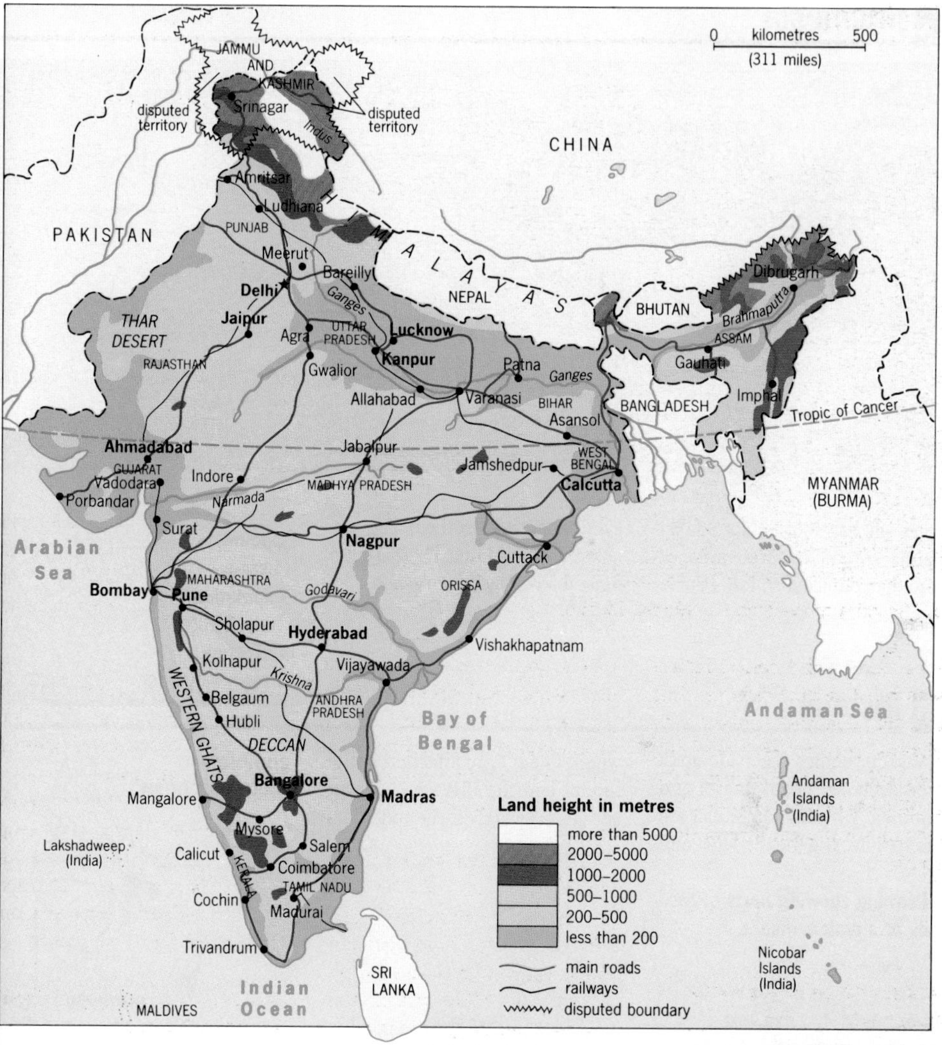

0 kilometres 500
(311 miles)

JAMMU AND KASHMIR
disputed territory
disputed territory
Srinagar
Indus
CHINA
PAKISTAN
Amritsar
Ludhiana
PUNJAB
HIMALAYAS
Meerut
Bareilly
Delhi
Ganges
NEPAL
BHUTAN
Dibrugarh
Brahmaputra
ASSAM
THAR DESERT
Jaipur
Agra
UTTAR PRADESH
Lucknow
Kanpur
RAJASTHAN
Gwalior
Patna
Ganges
Gauhati
Imphal
Allahabad
Varanasi
BIHAR
BANGLADESH
Asansol
Tropic of Cancer
Ahmadabad
Jabalpur
GUJARAT
WEST BENGAL
Jamshedpur
Vadodara
Indore
MADHYA PRADESH
Calcutta
MYANMAR (BURMA)
Porbandar
Narmada
Surat
Nagpur
Arabian Sea
Cuttack
MAHARASHTRA
ORISSA
Bombay
Pune
Godavari
Sholapur
Hyderabad
Vishakhapatnam
Kolhapur
Vijayawada
Krishna
WESTERN GHATS
Belgaum
ANDHRA PRADESH
Hubli
Andaman Sea
Bay of Bengal
DECCAN
Bangalore
Andaman Islands (India)
Mangalore
Madras
Mysore
Lakshadweep (India)
Calicut
Salem
KERALA
Coimbatore
TAMIL NADU
Cochin
Madurai
Trivandrum
SRI LANKA
Nicobar Islands (India)
Indian Ocean
MALDIVES

Land height in metres

- more than 5000
- 2000–5000
- 1000–2000
- 500–1000
- 200–500
- less than 200
- main roads
- railways
- disputed boundary

Industry is growing fast in India. Factories make aircraft, bicycles, cars, sewing machines and textiles.

◆ **Chandni Chowk, a famous street in Old Delhi.**

FACT FILE

Capital
New Delhi

Population
889,700,000

Currency
1 rupee = 100 paisa

Indonesia

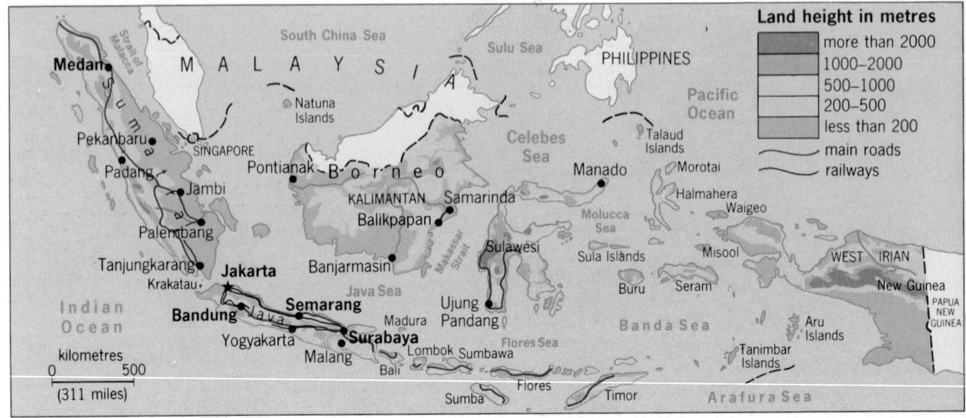

Indonesia has more than 13,000 islands spread over an area of more than 8 million sq km. People live on about 3,000 of them. They are all hot, wet and humid. There are also more than 100 active volcanoes.

Capital
Jakarta
Population
184,796,000
Currency
1 rupia = 100 sen

Insects

All insects' bodies are made up of three sections: head, thorax and abdomen. Eyes and antennae are attached to the head; legs and wings (if any) are attached to the thorax and the digestive system and sex organs are in the abdomen.

▼ **Drawing showing parts of the body of a typical insect.**

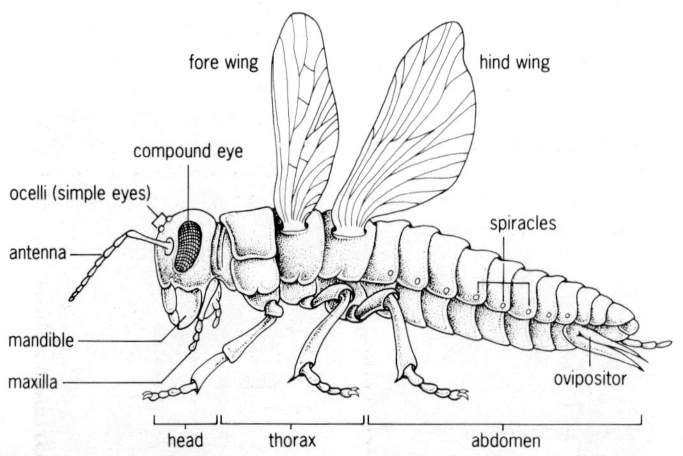

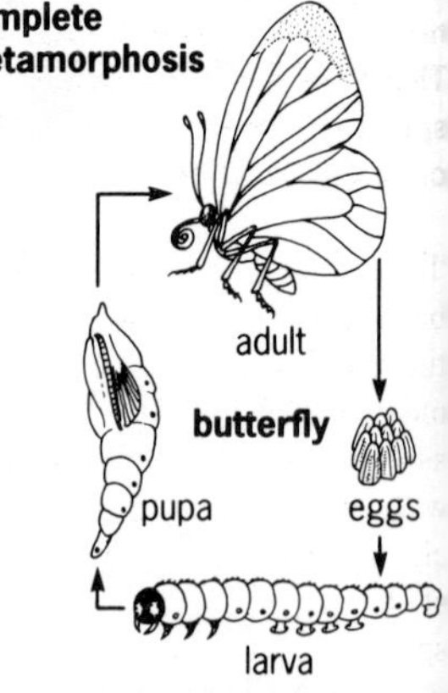

▲ **Many familiar insects undergo complete metamorphosis. They hatch from eggs as larvae, looking very different to their parents and feeding on separate food. When they are full grown they become pupae and change to the adult form.**

Invertebrates

amoeba

jellyfish

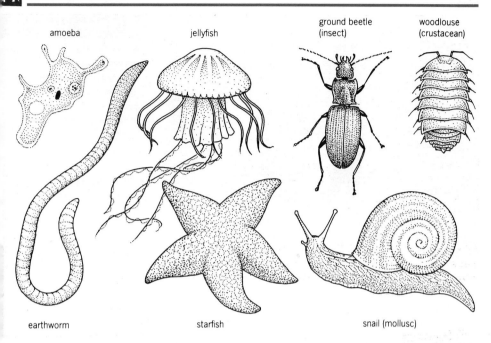

ground beetle (insect)

woodlouse (crustacean)

earthworm

starfish

snail (mollusc)

▲ Invertebrates are varied, numerous and widespread. There are about a million species of insects and crustaceans alone.

'Invertebrate' means 'without a backbone'. Most of the animals in the world are invertebrates. They include soft-bodied animals, such as worms and octopuses; animals with shells, such as snails and clams; and those with jointed outer skeletons, such as insects and spiders.

■ Not all invertebrates are small: the largest octopus, the Pacific octopus, has an armspan of about 7 m.

Iran

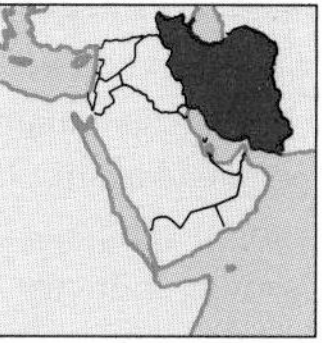

Iran is the biggest non-Arab country in the Middle East. In the north there are high mountains. Further south are deserts and oil wells, which give Iran most of its wealth. Iran used to be called Persia and was ruled by a shah. The last shah was overthrown in 1979 when Iran became an Islamic republic.

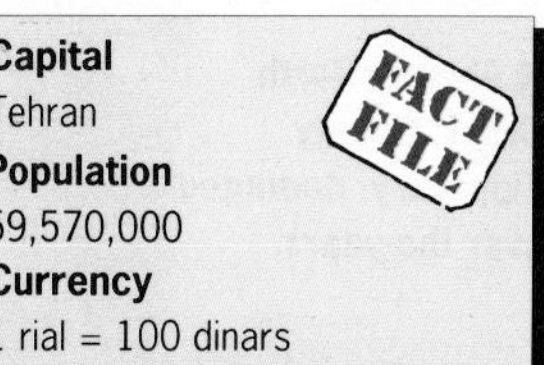

Capital
Tehran
Population
59,570,000
Currency
1 rial = 100 dinars

FACT FILE

Iraq

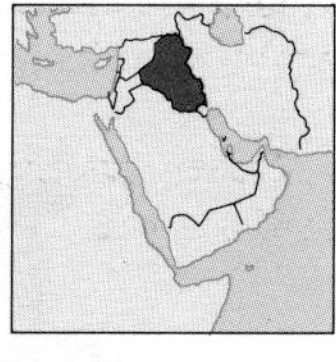

Iraq is one of the biggest and most powerful of Arab states. Many Iraqis work on the land, but most of the country's wealth comes from oil.

Rows over oil led to the Iraqi invasion of Kuwait in 1990. The United Nations sent armed forces to defeat Iraq and free Kuwait in 1991.

Capital
Baghdad
Population
18,838,000
Currency
1 Iraqi dinar = 20 dirhams

Ireland's history

> **Did you know?**
>
> ■ **The 1921 treaty set up two governments in Ireland. Twenty-six counties formed the Irish Free State. Six counties formed Northern Ireland and stayed in the UK.**

◀ **The suffering caused by the potato famine was immense.**

Ireland's first settlers probably crossed from Britain in about 6000 BC. In about 300 BC the Celtic people arrived. By the 5th century bishops such as St Patrick made it a Christian country. Viking raiders in the 9th century founded Dublin and other major ports.

The English often invaded Ireland. After the Reformation they tried to make it a Protestant country. In 1690 William III won the battle of the Boyne to establish British rule.

In the 19th century there was a potato famine that lasted three years. Whole families died and millions left Ireland. Many of those who stayed fought to free Ireland from British rule. This was finally achieved in 1921, but the Irish Republic was not set up until 1949.

Irish Republic

The Irish Republic is famous for its farm produce, linen, crystal glass, whiskey and beer. On the coast many people work in fishing and fish-farming industry.

Capital
Dublin
Population
3,519,000
Currency
1 punt =
100 pingine

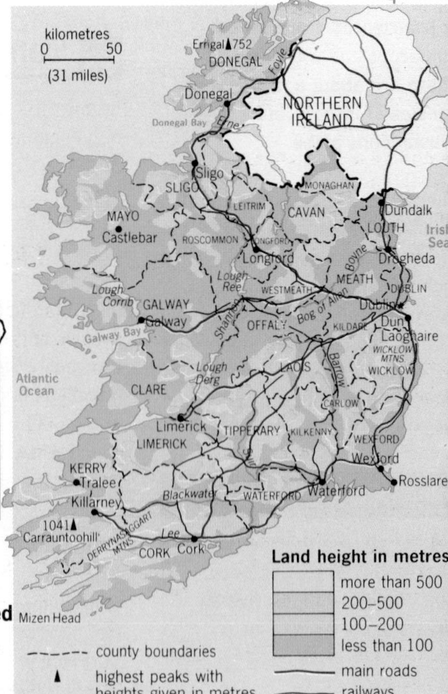

◀ **Ahenny North Cross, County Tipperary, damaged over the years.**

Iron and steel

Most iron is made by heating iron ore in a blast furnace. Iron ore, coke and limestone are heated to form iron and a waste material called slag. The liquid iron is either poured into moulds to make cast iron, or made into steel. Slag is used for road-building.

Steel is made by removing most of the carbon and other impurities from liquid iron. White-hot slabs of steel are then rolled into huge steelsheets.

Did you know?

- **Iron was first made by heating a mixture of iron ore and charcoal over a fire. The hot iron was beaten with a stone to make knives, axes and other tools.**
- **Iron was in use in about 2,000 BC in Anatolia (now Turkey).**

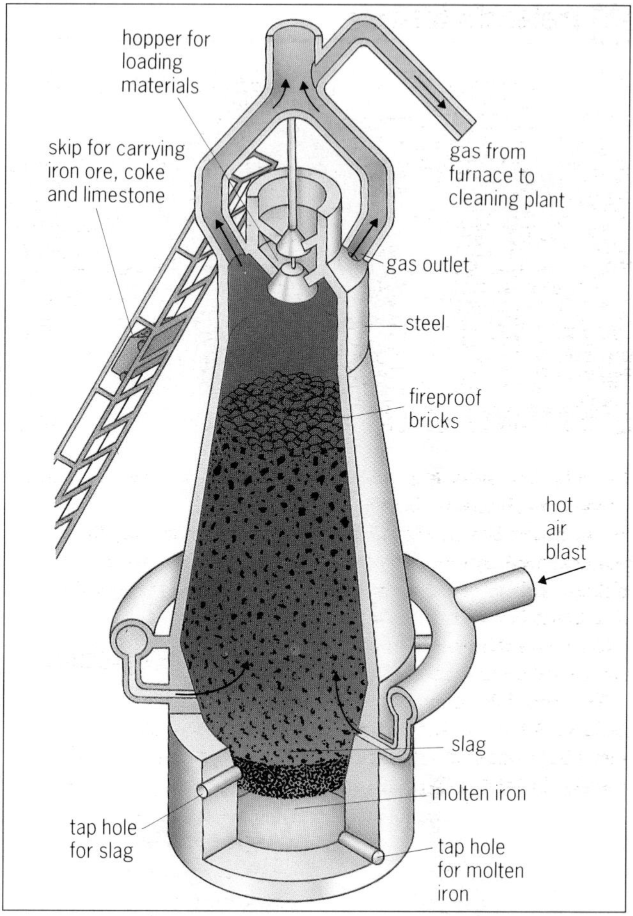

▸ In a blast furnace the iron ore, limestone and coke is heated by a continuous blast of hot air. Molten iron collects at the bottom and is drained off through a tap hole.

Islands

Some mountainous islands, such as the Caribbean islands, are really the tops of volcanoes on the ocean floor. Many low-lying islands in warm seas, such as the Maldive Islands, are made of coral. Other islands are formed simply because the sea-level has risen. Low areas are flooded, leaving the land in between as islands. The islands off the coast of Yugoslavia are like this.

Israel

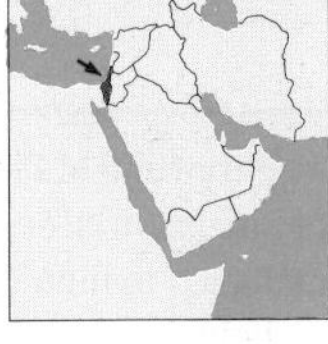

Israel was born in 1948. It is a country for Jewish people from all over the world. But it is surrounded by Arab countries which did not want Israel to be there. Because of this there have been many rows and wars between Israel and her Arab neighbours. Israel still controls some of the territory which it captured in those wars.

Most Israelis live near the Mediterranean coast, where they grow fruit and vegetables. Most of Israel's businesses are there too.

Capital
Jerusalem
Population
5,239,000
Currency
1 shekel = 100 new agorot

Italy

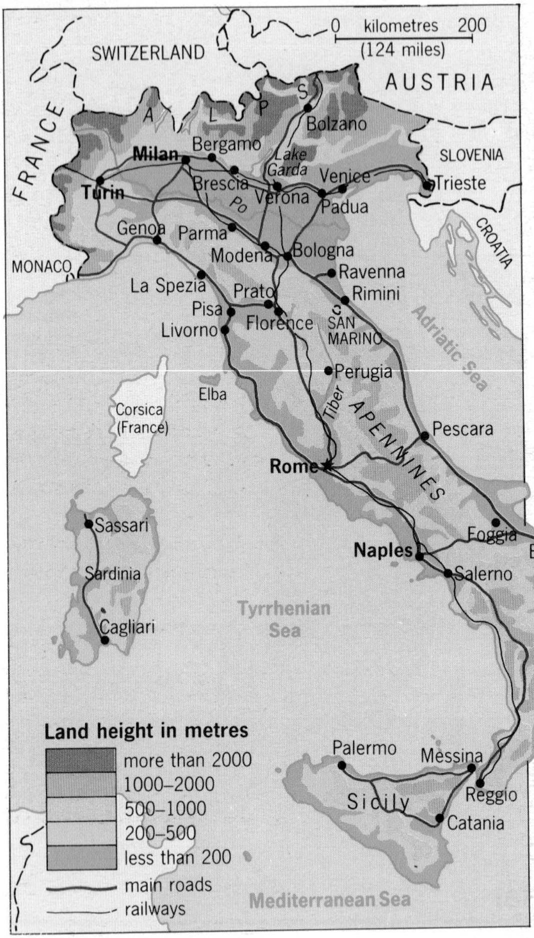

Italy is a long, narrow country in southern Europe. In Milan, Turin and other northern cities, there are factories producing cars, textiles and computers. The richest farmland is also in the north, in the flat valley area of the River Po. There are apple and pear orchards, fields of wheat, maize and sugar beet, and even rice on the wettest lowland.

In southern Italy and Sicily there is less work, and the stony soil is harder to farm. Olives for oil and vines for wine-making are grown. In Sicily there are orchards of almond trees, oranges and lemons.

Italians try to preserve their old buildings, so in Rome, Florence, Pisa, Venice and all the other ancient cities there is evidence of Italy's long history all round.

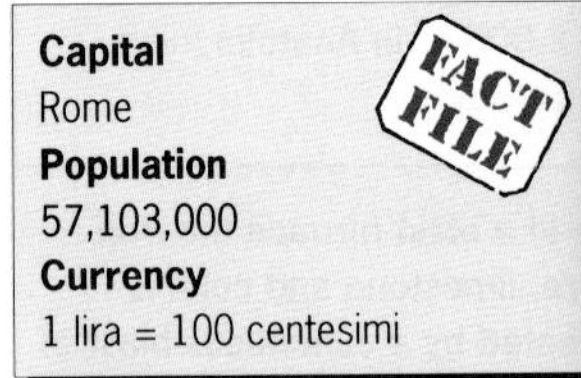

Capital
Rome
Population
57,103,000
Currency
1 lira = 100 centesimi

Italy's history

In ancient times Italy was at the centre of the Roman empire. But when the empire collapsed German tribes attacked Italy. Roman roads and buildings became ruins.

In the Middle Ages Venice and Florence grew rich from trade. The Pope ruled Rome. Italy was divided and remained so until the 19th century. Then the soldier Garibaldi led 1,000 troops into Italy. Together with the king of Piedmont and his prime minister, Cavour, he managed to unite Italy by 1870.

Italy fought with Germany in World War II. After their defeat, Italians voted in 1946 to get rid of their king.

▶ Niccolò Machiavelli (1469–1527) was one of the most important political figures of the Renaissance.

Japan

Japan is in the Pacific Ocean. Mountains and hills cover two thirds of the country and there are more than 60 active volcanoes.

Japan is a very crowded country. Three quarters of its people live in owns and cities close to the coast. Their homes are often small, but early every family has a refrigerator, television set and washing machine.

Japan leads the world in making motor vehicles, ships and elevisions.

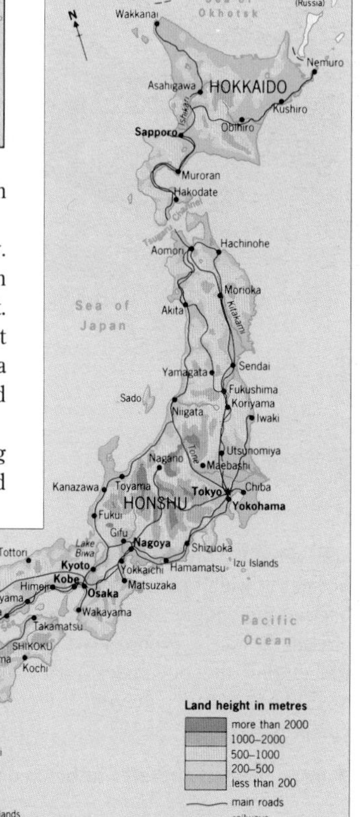

▲ **A Japanese family enjoying a meal at home. Japanese rooms tend to be fairly bare and plainly furnished. Meals are based mainly on rice and often include fish. Tea is drunk with the meal.**

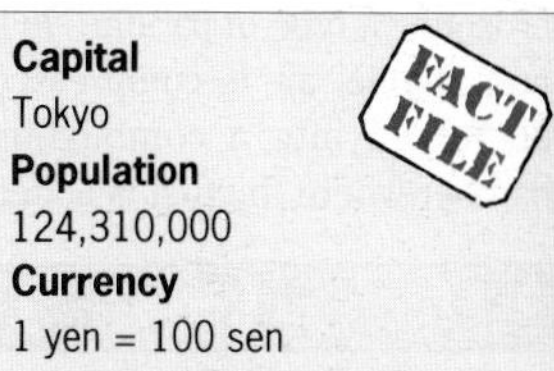

Capital
Tokyo
Population
124,310,000
Currency
1 yen = 100 sen

Jazz

azz was first played by black American musicians. It has become opular all over the world. Most azz players make up musical ideas nd play them as they go along. azz emphasises the off-beats in he music. This makes it bouncy.

The earliest jazz was played in New Orleans, by small groups. ater, people such as Duke llington and Count Basie led big ands.

Jellyfish

Jellyfish are not true fish; they belong to a group called *Cnidaria*. The jellyfish's tentacles are covered with powerful stinging cells. Each cell contains a coiled hollow tube with sharp hooks. When the trigger is touched, the tube shoots out like a harpoon. The hooks drill a hole in the prey's skin and poison is squirted in.

Did you know?

■ **The largest jellyfish measures over 2 m across, with tentacles over 65 m long.**

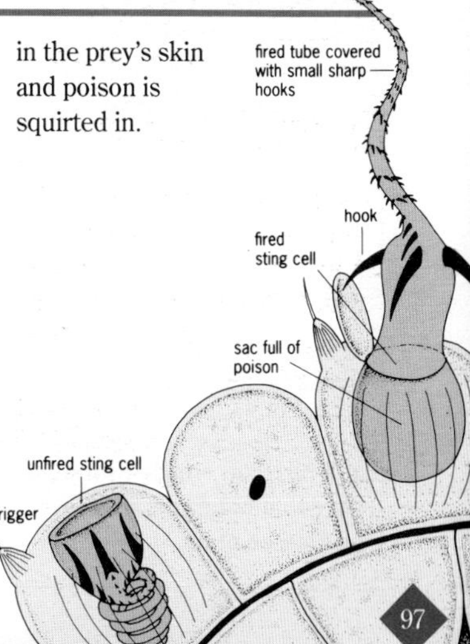

Jet engines

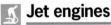

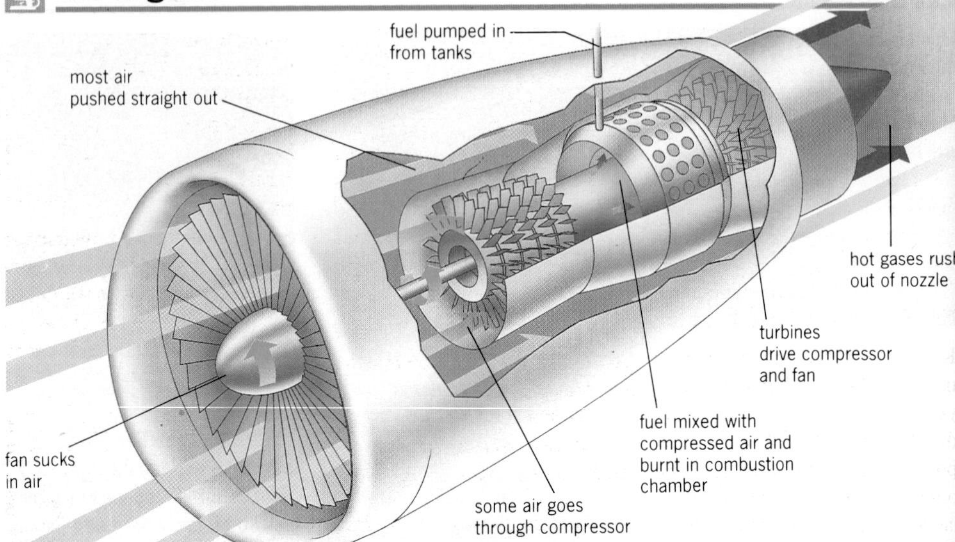

Jet engines are very powerful engines used mainly to drive fast aircraft. They burn a fuel called kerosene, a type of paraffin. In a basic engine, air is compressed and forced into a combustion chamber where the fuel is added and burned. This produces very hot gases which rush out of the back of the engine and drive the aircraft forwards. Before leaving the engine the hot gases turn a turbine which drives the compressor.

The first type of jet engine was the turbojet which was very noisy. Turbofan engines are quieter and are used in most large airliners. They have huge fans at the front to collect and blow out most of the air.

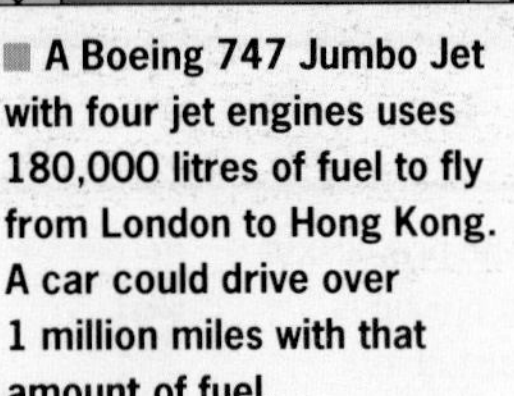

Did you know?

A Boeing 747 Jumbo Jet with four jet engines uses 180,000 litres of fuel to fly from London to Hong Kong. A car could drive over 1 million miles with that amount of fuel.

In 1983, Richard Noble reached a record speed of 1,019 km/h (633 mph) in a jet-powered car.

The first jet engine was tested in Britain in 1937 by Frank Whittle.

A turbofan engine pushes out some hot gases as well as masses of air.

▼ Inspecting an aircraft's turbofan engine.

Kangaroos

Kangaroos are marsupials, which means they give birth to their young before they are fully developed, and carry them in a pouch. They normally produce only one young at a time. The largest kangaroo, the red kangaroo (height 1·65 m, weight 90 kg), is only 2 cm long and 0·75g in weight, at birth. Baby kangaroos are called joeys. They stay in the pouch for about eight months.

▲ Tree kangaroos are found in the rainforests of Australia and New Guinea. Their strong forelimbs have sharp curved claws to help them climb.

Kenya

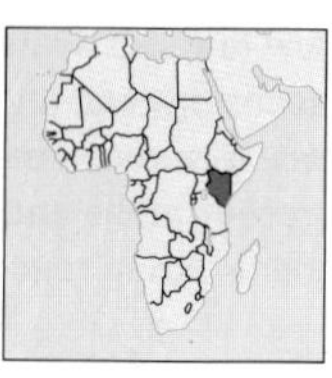

Kenya is on the Equator in East Africa. Most Kenyans live in the highlands where there is enough rain to grow crops such as maize and coffee. Many tourists go to Kenya's national parks to see the wildlife, which includes antelopes, elephants, giraffes, lions and zebras.

FACT FILE

Capital
Nairobi
Population
26,985,000
Currency
1 Kenya shilling = 100 cents

King, Martin Luther

As a church minister Martin Luther King Jr. helped black Americans to fight for their rights. But, like Gandhi, he believed in non-violence. In 1964 the Civil Rights Bill was made law. King was given the Nobel Peace Prize for his work. Sadly, in 1968, aged 39, he was shot dead by a sniper.

▲ Martin Luther King Jr. speaking in Washington.

Kings and queens

A king is a male ruler of a tribe or country. Usually when a king dies, his son becomes king after him. If there is no son, a daughter may become queen. Britain and the Netherlands both have queens today.

Some countries, such as Saudi Arabia, Morocco and Jordan, have powerful kings. But most kings and queens have handed their powers over to the country's elected parliament.

Did you know?

- **Most kings rule alone, but ancient Sparta had two kings who ruled together.**
- **Elizabeth II is the seventh queen in Britain.**

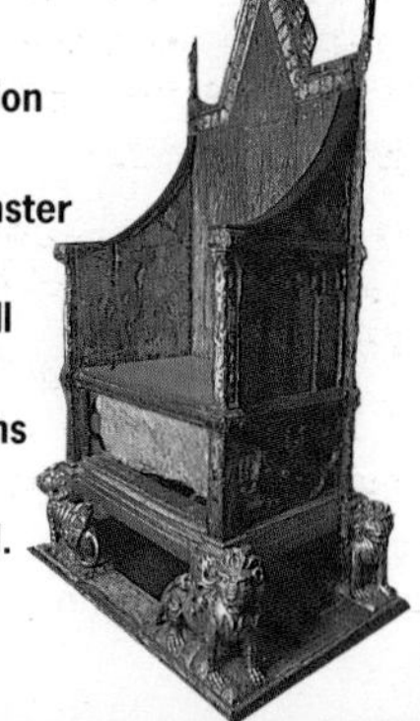

▶ The coronation chair in Westminster Abbey, where all British monarchs are crowned.

Kites

How to make a kite. Glue two pieces of wood together and twist wire round the joint. Cut grooves at the end of each spar and tie string round frame.

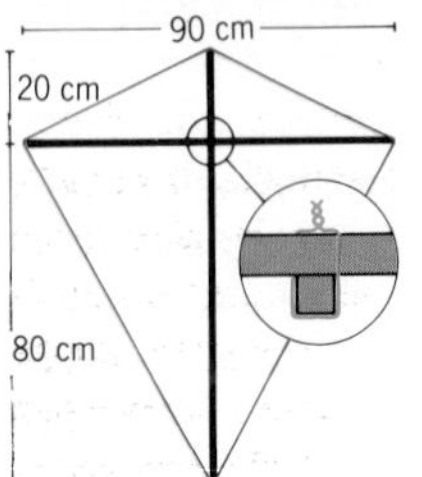

Cut diamond shape from strong paper, 4 cm larger than frame. Cut off corners and fold; glue paper over string.

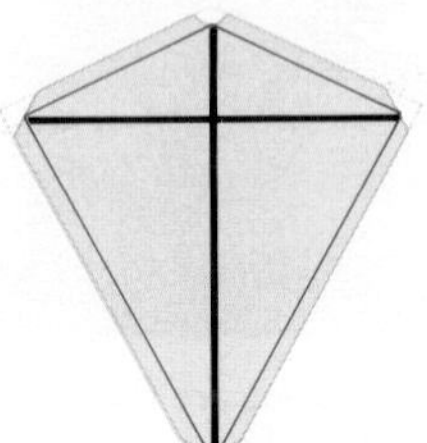

Make tail from 4 m of string and A4 sheets of paper. Attach a 1·3 m length of string to top and bottom of kite and attach flying line to this.

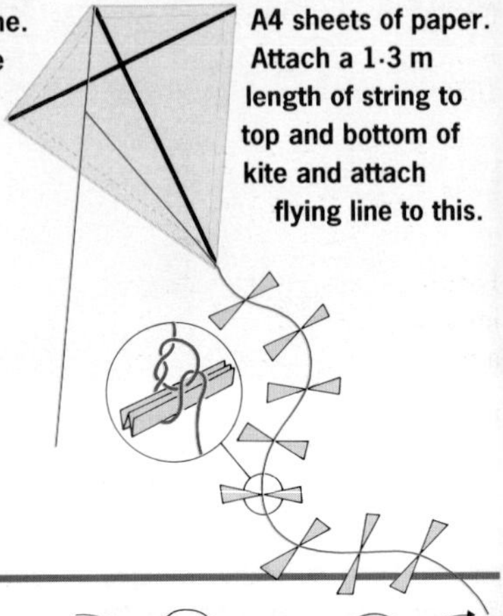

Knots

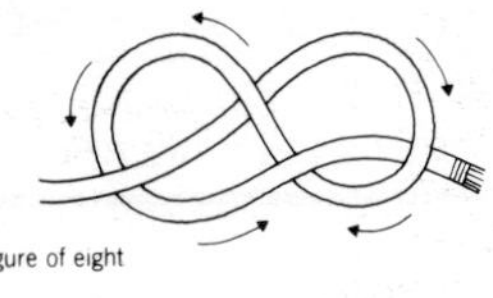

figure of eight

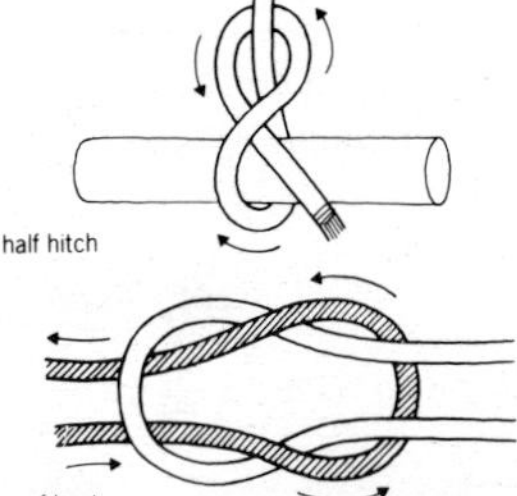

half hitch

reef knot

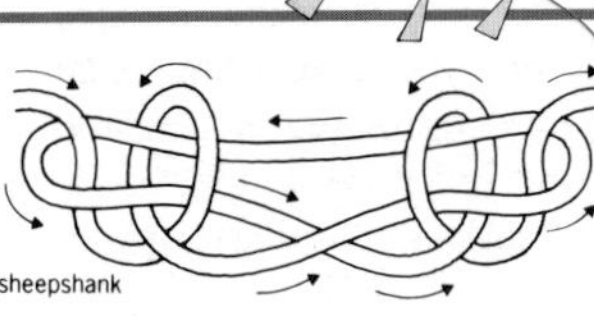

sheepshank

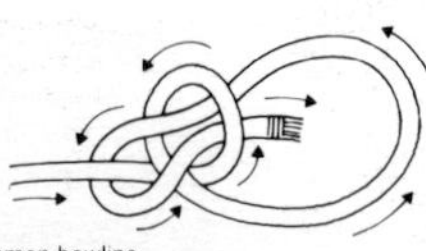

common bowline

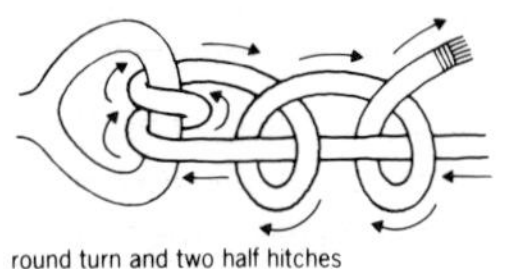

round turn and two half hitches

Koalas

◀ Koalas are climbing animals.

▶ They have two toes separated from the other three, to enable them to encircle a branch and cling tightly to it.

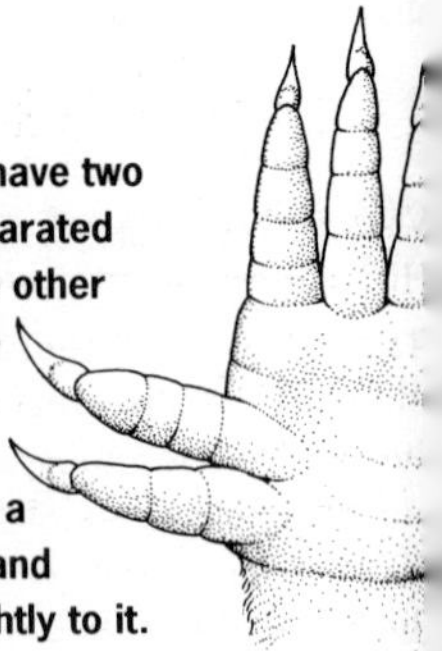

Koalas sleep for eighteen hours a day and are active mainly in the evening. They live in eucalyptus trees and feed on the young leaves and shoots. These contain a great deal of moisture, so koalas rarely need to leave the trees to look for water. 'Koala' is an Aborigine word meaning 'the animal that does not drink'.

Korean war

After World War II Korea was divided into two countries: North Korea and South Korea. In June 1950 the communist North invaded the South.

The USA, Britain and other countries joined in on South Korea's side. Later China joined North Korea. The war finally ended in July 1953 with about 5 million people dead.

Latitude and longitude

Latitude and longitude are imaginary lines that tell you where a place is on the Earth's surface.

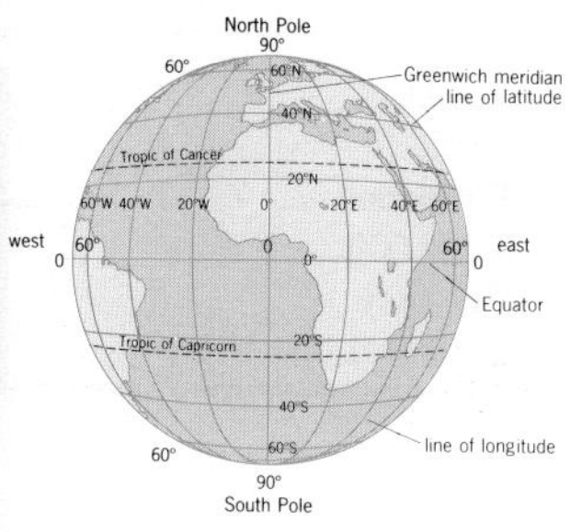

Latitude tells you how far it is north or south of the Equator. Longitude tells you how far it is east or west of a longitude line called the 'Greenwich Meridian', which goes through Greenwich in London.

Leaves

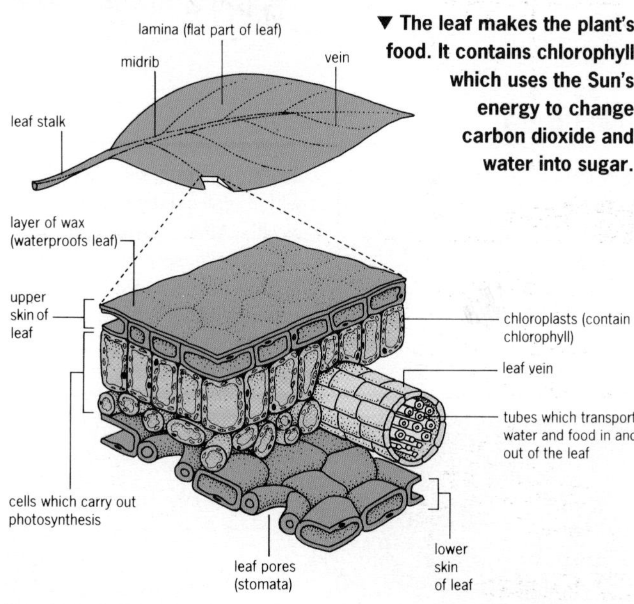

▼ The leaf makes the plant's food. It contains chlorophyll which uses the Sun's energy to change carbon dioxide and water into sugar.

Lenin (Vladimir Ilich Ulyanov)

Vladimir Ulyanov was born in 1870. His elder brother was hanged for trying to kill the tsar, and because of this Vladimir became a communist.

He was exiled to Siberia because of political activities and took the name 'Lenin' from the River Lena. In 1917 he returned to Russia and helped to lead the revolution. He died of a stroke in 1924.

► A poster of Lenin.

Leopards

Leopards are found in much of Africa and Asia in forests, grasslands and even deserts. Like all the big cats, they are becoming very rare.

Leopards are hunters, feeding mainly on small antelope and wild pig. But they will resort to smaller prey, such as rabbits, rats, or even insects. Usually they live alone, although cubs will remain with their mother until they are one to two years old.

Levers

We use levers to do jobs like lifting, pulling and turning. Scissors and door handles are two kinds of lever.

All levers have a place where you push or pull, a place where a force is put out, and a pivot.

▼ **These levers magnify force or movement.**

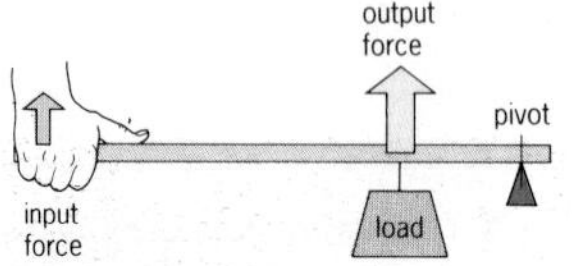

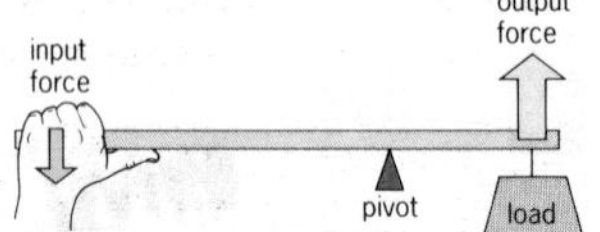

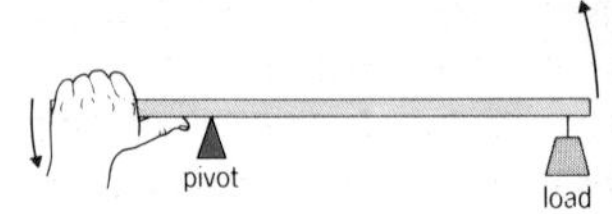

Libya

Libya is a very large North African country that is mostly desert. In the desert there is oil which gives Libya most of its wealth. Most Libyans live away from the desert on the fertile Mediterranean coast, where the land is good for farming.

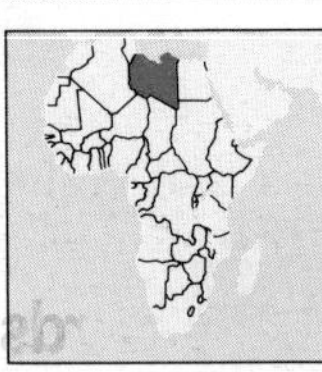

FACT FILE

Capital
Tripoli
Population
4,447,000
Currency
1 dinar = 1,000 dirhams

Light

▲ **A prism splitting white light into a spectrum.**

Light comes from the Sun or electric lights or from hot or burning things, like fires or flames. It travels through transparent substances like glass or water, but it is reflected by things that look solid. We see these objects when this reflected light enters our eyes.

The light from the Sun is really a mixture of colours. A triangular piece of glass, called a prism, will split sunlight up into a range of colours called a spectrum. The spectrum appears to be red, orange, yellow, green, blue and violet, but really the spectrum is a steady change of colour from beginning to end.

Lighting

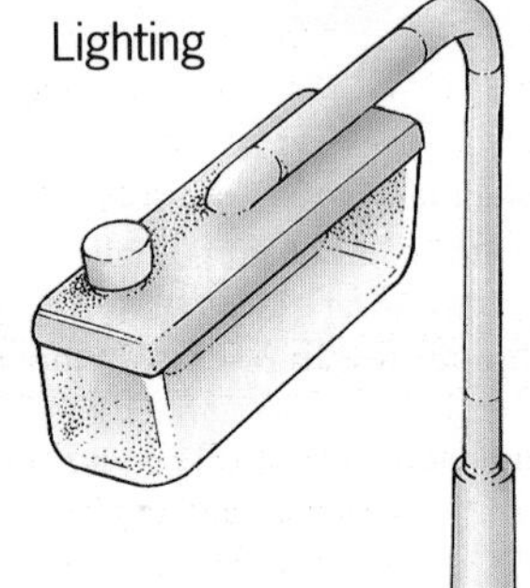

▲ **Street lights have gases in them which glow when electricity is passed through.**

▶ **An electric light bulb has a coiled wire called a filament. This glows white hot when electricity passes through it.**

Light years

The distances in space between stars and galaxies are so enormous that it is not convenient to measure them in kilometres or miles. Instead, they can be measured in light years. Light travels through space at a speed of 299,792 km (186,282 miles) per second. A light year is the distance light travels in 1 year. It is equal to 9·5 million million km (5·9 million million miles).

Lions

Lions live in groups called prides, usually made up of about a dozen animals. The females in a pride are usually sisters and remain together for life. Males rarely stay for more than three years. Lionesses do most of the hunting; only one hunt in four is successful. An adult male may eat 40 kg (90 lb) in a single meal, but then will not eat again for several days.

Lincoln, Abraham

Abraham Lincoln was born in 1809, in a log cabin into a poor family, but became president of the USA. During the Civil War he wrote a proclamation to free all US slaves. After the war, he wanted to heal the wounds between north and south. He was shot dead in a theatre in 1865 before he could do so.

Lizards

The largest lizard is the Komodo dragon which grows over 3 m long and weighs over 100 kg.

Livingstone, David

Livingstone (1813-1873) was a Scottish missionary and explorer whose three expeditions to Africa made him a Victorian hero. On his third expedition, to find the source of the Nile, he disappeared. The journalist H. M. Stanley found Livingstone at Lake Tanganyika and uttered the famous greeting, 'Dr Livingstone, I presume'.

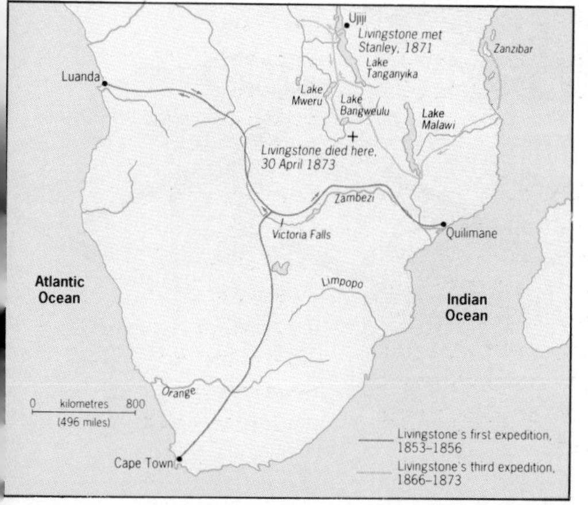

◀ **Map showing the routes of two of Livingstone's three African expeditions.**

▶ **The collar of the frilled lizard can be 25 cm across. It raises it when alarmed to make itself look bigger.**

Loch Ness Monster

Loch Ness is a very deep lake in Scotland. There are some people who think that a large animal lives in the waters of the loch. They call this monster the Loch Ness monster, or Nessie.

There have been photographs taken that are supposed to show a plesiosaur, an animal that existed in prehistoric times. But it is unlikely that such a big animal could find enough food in the cold waters of Loch Ness.

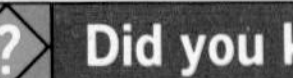

Did you know?

■ A plesiosaur was a large reptile with a long neck, a short tail and four large paddles.

Locks

Locks are used for raising or lowering boats and ships. They are needed where there are different water-levels on a canal. A boat can move from one water-level to another by passing through a pound lock. The boat in the diagram enters the lock when the lower gates are open. When all the gates are shut, water is let into the lock through a small flap called a sluice. When the water-level has risen, the upper gates are opened and the boat leaves the lock. The greatest height a canal boat can be raised in a lock is about 9 m (30 ft).

Locks are often built at dock entrances because it is difficult to load or unload a ship if the tide rises and falls more than about 4 m (12 ft). The ships are loaded in an enclosed dock but a lock is then needed to allow them to move between the dock and the sea.

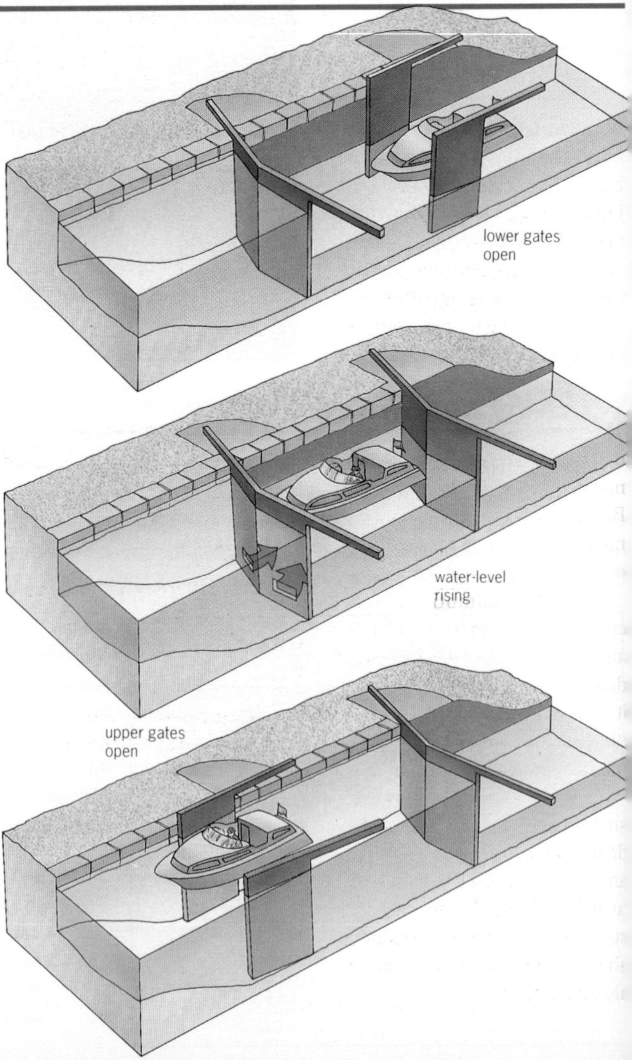

lower gates open

water-level rising

upper gates open

▶ A boat passing through a pound lock. The boat enters when the lower gates are open. When all gates are shut water is let in through a sluice. When the water-level has risen, the upper gates are opened and the boat leaves the lock.

Locomotives

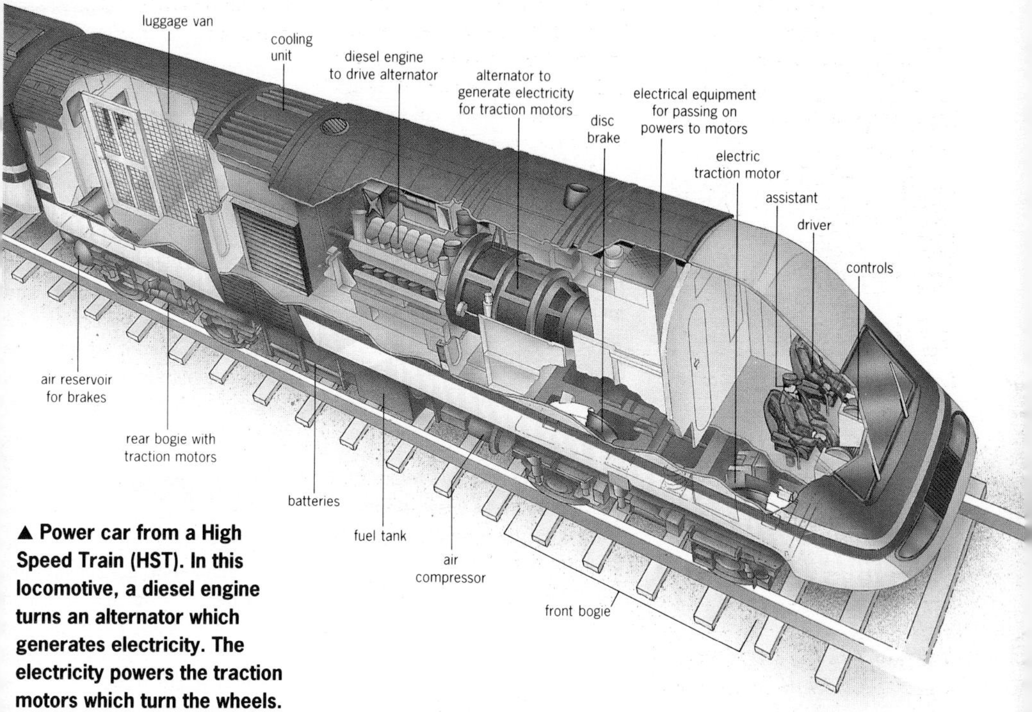

▲ Power car from a High Speed Train (HST). In this locomotive, a diesel engine turns an alternator which generates electricity. The electricity powers the traction motors which turn the wheels.

The earliest locomotives were driven by steam. Steam locomotives were widely used in Britain until the 1960s. Nowadays most railways use diesel or electric locomotives.

Diesel locomotives have engines similar to those in trucks and buses, but the engine does not drive the wheels directly. Instead, it turns a generator which supplies electricity to electric motors mounted between the wheels.

Electric locomotives can be small but powerful because they do not have to carry a large engine and a supply of fuel. Electric motors turn the wheels. The electricity is supplied from wires suspended above the track or from a third rail alongside the track.

Did you know?

- **The first steam locomotive was built in 1804 and ran in a Welsh ironworks.**
- **Railways were not used for carrying passengers until 1825.**
- **The world's largest working steam engine is Union Pacific's 'Challenger' number 3985.**
- **'Locomotive' means railway engine, but years ago it also meant road engine.**

Luxembourg

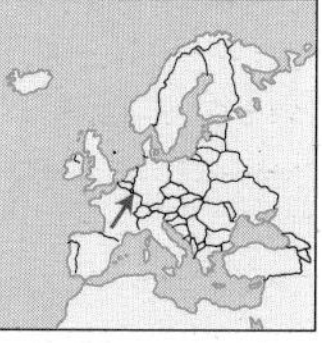

Luxembourg is a tiny country, ruled by a Grand Duke (or Duchess), to the north east of France. The north is wooded and hilly. In the south there is good land for farming. Wine, iron and steel are the main exports.

FACT FILE

Capital
Luxembourg
Population
387,000
Currency
1 Luxembourg franc = 100 centimes

Machines

Machines are devices that make work easier. They may be simple, like a pair of scissors, or more complicated, like a gearbox. Most mechanical things, however big or complicated, have parts based on five simple machines: the lever, the wheel and axle, the ramp, the screw and the pulley.

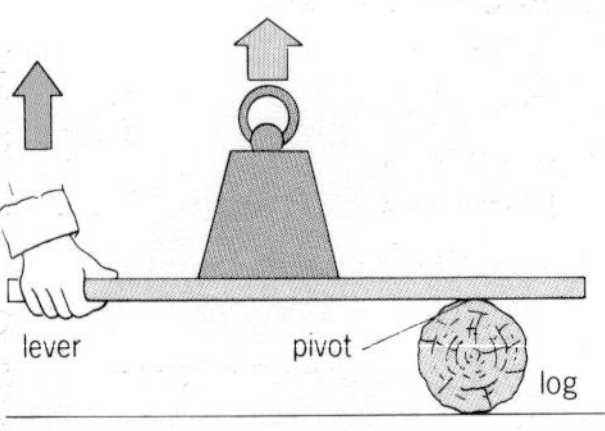

◀ **Levers can help us lift heavy things. With a long lever resting on a pivot, you can lift a heavy weight.**

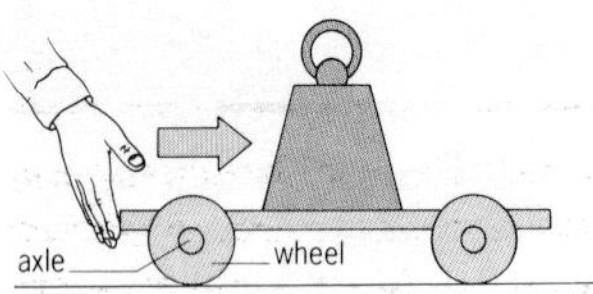

◀ **The wheel and axle make it possible to move loads along. The bigger the wheels the easier they are to turn. Long spokes act like levers.**

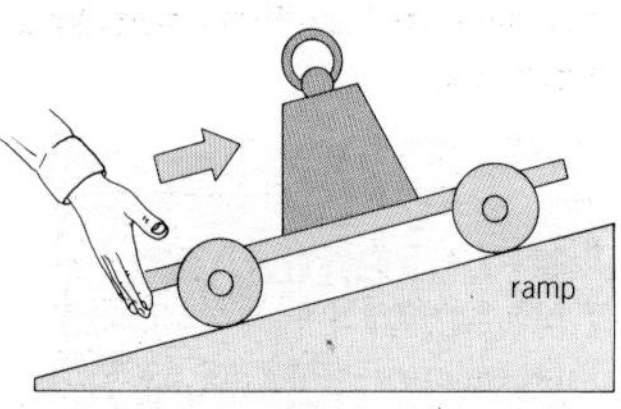

◀ **Ramps, or slopes, make it easy to go up a short distance by moving forward quite a long way.**

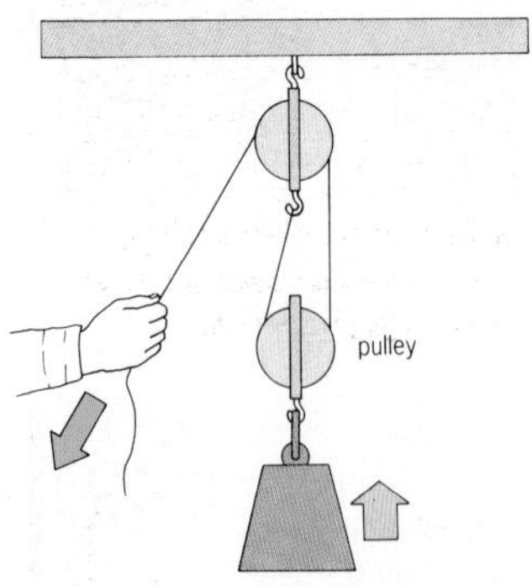

◀ **Pulleys raise heavy things by making it possible to pull downwards, which is much easier than pulling upwards.**

Magellan, Ferdinand

Ferdinand Magellan, born in 1480, wanted to find a sea route round South America to the east.

In 1519 he set out with five ships and 268 men. He had to face mutiny and terrible weather before he reached the Pacific Ocean. He was killed in 1521 on the return journey. Magellan's was the first expedition to sail round the world, and although he did not live to see the voyage completed it provided the first proof that the Earth is round. Only one ship returned to Spain, with a crew of just seventeen men.

Magnets

Magnets are found inside refrigerator doors and telephones, and in the electrical motors in food mixers and drills. Every magnet has a north pole and a south pole. Two north poles or two south poles push each other apart, but a north pole and a south pole attract each other.

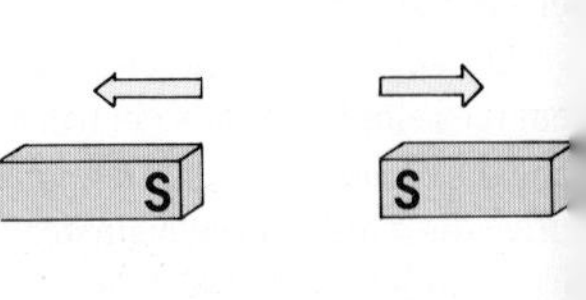

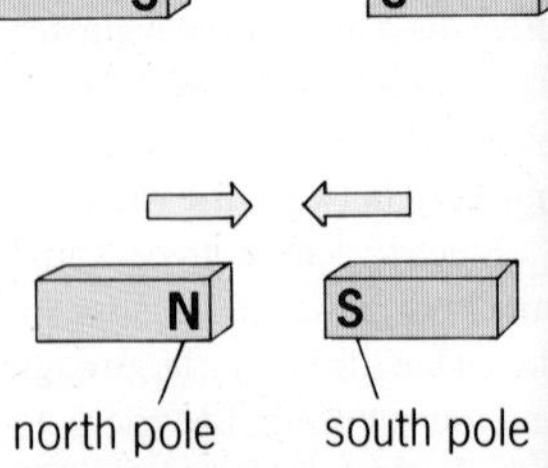

▲ **When the ends of two magnets are brought close, poles of the same kind repel, but poles of different kinds attract.**

Malaysia

Almost 800 km of sea divides Malaysia into two parts: the Malay Peninsula and the northern part of Borneo. It is very warm with heavy rain falls all year.

Malaysian people include Muslim Malays, Chinese, Indians and Borneo tribes.

FACT FILE

Capital
Kuala Lumpar
Population
18,630,000
Currency
1 ringgit (Malaysian dollar) = 100 sen

Mammals

All mammals have: bones including a backbone; lungs to breathe dry air, and some fur or hair. They all feed their babies on milk and they are warm-blooded.

There are about 4,000 species of mammal, divided into three groups depending on how the young develop. A very small number of animals hatch from eggs. These are the **monotremes**, found only in Australia and New Guinea. Some mammals are born very tiny and continue to grow in their mother's pouch. These are the **marsupials,** found mainly in Australia and New Guinea. Most mammals are **placentals** which means they remain in their mother's body for a long time .

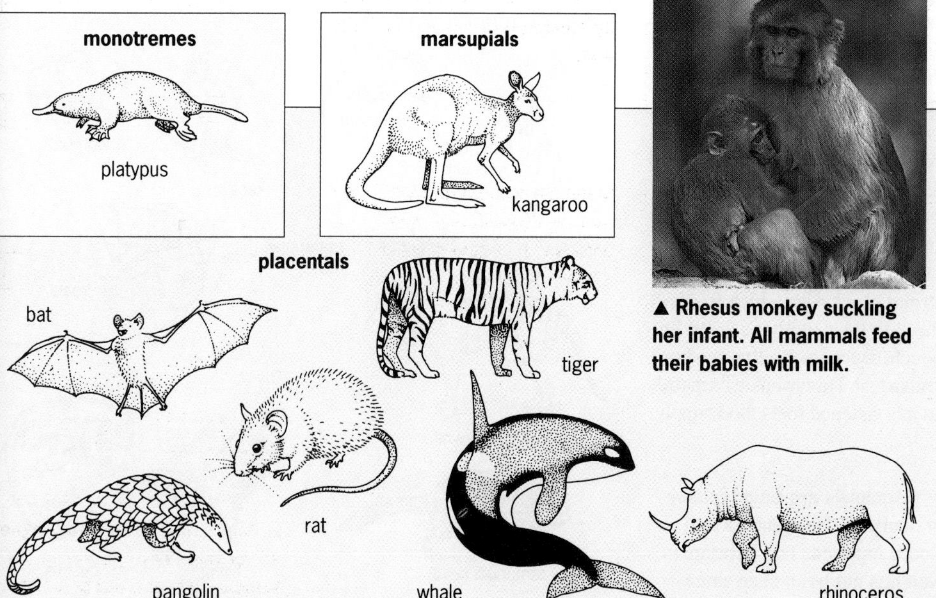

▲ **Rhesus monkey suckling her infant. All mammals feed their babies with milk.**

 Mao Zedong

Mao Zedong, was born in 1893. He was one of the first people to join the Chinese Communist Party in 1921. When the communists were being attacked in 1934, Mao led them on the 'Long March' of nearly 10,000 km over the mountains.

In World War II Mao's 'people's liberation army' fought the invading Japanese. The communists gained more support and took Beijing in 1949, setting up a People's Republic. Mao ruled China until he died in 1976.

 Maori

Maori are the people who first settled in New Zealand. They call it Aotearoa, 'land of the long cloud'. The Maori first arrived about 1,000 years ago after sailing from the Polynesian islands.

When Captain Cook reached New Zealand in 1769, many settlers followed. They took land from the Maori in the Land Wars of the 1860s. Many Maori also died of European diseases.

▶ Traditional Maori dancers.

Marsupials

Marsupials are sometimes called 'pouched mammals', as many of the females have a furry pouch on their underside. Baby marsupials grow inside their mother's body for only about six weeks, often less. When they are born they have hardly begun to develop. The largest is only 2 cm long and some are the size of a grain of rice. But they all have big forelimbs with strong claws with which to crawl through their mother's fur to her pouch. Once inside the newborn finds a teat. This swells in its mouth so it is fastened to its food supply.

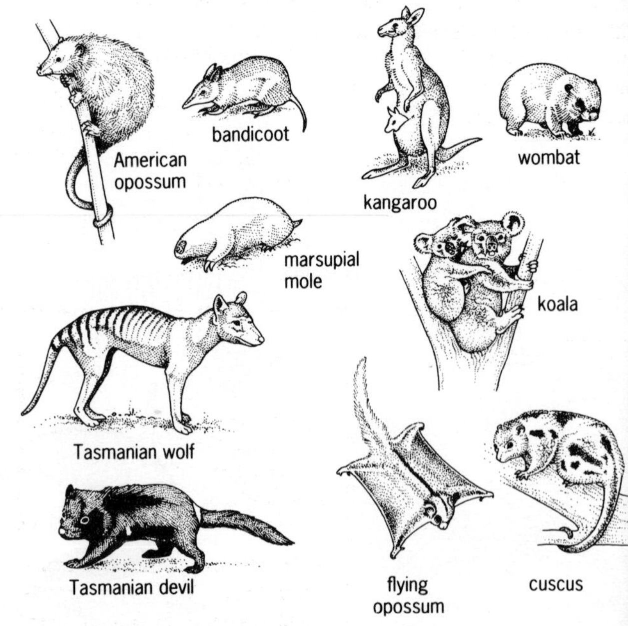

▶ Marsupials are found mainly in Australia, New Guinea and South America. The Tasmanian wolf has not been seen since 1936, so is probably extinct.

Marx, Karl

Karl Marx was born in 1818. He became a journalist and moved away from Germany. On his travels he met Friedrich Engels. Together they wrote *The Communist Manifesto* in 1848. In it they said that working people should rise up and take over the governments of the world.

Marx's ideas became very important to communists all over the world. He was still writing his main book, *Das Kapital* (Capital) when he died in 1883.

▶ **Portrait of Karl Marx.**

Metals

Almost three-quarters of the elements found in the Earth are metals. Some of these, such as platinum, gold, and some silver, are found in the ground in a pure state. Others are found in ores (mixtures of metals and other elements).

All pure metals, except one, are solid when they are kept at room temperature. Mercury is a liquid metal. With the exception of mercury, metals are strong and can be bent without breaking. They can be hammered or rolled into different shapes when hot, and stretched out to make wires. Metals are good conductors of heat and electricity.

Copper

Good conductor of heat and electricity. Used for wires and pipes for plumbing.

Iron

Very strong when made into steel. Rusts when exposed to air and moisture.

Lead

Heavy and poisonous. Used for waterproofing roofs.

Magnesium

Burns with a brilliant white flame and is used in fireworks. Makes strong light alloys for building aircraft and cars.

Mercury

Heavy and poisonous. Used in switches, pesticides and thermometers.

Platinum

Easily shaped and does not corrode. Used in jewellery and to reduce pollution from car exhausts.

Tungsten

Strong and hard. Used for light bulb filaments and to make steel for saws and drills.

Uranium

Rare radioactive metal used to provide energy in nuclear reactors.

Mexico

FACT FILE

Capital
Mexico City
Population
84,439,000
Currency
1 peso = 100 centavos

The Mexican landscape changes from tropical jungles to mountains, and volcanoes to deserts. There are frequent earthquakes. Over 14 million people live in its capital Mexico City.

Oil has been discovered off Mexico's east coast, but it has not made Mexico wealthy. There is widespread poverty and millions of Mexicans travel to work in the USA, both legally and illegally, for higher wages.

Middle Ages

▲ **A 13th-century picture of armoured knights fighting during a siege.**

The Middle Ages were the centuries from the end of the Roman empire to the Renaissance. The early part of this period is also known as the Dark Ages.

There were three classes or 'estates' of people in the Middle Ages. The first estate included churchmen, from mighty bishops down to poor monks and priests. Knights were in the second estate. They served kings and lords by fighting for them. Ordinary people were in the third estate. They had to work hard to support the churchmen and knights. In the 14th century there were revolts of the common people in England, France, Belgium and Italy.

English kings

Henry II
1154 – 1189

Richard I
1189 – 1199

John
1199 – 1216

Henry III
1216 – 1272

Edward I
1272 – 1307

Edward II
1307 – 1327

Edward III
1327 – 1377

Richard II
1377 – 1399

Henry IV
1399 – 1413

Henry V
1413 – 1422

Henry VI
1422 – 1461

Edward IV
1461 – 1483

Richard III
1483 – 1485

▲ **A peasant reaping corn.**

Middle East

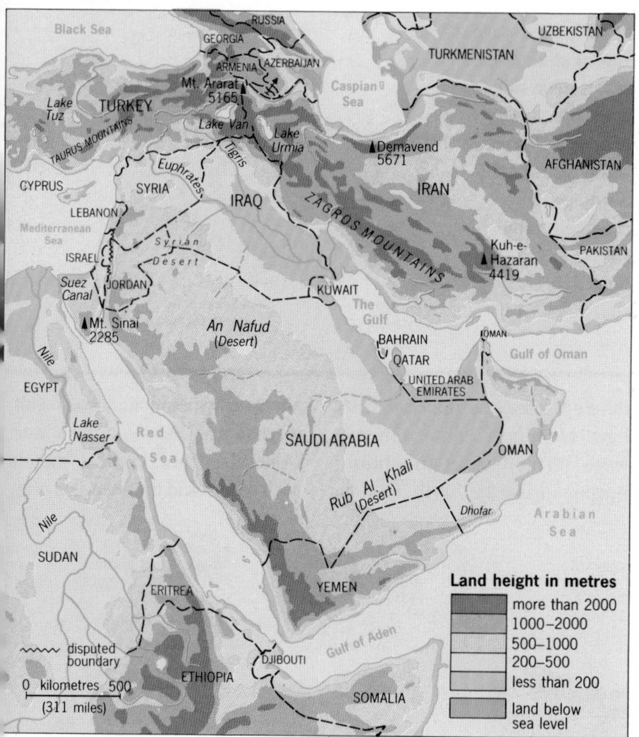

Europe, Asia and Africa meet in the Middle East, so called because it is halfway to the 'Far East'. Asians call the same area West Asia.

There are deserts and mountains in the Middle East and three of the world's great rivers, the Nile, Tigris and Euphrates, flow through it. The weather is hot and dry and temperatures can reach 50° C.

Most of the people are Arabs and Arabic is the main language. Some Middle Eastern countries have become very rich from oil. Farmers grow cotton, tobacco and fruits such as dates, grapes, oranges and olives.

Judaism, Christianity and Islam all started in the Middle East. Mecca in Saudi Arabia is the centre of the universe for Muslims.

◀ **Map showing the physical features of the Middle East and the borders of the countries.**

Milky Way

On a really dark, clear night, you may be able to see the Milky Way as a hazy band of light stretching across the sky. What you are seeing is millions of stars in our own Galaxy. The Sun belongs to this galaxy of 100,000 million stars. Dark clouds of gas and dust block off some of their light.

Our Galaxy is shaped like a flat disc with a bulge in the middle. In Britain we are looking out towards the rim of the Galaxy. In Australia more stars are visible because they are looking towards the centre of the Galaxy.

▶ **The brightest part of the Milky Way is in the constellation Sagittarius.**

Millipedes

Did you know?

■ The name 'millipede' means 'thousand feet'; millipedes actually have no more than 400 feet.

■ The largest millipede is about 30 cm long whilst the smallest is only 2 mm.

▶ Millipedes have a row of stink glands along their sides from which they produce chemicals when disturbed. Some protect themselves by rolling into a tight ball.

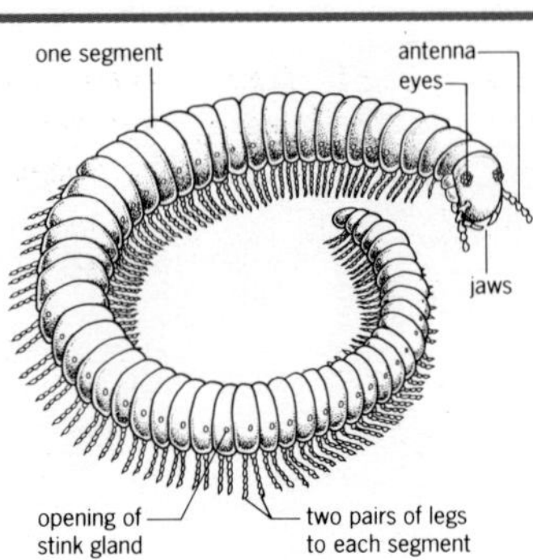

Minerals

Minerals are useful materials which can be mined from the ground. Gold, diamonds, talc and china clay are some of the 2,500 different minerals that scientists have identified. Some minerals were formed from the liquid magma inside the Earth. Others, such as gypsum and rock salt, were once dissolved in water. Minerals which contain metals such as lead and tin, are called ores.

Molecules

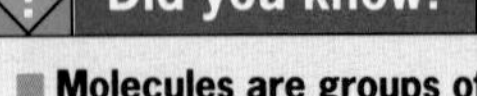

Did you know?

■ Molecules are groups of atoms.

■ A hydrogen molecule has only two hydrogen atoms and is the smallest molecule.

■ Molecules in the air have an average speed of about 1,800 km/h (1,100 mph).

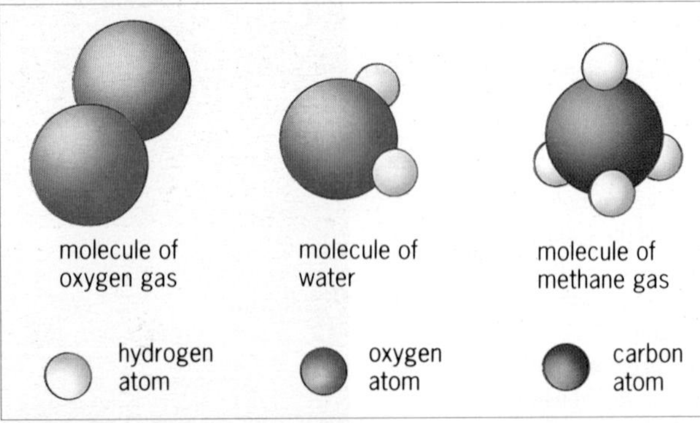

▲ Models showing how atoms group together to form molecules.

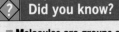

Molluscs

Many molluscs have shells. Their bodies are soft and usually include a head, a muscular foot, breathing, digestive, and sex organs. These are covered by a flap of skin, called the mantle, which makes the shell.

▼ **Different types of mollusc.**

Gastropoda
snail

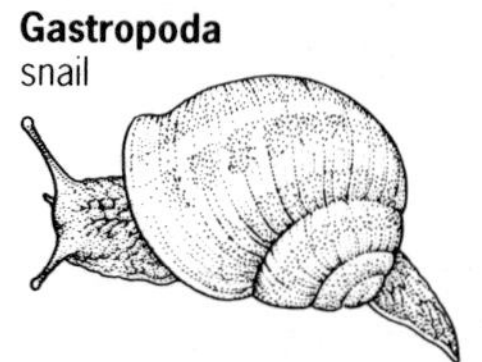

Polyplacophora
chiton

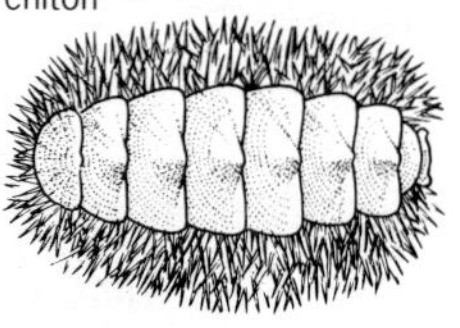

Bivalvia
scallop

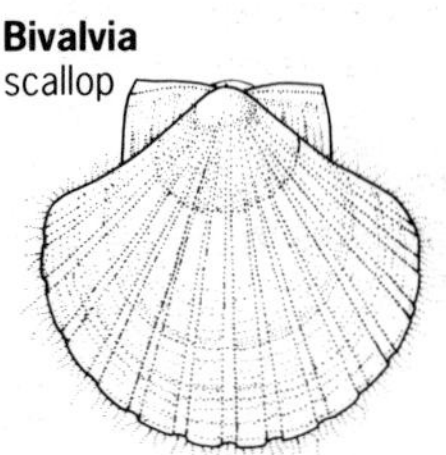

Monoplacophora
Neopilina

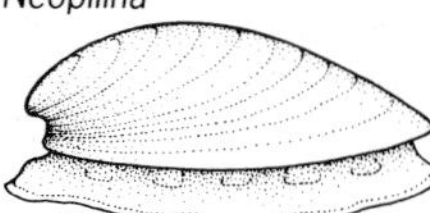

Cephalopoda
octopus

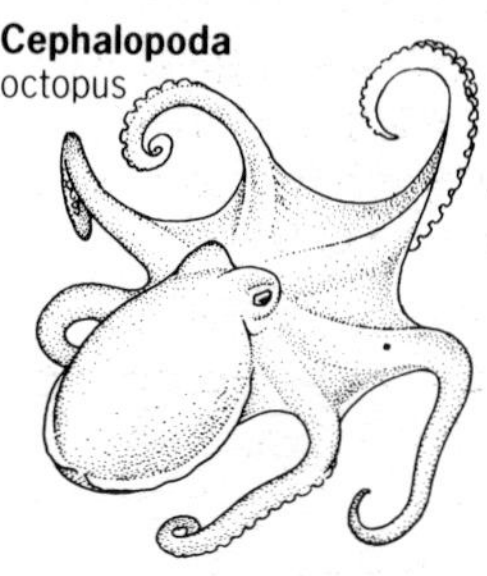

Scaphopoda
tusk shell

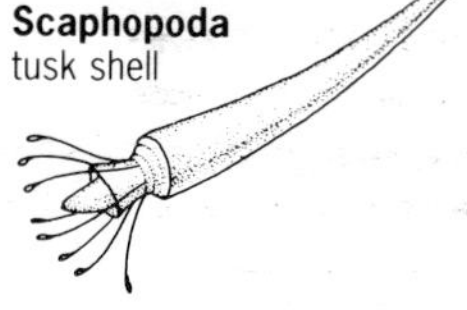

Monkeys

There are two main groups of monkeys. Those from South America live in the treetops, and many have a gripping tail which acts as an extra hand. The others are found in Africa and the warm parts of Asia. None of these has a gripping tail, and some live mainly on the ground.

▶ **South American monkeys have flat noses with nostrils set wide apart and opening to the side. African and Asian monkeys have nostrils closer together and front opening.**

New World monkey
weeper capuchin from South America

Old World monkey
king colobus from Africa

Moon

The Moon is a satellite of the Earth. It is a totally lifeless place with no air and no water, which means that there is no wind or weather on the Moon. The Moon takes about a month to orbit once round the Earth. In that time, its shape seems to change from a thin crescent through to a full Moon and back again. The different shapes are called the Moon's phases.

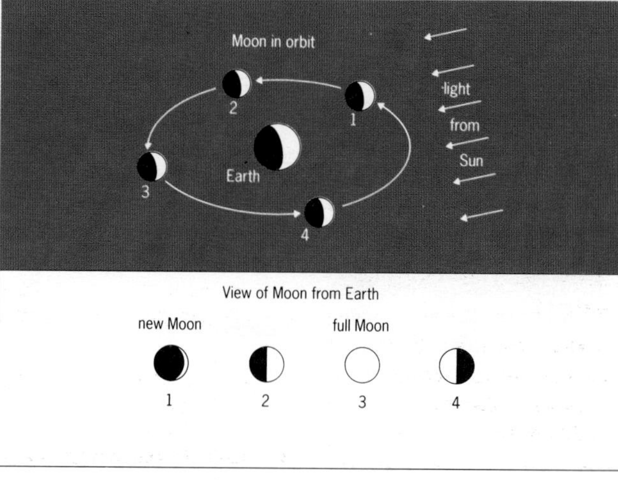

▶ **The phases of the Moon.**

Motor cars

There are more than 400 million cars in the world today. The first petrol-driven cars were made in Germany in the 1880s. But early motoring was expensive, until Henry Ford in America began to mass produce a cheap reliable car, the Model T, in 1907.

A car has over 20,000 parts, grouped into four main sections: the body, the engine, the transmission system and the controls.

The world's largest car is a limousine which is over 30 m long. It has 26 wheels and a swimming pool. It is used mainly for films and exhibitions.

▼ **1958 Cadillac Biarritz**

Suspension

This joins each wheel to the car and helps the car to go over bumps smoothly. Shock absorbers in the suspension stop the car bouncing up and down.

Steering

The steering-wheel is connected to the wheels by a steering-box and two rods which move from side to side.

Electrics

A battery provides electricity for the starter motor and spark-plugs when starting the engine. It also powers the lights and the radio. Once started, the engine drives an alternator which powers the lights and plugs and recharges the battery.

Driveshafts

These are metal rods which transmit the turning force from the engine and the gearbox to the wheels. This car has front-wheel drive. Some cars have rear-wheel drive and others have four-wheel drive.

Gearbox and clutch

Most cars have four or five forward gears and one reverse gear. When you press a foot pedal, the clutch disconnects the engine from the gearbox while you change gear.

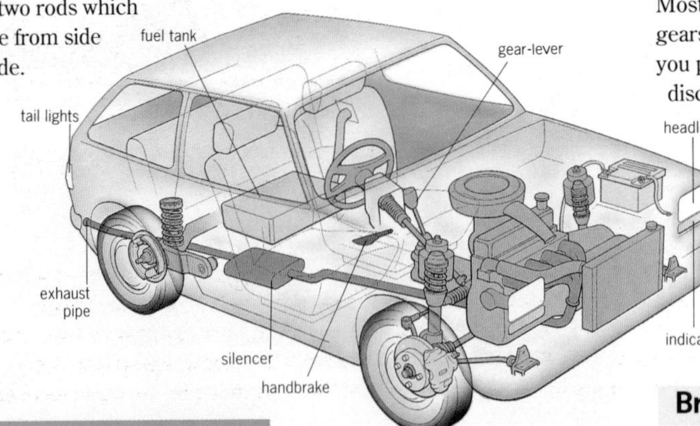

Cooling system

The cooling system pumps water around the engine to stop it overheating. The hot water is then pumped through the radiator where it is cooled by a rush of air or by a fan.

Engine

Most cars have an internal combustion engine which burns either petrol or diesel fuel. Some cars have the engine at the rear.

Brakes

These are attached to the wheels and suspension. The foot-brake pedal works on all four wheels. The hand brake works on two wheels and is used for parking. Most cars have disc brakes at the front and drum brakes at the back.

Mountains

Mountains are higher and steeper than hills. The soil is often thin because it has been washed down the slopes. High in the mountains trees cannot grow. Animals living there, such as mountain hares, have extra thick coats in winter. The weather can change quickly. As clouds rise over the mountains, they drop rain.

Did you know?

- **As you climb a mountain the temperature falls 1°C for every 150 m.**
- **Although Everest is the highest mountain at 8,863 m, Mauna Kea in Hawaii has 4,205 m above sea level and 6,000 m below the sea.**

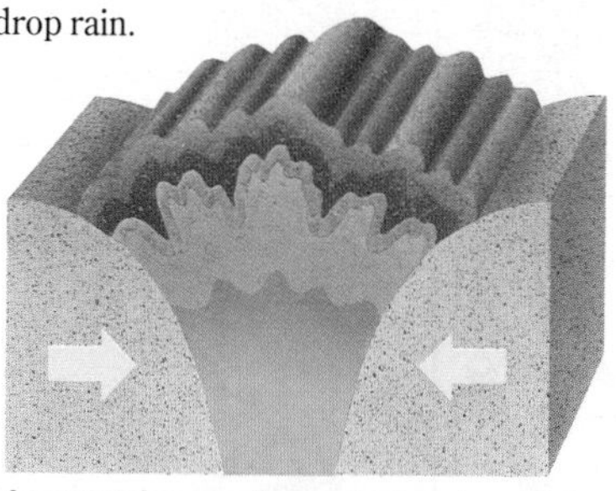

▲ Fold mountains are formed when two plates of the Earth's crust move together squeezing sediments upwards from the ocean floor. The Alps, Himalayas, Andes and Rocky Mountains are fold mountains.

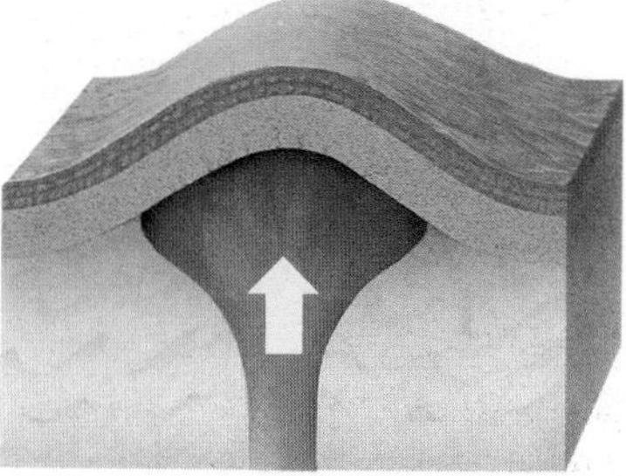

▲ Dome mountains are formed if the rocks above the molten lava do not give way but bulge upwards instead. The Black Hills of South Dakota (USA) are the eroded remains of a dome mountain.

▲ Block mountains: huge blocks of rocks can split and move up lines of weakness called faults. Great masses of rock may be lifted above neighbouring rocks to form mountains. The Sierra Nevada mountains (USA) and Mount Ruwenzori (E. Africa) are block mountains.

▲ Volcanic mountains are formed when molten rock from deep inside the Earth rises to the surface. It pours out of the ground as lava which forms hard rock as it cools. Mount Fuji (Japan) and Mount Vesuvius (Italy) are volcanic mountains.

Mozart, Wolfgang Amadeus

Wolfgang Amadeus Mozart was born in 1756. As a child he was a brilliant musician. By the age of 14, he had toured Austria, Germany, France, England and Italy.

By the time he died in 1791 Mozart had written over 600 pieces including 27 piano concertos and 41 symphonies. He also wrote famous operas, such as *The Magic Flute*.

Musical Instruments

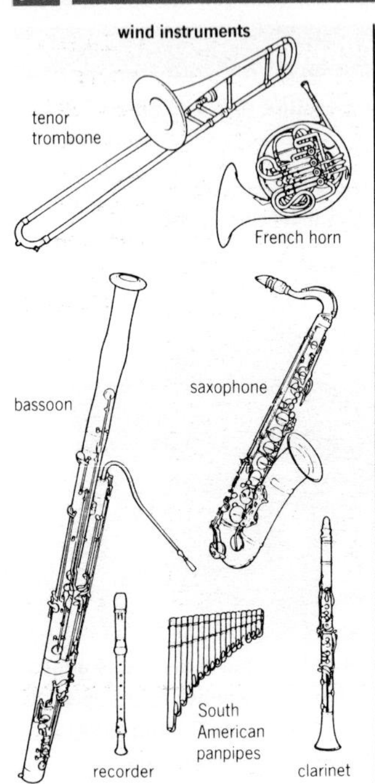

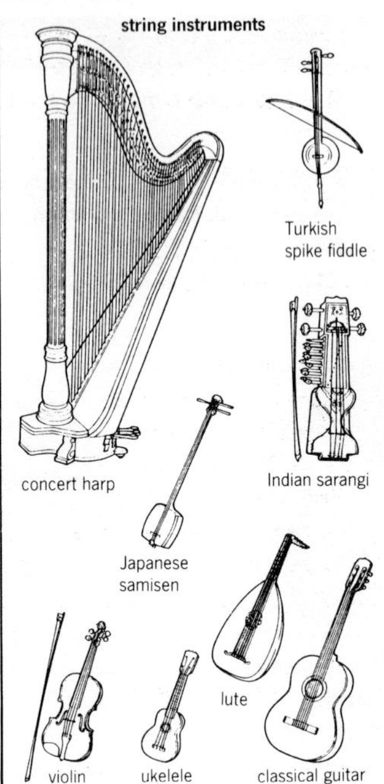

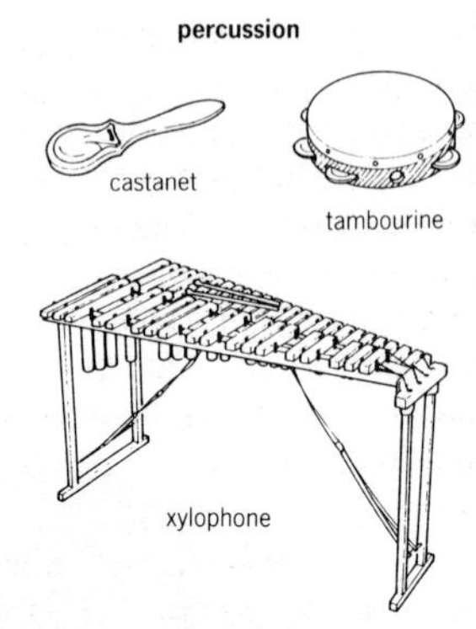

▲ **Musical instruments can be grouped into four main sorts, depending on how they produce sound: wind instruments, string instruments, keyboard instruments and percussion.**

Napoleon

Napoleon Bonaparte joined the French army at 15, and within eleven years had become a leading general. In 1799 he overthrew the government and became the leader of France.

By 1807 he had built the largest empire since Roman times, with himself as emperor. His worst mistake was to invade Russia in 1812. He was forced to retreat in winter and thousands of his men froze or starved to death.

Many French people were becoming weary of Napoleon's rule, and so when his army was defeated again, at the battle of Leipzig in 1814, Napoleon was exiled to the island of Elba in the Mediterranean. In 1815 he escaped and took power again.

Napoleon's final defeat came in 1815 at the battle of Waterloo. He was exiled to St Helena in the south Atlantic, where he died in 1821.

◀ ***Napoleon crossing the Alps* (1800), by Jacques Louis David.**

NATO

NATO is short for North Atlantic Treaty Organization. This began in 1949. A group of countries promised to help each other if they were attacked. Belgium, Canada, Denmark, France, Iceland, Italy, Luxembourg, the Netherlands, Norway, Portugal, the UK and the USA joined and NATO headquarters were set up in Brussels. France left NATO in 1966, but has remained in the Atlantic Alliance with the other NATO countries. Later Greece, Turkey, Germany and Spain joined too.

Nelson, Lord Horatio

At the age of 12 Horatio Nelson went on a long sea voyage to the Falklands with his uncle. Three years later he joined the navy, and at 21 was given his own ship to command.

When Britain declared war on France in 1793, Nelson soon became an admiral and won important battles against the enemy fleet.

His most famous victory was at the battle of Trafalgar in 1805. Nelson led 27 ships against 33 French and Spanish ships. he signalled to his own fleet: 'England expects that every man will do his duty.'

But during the battle Nelson was shot by a French sniper. He died on the deck of his ship *Victory*.

Did you know?

- **Nelson lost his right eye in 1794 and his right arm in 1797.**
- **Nelson's commander ordered him to withdraw at the battle of Copenhagen in 1801. Nelson put his telescope to his right eye and said, 'I really do not see the signal!'**

◀ Nelson's column standing in London's Trafalgar Square is a memorial known worldwide.

Nervous system

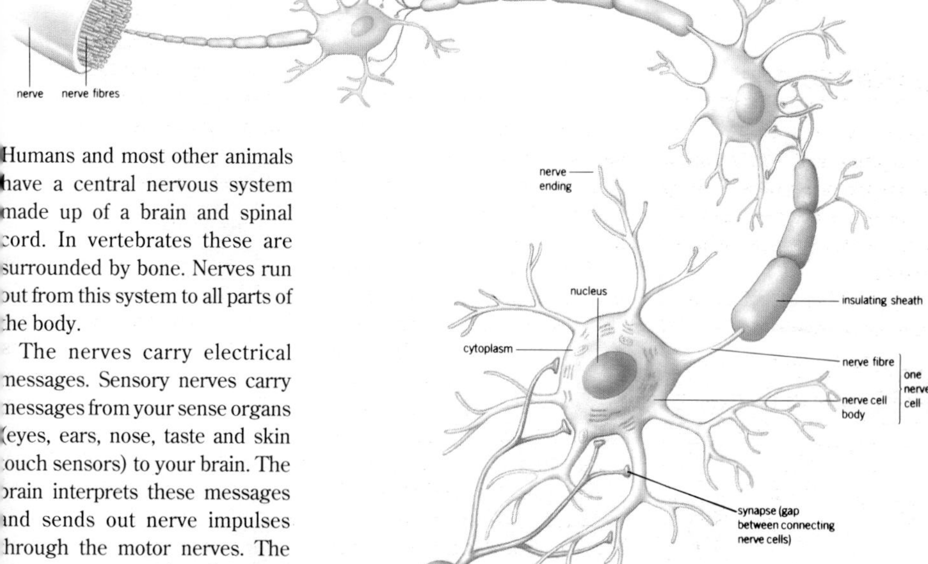

Humans and most other animals have a central nervous system made up of a brain and spinal cord. In vertebrates these are surrounded by bone. Nerves run out from this system to all parts of the body.

The nerves carry electrical messages. Sensory nerves carry messages from your sense organs (eyes, ears, nose, taste and skin touch sensors) to your brain. The brain interprets these messages and sends out nerve impulses through the motor nerves. The motor nerves carry impulses from the brain to the part of the body where action is needed, such as a muscle or a gland.

▲ A nerve is made up of a bundle of nerve fibres. The nerve fibres carry messages in the form of electrical impulses and so are insulated by a fatty sheath. Nerve cells connect end to end across gaps called synapses.

Netball

Netball is a seven-a-side game played on a court. The aim is to score goals by shooting the ball into the other team's goal net. This is a metal hoop on a pole.

Running with the ball is not allowed. The ball must be passed until it reaches the 'goal shooter' or 'goal attack'. They are the only players allowed to shoot.

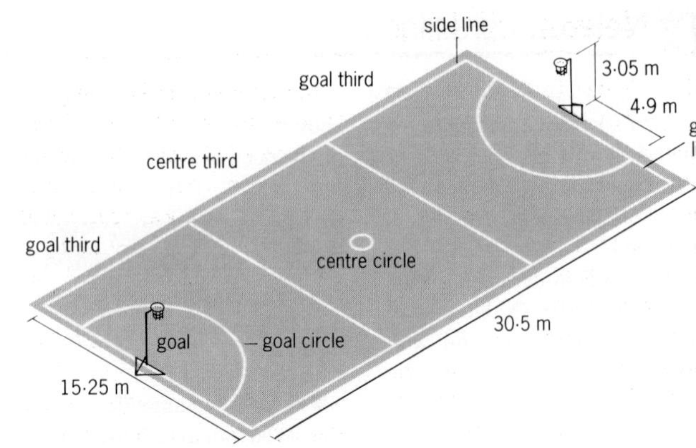

Netherlands

The name Netherlands means 'low lands'. The people and the language are Dutch. Much of the Netherlands was once covered by water, but much has been drained for farming.

The Netherlands is one of the most crowded countries in the world. Rotterdam, the largest city, is the world's biggest port.

Capital
Amsterdam
Population
15,163,000
Currency
1 guilder = 100 cents

FACT FILE

New Zealand

New Zealand is south east of Australia, and made up of two islands. There are active volcanoes in North Island. South Island has very high mountains and glaciers.

Capital
Wellington
Population
3,481,000
Currency
1 NZ dollar = 100 cents

FACT FILE

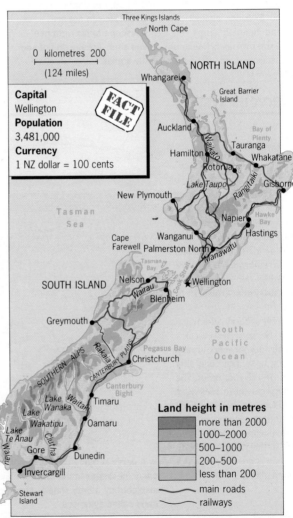

▶ **Map of New Zealand.**

Newton, Sir Isaac

The scientist Sir Isaac Newton (1642-1727) is best known for his ideas on gravity. Many people know the story of when he was sitting in an orchard and saw an apple fall off a tree. He realized that the force of gravity had pulled the apple down to the ground. At this time, when he was only 23, he was already trying to work out how the Earth, the Moon and the planets moved. He realized that it is gravity which keeps the Moon in orbit around the Earth.

Newton tried to make a telescope to study the stars but found that the lenses in it made the images have coloured edges. In trying to find out why this was he invented the first mirror telescope. Many of our present-day telescopes are based on Newton's design.

Newton's greatest book, *The Principia*, was written in Latin. It has had an enormous effect on the way scientists have thought ever since.

Did you know?

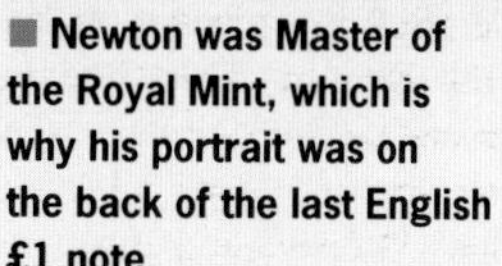

- **Newton was Master of the Royal Mint, which is why his portrait was on the back of the last English £1 note.**
- **Newton had to abandon his studies at Cambridge University and return home for two years because of the great plague of 1661.**
- **Without gravity the Moon would fly off into space.**

Nigeria

Nigeria has a bigger population than any other African country. The people can be divided into about 400 groups. The four main ones are the Hausa and the Fulani in the north, and the Yoruba and Ibo in the south. These four groups make up two thirds of Nigeria's population.

Much of Nigeria is hot and wet. The river Niger is the third longest river in Africa. Most Nigerians live in farming villages where they grow beans, maize, rice and yams.

Oil is Nigeria's main export and the money from this has been used to set up new industries.

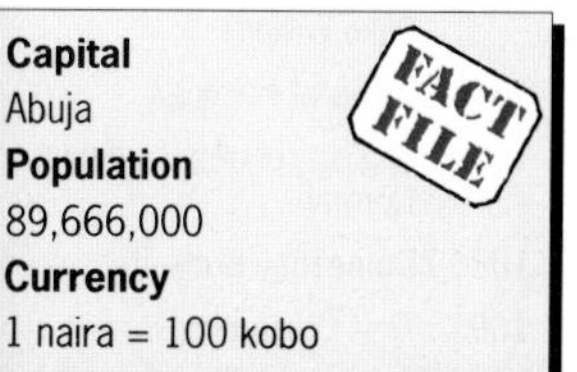

Capital
Abuja
Population
89,666,000
Currency
1 naira = 100 kobo

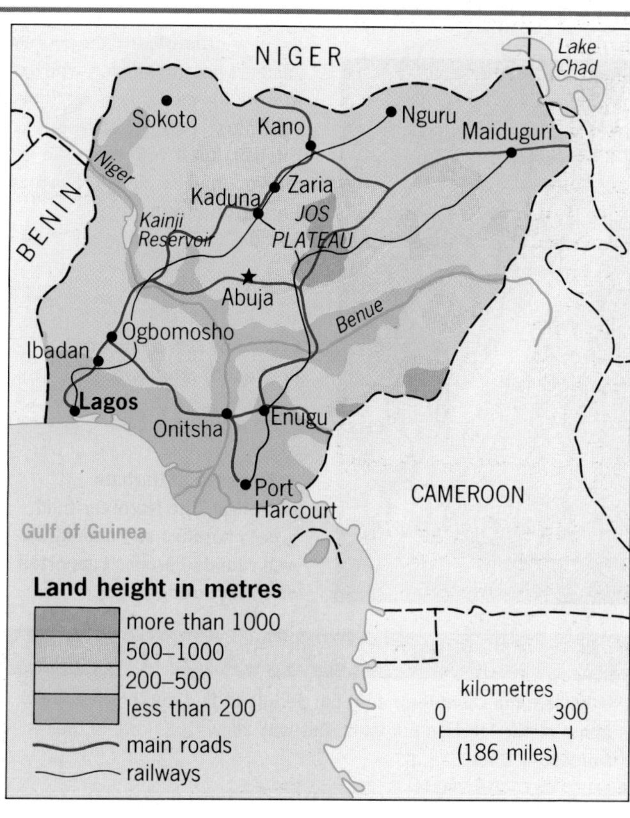

Normans

Normans were Vikings who moved to northern France. In 911 their leader, Rolf, was given some land round Rouen. This became Normandy. The Normans soon became rich.

They were good fighters, especially on horses, and travelled in search of conquests. Normans ruled Sicily until 1194. In 1066 the Norman Duke William defeated King Harold of Wessex to become the king of England. Later, Normans joined the crusades and helped to capture Jerusalem.

After the Norman Conquest there were great changes for English people. Anglo-Saxon lords were replaced by Norman barons.

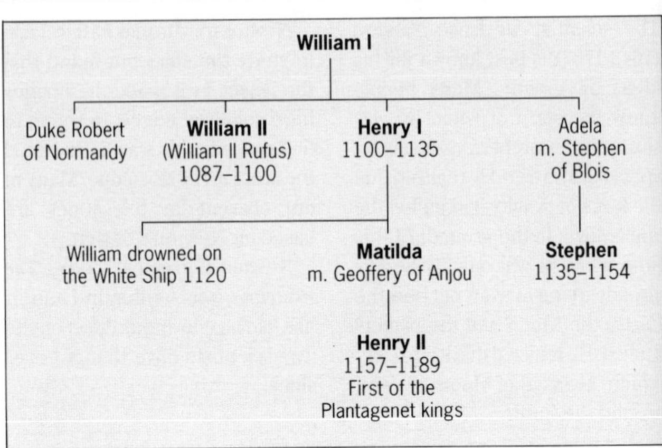

▲ **Family tree of the Norman kings of England, with the dates of their reigns.**

Many free men lost their land to the new lords. Most of the poorest villagers became villeins, who had to work for the lords at set times. Ordinary people still spoke English, but if you wanted to get on you had to speak Norman French and Latin.

▶ **Window with a chevron (V-shaped) ornament.**

◀ **The nave of Durham cathedral. The Normans built great churches and cathedrals with rounded arches supported on thick, strong pillars.**

1030	Normans began to take over Sicily and Southern Italy
1051	Edward the Confessor promised English throne to Duke William
1066	Battle of Hastings
1070	English rebellions against Normans
1086-7	Domesday Book
1095	First Crusades
1106	Henry I ruled Normandy
1120	White Ship sank
1140	Civil War: Stephen v Matilda
1154	Henry II King of England

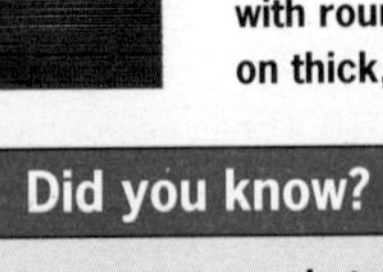

Did you know?

- **William the Conqueror sent out people to find out information about all the lands in England. This was all written down in the Domesday Book.**
- **After the Norman conquest, rich and educated people in England spoke Norman French and Latin.**

North America

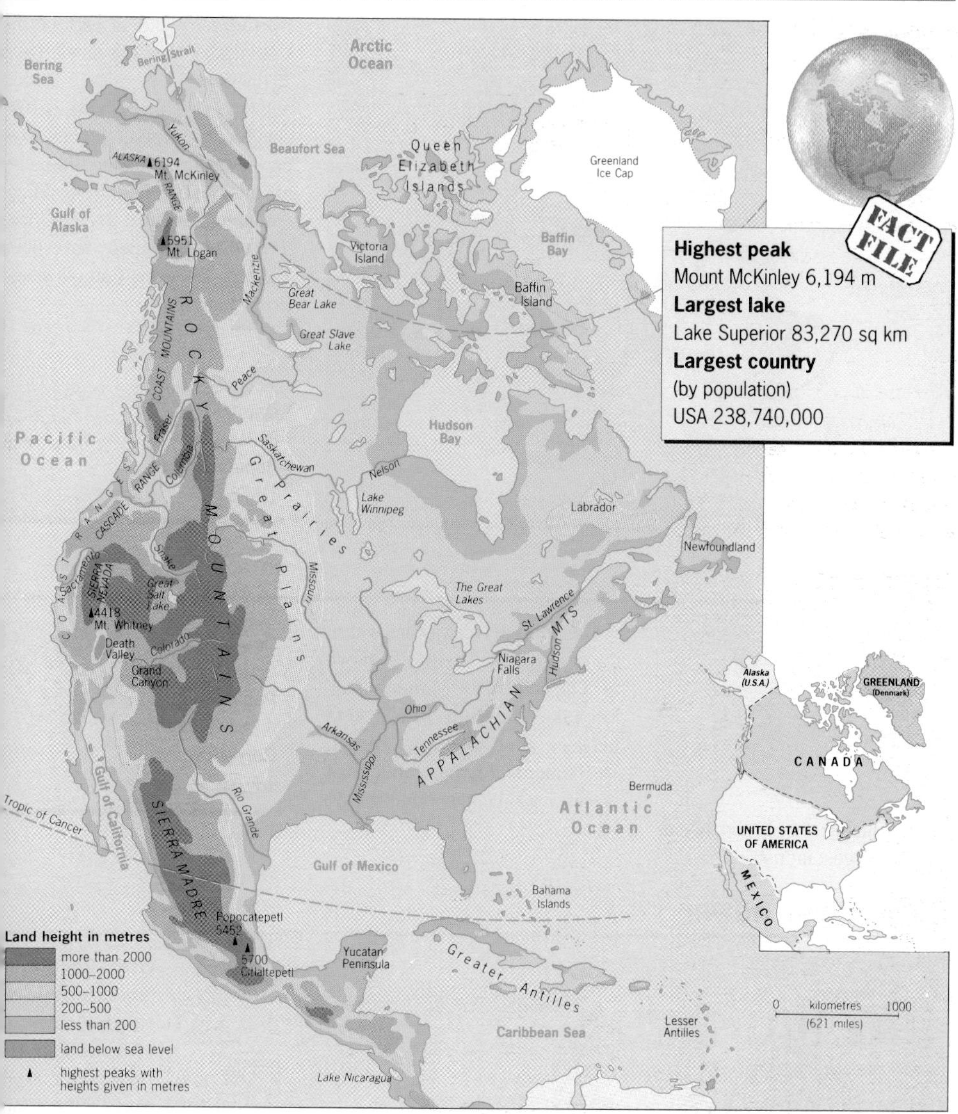

FACT FILE

Highest peak
Mount McKinley 6,194 m

Largest lake
Lake Superior 83,270 sq km

Largest country
(by population)
USA 238,740,000

North America is made up of three countries: Canada, the USA and Mexico. There are many valuable resources there, including timber, gold, oil, and gas. These help to make North America wealthy.

The Rocky Mountains run like a backbone from Alaska to Mexico. The Appalachian Mountains are in the east. Between these two are huge plains, across which the Missouri and Mississippi rivers run.

Almost all parts have hot summers. In winter some places are bitterly cold. Deserts in Mexico and the west of the USA get very little rain. Death Valley in California is the hottest and lowest place in North America.

The people are a complete mixture, including Native Americans ('Indians'), African Americans, Europeans, and Asians. English, Spanish and French are the main languages spoken.

Northern Ireland

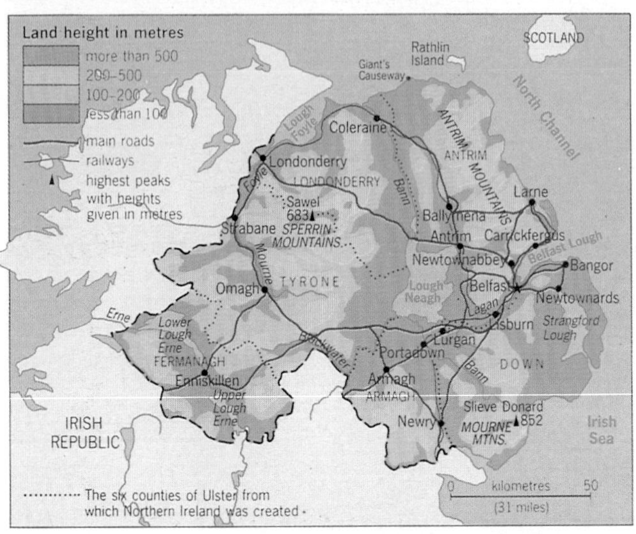

Northern Ireland is part of the United Kingdom. It is divided into 26 districts.

Farmers there keep cattle, sheep, pigs and poultry. They grow barley, oats and potatoes. Industry includes textiles and shipbuilding.

Since Northern Ireland was formed in 1921 there have been troubles between Catholics and Protestants.

Capital
Belfast
Population
1,578,000

Norway

Norway is a Scandinavian country in Northern Europe. It has many mountains, glaciers and fjords. Oil and fishing are the biggest industries.

One third of Norway lies within the Arctic Circle. This part is known as 'The Land of the Midnight Sun' because the Sun never sets between June and July. During December and January though, it is dark for almost 24 hours a day.

Capital
Oslo
Population
4,283,000
Currency
1 krone = 100 øre

Nuclear power

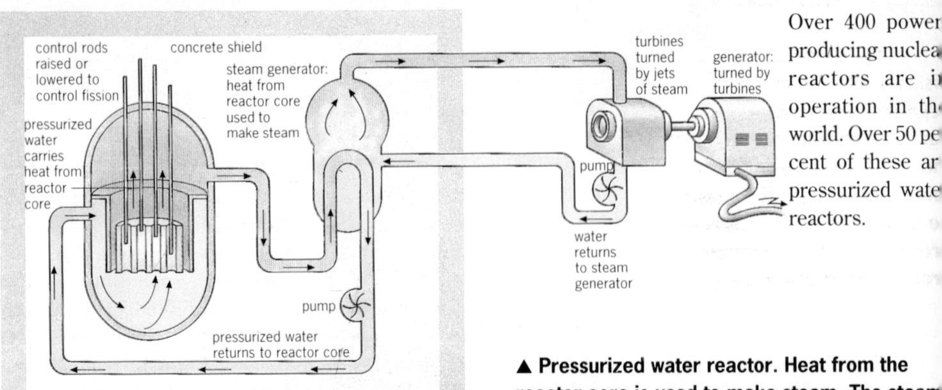

Over 400 power producing nuclea reactors are i operation in th world. Over 50 pe cent of these ar pressurized wate reactors.

▲ Pressurized water reactor. Heat from the reactor core is used to make steam. The stear turns the turbines which drive the generator.

Oceans and seas

Oceans cover over 70 per cent of the Earth's surface and can be as deep as 11,000 m (36,000 ft) in places. On the ocean floor there are plains, mountains and trenches. The mountains sometimes push up through the water's surface as islands. Many are active or extinct volcanoes.

The ocean's waves are caused by wind blowing over the water's surface. When a wave reaches shallow water, the water at the bottom slows down and is overtaken by the crest, which crashes to form a breaker.

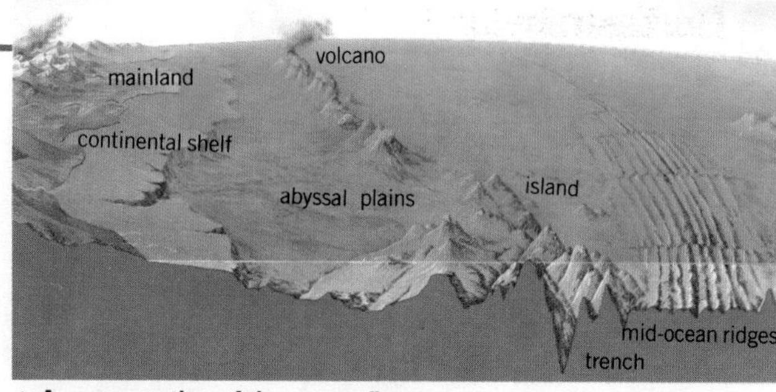

▲ A cross-section of the ocean floor.

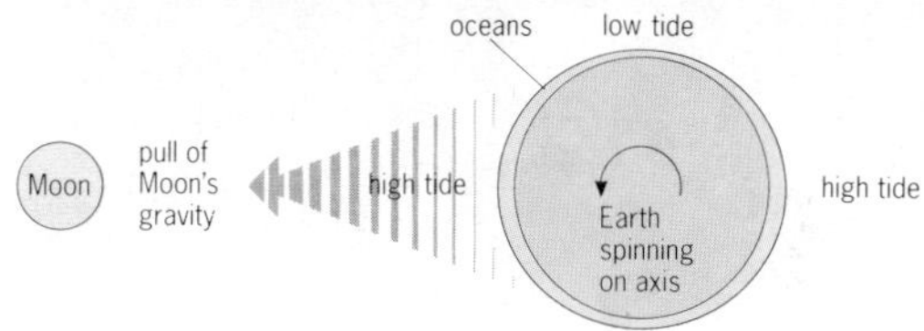

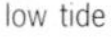

The Moon's gravity makes two bulges in the Earth's oceans. As the Earth spins places move in and out of the bulges and so get high and low tides.

Oil

Oil is the remains of tiny plants and animals which sank to the sea-bed millions of years ago They were buried by sediment, and slowly changed into oil and natural gas. The oil is often found under thousands of metres of rock, sometimes under the sea. At the refinery, crude oil is separated into different substances, including petrol and diesel, by a process called fractional distillation.

Fractional distillation. In a distillation tower, crude oil is separated into its different parts, called fractions. Some of the liquids from the distillation tower are too thick and heavy to be used as they are. These are broken down by a chemical process called cracking.

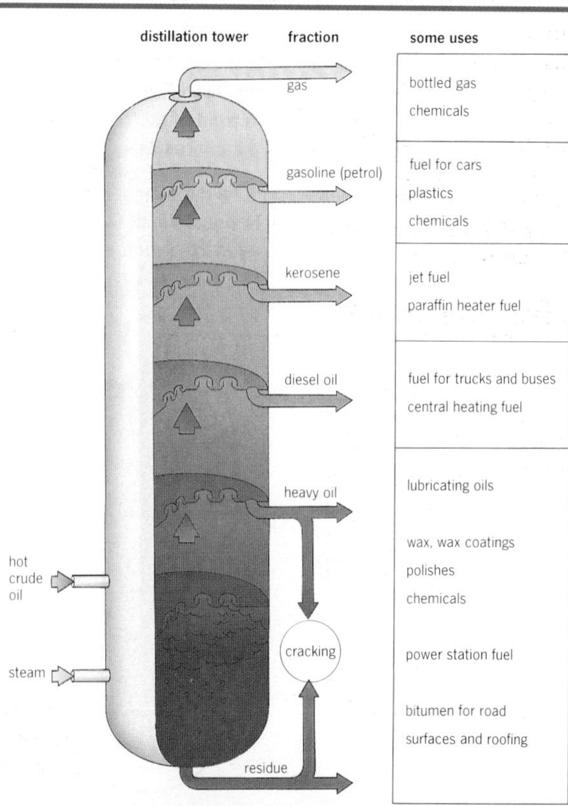

Orchestras

An orchestra is a big group of musicians who play their instruments together. They range in size from chamber orchestras with about 20 players to large symphony orchestras with as many as 120 players.

In a symphony orchestra there are four groups of instruments: strings, brass, woodwind and percussion.

Most orchestras have conductors who guide the orchestra's sound. Conductors also train the orchestra at rehearsals. The leader of the orchestra is the senior violinist.

Today many of the best known orchestras are based in specific places, such as the New York Philharmonic and the Melbourne Symphony.

Did you know?

- **In ancient Greek theatres the 'orchestra' was the area in front of the stage where the chorus sang.**
- **All the members of the UK National Youth Orchestra are aged 20 or below and can be as young as 10.**

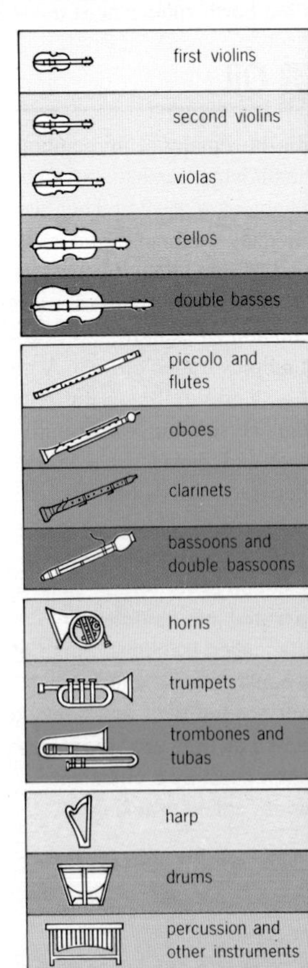

Origami

Origami is the Japanese art of paper folding. In Japan it is a children's game, but it is also used to decorate gifts and religious shrines.

Paper models are made from squares of paper by a series of folds. Some of these have traditional names such as rabbit-ear, petal or squash fold.

Experts spend many hours creating new models. Flowers, animals and puzzles can all be made.

▼ How to make a traditional Japanese bird from a square piece of paper.

Fold paper in half along diagonal. Open ut. Fold corners to meet middle fold.

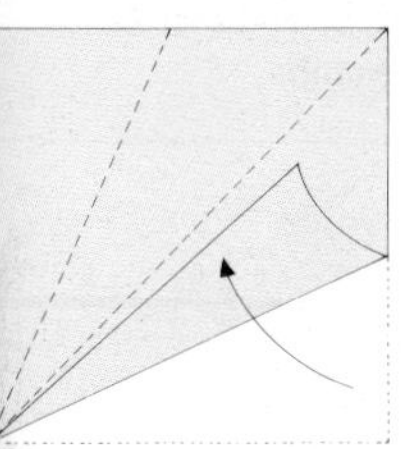

Fold kite corners in to form iamond. Turn diamond over.

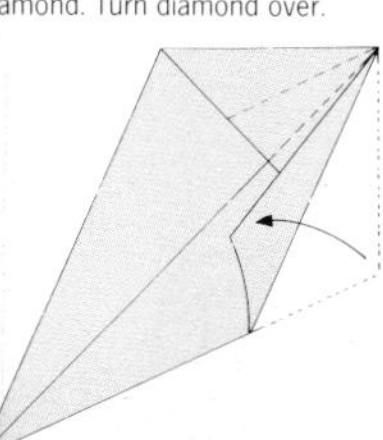

3 Fold diamond in half to make triangle.

4 Fold corner of triangle into the middle to make the bird's neck.

5 Fold tip back and crease on both sides. Then flatten again. Pull tip upwards to make neck.

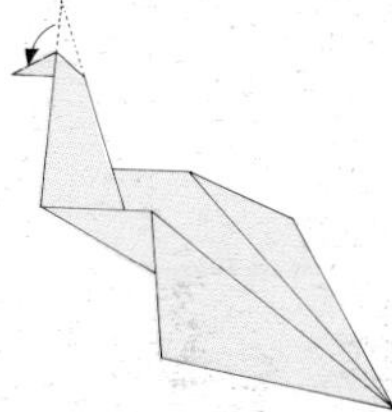

6 Finished bird.

Pakistan

FACT FILE

Capital
Islamabad
Population
130,129,000
Currency
1 rupee = 100 paisa

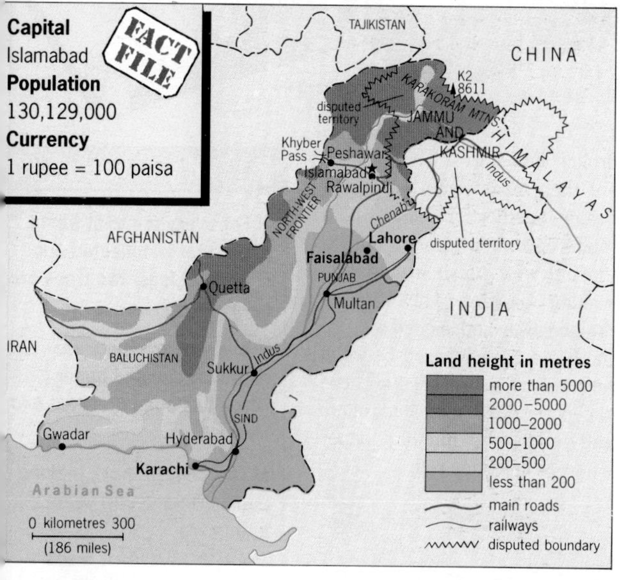

Pakistan was created in 1947, when British India was granted independence and divided into Pakistan and India. In Urdu *pak* means 'pure' and *stan* means 'land'. Most Pakistanis are Muslims.

In the north are high mountains, such as K2 which is the second highest mountain in the world. The plains round the River Indus are hot and wet, especially in the mid-July monsoon season. In the south west there are deserts with large gas fields. Gas is piped from here to the cities. The largest city in Pakistan is Karachi, a busy port where over 5 million people live and work.

Palestine

Palestine is at the eastern end of the Mediterranean Sea. In 1948 it was divided to create the new Jewish state of Israel. Hundreds of thousands of Arabs have left Israel since then. The division of Palestine is at the heart of the troubles in the middle East, although many Palestinian Arabs have now achieved self-rule in Israeli-controlled areas.

Pandas

Giant pandas are some of the rarest animals in the world. They live only in high mountain ranges in three isolated parts of China. Their main food is bamboo and they spend about twelve hours a day feeding. Many pandas starve if the bamboo crop fails, and their rarity is mainly due to changes in climate and vegetation, rather than to human activity.

Did you know?

- **There may be as few as 500 giant pandas left in the wild.**
- **Giant pandas have an extra bone in their hands which they use, much as we use our thumbs.**

Paper

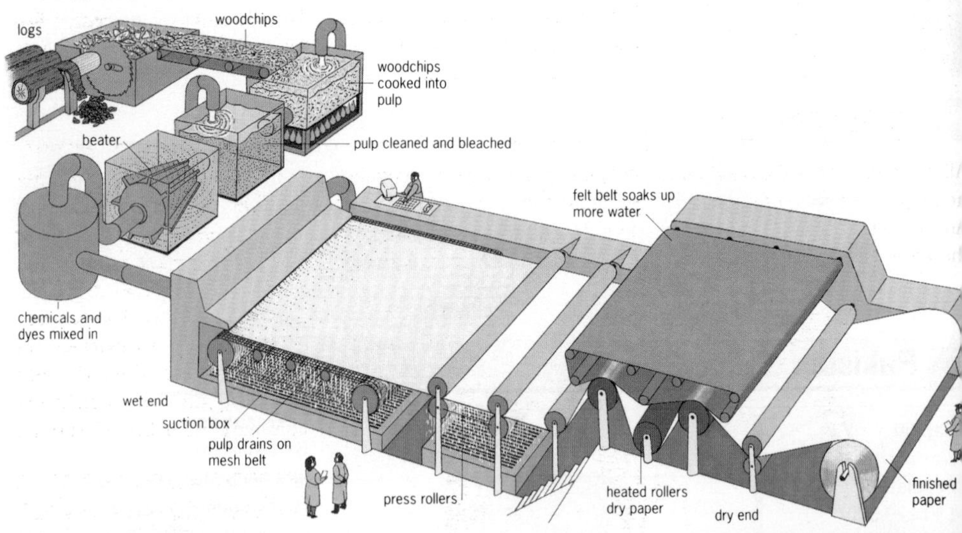

Paper is made from plant fibres that are matted together to form a sheet. Until the 19th century the fibres were obtained from pulped linen and cotton, making paper a rare and expensive item. Then it was discovered that paper could be produced from wood pulp. Most wood pulp now comes from coniferous trees such as pines, spruces and firs.

At a pulp-mill the bark is stripped off the logs and the wood is broken into fibres. These fibres are then mixed with water and beaten together. This slushy pulp mixture is then poured onto a moving wire mesh in a paper-making machine. The water is drained away and sucked off, and the fibres are squeezed between huge rollers to form sheets. These sheets are dried on heated rollers and finally the finished paper emerges in a huge roll.

Did you know?

- **For every tonne of waste paper that is collected and reused, at least two trees are saved.**
- **Many newspapers are made of recycled paper which has been de-inked and cleaned.**
- **The Chinese were making paper about 1,900 years ago.**

Parrots

All parrots have a curved bill and a short neck, and most are brightly coloured. There are more than 300 different species of parrot, ranging in size from the macaws which are about a metre high (including tail feathers), to the buff-faced pygmy parrot at 8·4 cm. Many parrots are prized as pets because of their ability to mimic the human voice. Most pets are home-bred now, rather than imported.

◀ **Scarlet macaws.**

Did you know?

■ Parrots are very long-lived: a sulphur-crested cockatoo was believed to be 120 years old when it died.

Pasteur, Louis

The great scientist Louis Pasteur (1822-1895) discovered that bacteria cause disease. He showed that living organisms, which we now call bacteria or 'germs', carry disease from one person, or animal, to another. He also made a life-saving vaccine for treating and preventing rabies.

In 1856 the French wine industry asked Pasteur to find out why so much of its wine was turning sour. He showed that this was caused by a yeast which could be killed by heat. This heating process, called 'pasteurization', is used today to make milk safe to drink.

Penguins

All penguins live in the southern hemisphere and emperor and Adelie penguins actually live on the ice of Antarctica. The emperor penguin is the largest penguin, standing over 1 m in height. It lays its eggs at the start of the Antarctic winter, so it endures some of the worst weather conditions experienced by any bird. Temperatures may fall below -40° C with hurricane force winds. Snow continually blows and there is no food. Males incubate the eggs on their feet, hidden under folds of skin, for 60 days. The males lose about half their body weight and only one chick in five will survive.

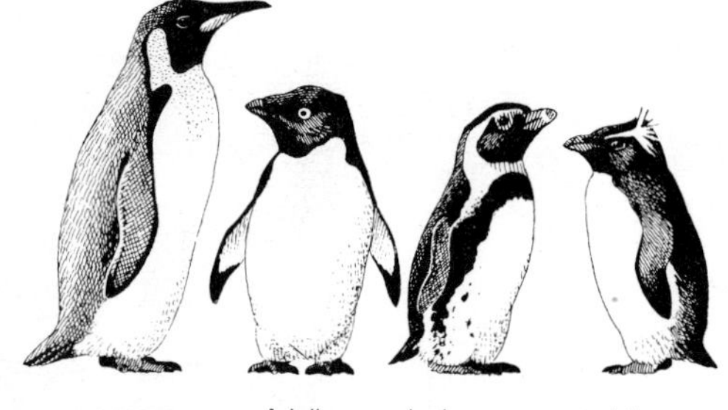

All penguins are mainly black and white but size and head patterns differ. The penguins are not drawn to scale.

Did you know?

■ Emperor penguins can dive to depths of 265 m (870 ft) and stay underwater for nine minutes.

Philippines

There are 7107 islands in the Philippines. Many of them are covered by rainforests. Earthquakes are common and there are also typhoons and several active volcanoes. The largest island is Luzon. Timber is an important export and rice is the main food crop.

FACT FILE

Capital
Manila

Population
63,609,000

Currency
1 peso = 100 centavos

Photography

The main skill of good photography is to compose the picture so that it is pleasing and shows what you wanted. Modern cameras adjust automatically to focus on the subject and to let in the right amount of light. They can even take a clear picture in focus if the subject is moving. The first photograph was taken in 1826.

Here are some guidelines for taking better photographs:

- Frame your picture carefully and do not cut off heads or feet.
- Think about the composition of your shot. Would it be better with the camera upright or horizontal?
- Stand close to your subject and fill the frame, or the background will dominate the picture.
- Do not always take people facing the camera. A side-view can be interesting.
- Do not have people looking straight at the camera when using the flash; it causes 'red eye'.
- To get a sharp picture of a moving subject, follow it with your camera. This is called panning.

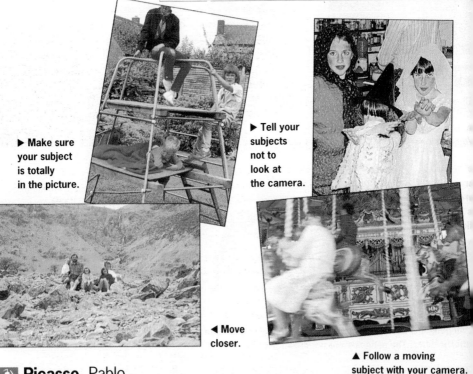

▶ **Make sure your subject is totally in the picture.**

▶ **Tell your subjects not to look at the camera.**

◀ **Move closer.**

▲ **Follow a moving subject with your camera.**

Picasso, Pablo

Pablo Picasso was born in Spain in 1881. At school he loved painting and worked at nothing else.

He grew up to become one of the most famous modern artists and his pictures are known and admired by millions of people. He died in 1973.

? Did you know? ?

■ **Picasso learned to draw before he could talk.**

▶ **Still life in cubist style.**

Planets

The nine major planets that orbit the Sun are Mercury, Venus, Earth, Mars, Jupiter, Saturn, Uranus, Neptune and Pluto. Some planets, such as the Earth, are balls of rock, while others, like Saturn, are giant balls of gas.

Jupiter, the largest of the nine, is over 1,000 times more massive than the Earth. Its four largest moons can be seen through an ordinary telescope. The most distant planet, Pluto, is between 7,400 and 4,400 million km (4,600 and 2,700 million miles) from the Sun. It orbits the Sun once in 248 years.

▲ Three separate photographs taken by the spacecraft *Voyager 1* were used to construct this picture of Saturn.

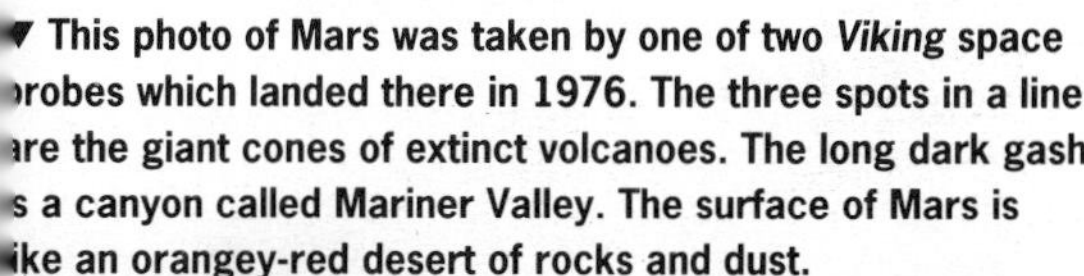

▼ This photo of Mars was taken by one of two *Viking* space probes which landed there in 1976. The three spots in a line are the giant cones of extinct volcanoes. The long dark gash is a canyon called Mariner Valley. The surface of Mars is like an orangey-red desert of rocks and dust.

▼ This image of Mercury was made from photographs taken by the space probe *Mariner 10* in 1974. The photos were taken from a distance of about 210,000 km (130,000 miles).

▼ Views from the *Voyager* spacecraft were put together to make this imaginary picture of the planet Jupiter and its four biggest moons, Io, Europa, Ganymede and Callisto.

Plants

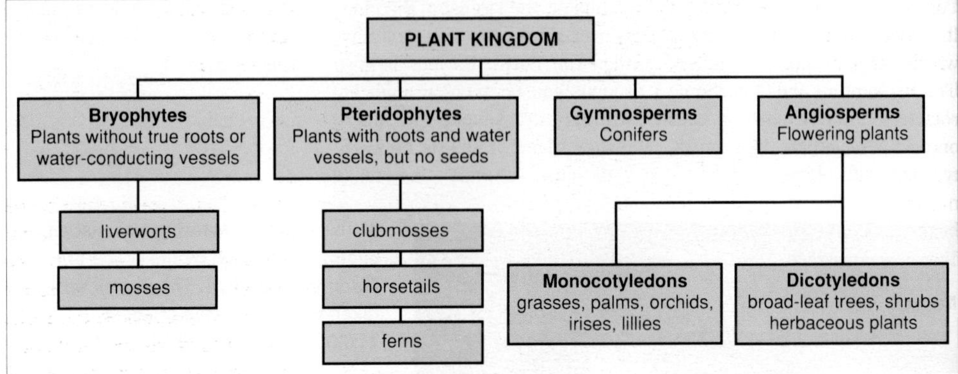

Poland

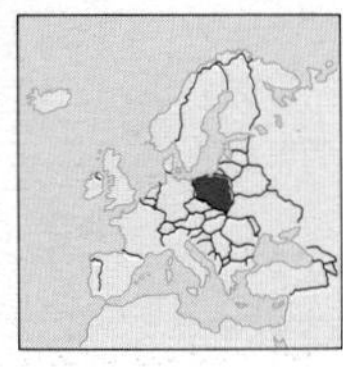

Poland is in north eastern Europe. Its longest river is the Vistula, which flows from the mountains of the south to the northern coast.

About a third of the people work on farms growing potatoes, sugar beet and cereal crops. In Silesia there are coal mines. Gdansk, Gdynia and Szczecin are ship-building cities.

A trade union called *Solidarnosc* (Solidarity) began in the shipyards of Gdansk when the communists ruled Poland. Eventually there were free elections in 1989. *Solidarnosc* won these and became the government of Poland. The leader of *Solidarnosc*, Lech Walesa, was elected president in 1990.

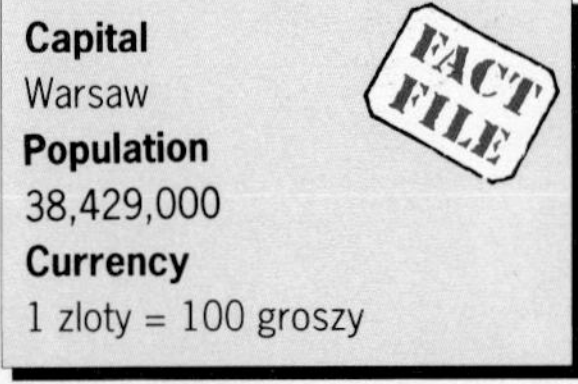

Capital
Warsaw
Population
38,429,000
Currency
1 zloty = 100 groszy

Polo, Marco

Marco Polo was 18 when his father and uncle took him on a journey to China. They set out in 1271 and the whole journey took four years.

Marco worked for the emperor of China, Kublai Khan, who sent him on missions to India, Burma and Sri Lanka.

After 24 years he returned to Venice, with a fortune in jewels.

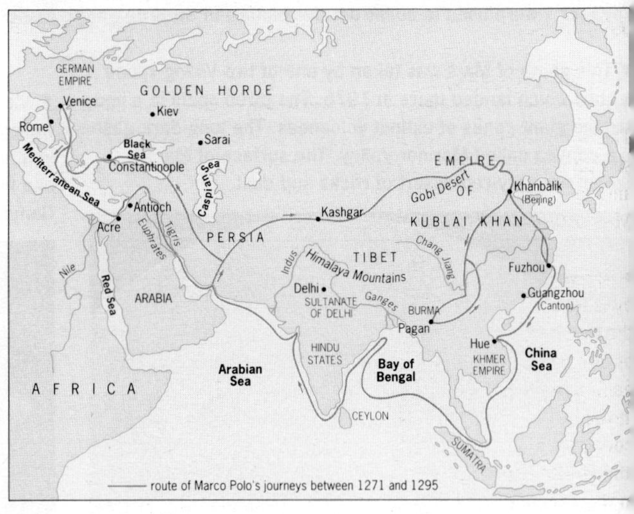

Pop and rock music

Pop is short for popular. It is used about music which lots of people like. Rock, or rock'n'roll, is one of the main types of pop music. It began in about 1955.

Michael Jackson.

▲ INXS.

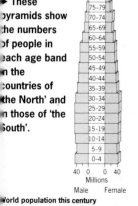

Annie Lennox.

▲ Bono, U2.

▲ Madonna.

Portugal

Portugal is in south west Europe next to Spain. Lisbon is at the mouth of the river Tagus. To the north of the Tagus there are mountains which are cold and wet. In the south the Algarve is a semitropical resort which is very popular with tourists.

Portugal is famous for its port wine, which comes from Oporto. It also exports textiles, cork, wood and sardines.

Capital
Lisbon
Population
9,844,000
Currency
1 escudo = 100 centavos

Population

The world's population has risen sharply since the mid-18th century, and very sharply since the 1950s. Most of this growth is in 'the South' (parts of Africa, Asia and Latin America). China has the world's biggest population: over one billion (1,000 million) people.

▶ These pyramids show the numbers of people in each age band in the countries of 'the North' and in those of 'the South'.

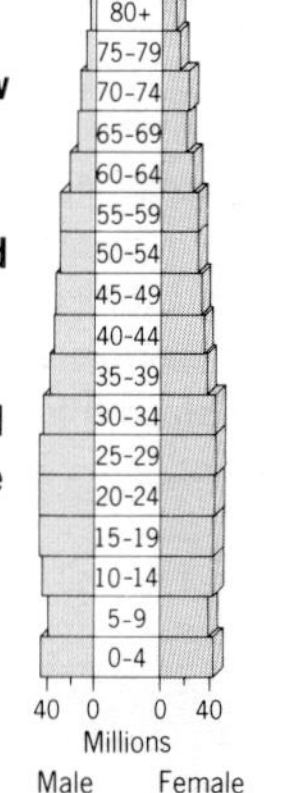

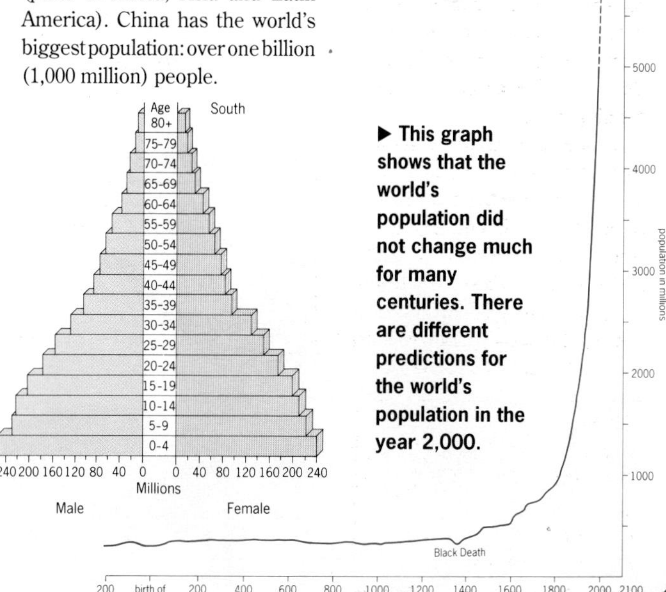

▶ This graph shows that the world's population did not change much for many centuries. There are different predictions for the world's population in the year 2,000.

World population this century

1900	1,550 million	1960	3,003 million
1930	2,070 million	1993	5,512 million

Postal services

1 Sending a letter to Australia.
2 The letter is taken to a sorting office.
3 The mail is sorted according to destination, and bundles of mail are put onto vans or trains.
4 As the mail is going overseas it has to be taken there on a boat or a plane.
5 The bundles of mail are unloaded onto vans and taken to the local sorting office.
6 Bundles of letters are loaded onto small vans for different delivery areas.
7 The local postal service delivers the letter.

All countries have postal services which deliver mail. In some countries letters are delivered to people's homes. In others, the people must collect them from the post office. If an item is properly addressed and paid for, it can be sent anywhere in the world. Today items can also be sent by fax machines and electronic mail systems.

Did you know?

■ **The Penny Black stamp for posting letters was first issued in Britain in 1840. In 1874 the General Postal Union set up co-operation between postal services in different countries.**

Prehistoric animals

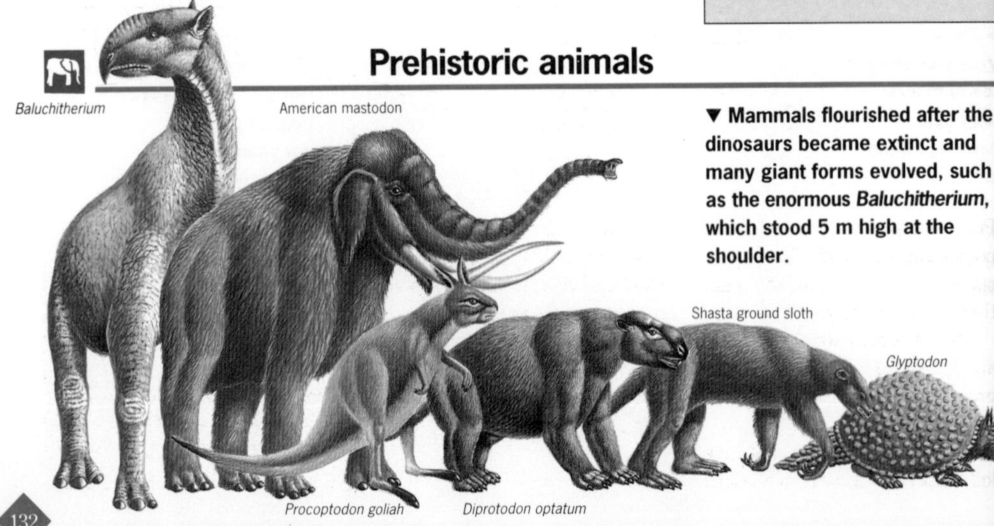

▼ **Mammals flourished after the dinosaurs became extinct and many giant forms evolved, such as the enormous *Baluchitherium*, which stood 5 m high at the shoulder.**

Prehistoric people

Prehistory is the time before written records. The earliest people lived in East Africa. They hunted animals and gathered plants for food. By 9000 BC people were planting crops in the Middle East.

Most tools were made from wood and stone.

Later people learnt how to use metals. Copper was first used in 6000 BC in West Asia. People in Turkey used iron in 2000 BC.

Prehistoric people also invented the wheel, pottery, spinning and weaving. They also developed their own art, from cave painting to carving.

▼ Archaeologists believe this is what a hunters' camp may have looked like in England in 7500 BC.

Printing

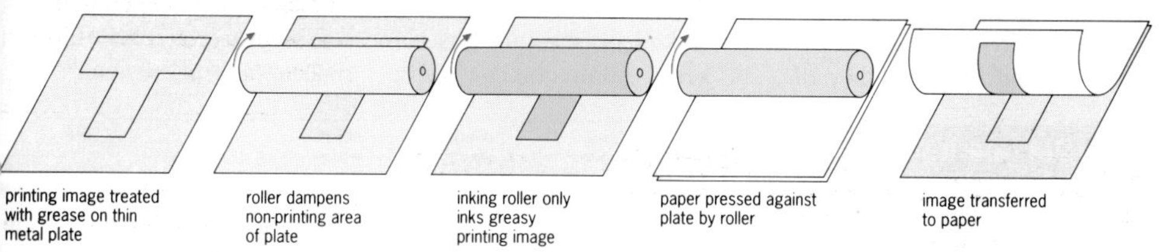

printing image treated with grease on thin metal plate
roller dampens non-printing area of plate
inking roller only inks greasy printing image
paper pressed against plate by roller
image transferred to paper

Printing is a way of making identical copies from one original. For every stamp, poster, book or bus ticket there was one original.

The three main ways of printing are letterpress, lithography and gravure. This book was printed by lithography.

Printing was known in China long before it was used in western countries. The first books were made in China by carving flat blocks of wood, inking them and pressing paper against them.

It was in about 1450 that Johann Gutenberg of Germany made a printing press with metal letters that could be used again and again.

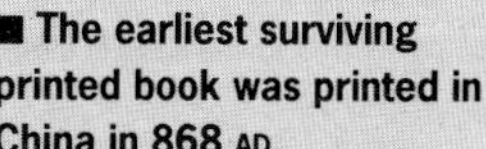

■ The earliest surviving printed book was printed in China in 868 AD.

■ William Caxton set up the first printing press in England in 1476.

Radar

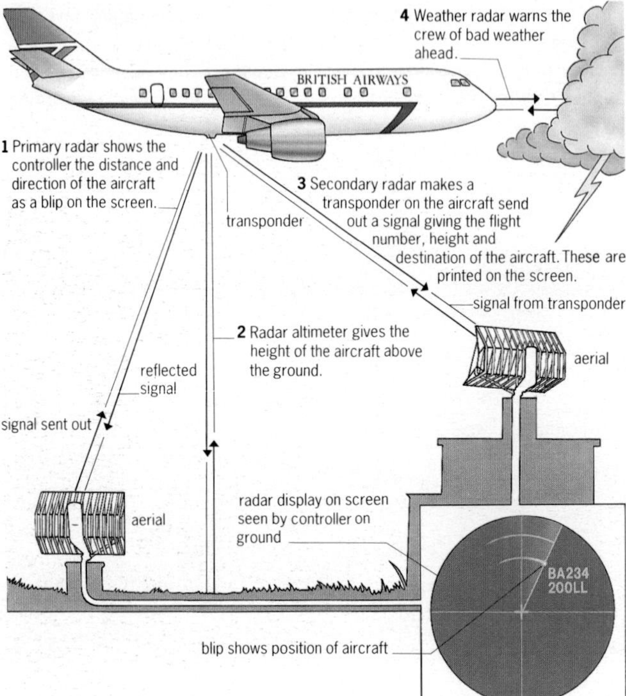

4 Weather radar warns the crew of bad weather ahead.
BRITISH AIRWAYS
1 Primary radar shows the controller the distance and direction of the aircraft as a blip on the screen.
3 Secondary radar makes a transponder on the aircraft send out a signal giving the flight number, height and destination of the aircraft. These are printed on the screen.
transponder
signal from transponder
2 Radar altimeter gives the height of the aircraft above the ground.
aerial
reflected signal
signal sent out
aerial
radar display on screen seen by controller on ground
BA234
200LL
blip shows position of aircraft

Radiation

Radiation is energy on the move. Heat, light, cosmic rays, ultraviolet light and sound are different types of radiation. Radiation travels as invisible waves, or tiny particles. Electromagnetic waves, such as light and radio waves, travel at 300,000 km/sec (186,000 miles/sec). Nothing can go faster than this.

An accident at a nuclear power-plant can release radioactive materials with enough radiation to kill people nearby, and to cause cancer, often many years later. Nuclear power-plants have thick concrete walls to stop radiation escaping, and workers wear special protective clothing.

◀ Four types of radar in use. The information on the screen tells the ground controller that this is flight number BA234, flying to London (LL) at 20,000 feet (200).

Radio

Transmitters send out thousands, or even millions, of radio waves every second. The number of waves per second (the frequency) is marked on the tuning scale in kHz (kilohertz) or MHz (megahertz). 1 kHz means 1,000 waves per second; 1 MHz means 1 million waves per second.

Did you know?

- **The first regular public broadcasting began in 1920.**
- **A radio wave can travel around the world in the time it takes you to blink.**
- **Radio waves bounce between the ground and the ionosphere.**
- **You have to tune a radio receiver to select the frequency you want.**

Type of radio wave	long wave	medium wave	short wave	VHF (very high frequency)	UHF (ultra high frequency)
used for	national broadcasting; AM radio; long distance ship communication	national broadcasting	international broadcasting	national broadcasting; high quality two-way radios; car phones	TV transmission
typical frequency	200 kHz	1 MHz	10 MHz	100 MHz	1,000 MHz
typical wavelength	1,500 m	300 m	30 m	3 m	⅓ m

▼ Radio waves can travel thousands of kilometres round the Earth bouncing between the ground and the ionosphere

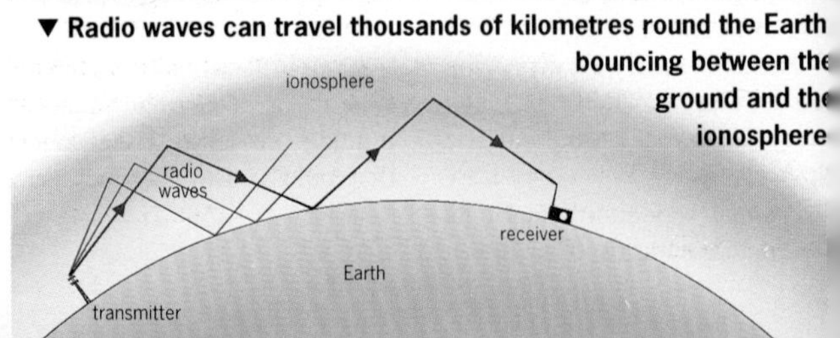

Railways

▲ French TGV express train at a station.

The first passenger railway opened between Stockton and Darlington, England, in 1825. Construction of others began in many parts of the world over the next 20 years.

A single locomotive can pull a load weighing thousands of tonnes. The heaviest load ever moved on rails is a church in what is now the Czech Republic, which was moved 730 m over a 4-week period in 1975.

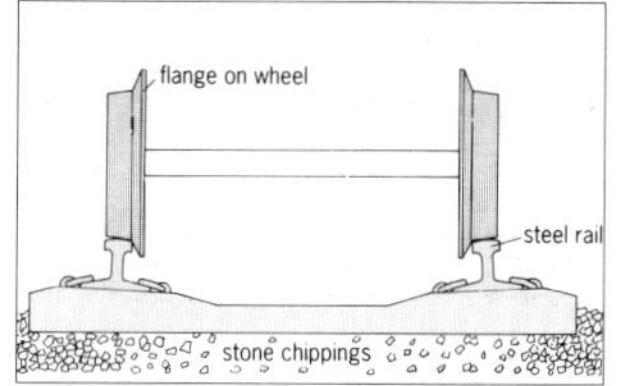

▲ Train wheels have flanges to keep them on the rails.

Did you know?

■ There are 97 stops on the world's longest railway, the Trans-Siberian Railway. The journey from Moscow to Nakhodka takes over 8 days.

■ The French high-speed passenger train, the TGV, reached a speed of 515 km/h (320 mph) in May 1990.

Rainbows

A beam of sunlight is split up as it goes into a raindrop. Only one colour from each raindrop reaches your eye, but because there are thousands of raindrops we can see the whole rainbow.

Recycling

About 60 per cent of the material in the average family dustbin could be recycled. Glass is unique because it can be used over and over again without any loss of quality.

Throwing away an aluminium can is like throwing away the same amount of energy as in half a can of petrol. An estimated 80 per cent of all the aluminium used could be recycled.

Red Cross

The Red Cross is a charity which gives help to the victims of war. It was set up in 1864. Those countries that signed the Geneva Convention promised not to fire on people, ambulances and hospitals showing the Red Cross.

The Red Cross also looks after prisoners of war. It helps to find them and also sends food parcels.

In Muslim countries a Red Crescent is used instead. There are Red Cross and Red Crescent Societies in 146 countries.

Refrigerators

Refrigerators keep food at a temperature of about 5°C. They take heat from the inside, which becomes colder, and give it to the outside which gets warmer. The cooling is done by evaporating a substance called a refrigerant. A compressor pumps the liquid refrigerant round a sealed system of pipes. When it passes through the expansion valve it turns to vapour and produces a cooling effect. The vapour turns back to liquid in the condenser.

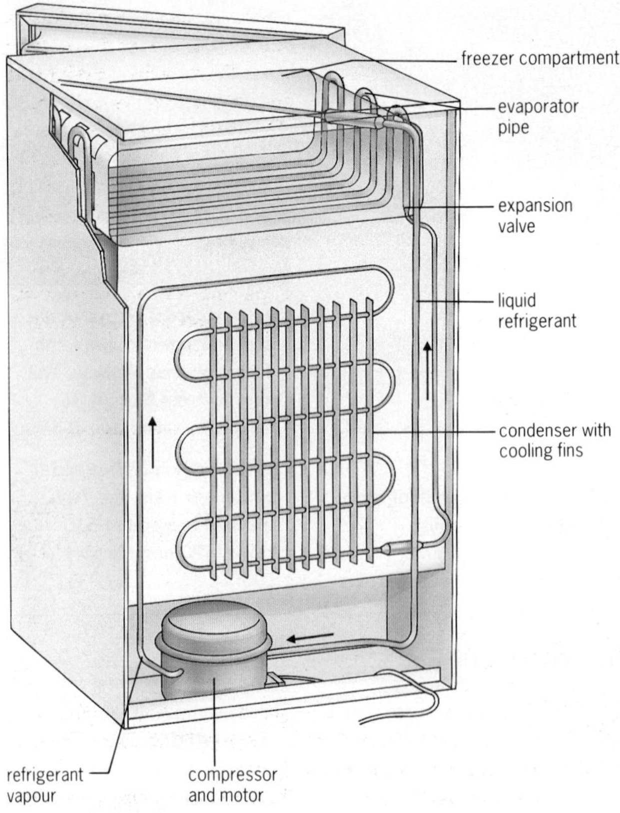

Reggae

Reggae is a kind of pop music. It began in Jamaica in the 1960s and quickly spread to other countries.

Reggae has a special rhythm, with a heavy beat on the second and fourth counts of every bar (one-**two**-three-**four**). Reggae words are usually in Jamaican dialect.

▼ Bob Marley, a Jamaican who made reggae popular throughout the world.

Renaissance

Renaissance means rebirth. It is the word used for the discoveries in science and art that were made in the 15th and 16th centuries. A lot of ideas came from studying the ancient Greeks and Romans. That is why it is called a rebirth.

Artists such as Raphael and Michelangelo used light and shadow to make paintings and sculptures more life-like. Scientists found out more about the world, such as Galileo who studied the movements of the planets. Architects looked at ancient buildings and learnt how to build magnificent domes and arches.

Reptiles

There are four orders of reptile alive today: crocodiles and their relatives; lizards and snakes; turtles and tortoises; and rhynchocephalia which contains only one species the tuatara. The tuatara is the only survivor of a big group of reptiles important during the days of the dinosaurs.

There are about 6,000 species of reptiles.

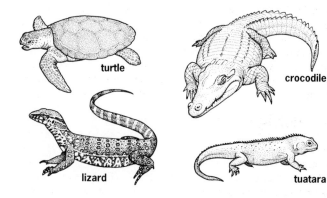

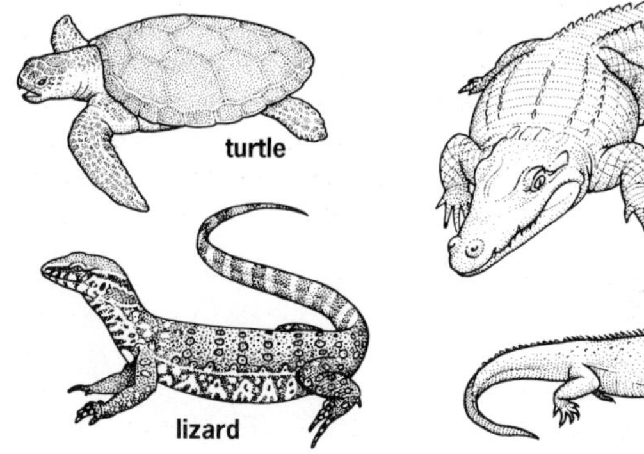

Rivers

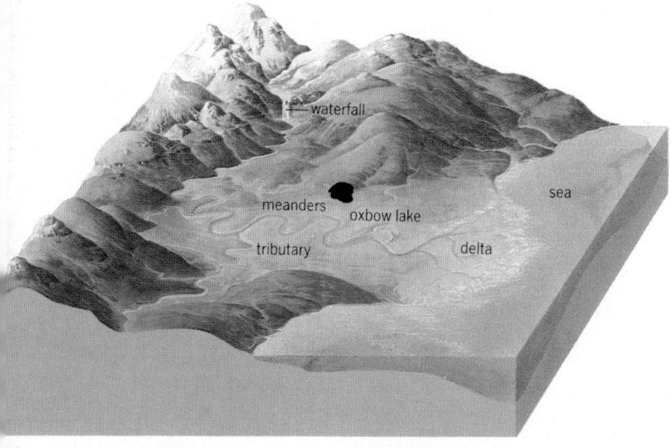

Rain or melting snow runs off the land to form trickles of water. These trickles merge to form streams which join up to form rivers. On its way to the sea a river cuts into the land, creating valleys and gorges. The Colorado River, USA, has cut a gorge 1·5 km (1 mile) deep. The world's longest river is the River Nile, which is 6,695 km (4,160 miles) long.

◀ The course of a river from its source in the mountains to its estuary at sea.

Robin Hood

'here have been many stories .bout Robin Hood since the 14th entury. He and his 'merry men' vere outlaws who lived in herwood Forest. They 'stole from he rich and gave to the poor'. The nerry men included Little John, 'riar Tuck and Will Scarlet. The ove of Robin Hood's life was Maid Marian.

Robin Hood might have really xisted, but the stories are robably based on several real utlaws.

Robots

▲ Robot arms in use on a car assembly line.

The robots you see on TV and in films do not look anything like the industrial robots used in factories. These robots are usually just big arms fixed to the floor and controlled by computers.

Rockets

The huge rockets that send satellites into space work using the same principle as firework rockets. Their fuel burns and produces hot gases which expand and push the rocket upwards. The German V2 war rocket, made in 1942, was the first rocket powerful enough to reach space.

▼ The Ariane rocket can launch 2 or 3 satellites into orbit at the same time.

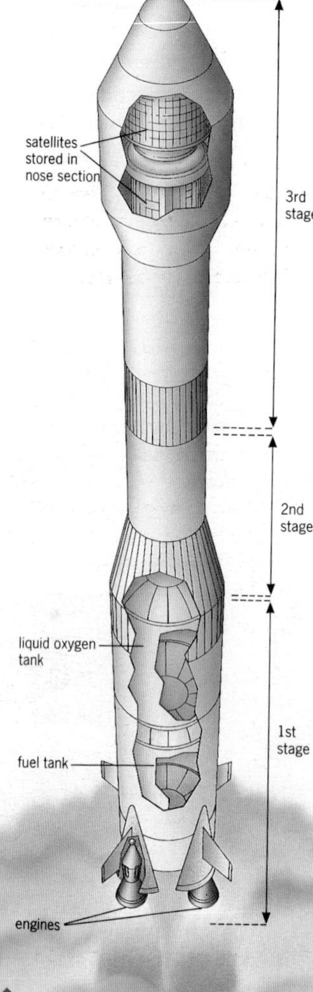

Rocks

Igneous rocks are formed from the liquid magma inside the Earth, or magma which has cooled on the surface as volcanic lava. Sedimentary rocks are formed from sand and mud, while metamorphic rocks are made when existing rocks are changed by heat, or by heat and pressure together.

Igneous

Granite contains many large crystals of the mineral quartz.

Basalt is a volcanic rock which is formed on the Earth's surface. It is fine grained because the liquid magma cooled quickly in the air.

Metamorphic

A folded and refolded specimen of Lewisian gneiss.

Sedimentary

Millstone grit is a coarse sandstone which was once used to make millstones for grinding corn.

Chalk is a soft white porous rock. It is made from the remains of chalky algae and often contains lumps of flint.

Shelly limestone is made from the piled-up skeletons of sea animals. Sometimes these fossil shells are perfectly preserved.

 Romania

Romania is in south-east Europe. The river Danube separates it from Bulgaria. Most of Romania is farmland growing cereals, sunflowers and sugar beet. Important industries include iron and steel, engineering and chemicals.

Capital
Bucharest
Population
23,332,000
Currency
1 leu = 100 bani

Romans

In 509 BC a tribe called the Latini took over the town of Rome. They became the Romans and spread their Latin language and their way of life throughout Italy and most of Europe.

They built well-planned towns. Water was piped to markets, fountains and public baths. They also built proper drains. Romans could visit the theatre or watch chariot racing and gladiator fights at a stadium. There were even take-away shops.

▲ A Roman coin with the head of the Emperor Hadrian.

The first emperor, Augustus, came to power in 27 BC. This marked the beginning of the Roman empire. Under the emperors, Rome conquered even more lands.

By the 5th century AD the western part of the empire had fallen to the Goths, Huns and Vandals. The eastern empire became the Byzantine empire.

▲ Part of a mosaic floor found in Cirencester.

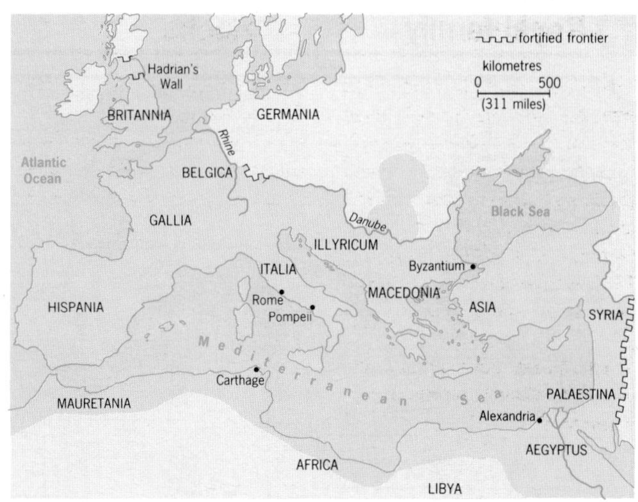

Roman Britain

Julius Caesar first invaded Britain in 55 BC. Nearly a century later in 43 AD, the Emperor Claudius began the real conquest of Britain.

The Romans built roads, towns, and forts to control the country. The Emperor Hadrian built a wall across northern England to act as a frontier barrier against people in the north.

▲ This temple was built in Colchester to worship the Emperor Claudius as a god.

Royal family

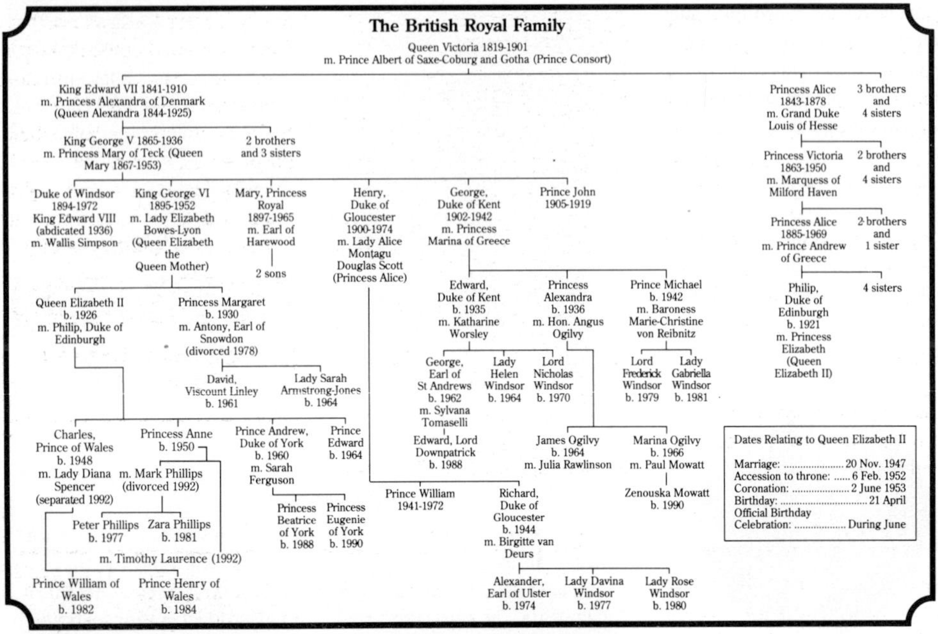

The British Royal Family

Queen Victoria 1819-1901
m. Prince Albert of Saxe-Coburg and Gotha (Prince Consort)

King Edward VII 1841-1910
m. Princess Alexandra of Denmark
(Queen Alexandra 1844-1925)

Princess Alice
1843-1878
m. Grand Duke
Louis of Hesse

3 brothers
and
4 sisters

King George V 1865-1936
m. Princess Mary of Teck (Queen
Mary 1867-1953)

2 brothers
and 3 sisters

Princess Victoria
1863-1950
m. Marquess of
Milford Haven

2 brothers
and
4 sisters

Duke of Windsor
1894-1972
King Edward VIII
(abdicated 1936)
m. Wallis Simpson

King George VI
1895-1952
m. Lady Elizabeth
Bowes-Lyon
(Queen Elizabeth
the
Queen Mother)

Mary, Princess
Royal
1897-1965
m. Earl of
Harewood

2 sons

Henry,
Duke of
Gloucester
1900-1974
m. Lady Alice
Montagu
Douglas Scott
(Princess Alice)

George,
Duke of Kent
1902-1942
m. Princess
Marina of Greece

Prince John
1905-1919

Princess Alice
1885-1969
m. Prince Andrew
of Greece

2 brothers
and
1 sister

Queen Elizabeth II
b. 1926
m. Philip, Duke of
Edinburgh

Princess Margaret
b. 1930
m. Antony, Earl of
Snowdon
(divorced 1978)

David,
Viscount Linley
b. 1961

Lady Sarah
Armstrong-Jones
b. 1964

Edward,
Duke of Kent
b. 1935
m. Katharine
Worsley

Princess
Alexandra
b. 1936
m. Hon. Angus
Ogilvy

Prince Michael
b. 1942
m. Baroness
Marie-Christine
von Reibnitz

Philip,
Duke of
Edinburgh
b. 1921
m. Princess
Elizabeth
(Queen
Elizabeth II)

4 sisters

George,
Earl of
St Andrews
b. 1962
m. Sylvana
Tomaselli

Lady
Helen
Windsor
b. 1964

Lord
Nicholas
Windsor
b. 1970

Lord
Frederick
Windsor
b. 1979

Lady
Gabriella
Windsor
b. 1981

Charles,
Prince of Wales
b. 1948
m. Lady Diana
Spencer
(separated 1992)

Princess Anne
b. 1950
m. Mark Phillips
(divorced 1992)

Prince Andrew,
Duke of York
b. 1960
m. Sarah
Ferguson

Prince
Edward
b. 1964

Edward, Lord
Downpatrick
b. 1988

James Ogilvy
b. 1964
m. Julia Rawlinson

Marina Ogilvy
b. 1966
m. Paul Mowatt

Zenouska Mowatt
b. 1990

Peter Phillips
b. 1977

Zara Phillips
b. 1981

m. Timothy Laurence (1992)

Princess
Beatrice
of York
b. 1988

Princess
Eugenie
of York
b. 1990

Prince William
1941-1972

Richard,
Duke of
Gloucester
b. 1944
m. Birgitte van
Deurs

Prince William of
Wales
b. 1982

Prince Henry of
Wales
b. 1984

Alexander,
Earl of Ulster
b. 1974

Lady Davina
Windsor
b. 1977

Lady Rose
Windsor
b. 1980

Dates Relating to Queen Elizabeth II	
Marriage:	20 Nov. 1947
Accession to throne:	6 Feb. 1952
Coronation:	2 June 1953
Birthday:	21 April
Official Birthday Celebration:	During June

Queen Elizabeth II is the head of the British royal family. She became queen when her father, **George VI**, died. His widow is **Queen Elizabeth, the Queen Mother.**

In 1947, before she became queen, Elizabeth married **Prince Philip of Greece**. They both have the same great-great-grandmother, **Queen Victoria**. When he married Elizabeth, Philip was made **Duke of Edinburgh**. Elizabeth II and Prince Philip have four children.

Charles, Prince of Wales, is the heir to the throne. In 1981 he married Lady Diana Spencer, who became **Princess of Wales**, but they separated in 1992. They have two children, **Prince Harry** and **Prince William**. The Prince and Princess of Wales carry out a lot of official business. The Princess is especially interested in children's charities.

Anne, the Princess Royal, is an expert horsewoman. She married Mark Phillips in 1973, but they divorced in 1992. They have two children, Peter and Zara. The Princess Royal carries out over 500 engagements each year, and is President of the Save the Children Fund. She married Commander Timothy Lawrence in 1992.

Prince Andrew serves as a helicopter pilot in the Royal Navy. he took part in the Falklands War in 1982. In 1986 he married Sarah Ferguson and became **Duke of York.** They have two children, Beatrice and Eugenie. The couple separated in 1992.

Prince Edward joined the Royal Marines after going to university but he left after four months. He chose to work in the theatre.

Rubber

Natural rubber is made from latex, the juice of the rubber tree. Most rubber trees are in south east Asia.

Rubber tappers cut half way round the trees, and return later to collect the latex. They use the same trees for 15 days a month making a new cut each time. The latex is cleaned, rolled, squeezed and dried in the factory, then packed and sent to Europe and America.

Synthetic rubber is made from oil, gas and coal.

▶ As the white latex oozes from the rubber tree it drips down a spout into a cup.

Rugby

Rugby is played with an oval ball. Players can handle the ball and run with it, but are only allowed to pass it backwards. The aim is to score a try by grounding the ball behind the other team's goal line.

There are two types of rugby: Rugby Union (fifteen-a-side) and Rugby League (thirteen-a-side).

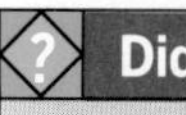

Did you know?

■ Rugby was first played at Rugby School.

Russia

Russia extends from the Arctic Ocean south to the Black Sea, and from the Baltic Sea east to the Pacific Ocean. It is the world's largest country, with an area of 17,075,400 sq km (6,592,849 sq miles), and it spans 11 time zones.

Russia is an industrial country. It produces all sorts of goods that are sold within the country and in eastern Europe. There are vast deposits of oil, natural gas, coal, copper, iron ore, gold, silver, platinum, lead and nickel.

In parts of Russia the climate is very severe. In the capital, Moscow, snow lies on the ground for five months of the year.

Russia was one of the four original countries that united to form the USSR in 1922. It regained its independence at the end of 1991, when the USSR ceased to exist.

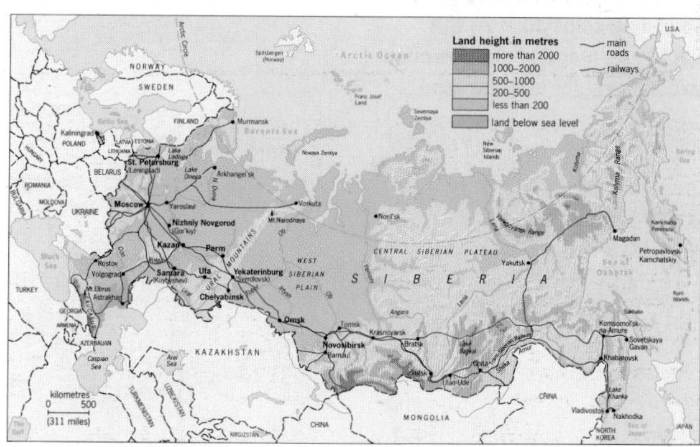

▲ Physical map of Russia after the break up of the USSR.

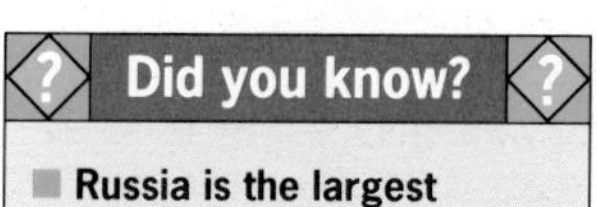

Did you know?

■ Russia is the largest country in the world.

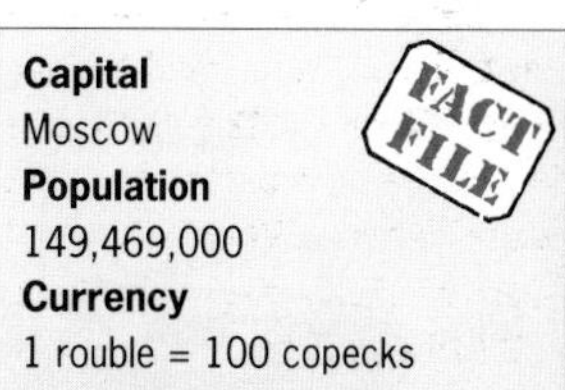

Capital
Moscow
Population
149,469,000
Currency
1 rouble = 100 copecks

FACT FILE

Sailing

Sailing boats use wind power to move. The sails used to be canvas, but are now made of synthetic material, such as nylon.

Before engines were invented, all ships had sails: the earliest had just one mast and sail, but as ships grew larger, more masts were added.

The fastest sailing ships were square-rigged clippers, so-called because they could 'clip' time off their sailing schedules.

Sailing ships are still used today: dhows in the Middle East, junks in the Far East, and yachts for sport worldwide.

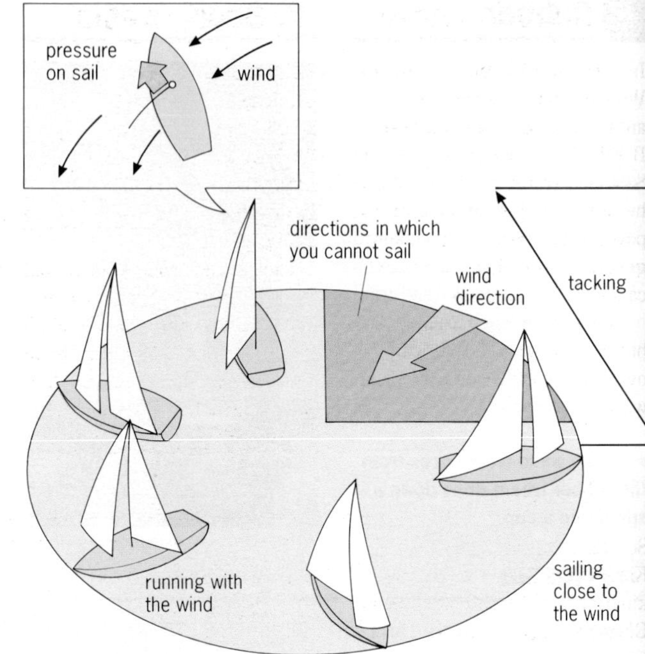

▶ **A sail is pushed sideways when the wind blows across it, so sailing ships such as this yacht can move in any direction except straight into the wind.**

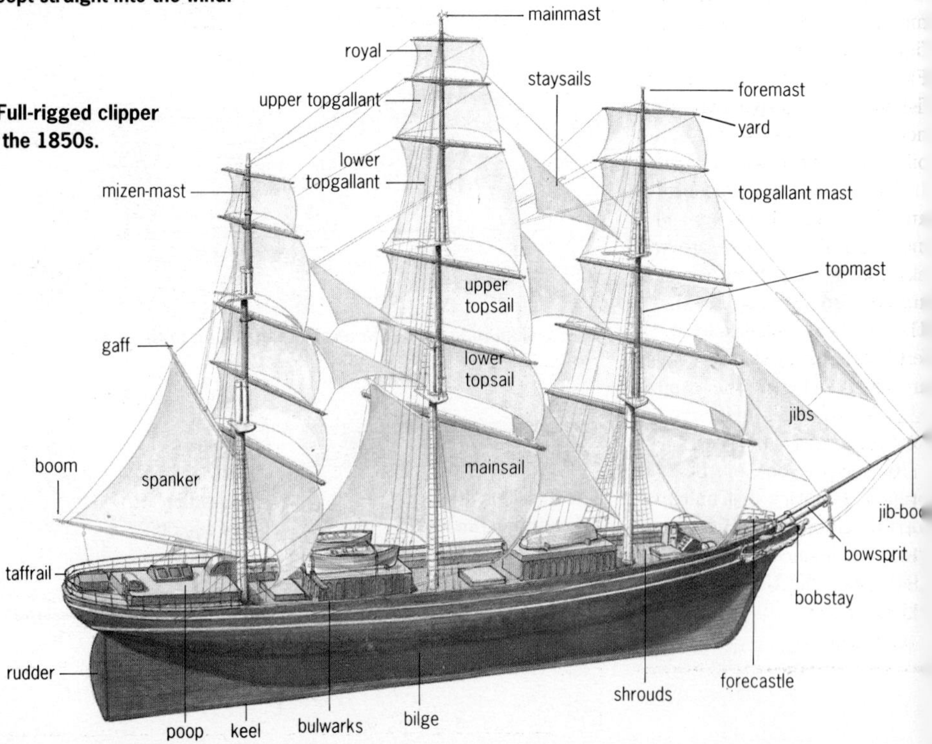

▶ **Full-rigged clipper of the 1850s.**

Salvation Army

In 1861 a Methodist minister, William Booth, decided to set up an organization to help poor people. Booth changed its name to the Salvation Army in 1878, because he was fighting a war against poverty. He became the Army's general, and it also had colonels, captains and corporals.

Today the Salvation Army has branches in 90 countries. It has over 25,000 officers to carry out its work.

Saudi Arabia

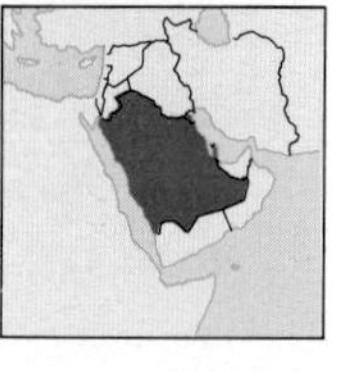

Saudi Arabia is a desert kingdom in the Middle East. It is about twice as big as Britain, France and Germany put together. It is the richest country in the Middle East because of oil under the desert. Money from oil has been used to build modern cities at Riyadh and Dammam. It is a Muslim country, and many pilgrims visit the city of Mecca where the prophet Muhammad lived. Saudi Arabians wear traditional clothes: women wear black robes and cover their heads in public, and men wear white robes and headdresses.

FACT FILE

Capital
Riyadh
Population
15,267,000
Currency
1 Saudi rial = 100 halalas

Scotland

Scotland is part of the United Kingdom. It used to be a separate kingdom, and it still has its own Church, legal system and education system.

In the Highlands there are mountains and hills. Farming and fishing are important there. Farmers rear cattle and sheep. The fishing fleet catches cod, mackerel, herring and other fish. North Sea oil is piped ashore at Aberdeen.

Further south are the Lowlands and Southern Uplands. New industries such as chemicals and electronics are replacing coal, steel and shipbuilding industries there. The Southern Uplands are more fertile than the Highlands, so farms are scattered throughout.

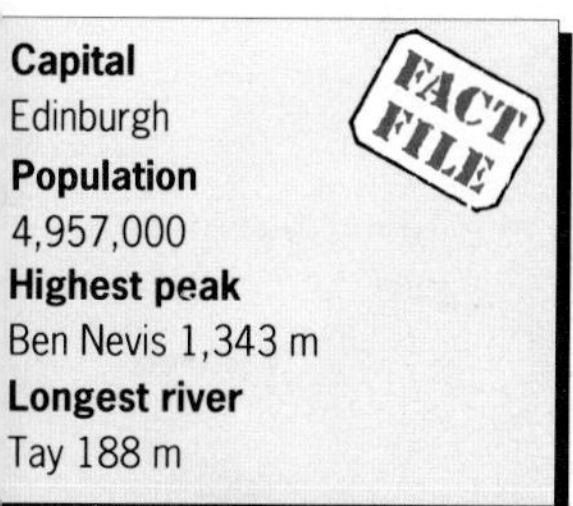

FACT FILE

Capital
Edinburgh
Population
4,957,000
Highest peak
Ben Nevis 1,343 m
Longest river
Tay 188 m

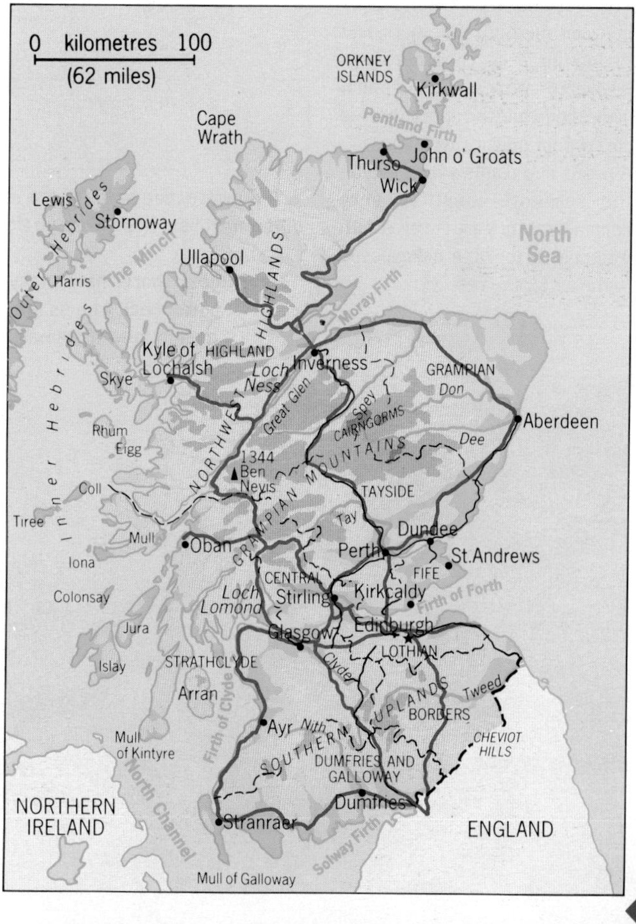

Scotland's history

▲ **Highlanders battling against English infantry in the battle of Culloden, 1746.**

In Roman times there were a number of warlike tribes in Scotland, and for centuries after the Roman departure Scotland remained a patchwork of peoples rather than a single kingdom. But in the year 843 AD the Scots became rulers of Scotland. There were many wars with England until 1603 when James VI of Scotland also became king of England. The two countries united in 1707.

Later, Scotland led the Industrial Revolution. New industries created wealth, but also misery. People were forced off their land in the Highlands and many went abroad.

Emigration continued in the 20th century as old industries declined. But North Sea oil and other new industries brought jobs.

Seashore

The seashore is part of the coast between the high tide mark and the low tide mark. The lower shore is covered with sea water for much of the day, while the upper shore is covered for only a short time. Animals and plants which live on the seashore must be very adaptable as they are covered with water part of the time and exposed to the air for the rest.

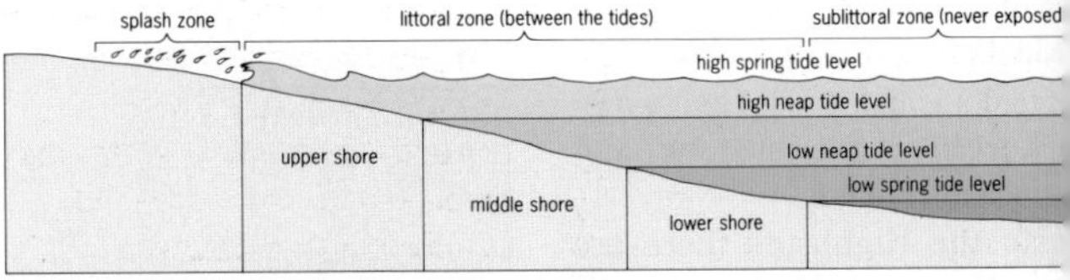

▲ **A cross-section of the shore showing how biologists divide it into different zones, depending on tide level.**

▼ **Rocky shores have many pools, each with its own community of animals.**

Did you know?

■ **There maybe as many as 100,000 animals per square metre living in the mud beneath a sandy shore.**

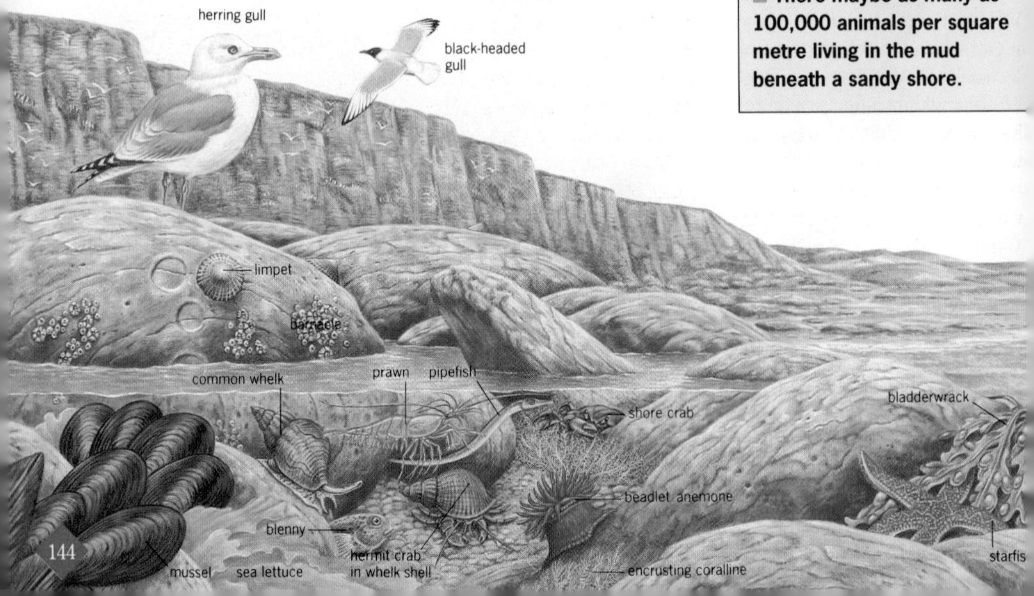

Seasons

The Earth travels round the Sun once each year. From March to September, the North Pole is tipped towards the Sun. Places in the northern hemisphere have spring and summer, while the southern hemisphere is having autumn and winter. From September to March things are the other way round.

The planet Mars has seasons too. We can see its ice-caps grow in winter and shrink in summer.

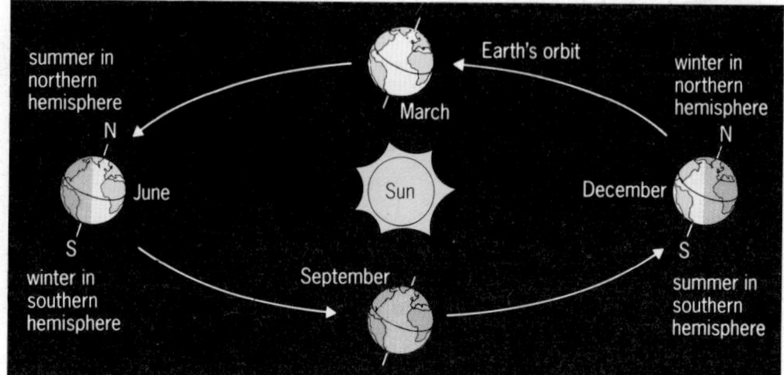

Seeds

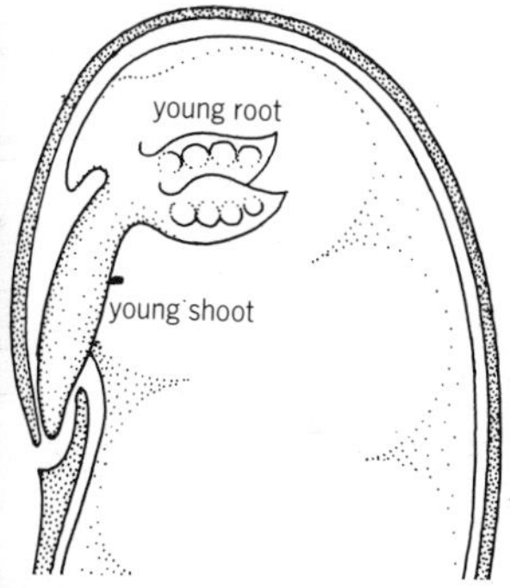

◀ If you soak a broad bean overnight it absorbs water, softens and swells. If you open it up you will see that, like all seeds, it contains a partly developed plant, complete with root, leaves and a supply of food. These are wrapped in a protective seed coat, the testa.

Seeds are produced by flowering plants and conifers. Each one, given the right conditions, can grow into a new plant. Seeds of flowering plants develop inside fruits, those of conifers develop inside cones. Nuts are fruits and the kernel, the part of the nut you eat, is actually a young plant. Seeds enable plants to survive harsh conditions, such as winter or drought, when normal growth is impossible.

Shakespeare, William

William Shakespeare was born in Stratford in 1564. When he was 18 he married Anne Hathaway. They had three children. By 1592 he was working as an actor and writer in London.

He wrote 37 plays, many of which became favourites with the audiences of his day. They included *Macbeth*, *Hamlet* and *Romeo and Juliet*. Shakespeare's plays are mostly written in verse. He also wrote 154 poems called sonnets.

Shakespeare's plays are still being performed all over the world, centuries after his death in 1616.

Did you know? 

■ Shakespeare took very little interest in the printing or publication of his work, and one or two of his plays may have got lost.

Sharks

Sharks that have attacked humans include hammerhead, tiger, grey, and great white sharks. There are fewer than 100 attacks a year.

▶ The great white shark, able to smell one part blood in a million parts water.

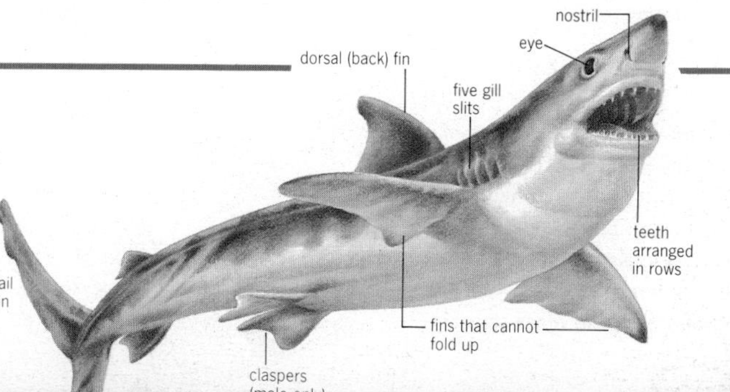

Skeletons

A skeleton is a stiff scaffolding which supports the soft parts of an animal. The vertebrates (fish, amphibians, reptiles, birds and mammals) have skeletons of bones and cartilage. They all have a backbone made up of a chain of vertebrae, and a skull. These support and protect the brain and the spinal cord.

Invertebrates do not have a bony skeleton. Worms, snails and shellfish, for instance, have taut, fluid-filled bags inside their bodies, to support them. Other invertebrates such as crabs, spiders and insects, have a surface skeleton. Their soft inner bodies are supported by a stiff jointed skin, called a cuticle. As the cuticle is hard it does not allow growth. So as the animal grows it must shed its external skeleton. Underneath is a new soft cuticle which allows growth until it hardens. The animal will shed its cuticle a number of times before it is fully grown.

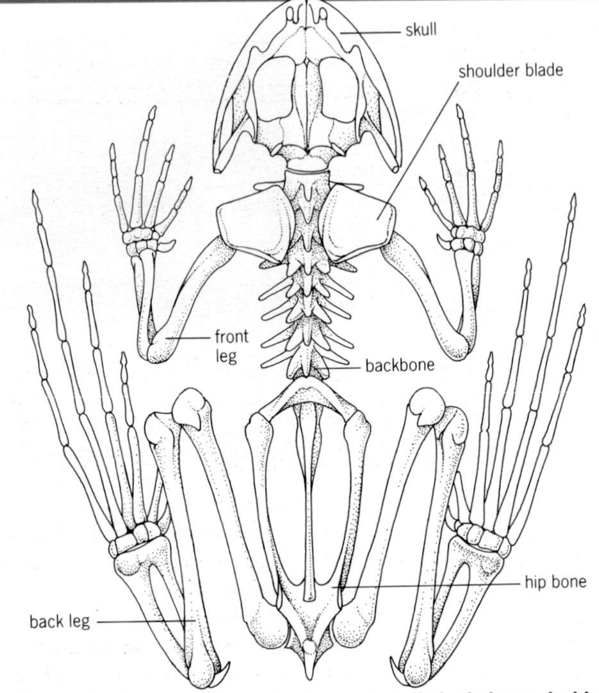

▲ Frogs, like other back-boned animals, have their skeletons inside their bodies. A frog has very large back legs to enable it to catch prey and escape danger.

Skin

The skin surface is made up of dead skin cells, and it wears away every time you touch anything. A layer of live dividing cells replaces it as fast as it is removed, and it is kept supple by an oily substance made by the skin. The skin also makes hairs and removes sweat from the blood.

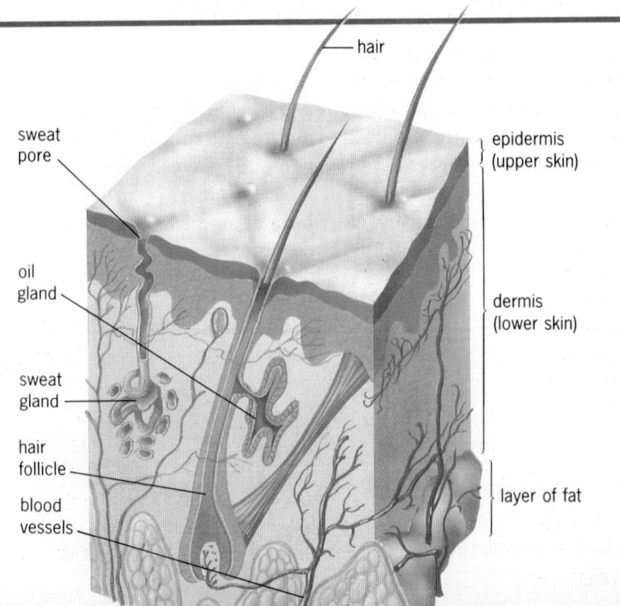

▶ A magnified section of skin. The upper dead layer wears away every time you touch everything. But a layer of live dividing cells replaces it as fast as it is removed. This also repairs cuts and other damage.

Slaves

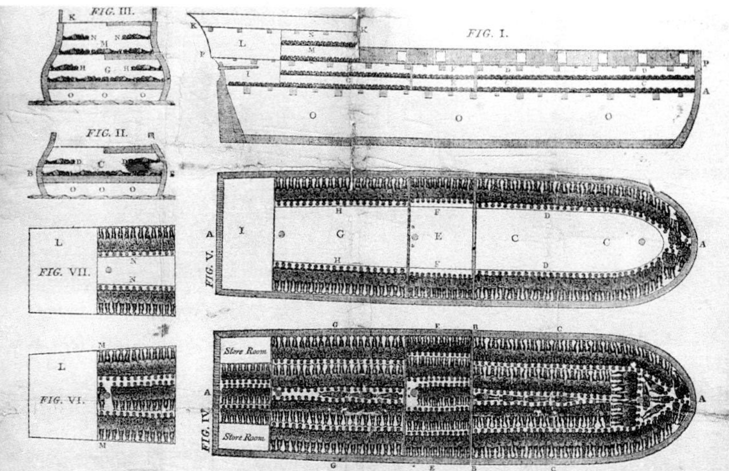

◀ **The plan of a slave ship that William Wilberforce, the anti-slavery campaigner, showed to Parliament, as part of his action to get slavery banned.**

Slaves are people who are somebody's property and so can be bought and sold. The ancient Greeks and Romans owned many slaves.

Centuries later Europeans sold African slaves to the Americas. These slaves cut sugar and picked tobacco and cotton.

Slaves did fight back. In Haiti an army of slaves set up a free country in 1804.

Eventually people began to see that slavery was wrong and it was abolished in the British empire in 1833, and in the USA in 1865.

Did you know?

- **Spartacus was a slave who led a slaves' rebellion in ancient Rome. Six thousand slaves were crucified following his defeat.**

Slovakia

In 1992 Slovakia became independent, when the central European country of Czechoslovakia divided in two. It has a growing timber and paper industry.

FACT FILE

Capital
Bratislava
Population
5,274,000
Currency
1 koruna = 100 halers

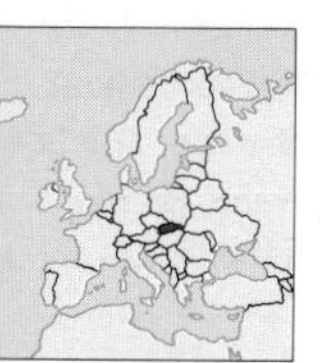

Snakes

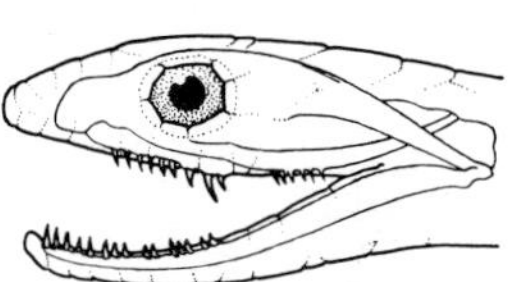

back-fanged boomslang

front-fanged viper

Snakes are reptiles. About a third of all snakes use poison to kill their prey. The poison glands are at the back of the upper jaw, and the poison is injected into the prey by hollow or grooved fangs. The fangs are at the back of the mouth in some, such as boomslangs, and at the front in others, such as vipers.

Did you know?

- **Anacondas can grow up to 10 m in length.**
- **Snakes have only one lung.**

Snooker

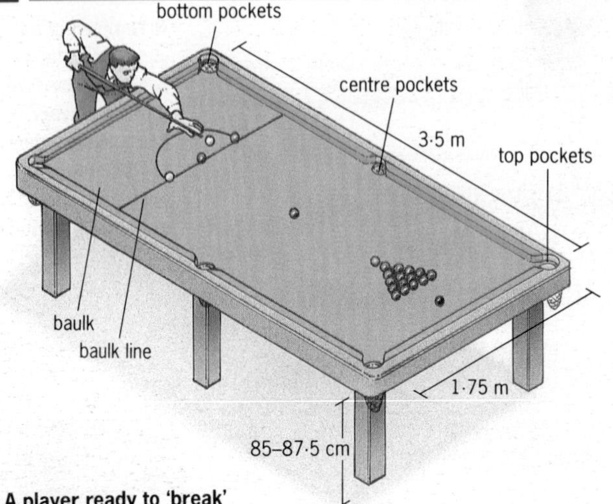

▲ A player ready to 'break' (start the game).

In snooker, there are 22 balls: 15 reds, 6 colours and the white cue-ball. The player must pot a red ball and then a colour ball, alternately. The colour ball is returned to the table. When all the reds are gone the colours are potted in a fixed order. The maximum break is 147:

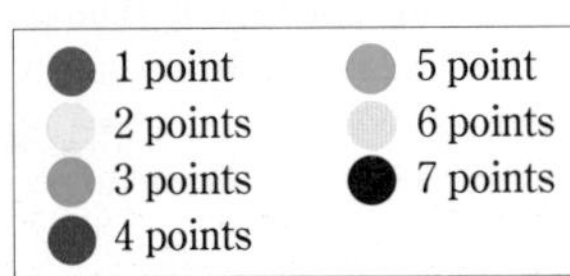

15 reds and 15 blacks, followed by all the colours.

Snow

▲ Snow crystals have many different shapes, but each has 6 spokes.

Snowflakes are made up of tiny ice crystals stuck together. Each crystal has six spokes, usually arranged symmetrically.

Snow can be a useful source of water, especially in hot dry countries where snow on high mountains acts like a reservoir, only thawing in very hot weather. The Nile River in Africa would dry up in hot weather without supplies of melting snow from the mountains.

Solar power

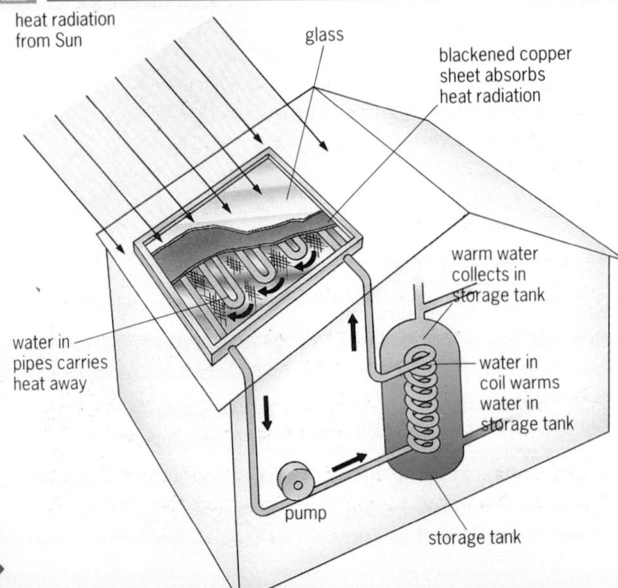

When we turn energy from the Sun into electricity or use it as heat, we call it solar power. On average every square metre (40 sq in) of the Earth's surface facing the Sun gets about 1,000 watts of power from the Sun: the same power as one bar of an electric fire.

Solar cells turn sunlight directly into electricity. In some remote areas, they help to pump water and to power fridges. Space satellites have huge panels of solar cells.

◀ A solar panel absorbs heat radiation from the sun. The heat helps to warm water for the house and so fuel bills are reduced.

Solar system

Pluto Neptune Uranus Saturn Jupiter Mars Earth Venus Mercury
distance from the Sun in million km
5,900 4,497 2,870 1,427 778 228 150 108 58
time to orbit Sun in days
90,502 60,275 30,660 10,767 4,343 687 365 225 88

▲ The major planets in order from the Sun. The planets are drawn to scale but the distances between them are not.

The Sun and all the things in orbit around it make up the Solar System, which is over 12,000 million km (7,500 million miles) across. The word 'solar' comes from the Latin word sol, meaning 'Sun'.

The largest objects in the Solar System, apart from the Sun, are the nine planets: Mercury, Venus, Earth, Mars, Jupiter, Saturn, Uranus, Neptune and Pluto. There are also thousands of minor planets in the Solar System, as well as hundreds of comets and streams of dust and pieces of rock. Astronomers believe that these things are left over from when the Sun formed from a cloud of gas about 5,000 million years ago. They all stay together in the Solar System because of the incredibly strong pull of the Sun's gravity.

Something to do

You can make a scale model of the Solar System to find out just how big it really is. You need to collect ten wide lollipop sticks. Then take them, together with a group of friends, to a park, a playground or a very long garden.

Near the end of one lollipop stick, draw a circle 9 mm across. This is the Sun. Draw a planet on each of the other sticks. Jupiter is a tiny circle 1 mm across, and Saturn is a little smaller. The other planets are dots like this . . .

Push the stick with the Sun on it upright into the the ground. Then position the planets at these distances from the Sun (1 metre equals one big step):

Mercury ⅓ m
Venus ¾ m
Earth 1 m
Mars 1·5 m
Jupiter 5 m
Saturn 10 m
Uranus 21 m
Neptune 32 m
Pluto 42 m

Did you know?

■ The spaces between the planets are huge. If the Sun were a football, the Earth would be a small pea 30 m (100 ft) away.

■ The planet Saturn has at least 23 moons. Titan, the largest, is the only moon in the Solar System that has an atmosphere.

■ Uranus was the first planet to be discovered with the help of a telescope. It was found accidentally by William Herschel in 1781.

Sound

Sounds are tiny vibrations that can travel through air and other materials. The loudness of a sound is measured in decibels (dB).

Typical sound levels in decibels

South Africa

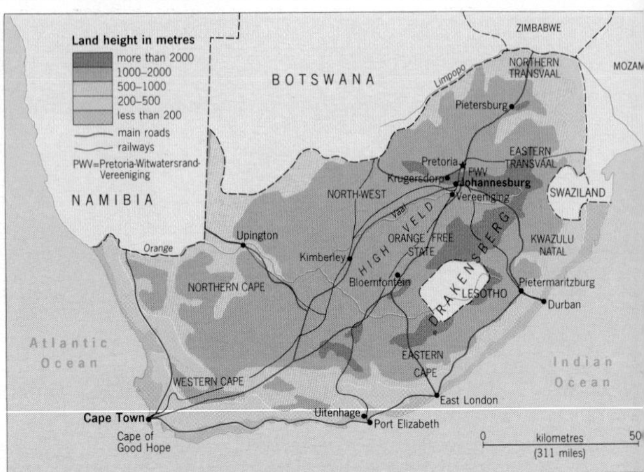

South Africa is the southern tip of the African continent. Inland there are huge, grassy plains called the veld, where lions, elephants and zebras live.

South Africa is Africa's richest country. It mines gold and diamonds, produces more food than it needs, and has many large factories.

Only 18 per cent of South Africans are white, but for many years they ruled the country. Now all races can vote, and there is a black president, Nelson Mandela.

▼ Soweto is a large township on the outskirts of Johannesburg.

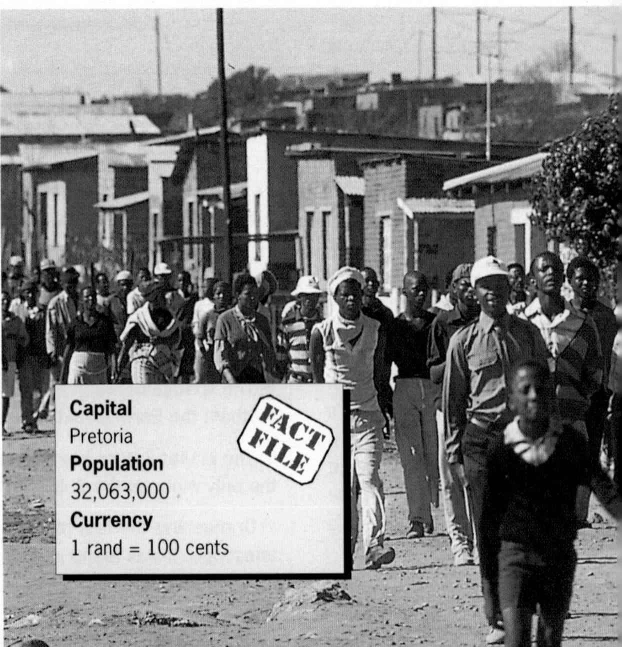

FACT FILE

Capital
Pretoria
Population
32,063,000
Currency
1 rand = 100 cents

South America

FACT FILE

Highest peak
Aconcagua 6,960 m
Largest lake
Maracaibo 13,000 sq km
Largest country
(by population)
Brazil 151,381,000

South America contains the longest mountain range in the world. The Andes is 7,100 km long. To its west is the driest place on Earth, a desert which runs from Ecuador to Chile.

The river Amazon, the world's second longest river, is surrounded by rainforest, which is hot all year and very wet. Many different trees, insects, monkeys and parrots live there. Away from the Amazon the forest thins out, and is replaced by grasslands further south.

Half of South America's population live in Brazil. Brazilians speak Portuguese. Most other South Americans speak Spanish.

Space exploration

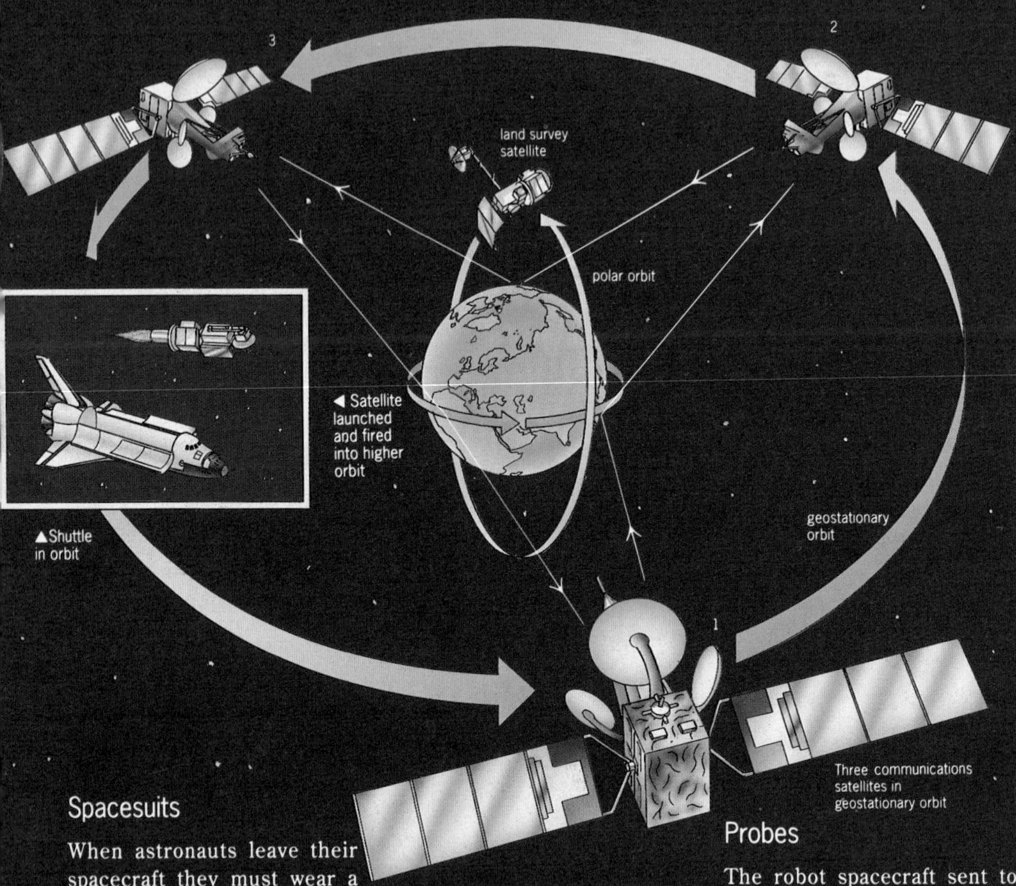

3

2

land survey satellite

polar orbit

◀ Satellite launched and fired into higher orbit

▲Shuttle in orbit

geostationary orbit

1

Three communications satellites in geostationary orbit

Spacesuits

When astronauts leave their spacecraft they must wear a spacesuit, together with a helmet and gloves. The suit's many layers protect against radiation and dust. Its life-support system supplies oxygen, power and water and keeps the astronaut cool.

Space stations

A space station contains everything the astronauts need, including food, air and water, which must all be brought up from the Earth. Large space stations where people can live for many months are built in space by adding extra sections sent up from Earth.

▲Shuttle glides back to Earth and lands.

Probes

The robot spacecraft sent to explore other planets are called probes. Between 1979 and 1989, the Voyager spacecraft flew past Jupiter, Saturn, Uranus and Neptune, sending close-up pictures of them back to Earth.

Communications satellites

These send TV and telephone signals across the oceans. In a 'geostationary' orbit about 35,000 km (22,000 miles) above the Equator their orbit matches the Earth's rotation; so they appear to be stationary in the sky.

Spain

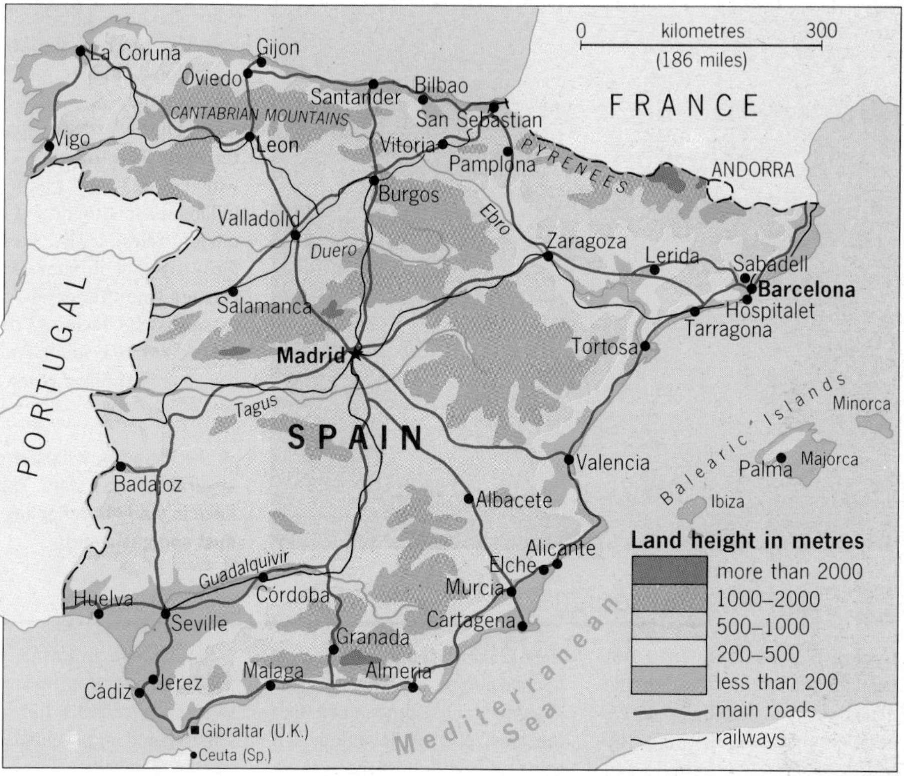

0 kilometres 300 (186 miles)

Land height in metres
- more than 2000
- 1000–2000
- 500–1000
- 200–500
- less than 200
- main roads
- railways

;pain is one of the most nountainous countries in Europe. Лadrid, at 646 m (2,119 ft), is ;urope's highest capital city. In he south Spain has very hot ummers, which attract tourists rom all over Europe. They visit the Mediterranean-facing south and east coasts.

In the North, countryside is green and lush. This is an important industrial area, too. Bilbao is the most important industrial town.

Capital
Madrid
Population
39,085,000
Currency
1 peseta = 100 centimos

FACT FILE

Spiders

ll spiders feed mainly on insects r other tiny creatures, although ne largest species catch prey as ig as mice and small birds. piders have pointed fangs with hich to inject their prey with enom. This not only paralyses the rey but also breaks down its flesh o liquid. The spider then feeds by ıcking.

Some spiders catch prey by building sticky webs, others such as wolf spiders, rely entirely on their speed and strength to overcome prey. Spitting spiders spit poisonous glue.

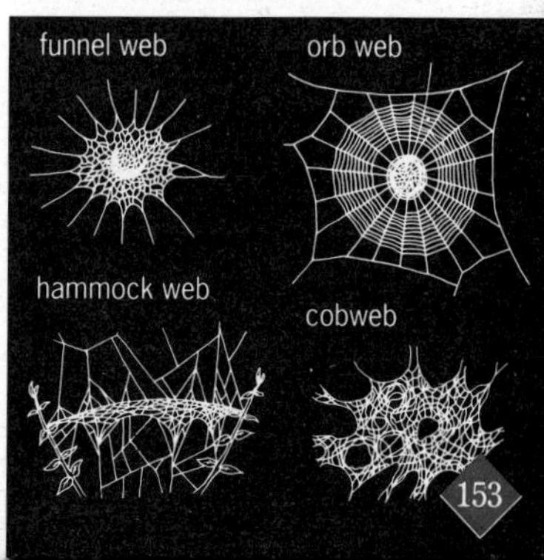

▶ **Different spider species spin different kinds of web to trap their prey.**

Stars

Stars are huge glowing balls of gas. The Sun is a star, but other stars look smaller and fainter because they are much farther away. The nearest star, apart from the Sun, is Proxima Centauri, which is 4·3 light years (40·85 million million km or 25·4 million million miles) away. Stars often form together in families, called clusters. One of the easiest clusters to see is the Pleiades. Its stars formed out of a cloud of dust and gas about 50 million years ago.

◀ The Pleiades, a cluster of several hundred stars. The blue haze is starlight reflecting off a dust and gas cloud.

Stephenson, George

George Stephenson (1781-1848) spent much of his working life designing and building railways and locomotives. He built the world's first public railway, and between 1814 and 1826 built at least 12 railway engines. His most famous engine, 'The Rocket', was designed for a competition to find the most efficient locomotive. It won first prize, but was in fact built by his son Robert.

Stephenson, a former miner, used the money from his invention to set up schools for miners' children and night-schools for the miners themselves.

Stone circles

Stone circles were set up in Europe from about 3000 BC to about 1200 BC. There are more than 900 stone circles in Britain. Some may have been used to observe the movement of the Sun and Moon. In this way, they could be used as a sort of calendar.

The circles took many years to build as the heavy stones had to be dragged to the site over large distances. Many were built inside a *henge*, an area surrounded by a ditch and a bank. Stonehenge had upright stones with capping stones on top. The Heel Stone at its entrance weighs over 20 tonnes. It is placed so that the Sun rises over it on Midsummer day.

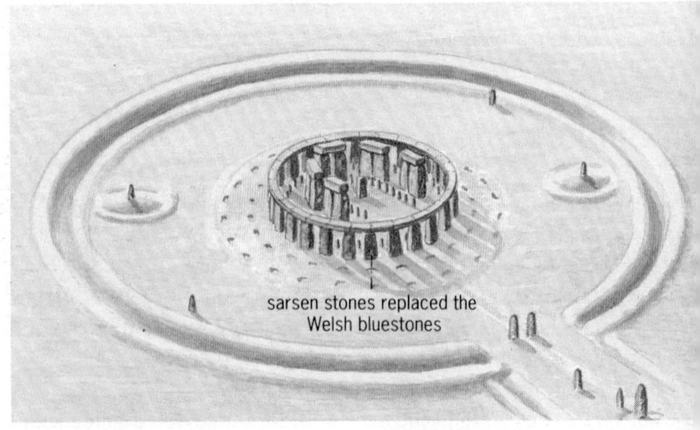

▲ Stonehenge as it would have looked in 1500 BC.

Streams

The speed at which a stream flows determines the kind of plants and animals which live in it. This is a slow-flowing stream.

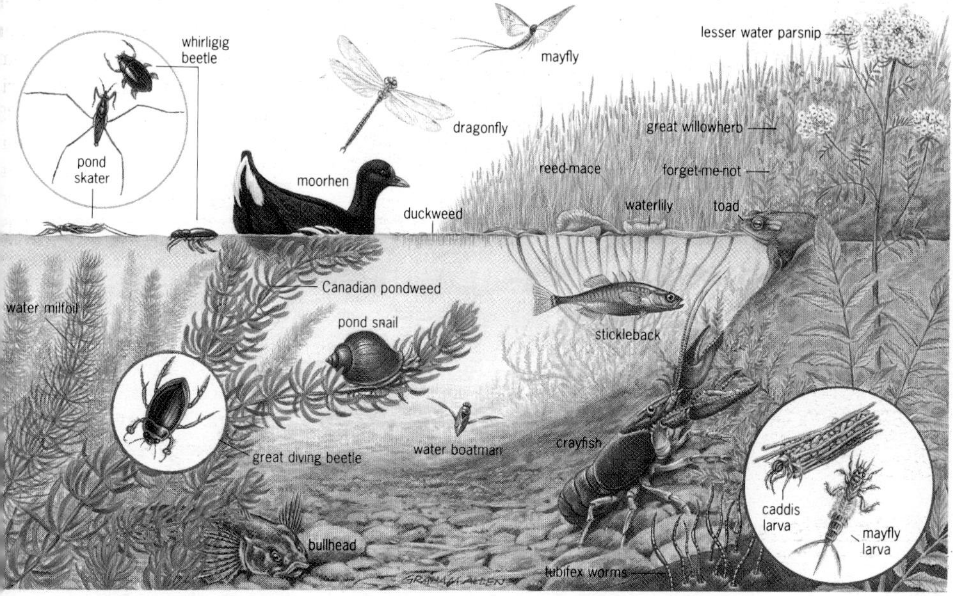

Stuart Britain

ames VI of Scotland became James of England when Elizabeth I ied. James and his son Charles I oth had trouble with Parliament ver money and religion. This led o the Civil War and the execution f Charles I.

From 1649 to 1660 Britain did ot have a king. It was called a Commonwealth' and from 1653 liver Cromwell ruled as Lord rotector. Then Charles II was nvited back to be king. His brother ames II was a Catholic who tried o rule without Parliament. He was orced out, and William and Mary ecame joint king and queen.

By the time of Queen Anne, the ast Stuart, the rulers had become onstitutional monarchs', which eant they had to keep the rules ade by Parliament.

▲ The execution of Charles I, 30 January, 1649. Many Roundheads who had fought against the king during the Civil War were horrified at his death.

Submarines

Submarines float or sink by emptying or filling their ballast tanks. Small submarines use electric motors, but larger ones are nuclear powered. The world's biggest submarines, the Russian Typhoon Class, weigh over 26,000 tonnes.

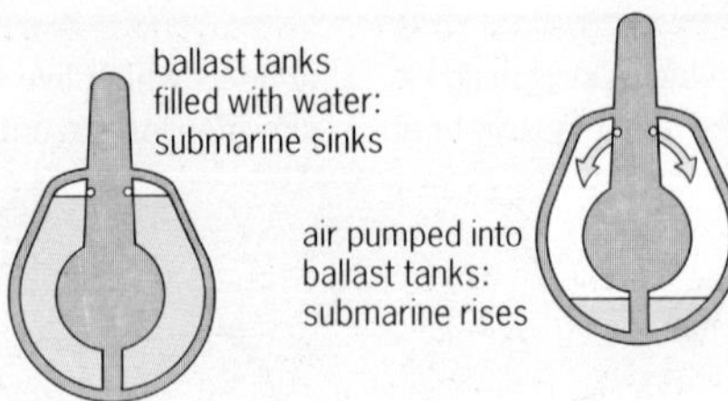

Sudan

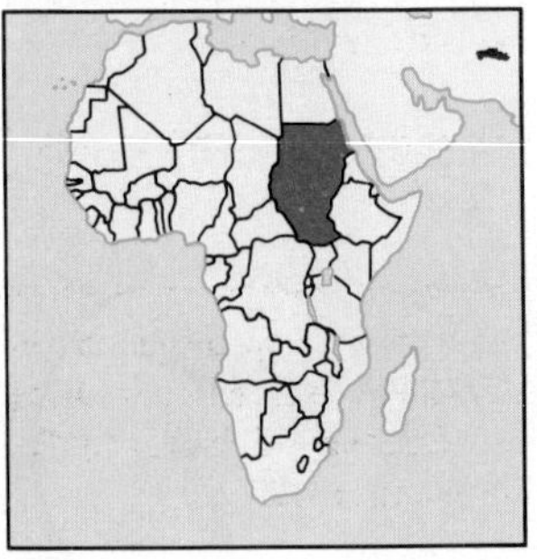

Sudan is the largest country in Africa. It is very poor, and suffers from drought.

FACT FILE

Capital
Khartoum
Population
29,971,000
Currency
1 Sudanese pound
= 100 piastres

Sugar

Sugar is made both from sugar cane and sugar beet. Sugar cane grows in tropical areas such as the Caribbean, Brazil and India. Sugar beet grows in temperate areas such as Britain.

Sugar is pure sucrose, a carbohydrate. It gives energy, but is also blamed for tooth decay.

Sun

Without the heat and light energy from the 5,000 million-year-old Sun, there would be no life on Earth. This giant ball of hot gas, 150 million km (93 million miles) away, measures as much as 109 Earths side by side. The temperature at its core is over 15 million °C.

◀ **The Sun, taken in 1973 from Skylab, a space station in orbit around the Earth.**

Sweden

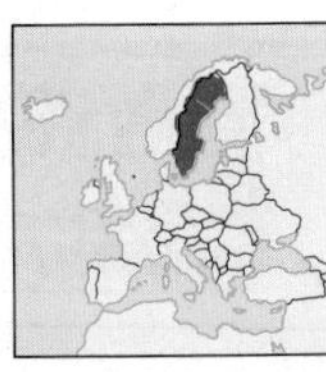

Sweden is in northern Europe. Over half of it is covered by thick forests, and there are over 95,000 lakes. It has many natural resources including timber and iron ore, which make it one of the richest countries in Europe.

Capital
Stockholm
Population
8,673,000
Currency
1 Swedish krona = 100 öre

Switzerland

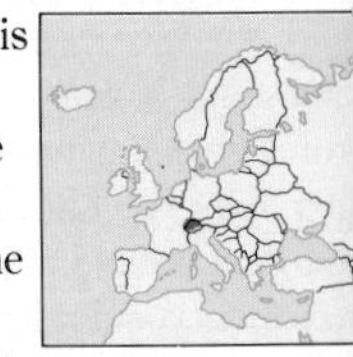

Switzerland is in central Europe. The Swiss Alps cover half the country. Tourists visit the Alps for skiing, climbing and sightseeing.

Farmers keep cattle for milk to be used in cheeses, such as Gruyère and Emmental. The milk is also used to make Swiss chocolate.

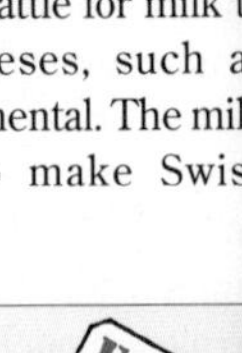

Capital
Bern
Population
6,911,000
Currency
1 Swiss franc = 100 centimes

Tanks

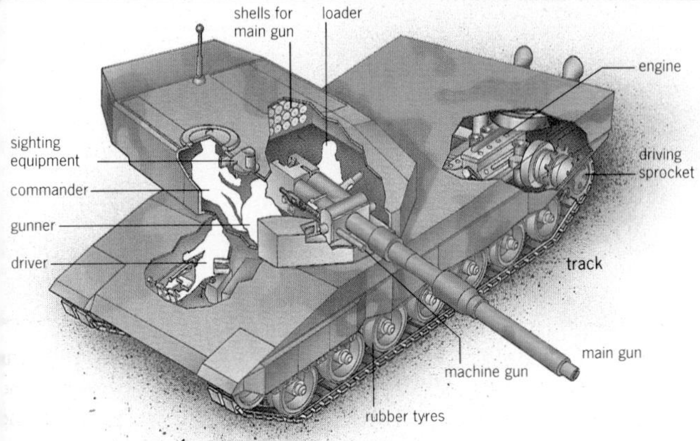

Tanks run on tracks, not wheels, so they can travel across rough and soft ground. Their armour is made of steel plate and can be as thick as 12 cm (4·5 in) at the front. The first tanks were used in World War I, for moving across muddy ground and breaking through barbed wire and trenches. They were developed in Britain and France from the idea of the new tracked farm tractors.

◀ **The layout of a modern tank.**

Tchaikovsky, Piotr

Piotr Tchaikovsky was born in Russia in 1840. He became a law student, but then, at the age of 23, he decided to give his life to music. He wrote his first symphony at 26 and went on to write his famous ballets, *Swan Lake*, *Sleeping Beauty*, and *Nutcracker*. *Swan Lake* was not appreciated during Tchaikovsky's lifetime; it was only performed once. Tchaikovsky died of cholera in 1893.

Teeth

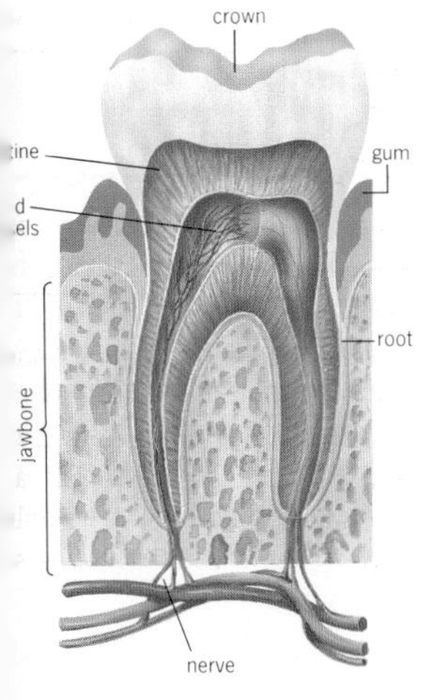

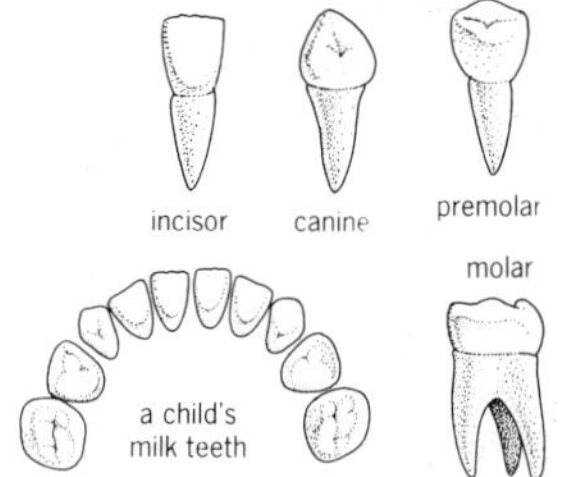

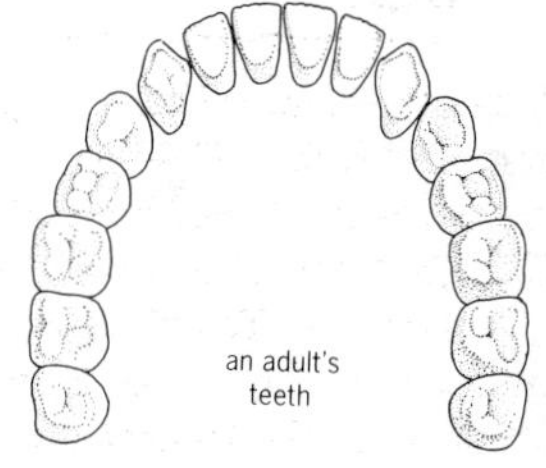

The part of the tooth you can see is called the crown. Below this, hidden in the gums, is the tooth's root which fixes the tooth firmly into the jawbone. Most of the tooth is made of a hard material called dentine. The crown is coated with even harder enamel. Inside the root is a cavity filled with pulp consisting of blood vessels and nerve fibres.

Babies are born with no teeth showing, but with two sets of tooth buds hidden in their gums. The first teeth, the milk teeth, appear during the first five years, and then are replaced by the permanent teeth.

Telephones

The first telephones were built in 1876 by the American Alexander Graham Bell. Now there are over 75 million telephones throughout the world, making the telephone the most widespread means of long-distance communication. A telephone conversation can travel from Britain to America in about a quarter of a second. It is sent via a satellite 36,000 km (22,000 miles) above the Atlantic Ocean.

Television

On a TV screen, what you actually see are lots of still pictures flashing on the screen one after another. In Britain, 25 complete pictures are put on the screen every second.

A colour TV picture is really separate red, green and blue pictures on top of each other, but they combine to give one full colour picture. The first colour TV programme was transmitted in the USA in 1951.

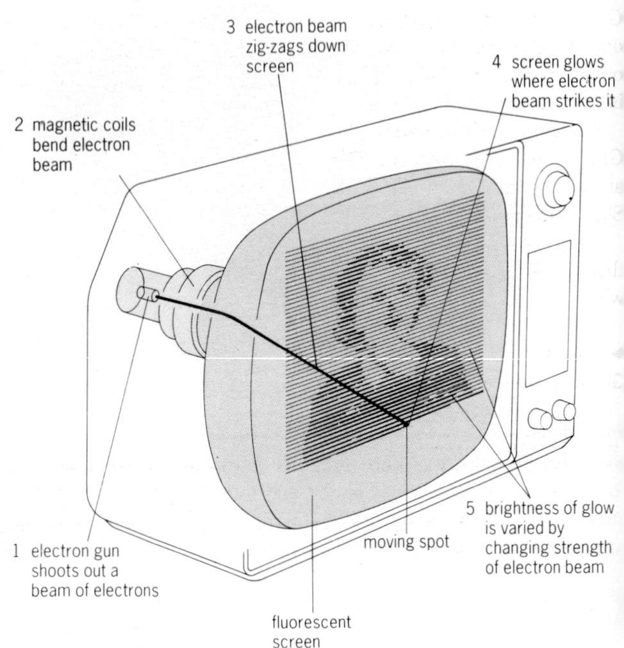

▶ The picture on a black-and-white screen is made up of hundreds of horizontal lines which change between light and dark along their length. The lines are made by a beam of electrons which strikes the back of the screen and makes it glow.

Tennis

Tennis is a game for two (singles) or four (doubles) played on a court. Players use rackets to hit the ball over a low net. The aim is to win points by hitting the ball so that your opponent cannot hit it back. Points make up 'games', and games make up 'sets'.

The most famous tennis tournament is Wimbledon, which began in 1877.

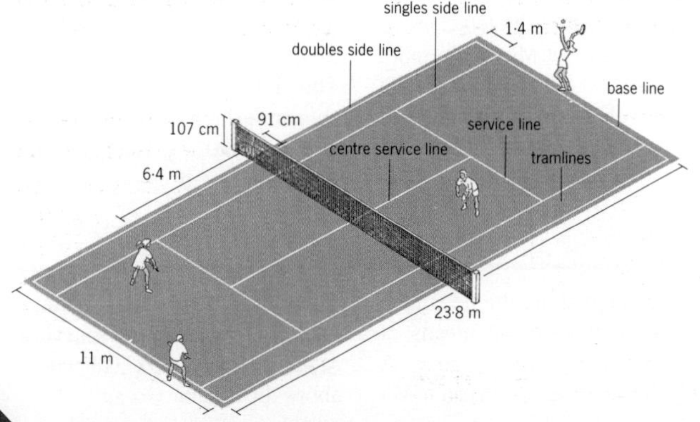

◀ Doubles players at the moment of service. The ball must go over the net and bounce in the service court opposite.

Thatcher, Margaret

Margaret Thatcher was born in 1925. She was elected to Parliament in 1959, and became leader of the Conservative Party in 1975.

Her party won the General Election in 1979, and so she became Britain's first woman prime minister. She held that post until 1990, when she resigned.

Theatres

The first theatres were built in Greece about 2,500 years ago as open-air theatres. Epidaurus has one with seats for 12,000 people. It is still used today.

Shakespeare's theatre, the Globe, was also open-air. The audience sat all round the stage, so Shakespeare called it a 'wooden O'.

After Shakespeare's time, most theatres were built as great halls with roofs.

Artist's reconstruction of the Globe in Shakespeare's time.

Tigers

Tigers are large and muscular cats; they can travel 12 km in a night, and leap 10 m, but 90% of their hunts will end in failure.

Time

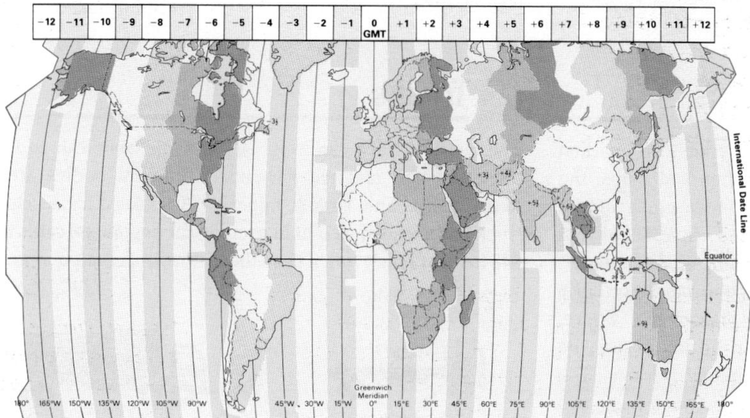

The world has 24 time zones. When you go west you put your watch back 1 hour for every time zone you cross. When you travel east you add 1 hour. At the International Date Line one day ends and another begins. The line has been adjusted so it does not cross a country.

Torches

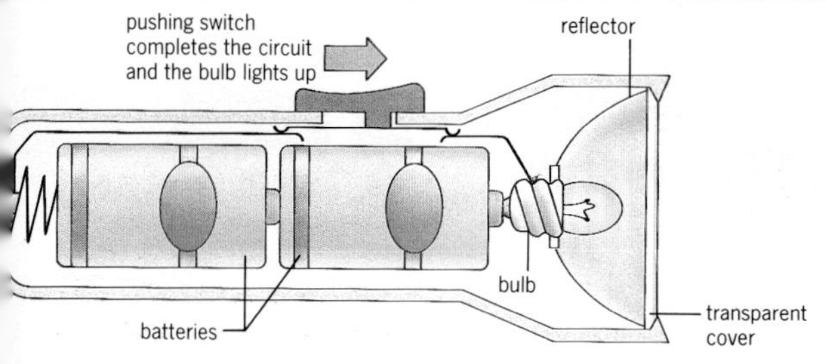

The Romans made torches out of twisted hemp or flax which was dipped in oil or fat to make it burn brightly. The word 'torch' comes from the Latin word *torquere* meaning 'to twist'. Modern torches are powered by electricity from cells inside a battery.

Trees

Only a small part of a tree trunk is living: a layer of dividing cells, the cambium, makes new bark, and another cambium layer makes new sapwood and phloem. The sapwood transports the water and minerals the tree needs and the phloem transports food made in the leaves. It is this second layer of cambium which gives rise to annual rings.

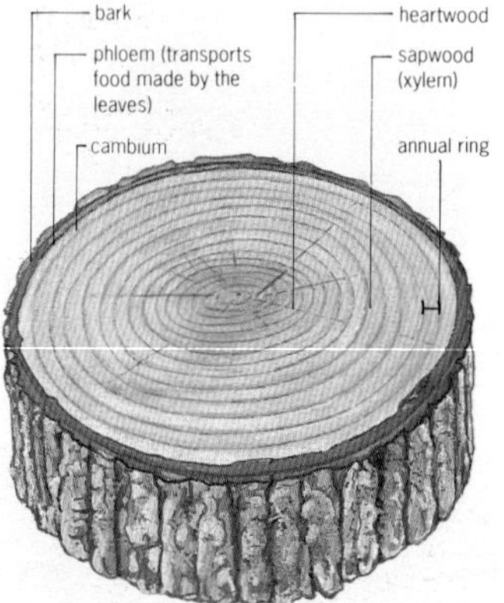

▲ **Trees in winter.**

Did you know?

■ The largest living tree is a giant sequoia in the Redwood National Park, California, USA. It is over 111 m (366 ft) tall.

Tropics

Two imaginary lines are marked on world globes and maps: the Tropic of Cancer north of the Equator, and the Tropic of Capricorn south of the Equator. These mark the most northerly and southerly positions where, depending on the time of year, the Sun can be directly overhead. The tropical areas between these two lines are hot all year round but with varying amounts of rainfall. At the Equator plenty of rain falls every month.

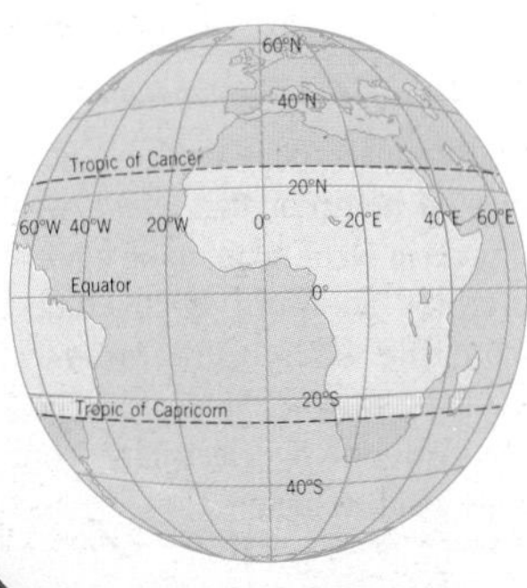

Trucks

The heaviest truck can weigh 40 tonnes or more and may have up to 16 gears. The largest tipper truck has a loaded weight of over 548 tonnes. Trucks often have the same basic cab and chassis, but different bodies are bolted on. Articulated trucks have two parts: the engine and cab at the front, and the trailer at the rear.

flat bed truck

tanker for bulk liquids, powder or grain

truck with rubbish skip

truck with drawbar trailer

tipper

articulated truck with container

Tudor England

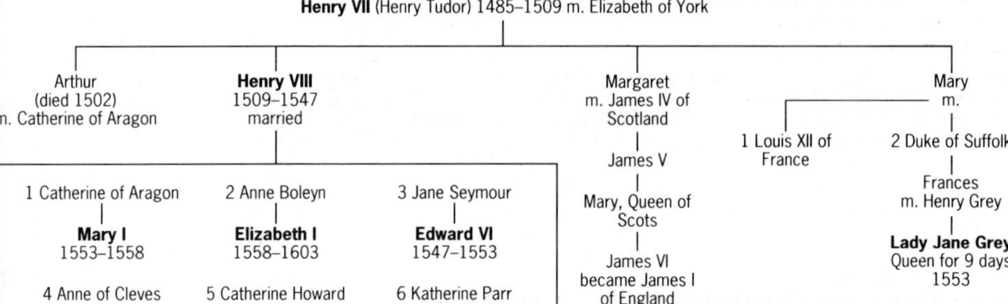

▲ **Tudor family tree showing the years of reign.**

Tudor England was a time of change. After Henry VIII's quarrel with the Pope over his divorce, England became a Protestant country.

Life was not easy for ordinary people in Tudor times. Diseases such as the bubonic plague killed many. Rising prices made food expensive and many people could not find work.

But some things improved. Books became easy to buy after William Caxton started printing in 1476. So many more people learned to read and write. Explorers such as Drake and Raleigh brought new goods back to England including potatoes and tobacco.

In 1588 the English navy defeated the Spanish Armada. And by 1601, the Poor Laws gave some help to those who were poor because they were too old, too young, or too ill, to earn a living.

 **Did you know?** 

- **When the Tudors ruled in England, the Stuarts ruled Scotland.**
- **About one baby in five died before its fifth birthday.**
- **In wartime more men died from diseases like typhus than from battle wounds.**

Turkey

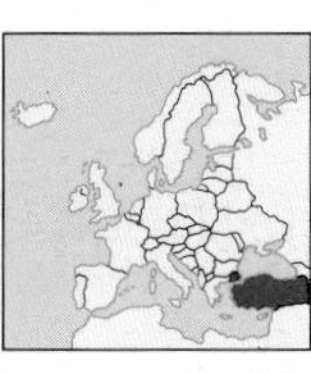

Turkey is at the eastern end of the Mediterranean. It is divided into two parts, Thrace and Anatolia, by the Sea of Marmara and two straits (the Bosporus and the Dardanelles). Thrace is in Europe. Anatolia is in Asia. Istanbul, built on the Bosporus, is the only city to be in two continents.

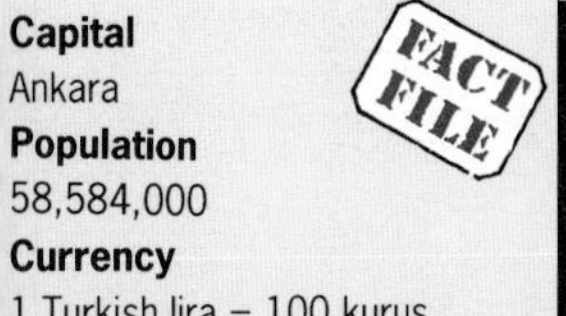

Capital
Ankara
Population
58,584,000
Currency
1 Turkish lira = 100 kurus

Turner, Joseph Mallord William

Joseph Turner was born in 1775. At 14 he became a student at the Royal Academy schools. Two years later his pictures were shown to the public.

For 50 years Turner went on sketching tours. He was influenced by new ideas from other artists and other countries.

He also worked very hard. As a result, he produced 500 oil paintings and more than 20,000 water-colours before he died in 1851. He left most of his pictures to the nation. They can be seen at the Tate Gallery in London.

Uganda

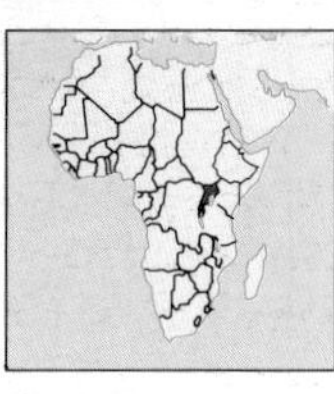

Uganda is in the middle of Africa. Rivers and lakes cover about one sixth of the country. Lake Victoria, which is shared with Kenya and Tanzania, is Africa's largest lake. There are about 40 different languages spoken in Uganda.

FACT FILE

Capital
Kampala
Population
17,194,000
Currency
1 Uganda shilling = 100 cents

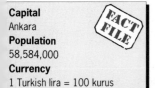

 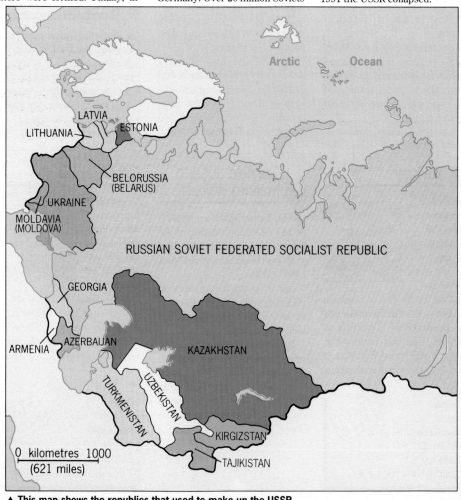 Union of Soviet Socialist Republics' history

For almost 70 years the Soviet Union was a powerful country, ruled by the Communist Party. Communists took power first in Russia in 1917, and after a civil war, the Russians created the USSR, by dividing the territories of the old Russian empire into republics: Russia itself, Belorussia, Ukraine, and a region later split into Georgia, Armenia and Azerbaijan. In central Asia the republics of Kazakhstan, Uzbekistan and others were formed. Finally, in 1940, the USSR forced the three Baltic states of Estonia, Latvia and Lithuania to join.

Russian Communists, led by Lenin till 1924, and then for nearly 30 years by Stalin, had great power. They reorganized the farms into huge cooperatives, so badly managed there was not enough food. In the 1930s millions starved.

In World War II the Soviet Union fought against Nazi Germany. Over 20 million Soviets were killed. By 1945 Soviet troops had occupied Poland, east Germany and other countries of eastern Europe. These nations also became Communist.

For 50 years the USSR built up armaments, and faced the USA in a Cold War. When Gorbachev became leader in 1985, he made changes. There were elections and the Communists gradually lost power. The different republics demanded independence, and in 1991 the USSR collapsed.

▲ **This map shows the republics that used to make up the USSR.**

United Nations

Nearly all the countries in the world belong to the United Nations (UN). It was set up in 1945 to provide a place where countries can discuss any world problems. The UN headquarters are in New York.

United States of America

There are 50 states in the United States of America. Forty-eight are together between Canada and Mexico. The 49th state, Alaska, is separated from the rest by Canada. The 50th, Hawaii, is over 3,700 km away in the Pacific Ocean. Each state has its own laws and government. The federal government in Washington, DC organizes the whole USA.

Because it is so large, different parts of the USA have very different features. Arizona and New Mexico have large deserts. Washington and Oregon have vast forests. Louisiana and Florida have swamps. California suffers from earthquakes.

But its size also gives the USA plenty of valuable resources. American farms produce maize, wheat, soya beans, tomatoes, cheese, fruit, beef and chickens. Their industries make goods which are sold all over the world, such as Ford cars and Coca Cola.

The Statue of Liberty was a gift from France in 1886. It was a symbol of hope and freedom to immigrants arriving by sea from Europe.

FACT FILE

Capital
Washington, DC
Population
255,414,000
Currency
1 dollar = 100 cents

Land height in metres
more than 2000
1000–2000
500–1000
200–500
less than 200
land below sea level
main roads
railways

Alaska and Hawaii are also in the U.S.A.

0 kilometres 500 (311 miles)

Universe

The Universe is everything that exists, from the Earth out to the farthest parts of space. It is filled with countless galaxies.

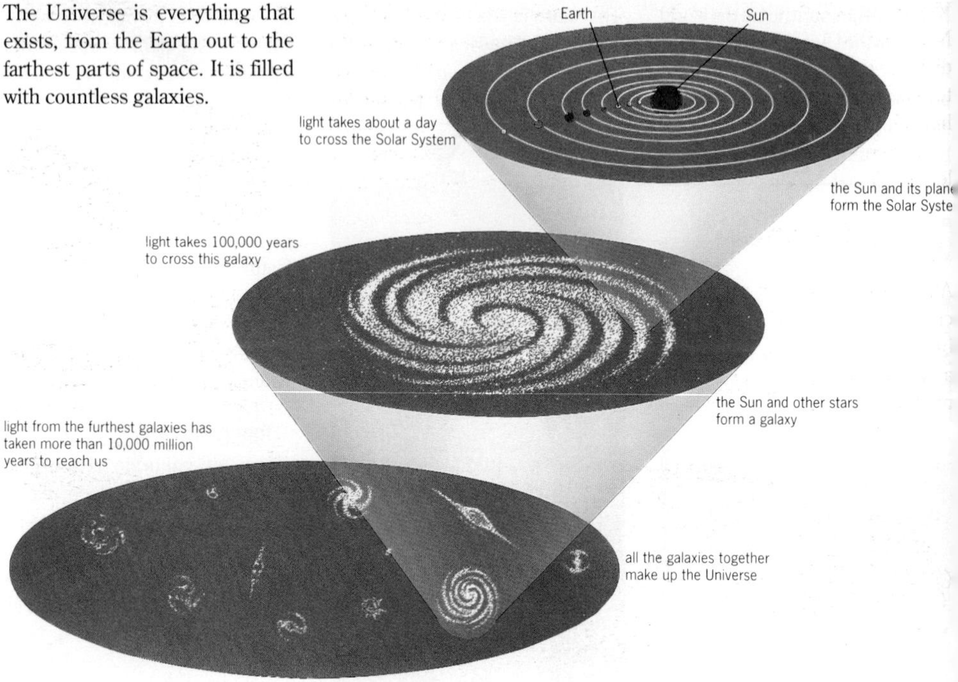

Earth
Sun
light takes about a day
to cross the Solar System
the Sun and its plane
form the Solar Syste
light takes 100,000 years
to cross this galaxy
the Sun and other stars
form a galaxy
light from the furthest galaxies has
taken more than 10,000 million
years to reach us
all the galaxies together
make up the Universe

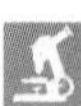

Vacuums

A vacuum is a completely empty space from which even the air has been removed. A vacuum is needed inside a television tube, so that the electron beam can move freely. Inside a Thermos flask there is a partial vacuum between two glass walls. This, together with the shiny surfaces and the stopper, helps reduce the movement of heat, keeping hot drinks hot and cold drinks cold.

Inside a vacuum cleaner a fan produces a part vacuum. Air rushes into this, carrying dust with it. The first vacuum cleaner, made in 1901, was pulled by a horse and parked outside people's homes. A long tube was passed into the house to clean the carpets.

Valves

handle
screw
thread
washer
blocks flow
washer
raised

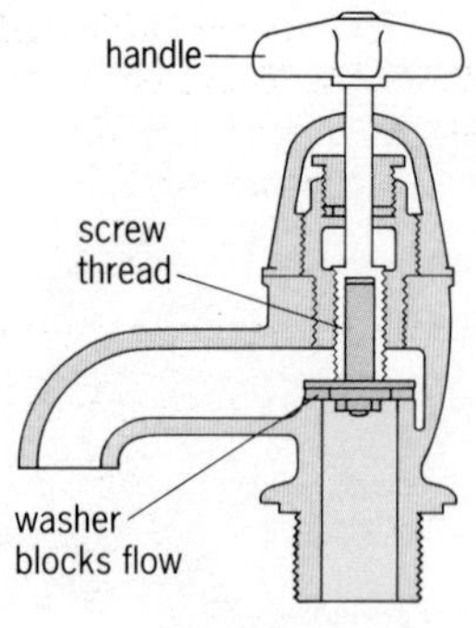

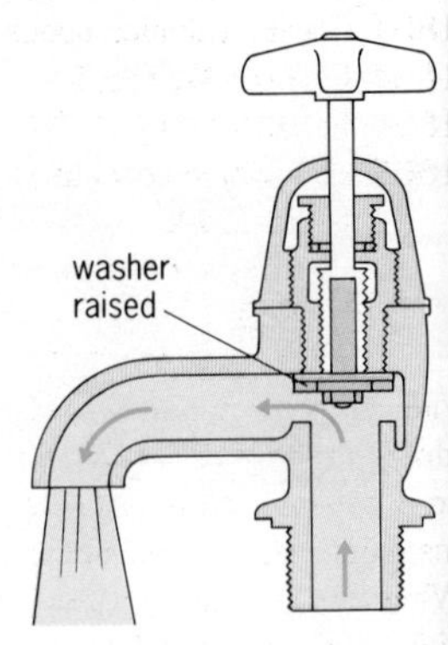

A tap is a type of valve which controls the flow of water into a sink or bath. All valves are used to control a flow, usually of a liquid or a gas. Valves in car engines open and shut to let gases in and out o the cylinders. Some valves allow a two-way flow whilst others, such as the ones on bicycle tyres, allow a flow in one direction only.

Van Gogh, Vincent

Vincent Van Gogh was born in the Netherlands in 1853. He was a difficult, moody child. He trained to be a missionary, and later taught himself to draw and paint.

He moved to France where he learned to use bright colours and bold brushwork in his paintings. He only sold one painting in his lifetime. Gradually he became more depressed and cut off his own ear. In 1890 he committed suicide. Van Gogh's paintings are now worth millions of pounds.

Vegetables

▼ Vegetables are edible plants. Different parts of the plant may be eaten.

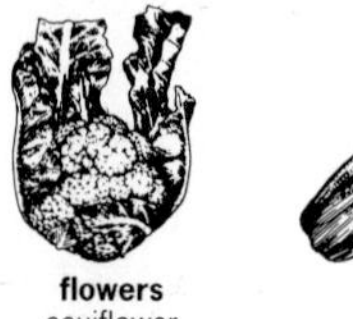

flowers
cauliflower

stems
celery

leaves
lettuce

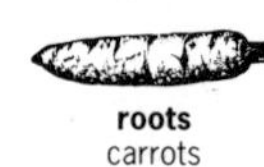

roots
carrots

Vertebrates

All animals with backbones are called vertebrates. There are five big classes of vertebrate: fish, amphibians, reptiles, birds and mammals.

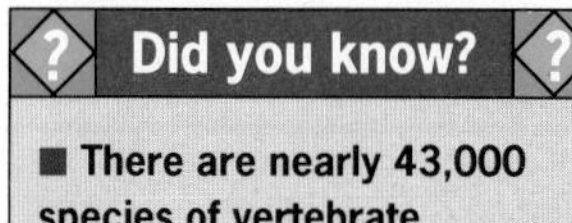

Did you know?

■ There are nearly 43,000 species of vertebrate.

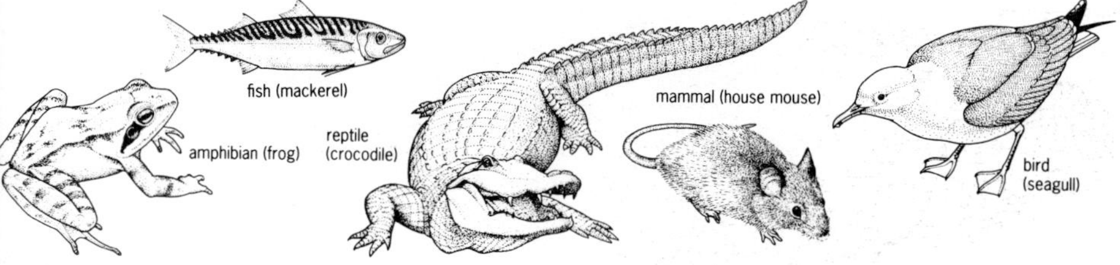

Victorian Britain

1837 Victoria becomes Queen
1840 Victoria marries Albert
1851 Great Exhibition opens
1854 Crimean War begins
1857 Indian 'Mutiny'
1865 First woman doctor begins work
1867 Many workers in towns get the right to vote
1870 Education Act
Trade Unions made legal
1875 Public Health Act
1884 Many workers in the country get the vote
1892 Keir Hardie elected as first socialist MP
1899 Boer War begins
1901 Death of Victoria

Video

Video recorders use the same basic idea as cassette players by storing sound and picture signals on magnetic tape inside cassettes. When the cassette is put inside the video recorder, the tape moves slowly past the recording/playback heads. Picture signals are recorded on the tape in diagonal stripes.

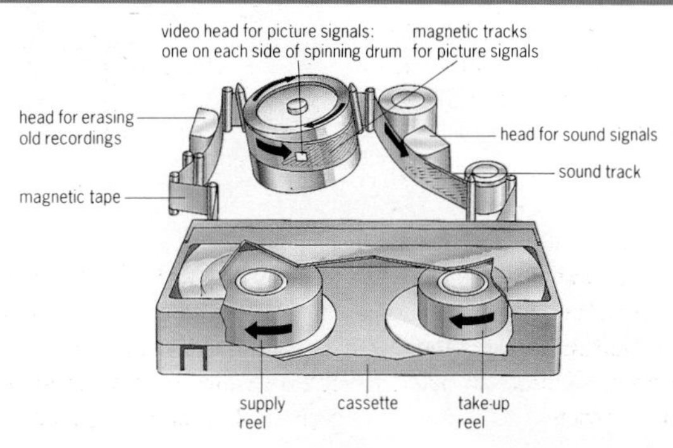

Video cassette inside a video recorder.

Vietnam

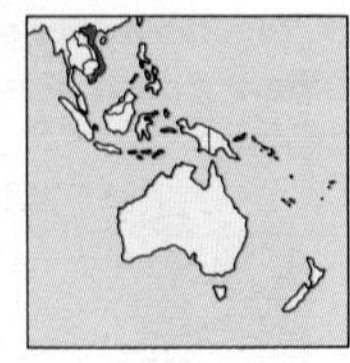

Vietnam is in south east Asia. It extends 1,600 km down from China. At its narrowest point it is only 50 km wide. Most of Vietnam is hot and wet. Nearly three quarters of its people work on farms. Fishing and forestry are also important industries.

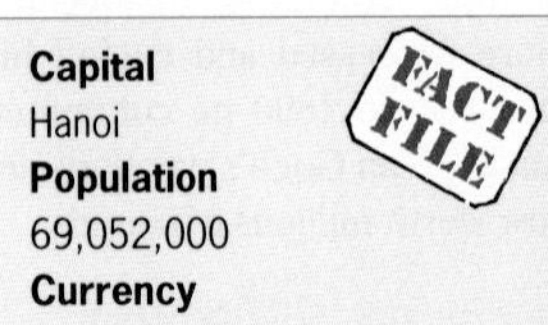

FACT FILE

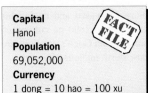

Capital
Hanoi
Population
69,052,000
Currency
1 dong = 10 hao = 100 xu

Vietnam War

From the 1950s communist guerrillas supported by North Vietnam tried to overthrow the non-communist government of South Vietnam. In 1964 the USA sent troops to help South Vietnam by dropping bombs and chemicals on the north. When the Americans realized they could not win, they left in 1973. The two Vietnams reunited in 1976.

Vikings

The Vikings lived in Norway, Denmark and Sweden. When they needed more land in the 8th century, they moved to other countries such as Britain and France.

Vikings were farmers who grew grain and vegetables, and kept cattle, sheep, pigs and chickens. A Viking farmhouse usually had a great hall where the family lived and cooked on an open fire.

We remember the Vikings for their daring journeys in longships. They raided other countries, and were also great traders and explorers.

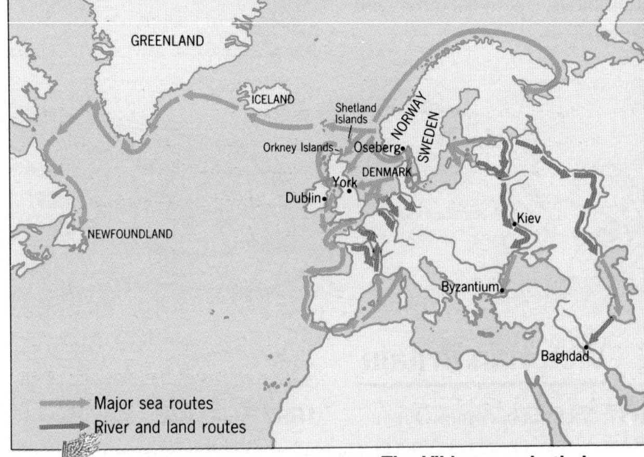

▲ The Vikings made their journeys between the years 780 and 1100.

◀ Viking longship.

1 Sail
2 Figurehead
3 Keel
4 Side rudder
5 Deck
6 Hull
7 Shields
8 Mastfish
9 Mast
10 Crutches

Did you know?

■ In about 1000 AD Leif Ericsson the Viking sailed across the Atlantic, about 500 years before Columbus.

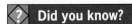

Vitamins

	Found in:	Used for:
A	Carrots, milk, butter, eggs, fish-liver oils, liver, green vegetables	Keeping skin and bones healthy, fighting disease and infection
B	Yeast, wholemeal bread, nuts, peas, beans, fish, meat, eggs, milk, cheese, green vegetables	Helping the body to release energy from food for growth, keeping skin and nerves healthy
C	Oranges, lemons, limes, tomatoes, blackcurrants, and green vegetables	Helping wounds to heal, keeping blood, gums and teeth healthy, protect against colds
D	Liver, butter, cheese, eggs, fish. Also made in the body by the effects of sunlight on the skin	Keeping bones and teeth strong and healthy. Important in childhood
E	Wholemeal bread, brown rice, butter, green vegetables	Believed to help cell growth and wound healing
K	Green vegetables, liver	Clotting blood

Voice

The basic sound of the human voice is produced by organs situated in the throat and mouth. We change that basic sound by altering the shape of our mouths, and by moving our tongues very quickly and precisely. In other animals the voice may be produced by different organs: crickets, for example, sing by rubbing their wings together.

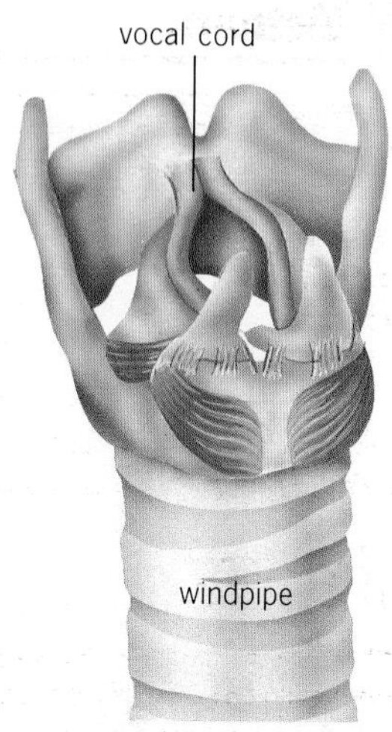

▲ The larynx (voice box) is a thickened part of the windpipe containing flaps called vocal cords. Air forced out over the vocal cords produces the basic sound of the voice.

Volcanoes

Some volcanoes give off clouds of ash and dust when they erupt. In others red-hot lava pours down the sides. Mauna Loa, the world's largest volcano, has its base on the ocean floor, 5,180 m (16,995 ft) below sea-level. When Krakatau in Indonesia erupted in 1883, it was heard 5,000 km (3,100 miles) away.

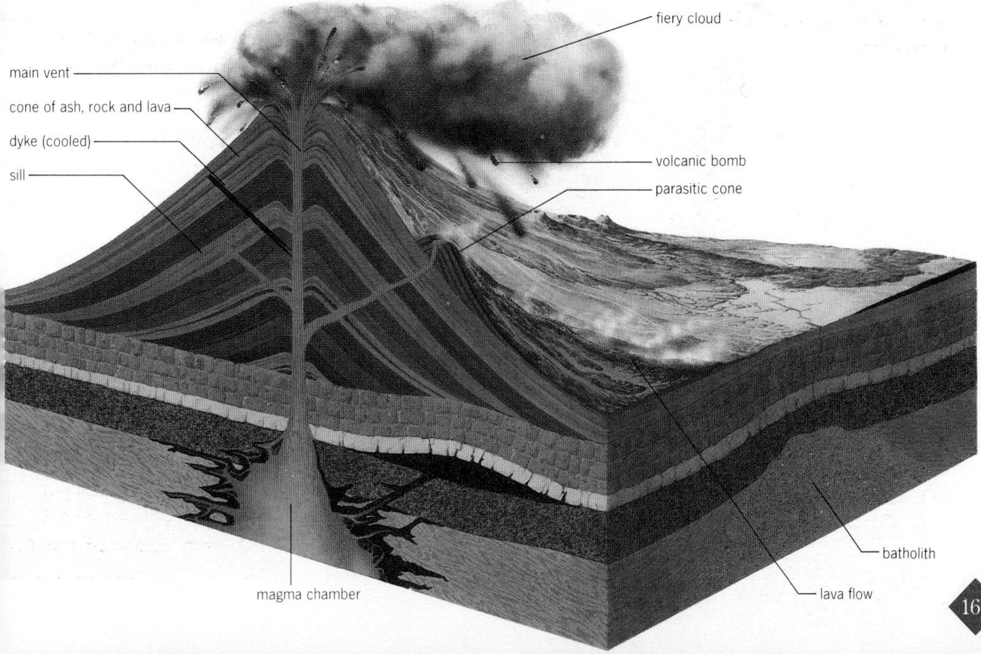

Wales

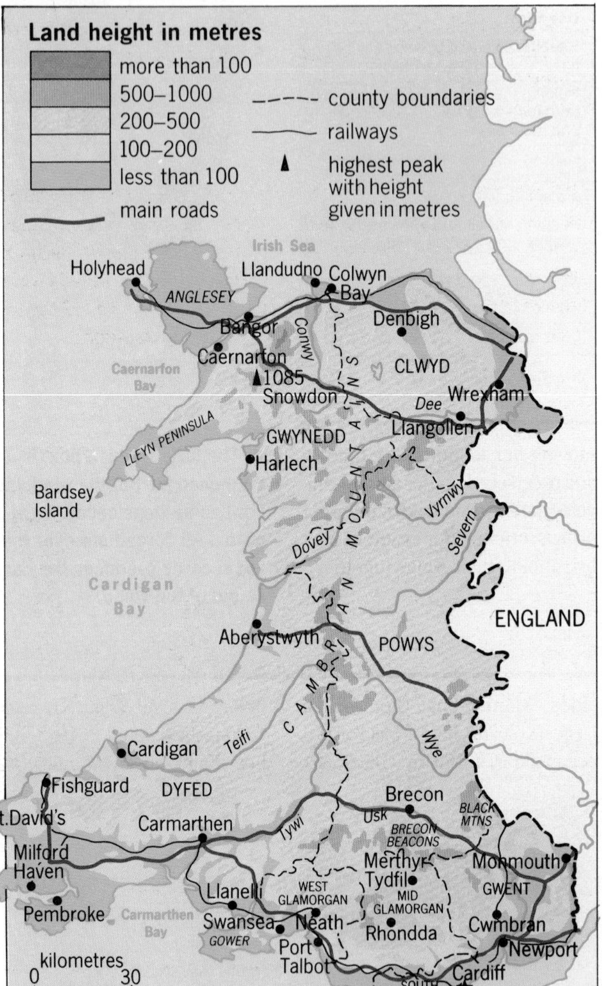

Land height in metres
more than 100
500–1000
200–500
100–200
less than 100
main roads
county boundaries
railways
highest peak with height given in metres

Irish Sea
Holyhead
ANGLESEY
Llandudno
Colwyn Bay
Bangor
Conwy
Denbigh
Caernarfon
Caernarfon Bay
1085
Snowdon
CLWYD
Wrexham
Dee
Llangollen
LLEYN PENINSULA
GWYNEDD
Harlech
Bardsey Island
Vyrnwy
Severn
Dovey
CAMBRIAN MOUNTAINS
Cardigan Bay
Aberystwyth
POWYS
ENGLAND
Cardigan
Teifi
Wye
Fishguard
DYFED
Brecon
BLACK MTNS
St.David's
Carmarthen
Tywi
Usk
BRECON BEACONS
Milford Haven
Merthyr Tydfil
Monmouth
Llanelli
WEST GLAMORGAN
MID GLAMORGAN
GWENT
Pembroke
Carmarthen Bay
Swansea
Neath
Rhondda
Cwmbran
GOWER
Port Talbot
Newport
kilometres
0 30
(18 miles)
Cardiff
SOUTH GLAMORGAN
Bristol Channel
Barry

Wales is part of the United Kingdom. It has many hills and mountains. The highest is Yr Wyddfa (Snowdon).

Its mountain rivers are used for hydroelectric power. Water from the lakes of mid-Wales is piped to English cities such as Birmingham and Liverpool.

About half a million people speak Cymraeg (Welsh) as well as English and a few speak only Cymraeg. Road signs and official documents are in both languages.

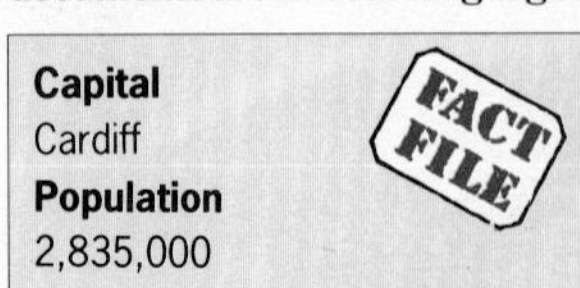

Capital
Cardiff
Population
2,835,000

Welsh history

When the Romans invaded Wales they could not defeat the Celts who had lived there for about 700 years. The Normans could not conquer the mountains either. Eventually Edward I defeated Llywelyn ap Gruffudd in 1282. He built castles throughout Wales and made his son the Prince of Wales.

England and Wales united in 1536. The Bible was printed in Welsh in 1588 and this helped to keep the Welsh language alive.

After 1850, many people moved to work in the coal mines, ironworks and slate quarries. These industries declined in the 20th century and a lot of jobs were lost.

Did you know?

■ **The patron saint of Wales is St David. He helped to defend Christianity in Wales from the pagan Anglo-Saxons.**

▼ The wives and daughters of miners in 1910, carrying coal home from the tip to use during a strike.

Washington, George

George Washington was born in America in 1732 when it was still ruled by Britain. He became the general who defeated the British and made America a free country.

In 1789 he was elected as first President of the USA. When he died in 1799 he was said to be 'first in war, first in peace, and first in the hearts of his countrymen'.

Water cycle

Water is constantly being recycled in a process called the water cycle. The oceans hold about 97 per cent of the world's water, and a further 2 per cent is frozen in the polar ice-caps. This means that only about 1 per cent of the world's water is going round and round the water cycle at any one time.

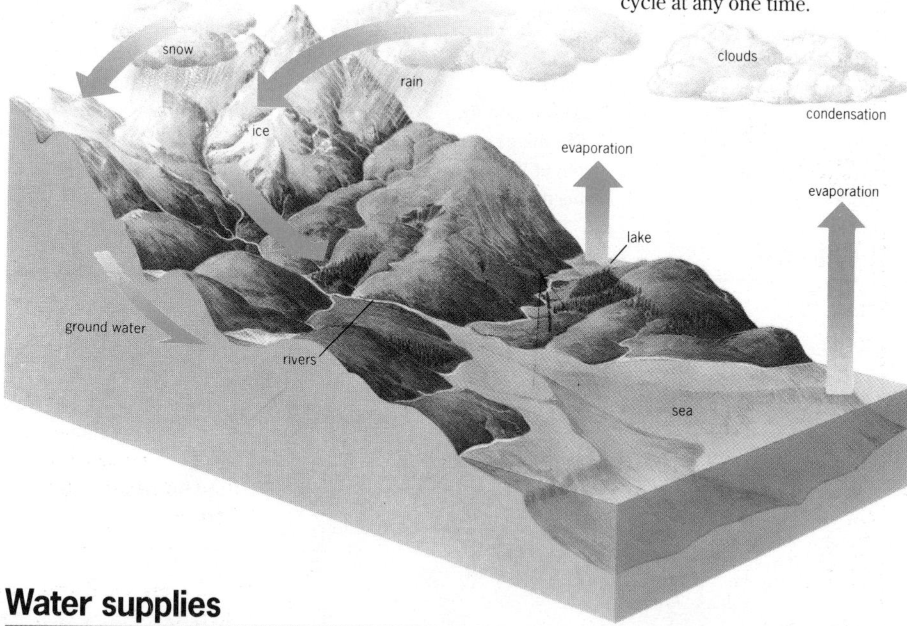

Water supplies

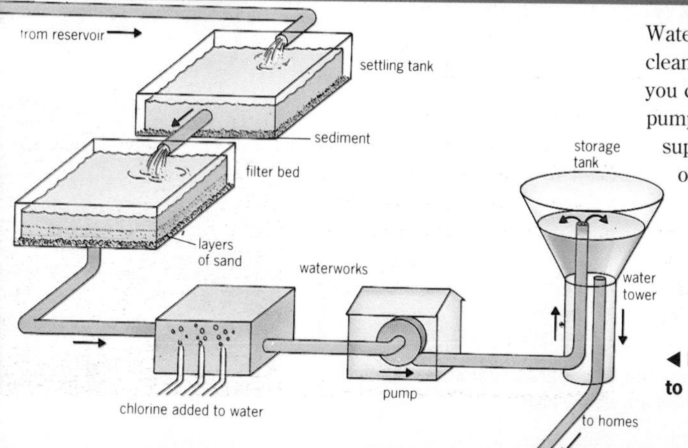

◀ **How rainwater is treated to make it safe to drink.**

Water from a reservoir must be cleaned at the waterworks before you can use it at home. It is then pumped to a storage tank which supplies homes, factories and other buildings in the area.

Wellington, Duke of (Arthur Wellesley)

Arthur Wellesley was born in Dublin in 1769. He joined the army at 18 and served in India, where he became a major-general, for eight years.

But it was in Spain and Portugal that he became really famous. He drove the armies of Napoleon back to France and was made the Duke of Wellington.

When Napoleon escaped from Elba, Wellington was asked to lead the armies against him. He won the battle of Waterloo in 1815.

Wellington then became a politician. He served in the government, and was prime minister from 1828 to 1830. Wellington died in 1852, aged 83.

▲ Cartoon from 1827: one of the things most people know about Wellington is that he gave his name to a type of boot.

Whales

Whales are mammals: they are warm-blooded and air-breathing, and they produce live young which they feed on milk. Yet they live all their lives in water and die if they are forced onto dry land, as their weight crushes their lungs. To keep warm in the water whales have an insulating layer of blubber. In the larger whales the blubber may be 60 cm (2 ft) thick.

Whales have poor eyesight and no sense of smell, but they can hear very well and communicate with one another by sounds we call whale songs. Some whale songs can carry many hundreds of kilometres under water.

Wildlife

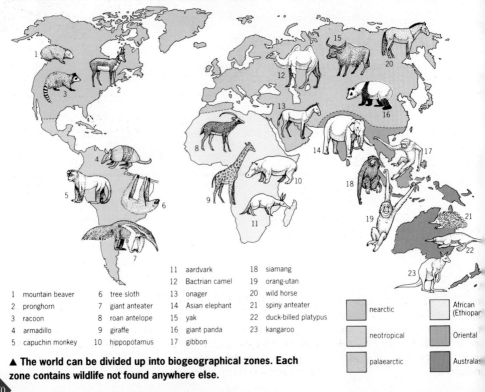

1 mountain beaver
2 pronghorn
3 racoon
4 armadillo
5 capuchin monkey
6 tree sloth
7 giant anteater
8 roan antelope
9 giraffe
10 hippopotamus
11 aardvark
12 Bactrian camel
13 onager
14 Asian elephant
15 yak
16 giant panda
17 gibbon
18 siamang
19 orang-utan
20 wild horse
21 spiny anteater
22 duck-billed platypus
23 kangaroo

nearctic
neotropical
palaearctic
African (Ethiopar
Oriental
Australas

▲ The world can be divided up into biogeographical zones. Each zone contains wildlife not found anywhere else.

Wind

When the Sun warms the ground, the air above it rises up. The cooler air which flows in to take its place is the wind. Weather forecasters use the Beaufort scale, which has 12 different wind speeds.

▼ The Beaufort scale which includes calm, with no wind.

Wool

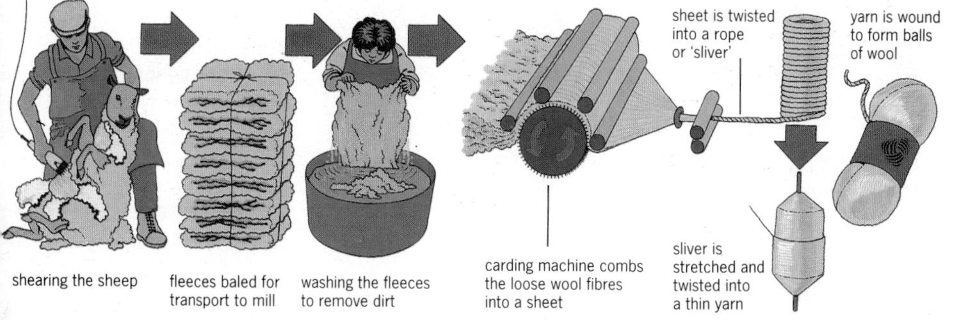

Vool comes from sheep and other nimals. It is used for making lothes as it is both soft and strong t the same time. Australia, New ealand, South Africa and rgentina are the main wool roducers.

Wordsworth, William

William Wordsworth was born in 1770 in the Lake District. His poetry was inspired by his love of nature. He lived briefly in France and Dorset, but was at his happiest in the Lake District, where he stayed until his death in 1850.

World War I

The 'Great War' started in August 1914. The countries of Europe had been arguing for some time. When Archduke Ferdinand of Austria was killed by a Serb, Austria threatened Serbia and the rows turned to war. On one side were Britain, Russia, France, Romania, Belgium, Italy, Serbia, Japan and Portugal. On the other were Germany, Austria-Hungary, Bulgaria and Turkey.

The Germans marched through Belgium, hoping to take France by surprise. The British and French armies stopped them. Both sides dug trenches which were hard to capture. Long battles were fought, and millions were killed or injured.

The same thing happened in the east where Austrian and German armies faced the Russians. Then after the Russian revolution in 1917 the Russians left the war.

But the Americans joined in that year against the Germans and their allies. Their fresh troops helped to bring victory. In 1918 an 'armistice' (end to the fighting) was called for at 11 am on 11 November. Over 7 million people had been killed before peace came.

▲ **Trenches provided some protection from enemy gunfire. The soldiers who guarded the trenches also had to live in them. Trenches were often water-logged and rat-infested.**

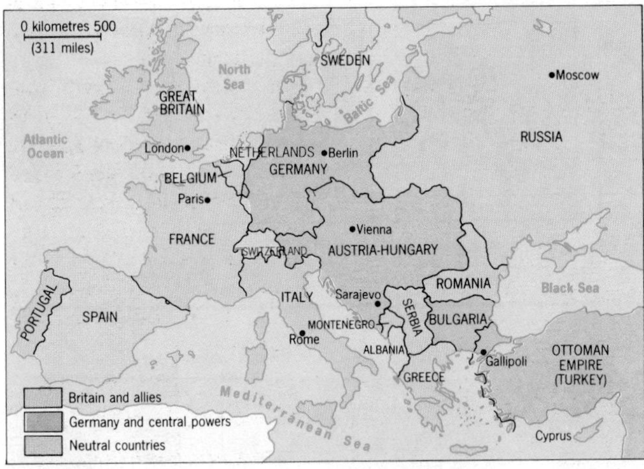

▼ **Sea battles did not play an important part in World War I as neither side wanted to risk serious damage to its fleet.**

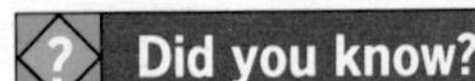

Did you know?

■ **There was only one really big sea battle in this war. This was at Jutland in the North Sea in 1916.**

■ **Aeroplanes were used only for scouting at first. Then they started shooting and dropping bombs.**

World War II

When Hitler came to power he gained popularity by saying that Germany should reclaim the land it lost in World War I. It started invading neighbouring countries. In 1938 Austria was taken. In 1939 Czechoslovakia fell and later that year Germany attacked Poland, and Britain and France declared war. Italy and Japan joined in on Germany's side.

▲ German troops marching into Prague, Czechoslovakia.

In 1940 Norway, Denmark, France, Belgium and the Netherlands all fell to Germany. The British army had to be carried away from Dunkirk by a fleet of ships and small boats. Germany prepared to invade Britain. They were stopped by the RAF in the 'Battle of Britain'.

The Germans attacked the USSR instead, breaking a peace treaty they had with the Russians. Millions of Russians died, but the Germans were held at Leningrad and Stalingrad. Meanwhile Japan attacked the USA, who then joined in on Britain's side.

▲ In 1940 Spitfires helped to defeat Germany in the Battle of Britain.

In 1944 the British and Americans invaded France on 'D-Day'. The Germans were pushed back to Berlin, the Russian Red Army invaded from Poland, and Germany surrendered in 1945. Japan also surrendered after atomic bombs were dropped on the cities of Hiroshima and Nagasaki.

Did you know?

■ **The atom bomb dropped on Hiroshima killed 80,000 people instantly.**

▲ The Nazis believed Jews to be inferior. They rounded them up and sent them to concentration camps.

▲ In 1945 the British air forces bombed Dresden, killing thousands of people.

▲ Millions of people were forced from their homes. This is a family of Italian refugees.

Worms

Earthworms' bodies are made up of segments. Each segment has small hairs on it which grip the worm's tunnel so the worm is difficult to dislodge. Some earthworms eat the soil as they burrow, and extract animal and plant material from it. Others pull leaves into their burrows. A football pitch may contain half a tonne of earthworms; in rich farmland there could be many more.

▶ Tapeworms, although called worms, are unrelated to earthworms and lugworms.

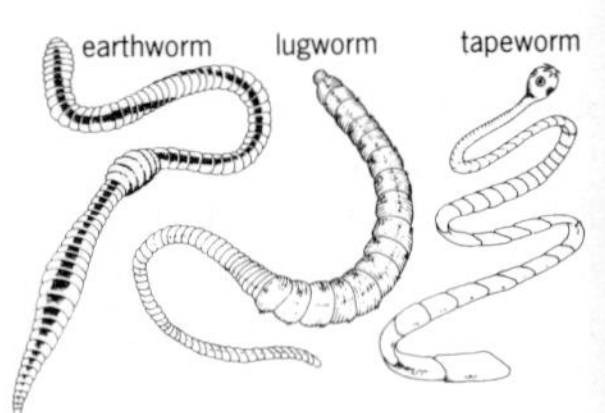

X-rays

X-rays are a kind of energy which travel at the same speed as light. They can go right through some solid things that light cannot penetrate. Doctors and dentists use X-rays to take pictures of broken bones and growing teeth inside your body. Doctors also use much stronger X-rays to treat cancers.

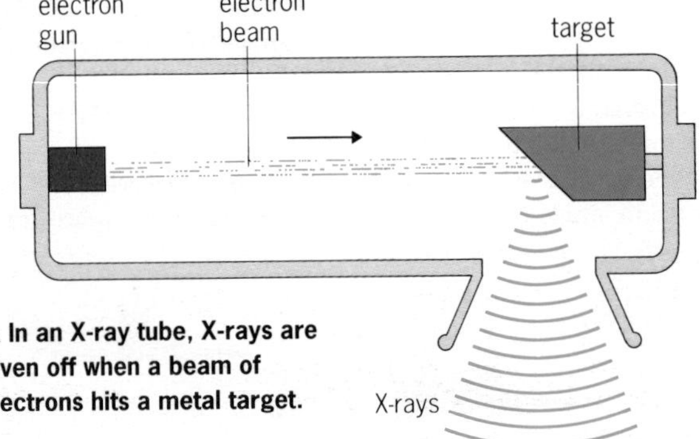

▲ In an X-ray tube, X-rays are given off when a beam of electrons hits a metal target.

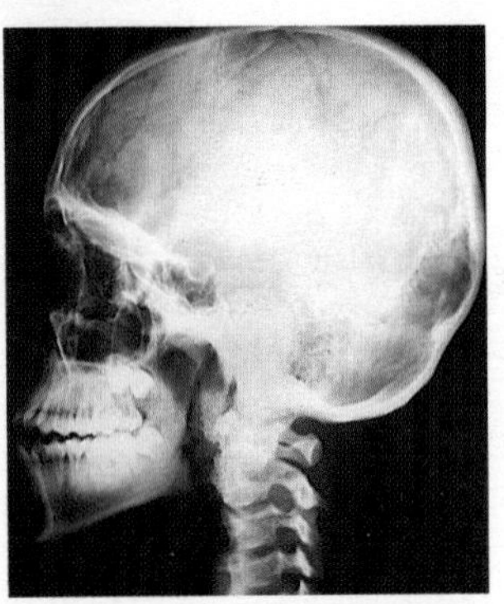

▲ X-ray of a normal human skull.

X-rays help engineers to find cracks or faults inside machinery, and X-rays from space can show astronomers where black holes might be located. X-rays are also used by security staff at airports to check the contents of luggage, to prevent terrorists taking weapons or bombs on to aircraft.

Yugoslavia

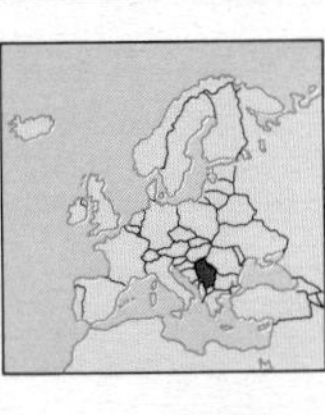

Yugoslavia was created in 1918 from 6 republics that had previously been independent. Slovenia and Croatia regained independence in 1991, Bosnia-Herzegovina in 1992, and Macedonia in 1993. Yugoslavia now consists only of Serbia and Montenegro. There has been civil war since 1991.

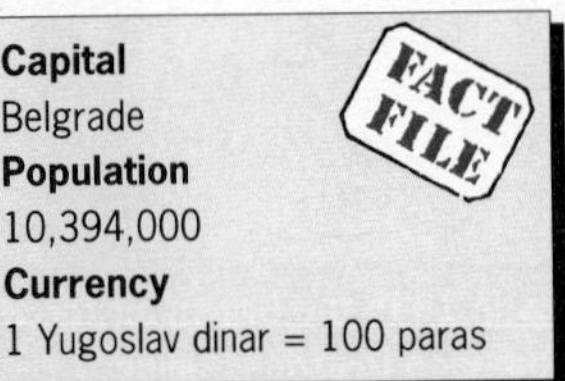

Capital
Belgrade
Population
10,394,000
Currency
1 Yugoslav dinar = 100 paras

Zebras

Zebras are related to horses an they are found in the Africa savannah. Plains zebras live i herds made up of many families Each family contains one stallion several mares and their foals. In big family there may be as many a six mares.

If a member of the famil becomes ill or is injured it will b protected by the others. Stallion can even fend off predators such a lions. When a foal is being born th stallion stands nearby to prote the mare. The foal is able to mov around an hour after birth.

No two zebras have the sam arrangement of stripes.

SPECIAL SECTION

Flags

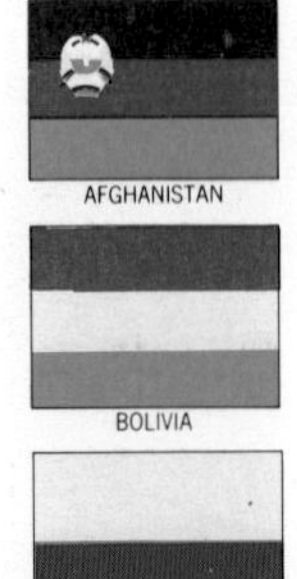

AFGHANISTAN ALBANIA ALGERIA ANGOLA ARGENTINA

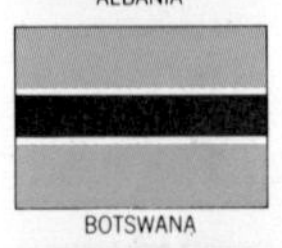

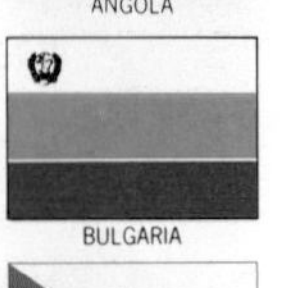

BOLIVIA BOTSWANA BRAZIL BULGARIA CAMBODIA

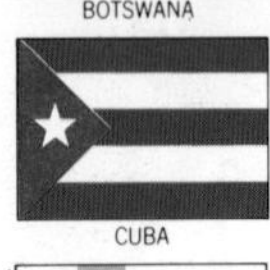
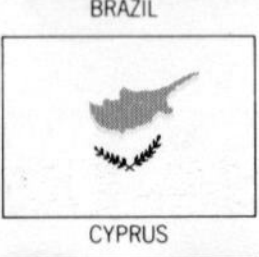
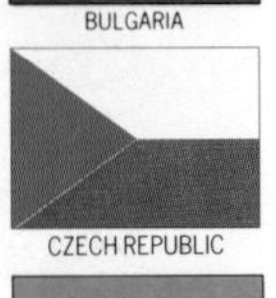

COLOMBIA CUBA CYPRUS CZECH REPUBLIC DENMARK

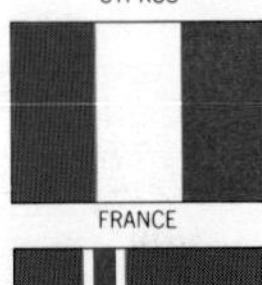
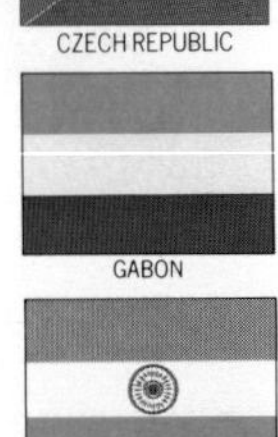
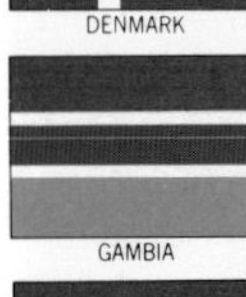

FIJI FINLAND FRANCE GABON GAMBIA

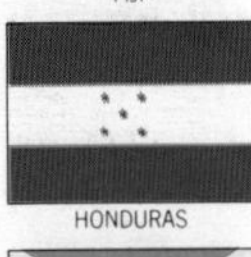

HONDURAS HUNGARY ICELAND INDIA INDONESIA

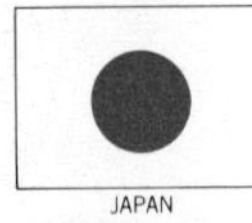

JAMAICA JAPAN JORDAN KENYA NORTH KOREA

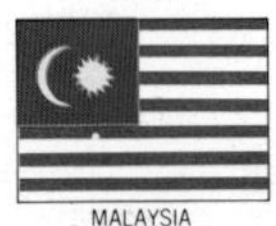
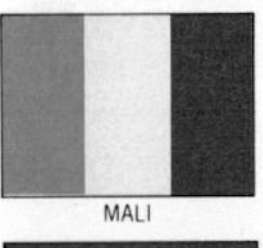
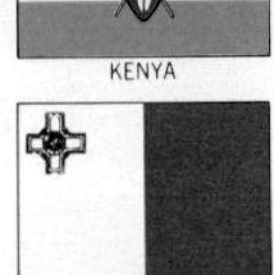

MALAWI MALAYSIA MALI MALTA MAURITANIA

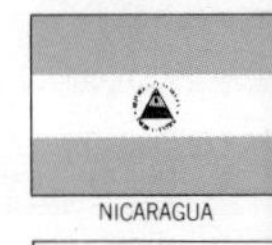

NAMIBIA NEPAL NETHERLANDS NEW ZEALAND NICARAGUA

PAPUA NEW GUINEA PARAGUAY PERU PHILIPPINES POLAND

SIERRE LEONE SINGAPORE SLOVAKIA SOMALIA SOUTH AFRICA

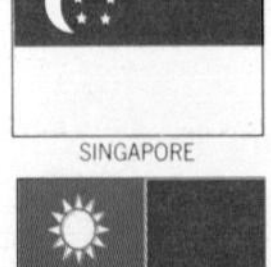

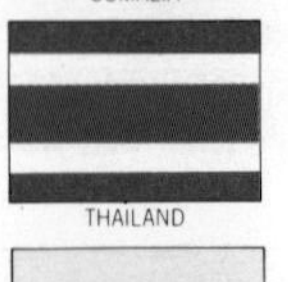

SYRIA TAIWAN TANZANIA THAILAND TRINIDAD AND TOBAGO

UNITED KINGDOM UNITED STATES OF AMERICA URUGUAY VENEZUELA VIETNAM

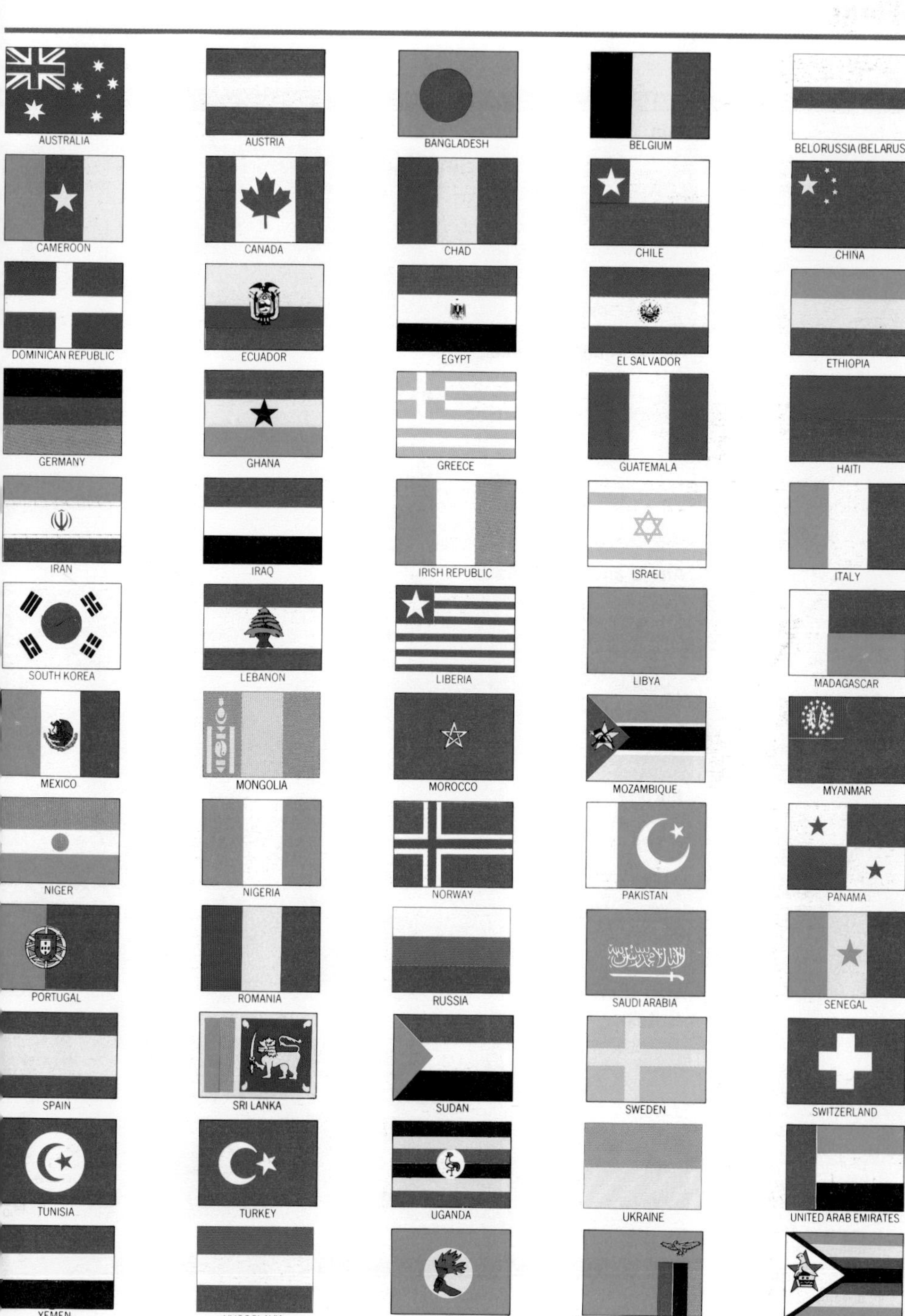
AUSTRALIA
AUSTRIA
BANGLADESH
BELGIUM
BELORUSSIA (BELARUS)
CAMEROON
CANADA
CHAD
CHILE
CHINA
DOMINICAN REPUBLIC
ECUADOR
EGYPT
EL SALVADOR
ETHIOPIA
GERMANY
GHANA
GREECE
GUATEMALA
HAITI
IRAN
IRAQ
IRISH REPUBLIC
ISRAEL
ITALY
SOUTH KOREA
LEBANON
LIBERIA
LIBYA
MADAGASCAR
MEXICO
MONGOLIA
MOROCCO
MOZAMBIQUE
MYANMAR
NIGER
NIGERIA
NORWAY
PAKISTAN
PANAMA
PORTUGAL
ROMANIA
RUSSIA
SAUDI ARABIA
SENEGAL
SPAIN
SRI LANKA
SUDAN
SWEDEN
SWITZERLAND
TUNISIA
TURKEY
UGANDA
UKRAINE
UNITED ARAB EMIRATES
YEMEN
YUGOSLAVIA
ZAIRE
ZAMBIA
ZIMBABWE

World history

	before 10000 BC	10000	9000	8000	7000
Asia	• Hunter-gatherers • From about 50,000 BC people were spreading through all continents with a variety of tools – knives, axes, scrapers, harpoons, needles	• Hunter-gatherers • Earliest pottery in Japan, flourishing coastal culture based on fishing	• Hunter-gatherers	• Rice farming in Thailand	• Rice and millet farming spreads
America and Oceania	• Hunter-gatherers • Cave drawings in Australia from about 20,000	• Hunter-gatherers • Sledges and canoes used	• Hunter-gatherers	• Hunter-gatherers	• Hunter-gatherers • Farming settlements in New Guinea
Africa and Middle East	• Hunter-gatherers • Engravings in south-west Africa from about 27,000	• Hunter-gatherers • Wild wheat gathered in Palestine • Domestication of dogs (wolves)	• Rock paintings in Sahara • Farming of cereals • Domestication of sheep and goats • Site of Jericho occupied • Pottery made in Syria • Wheat and barley ground on querns	• Farming skills spread through Middle East	• Wheel invented • Pottery and textiles used in Anatolia (Turkey) • Cattle domestic-ated • Jericho and Catal Hüyük walled towns
Europe	• Hunter-gatherers • Cave paintings from 30,000 • Female figurines of Great Goddess made across continent	• Hunter-gatherers • Cave paintings • Bow invented • Sledges and canoes used	• Hunter-gatherers	• Hunter-gatherers	• Farming in Balka and Greece • Domesticated sheep and goats • Cattle and pigs domesticated
Britain	• Hunter-gatherers • Cave dwellings	• Hunter-gatherers • Evidence of canoes for fishing and early trading	• Hunter-gatherers	• Hunter-gatherers	• Hunter-gatherers
		10000	9000	8000	7000

Archaeologists are working all the time and digging up new evidence. They often disagree on the period when new technology first developed so the dates given here are only approximate.

This represents 1,000 years: a millennium

	6000	5000	4000	3000	2000
Asia	• Farming in China and India • Pottery made in China	• Farming spreads in Huang He (Yellow River) valley, China • Wheat, barley, rice cultivated • Horses domesticated on steppes	• Ploughs used in China • Bronze worked in China and Thailand • Decorated pottery made in Japan • Jade worked in China	• Silk weaving in China • Cities of Harappa and Mohenjo-daro in Indus valley (now Pakistan) • Cotton grown in Indus valley	• Xia dynasty • Shang dynasty • Cities in China • Aryans invade north India • Hindu religion develops • Rice cultivated in Korea
America and Oceania	• Hunter-gatherers	• Maize cultivated in Mexico • Hunter-gatherers	• Pottery made in Guyana and Ecuador • Llamas domesticated in Andes	• Ceremonial centres built in Peru • Melanesian islands settled	• Metal working and cotton weaving in Peru • Olmec culture in central America • Burial mounds in Mississippi valley
Africa and Middle East	• Farming settlements in Mesopotamia • Copper used	• Sails used on Nile • Plough invented • Bronze worked and cast • Vines and olives cultivated	• Hieroglyphs in Egypt • Farming in central Africa • Cuneiform writing in Sumeria • Cities in Sumeria • Wheeled vehicles • Pottery in Sudan and East Africa	• Egyptian Old Kingdom ruled by Pharaohs • Pyramids built • Sumerian civilization • Cities in Iran • Troy founded	• Middle and New Kingdoms in Egypt • Hittite empire • Hammurabi king of Babylon • Jewish religion develops • Exodus of Jews from Egypt
Europe	• Copper and gold worked	• Megalithic tombs and standing stones • Flint mines • Horse domesticated in Ukraine	• Farming along Danube • Copper working spreads • Ploughs drawn by animals • Wheeled vehicles • Vines and olives cultivated around Mediterranean	• Sails used on Aegean Sea • Bronze worked in Crete • Megalithic tombs spread • Ox-drawn wagons and ploughs	• Minoan civilization on Crete • Mycenean civilization in Greece • Bronze begins to give way to iron
Britain	• Farming and fishing	• Early megalithic stones and tombs • Stone circles on uplands • Farming spreads to uplands	• Farming spreads • Circles built at Avebury • First circle made of wood at Stonehenge	• Megalithic burial mounds and stone circles • First stone circles built at Stonehenge • Bronze worked	• Stonehenge rebuilt • Farms on uplands abandoned

6000 5000 4000 3000 2000

World history

	1000	800	600	400	200 BC
Asia	• Zhou dynasty in China • Mahabharata composed in India	• Taoism founded in China • Zhou dynasty establishes legal system	• Iron working in China • Kongzi (Confucius) lived • Gautama Buddha lived	• Zhou dynasty ends • Qin dynasty • Great Wall of China • Alexander the Great of Macedon invades India • Ashoka, emperor of India	• Han dynasty • Roman envoys to China • Buddhism spreads to south-east Asia and China
America and Oceania	• Chavín village culture in Peru Pottery and cotton made • Settlements in Polynesia	• Olmec civilization in Mexico	• Hieroglyphic system of writing develops in Mexico	• Early Maya culture in Guatemala • Olmec civilization ends	• Foundation of Teotihuacán in Mexico
Africa and Middle East	• Kingdom of Kush in Africa • Assyrian empire • Phoenician alphabet • Kingdom of Israel • Carthage founded	• First coins in Lydia (Turkey) • Babylonian empire of Nebuchadnezzar • Assyrians conquer Israel • Zoroastrian religion in Iran	• Persian empire ruled by Cyrus, Darius and Xerxes • Persians conquer Egypt • Old Testament of Bible completed • Jews exiled to Babylon	• Nok culture in Africa • Carthage powerful • Persian empire conquered by Alexander the Great • Egypt ruled by Ptolemy dynasty	• Carthage destroyed and Syria, Palestine, Egypt conquered by Roman armies • Jesus born
Europe	• Celtic tribes migrate to Germany and France • Etruscans settle in north Italy	• Greek alphabet develops • Homer's poems composed • Rome founded	• Greek city states • Athens defeats Persians • Pericles lived • Socrates lived • Parthenon and other temples • Roman republic founded	• Philip of Macedon conquers Greece • Alexander the Great rules Greece and conquers Persians • Plato lived • Romans conquer Etruscans, rule all Italy and conquer Spain	• Greece ruled by Romans • Romans conquer Gaul • Civil war between Roman rivals • Augustus first Roman emperor
Britain	• Ox-drawn plough used • Bronze worked	• Celtic tribes invade and settle • Iron worked	• Hillforts built	• Trade increases with continent of Europe	• Belgae settle in south • Romans invade

1000 | 800 | 600 | 400 | 200 BC

This represents 200 years: two centuries

	1AD	200	400	600	800
Asia	• Han dynasty in China • Paper invented in China • Magnetic compass used • Emperors in Japan	• Gupta empire, India • Great Wall of China built	• Sui dynasty, China • Horse collar harness used • Mathematics develops in India	• Tang dynasty, China • Block printing invented in China • Kyoto capital of Japan	• Song dynasty, China • Gunpowder invented in China • Khmer empire in south-east Asia • Fujiwara family dominates Japan • Burma unified
America and Oceania	• Pyramids, palaces, temples built in Peru	• Maya civilization in central America	• Teotihuacán temples in Mexico • Complex cities and temples built in Mexico	• Maya astronomical congress	• Vikings sail to North America • Toltec civilization in northern Mexico
Africa and Middle East	• Iron working in Zambia • Jesus crucified • St Paul's missions • New Testament written • Jews expelled from Jerusalem	• Ethiopians become Christians • Text of Bible agreed • Byzantium becomes capital of Roman empire	• Sassanid empire in Persia • Byzantine empire powerful	• Muhammad founds Islam • Text of Koran established • Muslims conquer north Africa • Umayyad caliphs rule from Damascus • Arabs develop algebra	• Bantu tribes move into south Africa • Muslim religion spreads • Abbasid caliphs rule from Baghdad
Europe	• Roman empire most powerful • Emperors Trajan and Hadrian • Christianity spreads	• Franks, Huns, Goths, Vandal tribes attack Roman empire	• Roman empire in west collapses • Dark Ages	• Spain conquered by Muslims • Charles Martel defeats Muslims near Poitiers, France • Vikings raid and trade in France, Russia and Mediterranean	• Vikings settle Normandy, France • Charlemagne emperor • Magyars settle Hungary • Bulgars and Russians become Christian • Kingdom of Poland established
Britain	• Romans conquer Britain	• Villas built • Saxon raids begin • Christian missionaries in Britain	• Romans leave • Angles, Saxons, Jutes settle England • Celts retreat to Wales and Cornwall • Irish missions to Scotland	• Angle and Saxon kingdoms • Christianity spreads • Christians accept authority of Roman Church	• Vikings raid and settle Danelaw • Alfred defeats Danes • England unites into one kingdom

1AD 200 400 600 800

World history

	1000	1100	1200	1300	1400
Asia	• Song dynasty • Movable type printing • Muslim conquests in north India	• Song dynasty • Khmer empire powerful in south-east Asia • Many kingdoms in India	• Genghis Khan extends Mongol empire • Kublai Khan conquers China, Burma, Korea, founds Yuan dynasty • Marco Polo in China	• Ming dynasty in China • Tamerlane extends Mongol empire in central Asia • Muslim sultans rule north India • Black Death	• Ming dynasty • Mongols defeated by Ivan III of Russia • Vasco da Gama to India
America and Oceania	• Polynesian Maori settle in New Zealand • Chimú civilization in Peru	• Inca empire develops • Aztecs move into Mexico	• Easter Island statues • Aztec empire develops in Mexico	• Aztec empire powerful	• Inca empire powerful • Cabot in Newfoundland • Columbus in Caribbean
Africa and Middle East	• Zimbabwe • Kingdom of Ghana, West Africa • Turks invade Byzantine empire and occupy Palestine	• Turks conquer Egypt • Turks attacked by Christian crusaders	• Empire of Mali, West Africa • Mongols attack Baghdad • Turks defeat crusaders and rule Palestine	• Empires of Benin and Mali in West Africa powerful • Ottoman Turks conquer Anatolia and the Balkans • Black Death	• Songhai empire in West Africa • Portuguese explore coast of Africa • Ottoman Turks capture Constantinople 1453
Europe	• Normans rule Sicily and south Italy • Roman Catholic and Greek Orthodox churches split 1054 • First universities • First crusade	• Romanesque architecture • Cistercian monasteries • Crusades establish Christian state in Palestine	• Gothic architecture • Franciscan and Dominican friars founded • Golden Horde of Mongols conquer Russia • French kingdom expands • Cnristians defeat Muslim states in Spain	• Black Death • Hundred Years War • Venice, Florence, Genoa powerful city states	• Printed books made • Renaissance in Italy • Muslims driven from southern Spain • Russians drive out Mongols
Britain	• Norman conquest 1066 • Domesday Book	• Henry II rules Angevin empire in France • Norman (Romanesque) architecture	• Edward I conquers Wales, builds castles • Early English (Gothic) architecture	• Scots defeat English at Bannockburn 1314 • Black Death • Peasants' Revolt 1381 • Decorated (Gothic) architecture • Chaucer	• Wars of Roses • Perpendicular (Gothic) architecture

1000 1100 1200 1300 1400

This represents 100 years: a century

	1500	1600	1700	1800	1900
Asia	• Ming dynasty ends • Babur founds Mughal empire, north India • Sikh religion founded	• Qing (Manchu) dynasty in China • Dutch found empire in East Indies • Taj Mahal built	• Qing (Manchu) dynasty • Chinese export porcelain, silk and tea to Europe • Dutch trade increases • British fight French for control of India	• Opium war • USA forces trade with Japan • Britain founds Singapore and takes Hong Kong • India part of British empire • Independence movement starts in India	• China becomes republic 1911, communist 1949 • Japan defeats Russia 1905 • Rise and fall of Japanese empire • India becomes independent 1947 • Vietnam War
America and Oceania	• Aztec and Inca empires conquered by Spaniards • Spanish capture Caribbean islands and establish colonies • Magellan's fleet sails round world	• Europeans found colonies in north America • Slavery grows in America	• British defeat French in Canada • American Revolution and Declaration of Independence • Cook explores coasts of Australia and New Zealand • Australia settled by convicts	• Spanish and Portuguese colonies independent • USA expands by Lousiana Purchase and Mexican wars • Civil War • Slavery ends • Australia and New Zealand settled	• USA becomes world power • Technological revolution in industry, transport and communications • Civil rights and black power movements •Caribbean countries independent
Africa and Middle East	• Slave trade from West Africa to Caribbean and America begins • Suleiman the Magnificent rules Ottoman empire	• Slave trade expands • Dutch settlers (Boers) in South Africa	• Asante kingdom in West Africa • Slave trade continues	• Europeans explore and colonize Africa • Slave trade abolished • Boers fight British in South Africa • Ottoman empire declines	• African states gain independence • South African policy of apartheid till 1993 • Ottoman empire ends • Turkey and Arab states independent • Israel founded
Europe	• Reformation • Protestants break from Catholic Church • Wars of Religion • Ivan the Terrible rules Russia	• Dutch fight Spaniards and gain independence • French power grows under Louis XIV • Spanish power declines	• Russian power grows under Peter the Great and Catherine the Great • Poland partitioned • French Revolution 1789	• Napoleonic wars • Russian empire expands • Crimean War • Italian unification • German unification • Industrialization and growth of railways	• World War I 1914–1918 • Russian revolution 1917 • USSR 1922–1991 • World War II 1939–1945 • Communist domination of eastern Europe 1945–1989 • European Union (formerly European Community)
Britain	• Tudors fight Irish kings • Protestant Church of England founded • Shakespeare	• English colonists to North America and Caribbean • Civil War • Ireland conquered • St Paul's Cathedral built	• Union of England and Scotland 1707 • Agricultural and Industrial revolutions • Parliament's power grows • Canals constructed	• Emigration to USA and colonies • Industrialization and growth of cities • Empire powerful • House of Commons' power grows • Crimean War	• World War I • World War II • Colonies become independent members of Commonwealth • Welfare State developed • Industrial power declines • Joins European Community

1500 1600 1700 1800 1900

Geological time

Era	Period	Epoch	Millions of years ago	Evolution and events
CAINOZOIC	QUATERNARY	Holocene Pleistocene	2	The Great Ice Age. Modern humans appear
	TERTIARY	Pliocene Miocene Oligocene Eocene Palaeocene	66	Many mammals appear Alpine earth movements create Alps, Himalayas and Rockies
MESOZOIC	CRETACEOUS		135	Dinosaurs die out Chalk deposited
	JURASSIC		205	Many dinosaurs
	TRIASSIC		250	First dinosaurs and mammals
PALAEOZOIC	PERMIAN		290	Continents move together to form the giant landmass Pangaea
	CARBONIFEROUS		355	Great coal swamp forests
	DEVONIAN		412	Caledonian earth movements. Ferns and fish
	SILURIAN		435	First land plants
	ORDOVICIAN		510	Animals without backbones
	CAMBRIAN		550	Trilobites. First shellfish
PROTEROZOIC	PRECAMBRIAN			First jellyfish and worms. Algae

Chemical elements

When discovered	The elements: names and chemical symbols					
Prehistoric times	Carbon	C	Iron	Fe	Silver	Ag
	Copper	Cu	Lead	Pb	Sulphur	S
	Gold	Au	Mercury	Hg	Tin	Sn
Before AD 1650	Antimony	Sb	Arsenic	As		
1650–1699	Phosphorus	P				
1700–1749	Cobalt	Co	Platinum	Pt	Zinc	Zn
1750–1799	Bismuth	Bi	Nickel	Ni	Titanium	Ti
	Chlorine	Cl	Nitrogen	N	Tungsten	W
	Chromium	Cr	Oxygen	O	Uranium	U
	Hydrogen	H	Strontium	Sr	Yttrium	Y
	Manganese	Mn	Tellurium	Te	Zirconium	Zr
	Molybdenum	Mo				
1800–1849	Aluminium	Al	Iodine	I	Rhodium	Rh
	Barium	Ba	Iridium	Ir	Ruthenium	Ru
	Beryllium	Be	Lanthanum	La	Selenium	Se
	Boron	B	Lithium	Li	Silicon	Si
	Bromine	Br	Magnesium	Mg	Sodium	Na
	Cadmium	Cd	Niobium	Nb	Tantalum	Ta
	Calcium	Ca	Osmium	Os	Terbium	Tb
	Cerium	Ce	Palladium	Pd	Thorium	Th
	Erbium	Er	Potassium	K	Vanadium	V
1859–1899	Actinium	Ac	Helium	He	Radium	Ra
	Argon	Ar	Holmium	Ho	Rubidium	Rb
	Caesium	Cs	Indium	In	Samarium	Sm
	Dysprosium	Dy	Krypton	Kr	Scandium	Sc
	Fluorine	F	Neodymium	Nd	Thallium	Tl
	Gadolinium	Gd	Neon	Ne	Thulium	Tm
	Gallium	Ga	Polonium	Po	Xenon	Xe
	Germanium	Ge	Praseodymium	Pr	Ytterbium	Yb
1900–1949	*Americium*	*Am*	Francium	Fr	Promethium	Pm
	Astatine	At	Hafnium	Hf	Protactinium	Pa
	Berkelium	*Bk*	Lutetium	Lu	Radon	Rn
	Curium	*Cm*	Neptunium	Np	Rhenium	Re
	Europium	Eu	Plutonium	Pu	*Technetium*	*Tc*
1950–1954	*Californium*	*Cf*	*Einsteinium*	*Es*	*Fermium*	*Fm*
1955–1960	*Mendelevium*	*Md*	*Nobelium*	*No*		
After 1960	*Lawrencium*	*Lr*	*Unnilquadium*	*Unq*	*Unnilseptium*	*Uns*
			Unnilpentium	*Unp*	*Unniloctium*	*Uno*
			Unnilhexium	*Unh*	*Unnilennium*	*Une*

Those elements in *italics* were made in laboratories.

Countries and capitals of the world

Europe

country	capital
Albania	Tiranä
Andorra	Andorra la Vella
Austria	Vienna
Belarus	Minsk
Belgium	Brussels
Bosnia-Herzegovina	Sarajevo
Bulgaria	Sofia
Croatia	Zagreb
Cyprus	Nicosia
Czech Republic	Prague
Denmark	Copenhagen
Estonia	Tallinn
Finland	Helsinki
France	Paris
Germany	Berlin, Bonn
Greece	Athens
Hungary	Budapest
Iceland	Reykjavík
Irish Republic	Dublin
Italy	Rome
Latvia	Riga
Liechtenstein	Vaduz
Lithuania	Vilnius
Luxembourg	Luxembourg
Macedonia	Skopje
Malta	Valletta
Moldova	Chisinau (Kishinev)
Monaco	Monaco-ville
Netherlands	Amsterdam, The Hague
Norway	Oslo
Poland	Warsaw
Portugal	Lisbon
Romania	Bucharest
Russia	Moscow
San Marino	San Marino
Slovakia	Bratislava
Slovenia	Ljubljana
Spain	Madrid
Sweden	Stockholm
Switzerland	Bern
Ukraine	Kiev
United Kingdom	London
Vatican City	—
Yugoslavia	Belgrade

America

country	capital
NORTH AMERICA	
Canada	Ottawa
Mexico	Mexico City
United States of America	Washington DC
CARIBBEAN	
Antigua and Barbuda	St John's
Bahamas	Nassau
Barbados	Bridgetown
Cuba	Havana
Dominica	Roseau
Dominican Republic	Santo Domingo
Grenada	St George's
Haiti	Port au Prince
Jamaica	Kingston
St Kitts and Nevis	Basseterre
St Lucia	Castries
St Vincent and the Grenadines	Kingstown
Trinidad and Tobago	Port of Spain
CENTRAL AMERICA	
Belize	Belmopan
Costa Rica	San José
El Salvador	San Salvador
Guatemala	Guatemala City
Honduras	Tegucigalpa
Nicaragua	Managua
Panama	Panama City
SOUTH AMERICA	
Argentina	Buenos Aires
Bolivia	La Paz
Brazil	Brasilia
Chile	Santiago
Colombia	Bogotá
Ecuador	Quito
Guyana	Georgetown
Paraguay	Asunción
Peru	Lima
Surinam	Paramaribo
Uruguay	Montevideo
Venezuela	Caracas

Africa

country	capital
Algeria	Algiers
Angola	Luanda
Benin	Porto Novo
Botswana	Gaborone
Burkina Faso	Ouagadougou
Burundi	Bujumbura
Cameroon	Yaoundé
Cape Verde	Praia
Central African Republic	Bangui
Chad	N'Djamena
Comoros	Moroni
Congo	Brazzaville
Côte d'Ivoire (Ivory Coast)	Yamoussoukro

country	capital
Djibouti	Djibouti
Egypt	Cairo
Equatorial Guinea	Malabo
Eritrea	Asmara
Ethiopia	Addis Ababa
Gabon	Libreville
Gambia	Banjul
Ghana	Accra
Guinea	Conakry
Guinea-Bissau	Bissau
Kenya	Nairobi
Lesotho	Maseru
Liberia	Monrovia
Libya	Tripoli
Madagascar	Antananarivo
Malawi	Lilongwe
Mali	Bamako
Mauritania	Nouakchott
Mauritius	Port Louis
Morocco	Rabat
Mozambique	Maputo
Namibia	Windhoek
Niger	Niamey
Nigeria	Abuja
Rwanda	Kigali
São Tomé and Principe	São Tomé
Senegal	Dakar
Seychelles	Victoria
Sierra Leone	Freetown
Somalia	Mogadishu
South Africa	Cape Town, Pretoria, Bloemfontein
Sudan	Khartoum
Swaziland	Mbabane
Tanzania	Dodoma
Togo	Lomé
Tunisia	Tunis
Uganda	Kampala
Zaire	Kinshasa
Zambia	Lusaka
Zimbabwe	Harare

Asia

country	capital
Afghanistan	Kabul
Armenia	Yerevan
Azerbaijan	Baku
Bahrain	Manama
Bangladesh	Dhaka
Bhutan	Thimphu
Brunei	Bandar Seri Begawan
Cambodia	Phnom Penh
China	Beijing
Georgia	Tbilisi
India	New Delhi
Indonesia	Jakarta
Iran	Tehran
Iraq	Baghdad
Israel	Jerusalem
Japan	Tokyo
Jordan	Amman
Kazakhstan	Alma Ata
Kirgyzstan	Bishkek (Frunze)
Korea, North	Pyongyang
Korea, South	Seoul
Kuwait	Kuwait
Laos	Vientiane
Lebanon	Beirut
Malaysia	Kuala Lumpur
Maldives	Malé
Mongolia	Ulan Bator
Myanmar (Burma)	Yangon
Nepal	Kathmandu
Oman	Muscat
Pakistan	Islamabad
Philippines	Manila
Qatar	Doha
Saudi Arabia	Riyadh
Singapore	Singapore
Sri Lanka	Colombo
Syria	Damascus
Taiwan	Taipei
Tajikistan	Dushanbe
Thailand	Bangkok
Turkey	Ankara
Turkmenistan	Ashkabad
United Arab Emirates	Abu Dhabi
Uzbekistan	Tashkent
Vietnam	Hanoi
Yemen	Aden, San'a

Oceania

country	capital
Australia	Canberra
Fiji	Suva
Kiribati	Bairiki
Marshall Islands	Dalap-Uliga-Darrit
Micronesia	Kolonia
Nauru	Yaren
New Zealand	Wellington
Papua New Guinea	Port Moresby
Solomon Islands	Honiara
Tonga	Nuku'alofa
Tuvalu	Funafuti
Vanuatu	Vila
Western Samoa	Apia

Prime ministers of Great Britain and of the United Kingdom

Prime minister	Party	Term
Sir Robert Walpole	Whig	1721–1742
Earl of Wilmington	Whig	1742–1743
Henry Pelham	Whig	1743–1754
Duke of Newcastle	Whig	1754–1756
Duke of Devonshire	Whig	1756–1757
Duke of Newcastle	Whig	1757–1762
Earl of Bute	Tory	1762–1763
George Grenville	Whig	1763–1765
Marquis of Rockingham	Whig	1765–1766
Earl of Chatham	Whig	1766–1768
Duke of Grafton	Whig	1768–1770
Lord North	Tory	1770–1782
Marquis of Rockingham	Whig	1782
Earl of Shelburne	Whig	1782–1783
Duke of Portland	coalition	1783
William Pitt	Tory	1783–1801
Henry Addington	Tory	1801–1804
William Pitt	Tory	1804–1806
Lord William Grenville	Whig	1806–1807
Duke of Portland	Tory	1807–1809
Spencer Perceval	Tory	1809–1812
Earl of Liverpool	Tory	1812–1827
George Canning	Tory	1827
Viscount Goderich	Tory	1827–1828
Duke of Wellington	Tory	1828–1830
Earl Grey	Whig	1830–1834
Viscount Melbourne	Whig	1834
Duke of Wellington	Tory	1834
Sir Robert Peel	Conservative	1834–1835
Viscount Melbourne	Whig	1835–1841
Sir Robert Peel	Conservative	1841–1846
Lord John Russell	Whig	1846–1852
Earl of Derby	Conservative	1852
Earl of Aberdeen	coalition	1852–1855
Viscount Palmerston	Liberal	1855–1858
Earl of Derby	Conservative	1858–1859
Viscount Palmerston	Liberal	1859–1865
Earl Russell	Liberal	1865–1866
Earl of Derby	Conservative	1866–1868
Benjamin Disraeli	Conservative	1868
William Gladstone	Liberal	1868–1874
Benjamin Disraeli	Conservative	1874–1880
William Gladstone	Liberal	1880–1885
Marquis of Salisbury	Conservative	1885–1886
William Gladstone	Liberal	1886
Marquis of Salisbury	Conservative	1886–1892
William Gladstone	Liberal	1892–1894
Earl of Rosebery	Liberal	1894–1895
Marquis of Salisbury	Conservative	1895–1902
Arthur Balfour	Conservative	1902–1905
Sir Henry Campbell-Bannerman	Liberal	1905–1908
Herbert Asquith	Liberal	1908–1916
David Lloyd George	coalition	1916–1922
Andrew Bonar Law	Conservative	1922–1923
Stanley Baldwin	Conservative	1923–1924
Ramsay MacDonald	Labour	1924
Stanley Baldwin	Conservative	1924–1929
Ramsay MacDonald	Labour/coalition	1929–1935
Stanley Baldwin	coalition	1935–1937
Neville Chamberlain	coalition	1937–1940
Winston Churchill	coalition	1940–1945
Clement Atlee	Labour	1945–1951
Sir Winston Churchill	Conservative	1951–1955
Sir Anthony Eden	Conservative	1955–1957
Harold Macmillan	Conservative	1957–1963
Sir Alexander Douglas-Home	Conservative	1963–196
Harold Wilson	Labour	1964–197
Edward Heath	Conservative	1970–197
Harold Wilson	Labour	1974–197
James Callaghan	Labour	1976–197
Margaret Thatcher	Conservative	1979–199
John Major	Conservative	1990–

Counties of the United Kingdom

The regional boundaries of Scotland and the county boundaries of England and Wales are currently under review. The new Welsh counties are due to come into effect in 1996.

England

Avon
Bedfordshire (Beds.)
Berkshire (Berks.)
Buckinghamshire (Bucks.)
Cambridgeshire (Cambs.)
Cheshire (Ches.)
Cleveland
Cornwall (Corn.)
Cumbria
Derbyshire (Derby.)
Devon
Dorset
Durham (Dur.)
East Sussex
Essex
Gloucestershire (Glos.)
Greater London
Greater Manchester
Hampshire (Hants)
Hereford and Worcester
Hertfordshire (Herts.)
Humberside
Isle of Wight (IOW)
Kent
Lancashire (Lancs.)
Leicestershire (Leics.)
Lincolnshire (Lincs.)
Merseyside
Norfolk
Northamptonshire (Northants)
Northumberland (Northumb.)
North Yorkshire
Nottinghamshire (Notts.)
Oxfordshire (Oxon.)
Shropshire
Somerset (Som.)
South Yorkshire
Staffordshire (Staffs.)
Suffolk
Surrey
Tyne and Wear
Warwickshire (War.)
West Midlands
West Sussex
West Yorkshire
Wiltshire (Wilts.)

Northern Ireland

Antrim
Armagh
Down
Fermanagh (Ferm.)
Londonderry
Tyrone

Scotland

Regions

Borders
Central
Dumfries and Galloway
Fife
Grampian
Highland
Lothian
Strathclyde
Tayside

Island Areas

Orkney
Shetland
Western Isles

Wales

Clwyd
Dyfed
Gwent
Gwynedd
Mid Glamorgan
Powys
South Glamorgan
West Glamorgan

Rulers of England and of the UK

Saxon kings

Alfred	871–899
Edward the Elder	899–925
Athelstan	925–939
Edmund	939–946
Eadred	946–955
Eadwig	955–959
Edgar	959–975
Edward the Martyr	975–978
Ethelred the Unready	978–1016
Edmund Ironside	1016

Danish (Viking) kings

Cnut (Canute)	1016–1035
Harold I	1035–1040
Hardicanute (Harthacnut)	1040–1042

Saxon kings

Edward the Confessor	1042–1066
Harold II (Godwinson)	1066

House of Normandy

William I (the Conqueror)	1066–1087
William II	1087–1100
Henry I	1100–1135
Stephen	1135–1154

House of Plantagenet

Henry II	1154–1189
Richard I	1189–1199
John	1199–1216
Henry III	1216–1272
Edward I	1272–1307
Edward II	1307–1327
Edward III	1327–1377
Richard II	1377–1399

House of Lancaster

Henry IV	1399–1413
Henry V	1413–1422
Henry VI	1422–1461

House of York

Edward IV	1461–1483
Edward V	1483
Richard III	1483–1485

House of Tudor

Henry VII	1485–1509
Henry VIII	1509–1547
Edward VI	1547–1553
Mary I	1553–1558
Elizabeth I	1558–1603

House of Stuart

James I of England and VI of Scotland	1603–1625
Charles I	1625–1649

Commonwealth (declared 1649)

Oliver Cromwell, Lord Protector	1653–1658
Richard Cromwell	1658–1659

House of Stuart

Charles II	1660–1685
James II	1685–1688
William III and Mary II (Mary d. 1694)	1689–1702
Anne	1702–1714

House of Hanover

George I	1714–1727
George II	1727–1760
George III	1760–1820
George IV	1820–1830
William IV	1830–1837
Victoria	1837–1901

House of Saxe-Coburg-Gotha

Edward VII	1901–1910

House of Windsor

George V	1910–1936
Edward VIII	1936
George VI	1936–1952
Elizabeth II	1952–

Conversion tables

Weights and measures

Note. The conversion factors are not exact unless so marked. They are given only to the accuracy likely to be needed in everyday calculations.

British and American, with metric equivalents

Linear measure

1 inch	= 25·4 millimetres exactly
1 foot = 12 inches	= 0·3048 metre exactly
1 yard = 3 feet	= 0·9144 metre exactly
1 (statute) mile = 1,760 yards	= 1·609 kilometres

Square measure

1 square inch	= 6·45 sq centimetres
1 square foot = 144 sq in	= 9·29 sq decimetres
1 square yard = 9 sq ft	= 0·836 sq metre
1 acre = 4,840 sq yd	= 0·405 hectare
1 square mile = 640 acres	= 259 hectares

Cubic measure

1 cubic inch	= 16·4 cu centimetres
1 cubic foot = 1,728 cu in	= 0·0283 cu metre
1 cubic yard = 27 cu ft	= 0·765 cu metre

Capacity measure
British

1 pint = 20 fluid oz = 34·68 cu in	= 0·568 litre
1 quart = 2 pints	= 1.136 litres
1 gallon = 4 quarts	= 4·546 litres
1 peck = 2 gallons	= 9·092 litres
1 bushel = 4 pecks	= 36·4 litres
1 quarter = 8 bushels	= 2·91 hectolitres

Avoirdupois weight

1 grain	= 0·065 gram
1 dram	= 1·772 grams
1 ounce = 16 drams	= 28·35 grams
1 pound = 16 ounces = 7,000 grains	= 0·4536 kilogram (0·45359237 exactly)
1 stone = 14 pounds	= 6·35 kilograms
1 quarter = 2 stones	= 12·70 kilograms
1 hundredweight = 4 quarters	= 50·80 kilograms
1 (long) ton = 20 hundredweight	= 1·016 tonnes

Metric with British equivalents

Linear measure

1 millimetre	= 0·039 inch
1 centimetre = 10 mm	= 0·394 inch
1 decimetre = 10 cm	= 3·94 inches
1 metre = 10 dm	= 1·094 yards
1 decametre = 10 m	= 10·94 yards
1 hectometre = 100 m	= 109·4 yards
1 kilometre = 1,000 m	= 0·6214 mile

Square measure

1 square centimetre	= 0·155 sq inch
1 square metre = 10,000 sq cm	= 1·196 sq yards
1 are = 100 sq metres	= 119·6 sq yards
1 hectare = 100 ares	= 2·471 acres
1 square kilometre = 100 hectares	= 0·386 sq mile

Cubic measure

1 cubic centimetre	= 0·061 cu inch
1 cubic metre = 1,000,000 cu cm	= 1·308 cu yards

Capacity measure

1 millilitre	= 0·002 pint
1 centilitre = 10ml	= 0·018 pint
1 decilitre = 10 cl	= 0·176 pint
1 litre = 10 dl	= 1·76 pints
1 decalitre = 10 l	= 2·20 gallons
1 hectolitre = 100 l	= 2·75 bushels
1 kilolitre = 1,000 l	= 3·44 quarters

Weight

1 milligram	= 0·015 grain
1 centigram = 10 mg	= 0·154 grain
1 decigram = 10 cg	= 1·543 grain
1 gram = 10 dg	= 15·43 grain
1 decagram = 10 g	= 5·64 drams
1 hectogram = 100 g	= 3·527 ounces
1 kilogram = 1,000 g	= 2·205 pounds
1 tonne = 1,000 kg	= 0·984 ton

Temperature

Fahrenheit:
Water boils (under standard conditions) at 212° and freezes at 32°.

Celsius or Centigrade:
Water boils at 100° and freezes at 0°.

Kelvin: Water boils at 373·15 K and freezes at 273·15 K.

Celsius	*Fahrenheit*
−17·8°	0°
−10°	14°
0°	32°
10°	50°
20°	68°
30°	86°
40°	104°
50°	122°
60°	140°
70°	158°
80°	176°
90°	194°
100°	212°

To convert Celsius into Fahrenheit:
multiply by 9,
divide by 5,
and add 32.

To convert Fahrenheit into Celsius:
subtract 32,
multiply by 5,
and divide by 9.

Presidents of the United States of America

George Washington	Federalist	1789–1797
John Adams	Federalist	1797–1801
Thomas Jefferson	Democratic-Republican	1801–1809
James Madison	Democratic-Republican	1809–1817
James Monroe	Democratic-Republican	1817–1825
John Quincy Adams	Independent	1825–1829
Andrew Jackson	Democrat	1829–1837
Martin Van Buren	Democrat	1837–1841
William H. Harrison	Whig	1841
ohn Tyler	Whig, then Democrat	1841–1845
ames K. Polk	Democrat	1845–1849
Zachary Taylor	Whig	1849–1850
Millard Fillmore	Whig	1850–1853
Franklin Pierce	Democrat	1853–1857
ames Buchanan	Democrat	1857–1861
Abraham Lincoln	Republican	1861–1865
Andrew Johnson	Democrat	1865–1869
Ulysses S. Grant	Republican	1869–1877
Rutherford B. Hayes	Republican	1877–1881
James A. Garfield	Republican	1881
Chester A. Arthur	Republican	1881–1885
Grover Cleveland	Democrat	1885–1889
Benjamin Harrison	Republican	1889–1893
Grover Cleveland	Democrat	1893–1897
William McKinley	Republican	1897–1901
Theodore Roosevelt	Republican	1901–1909
William H. Taft	Republican	1909–1913
Woodrow Wilson	Democrat	1913–1921
Warren G. Harding	Republican	1921–1923
Calvin Coolidge	Republican	1923–1929
Herbert Hoover	Republican	1929–1933
Franklin D. Roosevelt	Democrat	1933–1945
Harry S. Truman	Democrat	1945–1953
Dwight D. Eisenhower	Republican	1953–1961
John F. Kennedy	Democrat	1961–1963
Lyndon B. Johnson	Democrat	1963–1969
Richard M. Nixon	Republican	1969–1974
Gerald R. Ford	Republican	1974–1977
James Earl Carter	Democrat	1977–1981
Ronald W. Reagan	Republican	1981–1989
George H. W. Bush	Republican	1989–1993
William Clinton	Democrat	1993–

States of the United States of America

ith official and postal abbreviations

ate	*Capital*
abama (Ala., AL)	Montgomery
laska (Alas., AK)	Juneau
rizona (Ariz., AZ)	Phoenix
rkansas (Ark., AR)	Little Rock
alifornia (Calif., CA)	Sacramento
olorado (Col., CO)	Denver
onnecticut (Conn., CT)	Hartford
elaware (Del., DE)	Dover
orida (Fla., FL)	Tallahassee
eorgia (Ga., GA)	Atlanta
awaii (HI)	Honolulu
aho (ID)	Boise
nois (Ill., IL)	Springfield
diana (Ind., IN)	Indianapolis
wa (Ia., IA)	Des Moines
nsas (Kan., KS)	Topeka
ntucky (Ky., KY)	Frankfort
uisiana (La., LA).	Baton Rouge
ine (Me., ME)	Augusta
aryland (Md., MD)	Annapolis
ssachusetts (Mass., MA)	Boston
chigan (Mich., MI)	Lansing
nnesota (Minn., MN)	St Paul
ssissippi (Miss., MS)	Jackson
ssouri (Mo., MO)	Jefferson City

State	*Capital*
Montana (Mont., MT)	Helena
Nebraska (Nebr., NB)	Lincoln
Nevada (Nev.,NV)	Carson City
New Hampshire (NH)	Concord
New Jersey (NJ)	Trenton
New Mexico (N. Mex., NM)	Santa Fe
New York (NY)	Albany
North Carolina (NC)	Raleigh
North Dakota (N. Dak., ND)	Bismarck
Ohio (OH)	Columbus
Oklahoma (Okla., OK)	Oklahoma City
Oregon (Oreg., OR)	Salem
Pennsylvania (Pa., PA)	Harrisburg
Rhode Island (RI)	Providence
South Carolina (SC)	Columbia
South Dakota (S. Dak., SD)	Pierre
Tennessee (Tenn., TN)	Nashville
Texas (Tex., TX)	Austin
Utah (UT)	Salt Lake City
Vermont (Vt., VT)	Montpelier
Virginia (Va., VA)	Richmond
Washington (Wash., WA)	Olympia
West Virginia (W. Va., WV)	Charleston
Wisconsin (Wis., WI)	Madison
Wyoming (Wyo., WY)	Cheyenne

ACKNOWLEDGEMENTS

PHOTOGRAPHS

We should like to thank the following for their permission to include copyright material.

Aerofilms, p85 top; Aldus Archive, p155; Allsport, pp71, 82 (G. Vandystadt); Antiquities Museum, Newcastle, p139 top; Ashmolean Museum, Oxford, pp7, 37 left; B.T. Batsford Ltd, p76 bottom left; Biophoto Associates, pp75, 138 bottom right; Trustees of the British Museum, p12; Camera Press, London, p140 bottom left; Bruce Coleman, pp73 & 127 (H. Reinhard), 78 (J.R. Anthony), 99 top (F. Prenzel), 99 bottom (M. Freeman), 103 top (G. Ziesler), 112 top left (C. Ott); Colorific!, pp90 top left (Brian Boyd), 163 (Andrew Levin/ Black Star); Richard Cooke, p6 left; Cynon Valley Borough Council/ Central Library Aberdare, p168; DACS 1992, p128 (Pablo Picasso 1881-1973 'Still Life' Prado, Madrid/ Bridgeman Art Library, London); ET Archive, p20 (Museo Bibliografico, Bologna); Mary Evans Picture Library, p48; Chris Fairclough Colour Library, p30; Michael & Patricia Fogden, p 10; Fotomas Index, p170 (A.D.C. Allan); Dept of Geology, University of Wales, Cardiff, p138 bottom left; Robert Harding Picture Library, pp9 top (Hanbury-Tenison), 9 bottom, 33, 49, 91, 97 (N. Blythe); Michael Holford, pp4, 38 middle, 53, 54 top, 90 bottom left, 139 bottom; Hulton Picture Company, pp38 top, 74, 76 bottom, 99 middle, 173 top & bottom left; Illustrated London News Picture Library, p94 top; Trustees of the Imperial War Museum, London, p172 top; P. & P.F. James, p6 right; A.F. Kersting, p120; Frank Lane Picture Agency, pp29 (T.&P. Gardner), 83 (P. Haynes), 85 bottom; D. Malin, Royal Observatory & Anglo-Australian Telescope Board, p154; Metropolitan Police, p66; Museum of London, p165; NASA, pp51, 129 top left, 156; NHPA, pp19 (Stephen Dalton), 100 (Dave Watts), 107 (Patrick Fagot), 159 (Gerard Lacz); National Library of Jamaica, p32; National Motor Museum, Beaulieu, p114; National Portrait Gallery, London, pp28, 45, 84; Natural History Museum, London, pp72, 89, 112 top right, bottom left, bottom right, 138 top centre, top left, bottom centre, top right; Peter Newark's Western Americana, p8; Oxford Scientific Films, pp65 (K. Sandved), 103 bottom (K. Atkinson); The Pierpont Morgan Library, New York. M.638, f.23v upper detail, p110 top; Axel Poignant Archive, p108; Popperfoto, pp54 bottom, 109; Press Association, p140 bottom right (Chris Bacon); Commissioners of Public Works in Ireland, p94 bottom; QA Photos, p36 left; RMN, p116 (J.L. David 'Bonaparte Crossing the Saint Bernard' Versailles); Raleigh, p21; Retrograph Archive, London, p101 (Martin Breese); Rex Features, pp131 bottom left (Young), top left, top right (D. Hogan), bottom right, centre (Brooker), 136 (E. Adebari), 140 top, 150 (Durand/Sipa-Press); Rolls-Royce, p98; Royal Collection, St James's Palace c Her Majesty the Queen, p144; Scala, Florence, p96; Science Photo Library, pp17 top, 129 bottom right (NASA), 112 centre (Arnold Fisher), 148 (Claude Nuriosany & Marie Perennou), 174 (Science Source); Science Photo Library, p111 (Ronald Royer) Spectrum Colour Library, pp17 top, 90 top right, 103 centre; Sporting Pictures (UK), p15; Statni Zidovske Museum, Prague/Aldus, p173 bottom right; Tony Stone Photolibrary-London, pp80 top (G. Grigoriou), bottom (R. Wideson), 135 (C. Kapolka), 137 (A. Sacks); Swatch, p38 bottom; J.R. Tabberner, pp36 top & right, 90 bottom right; Topham Picture Source, pp172 bottom, 173 centre and bottom; The Master and Fellows of Trinity College, Cambridge, p110 bottom; U.S. Geological Survey, p129 bottom left; Wilberforce Museum, Hull, p147; Reg Wilson, p17 left; ZEFA, pp2 (D. Baglin), 17 right (Stockmarket), 31 (G. Heilman), 37 right, 86, 102 (Phototake), 117, 129 top right (Photri), 141 (Schwertner)

ILLUSTRATIONS

Andrew Robinson: 12; 48(B); 63; 64; 132(B). Brian Beckett: 10; 18(B); 20; 33(B); 34(BR); 35(T); 43(T); 46(T); 92; 92; 97; 100(B); 112(T); 153. Christyan Jones: 104(T). Dave Murray: 78(T); 126; 132(T); 171(B). Frank Kennard: 24; 24; 65; 83(TL); 83(TR); 88; 88; 88; 88; 88; 117. Gary Hincks: 34(BL); 39(T); 51(B); 115; 123(T); 137(B); 167(B); 169(T). Howard Twiner: 16; 41; 57. Jim Robbins: 14(R); 15(L); 19(T); 26; 45; 71; 71; 78(B); 102(B); 118; 148(T); 158(B). Jones Sewell Associates: 13(T); 43(B); 50(T); 84; 100(T); 100(M); 112; 116; 116; 116; 116; 116; 124. Linden Artists: 68(R); 69; 69; 69. Linden Artists: Chris Rothero: 73; 177. Linden Artists: David Moore: 72; 160(TL); 160(TL). Linden Artists: Gillian Kenny: 79. Linden Artists: Graham Allen: 144(B); 155. Linden Artists: Mel Wright: 133(T); 154. Linden Artists: Mick Loates: 66(R); 67; 67; 67; 67; 145(B). Linden Artists: Ray Hutchins: 49. Linden Artists: Richard Hook: 59. Linden Artists: Tony Gibbons: 142(B). Michael Woods: 7; 11(B); 23(BR); 29; 34(T); 35(B); 42(L); 52(R); 56; 62; 66(L); 75; 82(B); 85; 87(BL); 87(T); 93; 101(R); 107; 108; 113(T); 113(M); 120; 137(T); 145(M); 146(T); 157(BR); 165(T); 165(M); 174(T). Mike Saunders: 51(T); 146(B); 147; 157(BL); 167(T). Norman Arlott 22; 22; 23(BL); 23(TL); 23(TR); 50(B); 89; 127. Oxford Illustrators Ltd: 3; 5; 5; 5; 6; 11(T); 15(R); 18(T); 19(B); 21; 25; 30; 30; 35(M); 38; 40; 42(R); 44; 46(B); 47; 50(M); 52(L); 55(B); 55(T); 68(TL) 68(BL); 70; 82(T); 83(B); 87(BR); 95 98; 102(T); 104(B); 105; 107(L); 107(R) 112(B); 113(B); 114; 122; 123(M); 123(B); 125; 131; 133(B); 134; 134; 135 136; 138; 142(T); 144(T); 145(T); 148(B) 149; 152; 156; 157(T); 158(T); 159(B 160(B); 164(T); 164(B); 165(B); 169(B 174(B). Peter Connolly: 80; 81; 139. Peter Joyce: 74; 150; 171(T). Vaness Luff: 48(T). Victor Ambrus: 13(B).